An Introduction to

MUSIC THERAPY

Theory and Practice

William B. Davis, Ph.D., RMT
Colorado State University

Kate E. Gfeller, Ph.D., RMT
The University of Iowa

Michael H. Thaut, Ph.D., RMT
Colorado State University

second edition

An Introduction to MUSIC THERAPY

Theory and Practice

Boston Burr Ridge, IL Dubuque, IA Madison, WI New York San Francisco St. Louis
Bangkok Bogotá Caracas Lisbon London Madrid
Mexico City Milan New Delhi Seoul Singapore Sydney Taipei Toronto

McGraw-Hill

A Division of The ***McGraw-Hill*** *Companies*

AN INTRODUCTION TO MUSIC THERAPY:
Theory and Practice

This book is printed on acid-free paper.

8 9 0 DOC/DOC 0 9 8 7 6

ISBN-13: 978-0-697-38860-5
ISBN-10: 0-697-38860-3

Editorial director: *Phillip A. Butcher*
Sponsoring editor: *Christopher Freitag*
Editorial assistant: *Nadia Bidwell*
Marketing manager: *David Patterson*
Senior project manager: *Gladys True*
Manager, new book production: *Melonie Salvati*
Designer: *Kiera Cunningham*
Compositor: *ElectraGraphics, Inc.*
Typeface: *10/12 Times Roman*
Printer: *R. R. Donnelley & Sons Company*

Library of Congress Cataloging-in-Publication Data

Davis, William B. (William Barron)
An introduction to music therapy : theory and practice/William B. Davis, Kate E. Gfeller, Michael H. Thaut. — 2nd ed.
p. cm.
Includes bibliographical references (p.) and index.
ISBN 0-697-38860-3
1. Music therapy. I. Gfeller, Kate E. II. Thaut, Michael H.
ML3920.D28 1999
615.8'5154—dc21 98-29454

http://www.mhhe.com

For my wife Carol, my sons Philip and Andrew, my mother Myra McGregor, and the music therapy students at Colorado State University

WBD

Many people have helped me in this effort. My husband, Kyran Cook, provided unfailing support and helpful suggestions. My parents, Norman and Stella Gfeller, instilled in me curiosity and an excitement about learning. I am also grateful for the professional innovations and dedication of colleagues, and for the wonderful questions of my students, which have helped motivate this effort.

KEG

To my wife Corene and my parents, Dr. Rudolph and Irmgard Thaut, for their love and support; to my students whose enthusiasm and quest for knowledge have been the inspiration for writing and rewriting this book; and to the patients we serve through music therapy

MHT

Music exalts each joy, allays each grief,
Expels diseases, softens every pain,
Subdues the rage of poison and of plague.

John Armstrong, 1744

PREFACE TO THE SECOND EDITION

In the relatively short period of time since the publication of the first edition of *An Introduction to Music Therapy: Theory and Practice,* many changes have occurred in the music therapy profession. Most important was the merger between the National Association for Music Therapy and the American Association for Music Therapy to form the American Music Therapy Association. The new association creates a more visible presence for music therapy in the United States and has already led to numerous advances in the practice of music therapy.

The second edition of *An Introduction to Music Therapy: Theory and Practice* reflects recent changes in the profession and provides undergraduate students with an up-to-date working knowledge of music therapy. Based on feedback from students and teachers, we have retained aspects of the first edition deemed most useful.

This text presents an overview of state-of-the-art music practice, using the most current research findings and clinical techniques. We gathered and synthesized information from many disciplines, including music, psychology, counseling, medicine, rehabilitation, special education, biology, neurology, and physiology.

Although written primarily as an introductory text on music therapy, the book is also relevant in other undergraduate music therapy courses, including clinical populations and techniques, clinical practice, and research methods. In addition, this book can serve as a reference for music therapy clinicians who wish to learn about unfamiliar clinical populations, update their knowledge about the current state of music therapy, or prepare for the Board Certification exam.

In recent years, the special needs of disabled adults and children have become the shared responsibility of educators and health professionals. This interrelationship has increased the need to become familiar with the educational and therapeutic strategies of other disciplines. The text introduces music therapy to a broad range of health and human services students and professionals, such as those in special education, medicine, nursing, occupational therapy, physical therapy, psychology, recreational therapy, counseling, gerontology, psychology, social work, and human development.

Specifically, our goals for the second edition of this text were as follows:

To introduce the field of music therapy to the reader in a clear, straightforward manner, including the definition of music therapy, education and training of music therapists, clinical populations served by music therapists, and employment options

To provide a historical perspective on the development of the music therapy profession

To provide an understanding of human response to music

To describe characteristics and needs of those populations most commonly served by music therapists and to introduce music therapy interventions

To introduce the basic concepts of referral, assessment, treatment planning, intervention, and evaluation

To introduce the role of research and the most prominent research methods used in music therapy

To introduce key legislative and accreditation issues that impact health care delivery, especially those that relate to music therapy practice

To compile an extensive bibliography of research articles, books, and materials used by music therapists

ORGANIZATION

The book is organized into three major sections: An Overview of Music Therapy, Populations Served by Music Therapists, and Professional Issues in Music Therapy.

Part One, An Overview of Music Therapy, is comprised of three chapters that introduce the reader to the basic concepts of music therapy. The first chapter defines music therapy, provides an overview of the clinical settings and populations served by music therapists, and describes the education and training of a music therapist. Chapter 2 discusses the historical development of the use of music in therapy, focusing on the development of the profession in the United States during the nineteenth and twentieth centuries. Chapter 3 describes human response (social, psychological, and physiological) to musical stimuli. This chapter includes a discussion of music as a life-span activity.

Part Two, Populations Served by Music Therapists, makes up the majority of the text with 10 chapters devoted to this topic. In this section, we introduce the clinical populations most frequently served by music therapists. Special efforts were made to present concepts in a manner that may be easily understood by the beginning therapist. Each chapter is similarly structured, beginning with a definition and general information about the disability, followed by a discussion of the use of music therapy with that condition.

Chapters 4, 5, and 6 provide a thorough description of three population groups most frequently served by music therapists: people who are mentally retarded, mentally ill, and elderly. Chapters 7 through 13 describe other important clinical groups that music therapists work with, including people with physical disorders, autism, learning disorders, sensory impairments, medical conditions, stroke or traumatic brain injury, and those in prison.

Part Three, Professional Issues in Music Therapy, provides the reader with information about accountability, research, and future trends. Chapter 14 is devoted to professional accountability, including the responsibilities of assessing client strengths and weaknesses, planning therapeutic music activities based on goals and objectives, and evaluating treatment progress. Chapter 15, the final chapter, describes the importance of research in music therapy. Six major research methods—descriptive, experimental, single systems, qualitative, philosophical, and historical—are presented. In addition, we have included information about how to effectively read a research journal article.

In its whole, this book presents a comprehensive overview of the music therapy profession. It looks at where we have been, where we are today, and where we might be in the future. Efforts to enhance the lives of persons with disabilities demand the attention of many skilled professionals, the music therapist included. Technical skill and knowledge is but one component of helping disabled people recognize their full potential. Music therapy professionals must also believe in themselves and in their ability to make a contribution. This book was written especially for the dedicated students and professionals who believe they can make a difference in the lives of these special people.

SPECIAL FEATURES

An Introduction to Music Therapy: Theory and Practice includes a number of learning aids that will help the student study successfully.

Chapter Outlines

Each chapter begins with an outline, which allows the student to quickly surmise how the chapter is organized and what major topics are included.

Tables, Illustrations, and Photographs

Throughout the book, the reader will find tables and illustrations to help clarify ideas and assist in reviewing material. Photographs serve as a visual representation of ideas that are presented.

Chapter Summaries

At the end of each chapter, a concise summary helps the student grasp the major concepts. In addition, the reader may want to preview a chapter by reading the concluding statements.

Study Questions

Study questions at the end of each chapter allow the student to test his or her understanding of the information that was presented. The format of these questions is short answer/essay.

Selected Readings

For those readers who would like additional information about a specific topic or are in search of references for a research paper, we have included a list of books and articles that will be helpful in beginning the research project.

Glossary

Important terms used in each chapter are indicated in boldface type. These key words and phrases are defined and listed alphabetically at the end of the book, providing a convenient study aid for students who wish to review definitions of important terms.

Index

An index of the important topics and names is included at the end of the book. By consulting this reference tool, the reader can quickly and easily locate the page or pages containing a particular topic or name.

ACKNOWLEDGMENTS

We wish to thank the following professors who assisted us in the revision of *An Introduction to Music Therapy,* second edition:

Alicia Ann Clair
University of Kansas

Peggy A. Codding
Ohio University

Martha Estes
West Texas A&M University

Kaja Jensen
Southern Methodist University

Carol A. Prickett
University of Alabama

Dale B. Taylor
University of Wisconsin, Eau Claire

CONTENTS

PART ONE

AN OVERVIEW OF MUSIC THERAPY

1

CLINICAL PRACTICE IN MUSIC THERAPY

Kate E. Gfeller
William B. Davis

CHAPTER OUTLINE

WHAT IS MUSIC THERAPY?

WITH WHOM DOES A MUSIC THERAPIST WORK?

WHERE DO MUSIC THERAPISTS WORK?

WHAT ARE THE PERSONAL QUALIFICATIONS OF A MUSIC THERAPIST?

WHAT IS THE EDUCATIONAL PREPARATION OF A MUSIC THERAPIST?

WHAT IS THE OVERALL PROFILE OF THE MUSIC THERAPY PROFESSION?

Music therapy—what's that? This question is often asked by people with no musical background as well as by those with substantial training as musicians. Most people have a general idea of what professionals such as doctors, teachers, accountants, or construction workers do, because they have encountered numerous examples in everyday life. In contrast, the music therapy profession is relatively young and growing, so many people have little personal experience with this unique career and have questions concerning its scope and methods. We will begin this chapter with some brief examples of how music therapy is used in different settings and with different clientele.

John is a music therapist at New Horizons Rehabilitation Center. His clients come to the center because they have difficulty with basic physical movements such as walking, eating, writing, and other important tasks as the result of accidents or neuromuscular conditions. This afternoon, John is working with his gait training group, that is, a small group of adults who could once walk naturally and with ease, but who now have a labored and irregular gait (walking motion) because of neurological damage. Research has shown that a steady rhythmic beat can function as a timing cue that helps reestablish a more regular gait. Therefore, John and the center's physical therapists have their clients practice gait training to music that has a strong steady beat and that is at a suitable tempo. The clients also seem to be more motivated and less frustrated when they practice their gait training, which can be difficult and tedious, to music they really enjoy. Therefore, John takes into account the favorite musical styles of each client when selecting music for gait training. In summary, John uses music as a timing cue and to sustain the motivation level of adults in physical rehabilitation.

Across town, Lisa works as a music therapist in a preschool program for children who have language delays. Lisa and the children are singing a favorite childhood song, "The Wheels on the Bus." As they come to the verse, "the wheels on the bus go round and round" they all draw circles in the air with their fingers. Next, they bob up and down as they sing "the people on the bus go up and down." Although this looks much like any preschool group, Lisa has selected musical activities and song lyrics that illustrate or reinforce some of the language concepts being emphasized in speech therapy. However, because musical songs and games are such a natural part of young childhood, and because Lisa has done such a skillful job of selecting musical materials that are developmentally appropriate, these youngsters don't even realize that they are working hard on important language skills. If you ask them, music is just for fun!

Holly is a music therapist at Greenbriar Retirement Village, where her clients are all senior citizens. Some of the seniors are quite frail and need a lot of nursing care. However, this afternoon, Holly is working with a group of older adults who live in their own apartments, but who come to the social center at Greenbriar to participate in their weekly bell choir rehearsal. Each person is responsible for playing one or more of the bells. All together, they can create a complete song. They just finished giving a concert at the local civic center, and will start preparing for their next concert today. Violet, who has been with the group for several years now, has recently had a slight stroke. Consequently, she has difficulty using her left hand. Therefore, Holly has given Violet a part that requires her to use only one hand. In the coming months, Holly will check with Violet's physical therapist to determine if a specially adapted handbell might provide Violet with some motivation to practice regaining use of her left hand. Melvin has trouble with his eyesight, so Holly has given him a bell part that is rung less frequently, and she notates his part in extra large print. Harriet is a very active and alert senior who is looking for a challenge, so Holly assigns to Harriet four different bells. Harriet also helps with the choir's newsletter and concert schedule. The bell choir provides an enjoyable and musically satisfying context in which these seniors can maintain their physical dexterity (e.g., handle the bells), stay mentally alert (e.g., follow their part, and play only at the correct time), and keep involved socially.

Paul is a music therapist at the community mental health center. This afternoon, he is meeting with a group of adults who suffer from chronic depression. One of the first things you might notice about this group is that no one is talking! Rather, each member of the group is actively improvising on musical instruments, an interesting observation given the fact that none of the clients are trained musicians. As a music therapist, Paul has been trained to help people with all kinds of backgrounds and abilities participate in musical activities in meaningful and therapeutic ways. In this session, musical improvisation serves as a medium for self-expression, and the members of the group are using this nonverbal mode of communication to share how they are feeling today with other members of the group.

Kellie is a music therapist at the local general hospital, and in that capacity, she works with many different kinds of patients who have different health problems. Today, she is consulting with a Lamaze group, where a group of expectant mothers is learning techniques to help them cope with the pain that occurs in natural childbirth. Kellie is explaining how music can be used to assist with physical relaxation and as a focal point to help them during painful portions of labor. In cooperation with the Lamaze teacher and each mother-to-be, Kellie will prepare a personalized tape of music that each mother can use during labor. In addition, Kellie and the Lamaze teacher are instructing the women on how to use music to cue a relaxation response. Kellie is using well-researched principles of relaxation, cognitive pain management, and her knowledge of human response to music to help these women prepare for this important moment in their lives.

From these few examples, it should be clear that music can be used in a variety of ways with a variety of people and in different kinds of places. Consequently, the question, What is music therapy? does not easily lend itself to a short, concise answer. Using these examples as a point of departure, let's address some commonly asked questions about music therapy:

- What is music therapy?
- With whom does a music therapist work?
- Where do music therapists work?
- What are the personal qualifications of a music therapist?
- What is the educational preparation of a music therapist?
- What is the overall profile of the music therapy profession?

WHAT IS MUSIC THERAPY?

In music therapy, the word *music* is used to describe the particular medium used. Music is used as therapeutic medium, but its optimal benefit in therapy depends on the appropriate use by the therapist. It is not a panacea. For example, what would happen if we were to give musical recordings or concert tickets to people who have cerebral palsy, or depression. Those individuals may enjoy the music, or may even feel a temporary shift in mood as a result of enjoying the concert. However, it is unlikely that they would experience significant or lasting improvements in physical or emotional functioning as a result of those brief musical experiences. That sort of informal usage of music, which people can provide for themselves each day, does not take into account the underlying cause of the health problem. Nor is the music utilized in a manner consistent with well-tested theories of treatment. The effectiveness of music as a therapeutic tool that is applied for particular use depends on the skill and knowledge of the therapist.

In the examples at the opening of this chapter, different kinds of music were used in different ways. For example, in his work at the rehabilitation center, John uses recordings of highly rhythmic music as a timing cue and to enhance motivation. Lisa and the children in the preschool group are singing commonly known children's songs, but the choice of songs is, in part, due to the particular language concepts embedded in these particular songs. Paul's clients at the mental health center are actually creating their own music on the spot, and using their improvisation as nonverbal communication. Just as physicians use a variety of procedures and equipment (i.e., perform surgery, prescribe medicine, listen to people's problems, etc.), depending on the medical condition, so do music therapists tailor their uses of music to the individual needs of their clients.

Because music is a universal phenomenon, people of all ages and all cultures listen, perform, create, and enjoy it. Some music is highly complex and challenging to understand. Other music is very simple and easy to follow. Some people like to compose or perform music; others derive considerable pleasure simply by listening. The variety of musical styles and the manifold ways in which people can be involved make music a highly flexible therapeutic medium. (Chapter 3 describes different structural features of music, and its functions in society that contribute to music's effectiveness as a therapeutic tool.)

Now, let's consider the word *therapy*. This is a commonly used word that is often used to mean assisting or helping a person. Often, it is used in the context of physical or mental problems. As we know from everyday life, therapy can occur in a variety of forms. For example, psychologists primarily listen and talk to their clients, dieticians educate people on which foods are most nutritious and suitable for their individual needs, physical therapists assign various physical exercises or develop special splints or mobility devices. Surgeons use special tools like scalpels and clamps to repair damaged body parts. Music therapists use music and musical activities to facilitate therapeutic processes.

Given the various ways in which music is used as a therapeutic tool, it is difficult to articulate a brief yet comprehensive definition of music therapy. Certainly a number of different definitions have been proposed over the years as the profession has evolved. In the first decade of professional development, a brochure entitled, "Music Therapy as a Career" (National Association for Music Therapy, 1960), defined music therapy as "the scientific application of the art of music to accomplish therapeutic aims. It is the use of music and of the therapist's self to influence changes in behavior."

In the early days of the profession (see Chapter 2 for additional information on the history of the profession), music therapists were fewer in number and were trained in one of a handful of programs. Further, the variety of clientele served and procedures used in those early years were much more narrow than in present day. Thus, this rather brief and narrow definition of music therapy probably seemed fairly appropriate at the time.

Two decades later, that same professional organization had grown considerably in membership. By this time, new techniques and standards of practice had been developed to meet an ever more diverse client base. Thus it is no surprise that a new definition was in order. The 1980 brochure, "A Career in Music Therapy" (National Association for Music Therapy) described the profession in the following way:

> Music therapy is the use of music in the accomplishment of therapeutic aims: the restoration, maintenance, and improvement of mental and physical health. It is the systematic application of music, as directed by the music therapist in a therapeutic environment, to bring about desirable changes in behavior. Such changes enable the individual undergoing therapy to experience a greater understanding of himself and the world about him, thereby achieving a more appropriate adjustment to society. As a member of the therapeutic team the professional music therapist participates in the analysis of individual problems and in the projection of general treatment aims before planning and carrying out specific music activities. Periodic evaluations are made to determine the effectiveness of the procedures employed.

Since 1980, the music therapy profession has continued to evolve as new knowledge and new health care practices have emerged. In 1997 the American Music Therapy Association published the following definition of music therapy in their brochure regarding professional opportunities:

> Music Therapy is an established allied health profession using music and music activities to address physical, psychological, cognitive and social needs of individuals with disabilities. The profession was established in 1950 as a result of work done using music with patients in Veterans' Hospitals following World War II. Today, over 5,000 music therapists are employed throughout the United States in settings such as hospitals, clinics, day care facilities, schools, community mental health centers, substance abuse facilities, nursing homes, hospices, rehabilitation centers, correctional facilities and private practices. Nearly half a century of research in music therapy supports the effectiveness of music therapy in many areas such as facilitating movement and overall physical rehabilitation; motivating people to cope with treatment; providing emotional support for clients and families; providing an outlet for expression of feelings and providing process oriented psychotherapy. (AMTA Membership Brochure, 1997)

This definition of music therapy emphasizes various types of health problems assisted through music therapy, offers a brief historical perspective, and lists some of the health care settings in which music therapists are most often employed. However, this particular definition offers little information about other aspects of the profession (e.g., how music functions as a therapeutic tool). Music therapy means different things to different people and is shaped by the individual therapist's values, philosophy, training, clinical setting, and cultural background. It is likely that each music therapist might modify this particular definition a little or a lot, depending on his or her own professional experiences. As you read further in this book, you will find information about the various structural features and societal functions of music that contribute to its effectiveness as a therapeutic medium. You will also read about the many different ways in which music functions as a therapeutic tool with different clienteles. Once you have finished reading this book, you should have in mind a much more comprehensive idea of this profession.

WITH WHOM DOES A MUSIC THERAPIST WORK?

As the opening vignettes imply, there are a wide variety of people who can benefit from music therapy. For example, John works with people who have physical disabilities. Paul works with adults who have emotional disorders. Lisa works with little children who have delays in language development. These are only a few of the many clienteles served by music therapists today.

In the past, music therapists have most frequently worked with those who are mentally ill or mentally retarded. With increased emphasis on providing preventive health care, integrating disabled children into the public schools, and increasing services to the elderly population, music therapists are expanding into new clinical areas. Music therapy is now used in pain control, stress management, infant stimulation, adult day care, nursing homes, wellness programs, childbirth, prisons, and medical care.

As is the case in other health care professions (e.g., nursing, physical therapy, speech language pathology, etc.) music therapy methods and techniques vary greatly among these clinical settings. For example, Holly uses methods and materials that are suitable for both well and fragile older adults. Kellie's use of music with expectant mothers is based on principles of pain management and requires sensitivity to their physical needs during pregnancy. Lisa has to take into account normal patterns of child development, especially as related to language development, in planning her session. The therapeutic goals selected, and the interventions used are influenced by the individual client's needs, facility policies and programs, and input from other therapists. Therefore, music therapists need to learn not only basic music therapy methods, but also specialized techniques applicable for particular clienteles.

Below is a breakdown of the major populations served by music therapists based on a 1998 survey conducted by the American Music Therapy Association (AMTA).

- Elderly
- Developmentally disabled
- Mental health
- Physically disabled
- School-age
- Early childhood
- Substance abuse
- Sensory impaired
- Neurologically impaired
- Terminally ill

Approximately 40 percent of all music therapists work with clients who have mental disorders or developmental disabilities or with elderly people in nursing homes or other institutions. Historically, mental illness and mental retardation (developmental disabilities) have been the disabilities most prevalently served by music therapists but, recently, music therapists are serving a more diverse population of clienteles. In the past two decades, increasing numbers of music therapists are working with older adults. This is consistent with the overall growth of the elderly population and its need for increased medical and social services, including music therapy.

The types of clients served by music therapists continue to change over time. For example, only a few decades ago, many premature babies died shortly after delivery. Now, many of these at-risk babies survive, but may have special education and health care needs that could be addressed by a music therapist. Other trends, such as the AIDS epidemic, have also changed the type of clientele that music therapists serve. Therefore, this profile of clients served by music therapists will continue to change over time. These changes bring about modifications in professional training and job opportunities.

In order to learn more about the sorts of people served by music therapists, students can seek experience, such as in volunteer or paid positions. By working with children, adolescents, or adults with special needs, the aspiring therapist learns about one or more clinical populations and can make a more informed career choice (Henry et al. 1986).

WHERE DO MUSIC THERAPISTS WORK?

As the profiles of the music therapists at the beginning of this chapter suggest, music therapists work in a variety of settings. For example, the community mental health center where Paul works is a renovated Victorian home, which has been remodeled to include offices of counselors and larger rooms for group therapy. The clients do not live at the center, but rather, arrive when they have individual or group therapy. Kellie, on the other hand, works in a general hospital. Her office, where she does her planning, is in the activity therapy area, but often, she provides music therapy right in the patient's rooms or therapy areas on the different wards. Lisa's preschool classroom is at the end of one wing of the public school. The parents bring their children to preschool on weekday mornings. As you can see, music therapists do not necessarily work in hospitals. The type of treatment facility will vary greatly depending on the nature of the individual's health problem. However, these various options for provision of treatment have not always existed.

The places in which people receive treatment have changed dramatically over the centuries. In ancient times, we know that people who had mental or physical impairments were sometimes killed, abandoned, or left to fend for themselves as street beggars (Rudenberg 1981). In the 1800s, the public attempted to care for those with disabilities by establishing special institutions for the blind, the "feebleminded," the deaf, and the insane (Graham and Beer 1980). It was usual for very young children with severely disabling conditions to be sent to a residential institution where they would be raised and educated and perhaps spend their entire lives.

The quality of institutions varied greatly. Some were, unfortunately, little more than walls and beds and provided essentially custodial care. Other institutions, run by more enlightened administrators, included rehabilitation or recreational programs. Some institutions included music programs for the residents, including orchestra, band, chorus, or other groups. Often, exceptionally talented residents were identified and became lifelong members of the performance groups of the facility. These institutional music programs were sometimes organized by musically talented personnel or philanthropically minded music teachers. In other instances, music therapists were hired by the institution to develop a music program (Graham and Beer 1980).

The initial purpose of these music programs was to develop performance groups. As time went on, educators and health care specialists began to notice additional benefits of music programs for the disabled. For example, in programs for the mentally retarded, music was seen as an opportunity for developing speech and social skills. Early reports from schools for the deaf indicate that rhythmic activities were perceived as beneficial for training the residual, or usable, hearing of the residents (Darrow and Heller 1985; Graham and Beer 1980).

In the twentieth century, significant changes in educational and rehabilitative practices have occurred. People began to raise concerns about those institutions that provided poor care and further questioned whether people with disabilities should be isolated from their families and communities. Gradually, the general public became more concerned with the rights of individuals with physical and mental limitations (Graham and Beer 1980; Shore 1986; U.S. Department of Education 1988). In response to pressure by parents and advocacy groups who believed that the educational and social opportunities within the institutions were of lesser quality than programs found in the public schools (Biklen et al. 1987; Shore 1986), regulatory changes in the educational practices for disabled students occurred.

In 1975, the U.S. Federal Government passed a landmark bill, Public Law 94-142, entitled the Education for All Handicapped Children Act of 1975 (Shore 1986; U.S. Department of Education 1988). This bill called for sweeping changes in the education of children with disabilities, including appropriate placement within the public school setting (called mainstreaming); the development of individualized education plans (IEPs) was implemented in schools across the nation in 1978. (An IEP is a written statement for each child with disabilities that provides for individually designed instruction to meet the unique needs of each child.) So, rather than educating disabled students in remote residential institutions, children from the ages of 3 through 21 with wide-ranging disabilities were enrolled in local public schools (Graham and Beer 1980).

Today, music therapists are employed in a variety of health care and educational settings including medical hospitals, clinics, group homes, centers for the developmentally disabled, prisons, schools, and mental health facilities. Some music therapists engage in private practice or serve as consultants. Others teach, supervise music therapy interns, or become administrators.

The majority of music therapists are employed in inpatient psychiatric facilities and schools, with a significant number working in nursing homes, geriatric facilities, private practice, and universities (as teachers in music therapy programs). Job opportunities vary depending on geographic location, availability of funding, and other factors, such as regional and institutional practices.

According to the 1997 membership directory of NAMT, major growth areas for employment include working with adult day care, hospice, inpatient psychiatry, physical rehabilitation, and private practice. Employment opportunities can be expected to change with future developments in educational and health care trends. Music therapists' salaries are comparable to those of other professionals in allied health professions, such as special education teachers and social workers.

WHAT ARE THE PERSONAL QUALIFICATIONS OF A MUSIC THERAPIST?

A music therapist must be both a good musician and a good therapist. What does this mean? Musically, the individual must have excellent functional musical skills (e.g., the ability to play social instruments such as guitar, piano, etc.), have a broad knowledge of different styles of music (e.g., popular music, classical, jazz, religious, etc.), and should be able to use music flexibly, creatively, and in an aesthetically satisfying manner. Being a talented musician, however, is not enough. Some excellent musicians lack the interpersonal qualities so essential to a good therapist.

Because a therapist's work can be both physically and mentally demanding, certain personal characteristics are requisite to being a successful caregiver. Good physical health is important for stamina. Emotional stability is essential because a music therapist must relate effectively with many different types of people of all ages and should serve as a good role model. A sincere interest in helping others, patience, tact, understanding, and a good sense of humor are important. Because the music therapist works with particularly vulnerable individuals, it is especially important that the therapist be reliable, genuine, and ethical. For example, becoming a therapist primarily to have a steady job to fall back on, as opposed to having genuine interest and good therapeutic skills to offer, suggests that the therapist is using the client for her or his own financial security. This sort of "use" of the client is unethical.

The music therapist must accept that many of the rewards in a helping profession are intangible. He or she must be able to cope with frustration and must be able to look at situations with clinical objectivity. In short, the successful music therapist is a good musician as well as a creative and imaginative person; demonstrates excellent interpersonal skills with clients, supervisors, and peers; and is reliable, genuine, and ethical.

WHAT IS THE EDUCATIONAL PREPARATION OF A MUSIC THERAPIST?

As you will learn later in this chapter, the education and training of a music therapist is multidisciplinary, encompassing other subject areas in addition to music. The music therapy student can expect to learn about physiology, biology, psychology, counseling, anthropology, and movement/dance. As you can see, music therapy is a diverse field that is influenced by many factors. The training received by music therapists is unique among college programs, because it requires not only a thorough knowledge of music, but also in-depth education in the biological sciences, sociology, anthropology, psychology, and oral and written communication.

Music therapy programs are approved by the American Music Therapy Association (AMTA). Although there is some variation in the particular course titles and number of semester hours in each area from one program to the next, programs typically require course work in the following general areas: music therapy, music, behavioral/health/natural sciences, general education, and general electives. The content to be covered in these courses is summarized in the AMTA's list of professional competencies, knowledge and skills that should be included in the undergraduate program. Study in the area of music therapy includes courses in music therapy principles, the psychology of music, and practical clinical experiences (including a six-month internship). Typically, classes cover theories, observation, assessment and measurement techniques, research literature, methods and materials, and ethics. Students can expect to learn about the application of these topics to a variety of disability groups. The course work in music therapy is normally completed in four years if you are a full-time student and is followed by a six-month internship at a clinical facility.

Music courses include theory, history, performance on primary and secondary instruments, functional knowledge of orchestral and band instruments, and music leadership skills. Students in music therapy should expect to master a primary instrument (clarinet, piano, violin, voice, etc.) as well as gain functional skills on guitar, piano, voice, autoharp, and other instruments. The part of the program devoted to the behavioral/health/natural sciences includes course work in psychology, sociology, human development, and research methods. It is recommended that studies in physiology, kinesiology, neurology, and biology also be included. General education consists of those courses required by the individual institution. A school's general curriculum often includes math, English, philosophy, physical education, and basic computer skills. Additional course work in the humanities, such as art, dance, theater, and movement, is suggested. A small portion of the curriculum may be devoted to general electives: studies chosen by the student. These courses may be in the areas of music, behavioral/health/natural sciences, or additional work in music therapy.

After completing course work, the student enters into a six-month clinical internship at an AMTA-approved site. During the internship, the student refines his or her clinical skills under the supervision of a certified music therapist. This experience simulates a full-time job in music therapy and provides the student with practical experience in all aspects of music therapy practice. Once this phase of training is completed, the student is eligible to take the Certification Board exam. This exam is administered by the Certification Board for Music Therapist (CBMT), an independent accrediting organization. The test measures the candidate's knowledge about music therapy foundations and principles, clinical theories and techniques, general knowledge about music, and professional roles and responsibilities. Once the exam has been passed, the candidate becomes board certified and can apply for professional certification.

WHAT IS THE OVERALL PROFILE OF THE MUSIC THERAPY PROFESSION?

Currently, there are about 2,500 professional music therapists in the AMTA. Of the individuals responding to the 1997 survey, approximately 90 percent of the members are women and 10 percent are men. The membership profile by age is as follows: ages 20–29: 22 percent, ages 30–39: 20 percent; ages 40–49: 16 percent, ages 50–59: 5 percent, and 60 or older: 3 percent. Seventeen percent of the membership have masters or doctorates. Approximately 92 percent of the profession are Caucasian. African Americans make up slightly more than 2 percent of the AMTA membership, and Hispanics 1.2 percent. Thus, at this time, young women with undergraduate degrees make up the largest proportion of the profession. Increased diversity by gender and by ethnicity are important goals for the association, especially given the diverse population served and the fact that musical preferences and responses are related to cultural background.

SUMMARY

A career in music therapy offers challenge, opportunity, and reward to those interested in working with children and adults who require special services because of behavioral, learning, or physical disorders. We defined music therapy as a behavioral science concerned with changing unhealthy behaviors and replacing them with more adaptive ones through the use of musical stimuli. The person considering a career in music therapy should be a competent musician who is physically and mentally healthy with good interpersonal skills.

Music therapists work with a variety of clinical populations including, most frequently, the mentally ill, mentally retarded, and the elderly. Facilities that employ music therapists are equally diverse. Currently, many music therapists are employed in mental health centers, public schools, and in institutional settings for the mentally retarded. The American Music Therapy Association requires a rigorous educational and training program. Course work in music therapy, music, the health/behavioral/natural sciences, clinical techniques, and general courses comprise a typical program in which the aspiring music therapist will engage.

The following chapters of this book will elaborate on this basic information and, in addition, will discuss historical bases for the uses of music therapy and how music affects the emotional, psychological, and physical health of disabled populations. We will also consider the music therapy treatment process, the role of research in music therapy, and future trends in this unique field.

STUDY QUESTIONS

1 How is a music therapist different from a music educator?
2 Before deciding on a career in music therapy, why is it important to gain experience working with disabled populations?
3 The three clinical populations most frequently served by music therapists include people with mental retardation, mental illness, and ____________.
4 Describe the music programs found in early institutions. How did they differ from the music therapy programs offered today?
5 List at least four health care settings that employ music therapists.
6 What are three qualifications that a person should have to become a successful music therapist?
7 What is the purpose of the internship required by the American Music Therapy Association?
8 What is the function of the board certification exam? When is a music therapist eligible to take the exam?

REFERENCES

American Music Therapy Association. 1997. *1997 membership brochure.*

Biklen, D., S. Lehr, S. Searl, and S. Taylor. 1987. *Purposeful integration . . . inherently equal.* Syracuse, NY: The Center on Human Policy, Syracuse University.

Darrow, A. A., and G. N. Heller. 1985. Early advocates of music education for the hearing impaired: William Wolcott Turner and David Ely Bartlett. *Journal of Research in Music Education* 33:269–279.

Graham, R. M., and A. Beer. 1980. *Teaching music to the exceptional child.* Englewood Cliffs, NJ: Prentice Hall.

Henry, D., C. Knoll, and B. Reuer. 1986. *Music works: A handbook of job skills for music therapists.* Stephanville, TX: Music Works.

National Association for Music Therapy. 1960. *Music therapy as a career,* brochure. Washington, DC: National Association for Music Therapy.

———. 1980. *A career in music therapy,* brochure. Washington, DC: National Association for Music Therapy.

———. 1997. *1997 membership directory.* Washington, DC: The National Association for Music Therapy.

Rudenberg, M. T. 1981. *Music therapy for handicapped children: Orthopedically handicapped.* Washington, DC: National Association for Music Therapy.

Shore, K. 1986. *The special education handbook.* New York: Teachers College Press.

U. S. Department of Education. 1988. *Summary of existing legislation affecting persons with disabilities.* Washington, DC: U. S. Department of Education.

2

MUSIC THERAPY: A HISTORICAL PERSPECTIVE

William B. Davis
Kate E. Gfeller

CHAPTER OUTLINE

Scholars from diverse disciplines, including anthropology, psychology, musicology, and physiology, have long questioned why music has been in our behavioral repertoire for thousands of years (Hodges 1980; Winner 1982). Music has no apparent survival value, yet it has been an important part of all cultures, past and present. Music has been called *the universal language* and *the greatest good that mortals know.* Throughout recorded time, it has been credited with the power to solace the sick and weary and to express unspoken emotions (Stevenson 1967). It is remarkable that music has claimed such a valued role throughout history. This chapter will discuss the role of music in preliterate cultures, the relationship between music and healing during the advent of civilization, the early practice of music therapy in the United States, and the development of the music therapy profession.

MUSIC THERAPY IN PRELITERATE CULTURES

Preliterate societies are those that possess no system of written communication. Early nomadic people banded together in small groups for survival and eked out their living as hunters and food gatherers. They had no agriculture, political structure, or permanent housing. These small groups developed distinct customs and rituals that set them apart from other similar groups. We can only speculate about the musical component of prehistoric life, but we can gain some clues by studying how music is used in preliterate cultures that exist today. This knowledge helps us understand human response to music and provides some background about the close relationship between music and healing (Nettl 1956). Members of preliterate cultures generally believe they are controlled by magical forces and are surrounded by an evil, unpredictable environment. To remain healthy, they feel compelled to obey a complex set of regulations that protect them from the hostile forces of nature and their fellow human beings. They perceive magic as an integral part of a healthy and peaceful life (Sigerist 1970).

Members of preliterate cultures believe in the power of music to affect mental and physical well-being. Music is often connected with supernatural forces. For example, among certain preliterate societies, the songs used in important rituals are believed to have come from superhuman or unearthly sources (Merriam 1964; Sachs 1965). These songs, with their unexplainable powers, are used for entreating the gods and in all activities requiring extraordinary assistance, such as in religious or healing rites.

In some preliterate societies, an ill person is viewed as a victim of an enemy's spell. He or she is blameless and thus enjoys special treatment from the group. In other societies, however, it is believed that a person suffers illness to atone for sins committed against a tribal god. As long as the afflicted member continues to contribute to the well-being of the family and community, status does not change. If the person becomes too ill to uphold social responsibilities, he or she is considered an outcast and ostracized. In these cultures, the cause and treatment of disease is primarily determined by the "medicine man," who often applies elements of magic and religion in order to exorcise the malevolent spirit or demon from the patient's body. The type of music used is determined by the nature of the spirit invading the body. Because of slightly different concepts of disease among preliterate societies, the role of the musician/healer and style of music varies. In most instances, the tribal musician/healer holds a place of importance within society. It is this person's duty not only to determine the cause of the disease, but also to apply the appropriate treatment to drive the spirit or demon from the patient's body. Sometimes, music functions as a prelude to the actual healing ceremony. Drums, rattles, chants, and songs may be used during the preliminary ritual and also throughout the actual ceremony (Sigerist 1970). It is important to note that the musician/healer usually does not act alone. Preliterate societies recognize the power of the group and include family and society members in the ritual. Healing seances or choruses provide spiritual and emotional support in order to facilitate a quick recovery (Boxberger 1962).

MUSIC AND HEALING IN EARLY CIVILIZATIONS

The hunters and food collectors of preliterate cultures predominated for about 500,000 years. The advent of agriculture 8,000 to 10,000 years ago led to a more stable existence, the growth of larger populations, and the rise of civilization. Civilization is characterized by the evolution of written communication, the growth of cities, and technological achievement in areas that include science and medicine. It is a way of life for a large group of people living in a more or less permanent alliance with a particular set of customs and view of nature. The first civilizations appeared between 5,000 and 6,000 B.C. in an area that is now Iraq and became firmly established by 3,500 B.C. Music played an important part in **rational medicine** during this time as well as in magical and religious healing ceremonies.

USES OF MUSIC IN ANTIQUITY: HEALING RITUALS

With the advent of civilization, the magical, religious, and rational components of medicine began to develop along separate lines. In ancient Egypt (c. 5,000 B.C.), these elements existed side by side, but healers generally based a treatment philosophy on only one. Egyptian music healers enjoyed a privileged existence because of their close relationships with priests and other important government leaders. Egyptian priest-physicians referred to music as medicine for the soul and often included chant therapies as part of medical practice (Feder and Feder 1981).

During the height of the Babylonian culture (c. 1,850 B.C.), disease was viewed within a religious framework. The sick person suffered as penance for sins committed against a god and was viewed by society as an outcast. Treatment, if offered, consisted of religious ceremonies to placate the offended deity (Sigerist 1970). Healing rites often included music.

Music was regarded as a special force over thought, emotion, and physical health in ancient Greece. In 600 B.C., Thales was credited with curing a plague in Sparta through musical powers (Merriam 1964). Healing shrines and temples included hymn specialists, and music was prescribed for emotionally disturbed individuals (Feder and Feder 1981). The use of music for curing mental disorders reflected the belief that it could directly influence emotion and develop character. Among the notables of Greece who subscribed to the power of music were Aristotle, who valued it as an emotional catharsis; Plato, who described music as the medicine of the soul; and Caelius Aurelianus, who warned against indiscriminate use of music against madness (Feder and Feder 1981).

By the sixth-century B.C., rational medicine had almost completely replaced magical and religious rites in Greece. Although a minority still attributed illness to supernatural powers, the majority supported rational investigation into the causes of disease. For the first time in history, the study of health and disease was based on empirical evidence (Sigerest 1970).

The predominant explanation of health and disease became the theory of the four cardinal humors. This theory was described by Polybus, son-in-law of Hippocrates, in his treatise, *On the Nature of Man,* circa 380 B.C. The four humors were blood, phlegm, yellow bile, and black bile, and each element contained a unique quality. Good health was the result of maintaining a balance among the four humors, whereas an imbalance of two or more elements led to illness. Sick individuals were considered to be inferior. With only slight modification, this theory influenced medicine for the next 2,000 years, becoming most important during the Middle Ages.

MUSIC AND HEALING IN THE MIDDLE AGES AND RENAISSANCE

Although much of the splendor of classical Greece was lost during the Middle Ages, this time period (c. 476–1,450 A.D.) represents an important connection between antiquity and the present. After the fall of the Roman Empire, Christianity became a major force in Western civilization. The influence of Christianity prompted a change in attitudes toward disease. Contrary to earlier thinking, a sick person was neither inferior nor being punished by gods. As Christianity spread throughout Europe, societies began to care for and treat their sick members. Hospitals were established to provide humanitarian care to people with physical ailments. Sufferers of mental illness, however, were not as fortunate. Mentally ill people were believed to be possessed by demons and were often incarcerated and abused (Boxberger 1962).

Although Christian beliefs heavily influenced attitudes toward disease during the Middle Ages, the practice of medicine was still based on the theory of the four humors developed during Greek civilization. This framework also provided the basis for the role of music in treating illness. Numerous statesmen and philosophers believed in the curative powers of music, including Boethius, who claimed that music either improved or degraded human morals. Cassiodorus, like Aristotle, viewed music as a potent type of catharsis, whereas St. Basil advocated it as a positive vehicle for sacred emotion. Many believed hymns to be effective against certain unspecified respiratory diseases (Strunk 1965).

During the Renaissance, advances in anatomy, physiology, and clinical medicine marked the beginning of the scientific approach to medicine. Despite developments in the laboratory, however, treatment of disease was still based on the teachings of Hippocrates and Galen and a sophisticated interpretation of the four humors. During this period, there was some integration of music, medicine, and art. For example, it was not unusual to find writings, such as those of Zarlino (a musician) and Vesalius (a physician), that touched on the relationship between music and medicine (Boxberger 1962).

Music during the Renaissance was not only used as a remedy for melancholy, despair, and madness, but also prescribed by physicians as preventive medicine. Properly dispensed music was recognized then, as it is today, as a powerful tool to enhance emotional health. For those who could afford the luxury of attending live performances, music helped maintain a positive outlook on life. Optimism was particularly important during this time, because Europe was being ravaged by epidemics that sometimes decimated entire villages (Boxberger 1962).

During the Baroque period (1580–1750), music continued to be linked with the medical practice of the day, based as before on the theory of the four humors. In addition, the theory of temperaments and affections by Kircher (1602–80) provided a fresh viewpoint on the use of music in the treatment of disease. Kircher believed that personality characteristics were coupled with a certain style of music. For example, depressed individuals responded to melancholy music. Cheerful people were most affected by dance music, because it stimulated the blood (Carapetyan 1948). Thus it became necessary for the healer to choose the correct style of music for treatment. Supporting the use of music to treat depression, Burton, in his *Anatomy of Melancholy,* stated, "besides that excellent power it hath to expel many other diseases, it is a sovereign remedy against Despair and Melancholy, and will drive away the Devil himself" (Burton 1651). Other writers, such as Shakespeare and Armstrong, also included numerous examples of music as therapy in their plays and poems (Davis 1985).

By the late-eighteenth century, music was still advocated by European physicians in the treatment of disease, but a definite change in philosophy was underway. With increased emphasis on scientific medicine, music was relegated to special cases and applied by only a few physicians who viewed treatment from a holistic (multitherapeutic) framework. This shift was evident during the growth and development of music therapy in the United States.

MUSIC THERAPY IN THE UNITED STATES

The practice of music therapy in the United States has a long, storied history. Although music therapy as a profession became organized only in the twentieth century, music has been used in this country to treat physical and mental ailments since the late eighteenth century.

Eighteenth-Century Writings on Music Therapy

The earliest known reference to music therapy in the United States was an unsigned article in *Columbian Magazine* in 1789. The article, entitled "Music Physically Considered," presented basic principles of music therapy that are still in use today and provided evidence of music therapy practice in Europe. Mainly using the ideas of Descartes (a French philosopher), the anonymous author developed a case for using music to influence and regulate emotional conditions. An interesting conclusion drawn by the author was that a person's mental state may affect physical health. The author also asserted that music, because of its effect on emotions, was a proven therapeutic agent. One other important point in this article was the author's advice that the skilled use of music in the treatment of disease required a properly trained practitioner. This advice is as pertinent now as it was in 1789 (Heller 1987).

Another article published during this period was entitled "Remarkable Cure of a Fever by Music: An Attested Fact." This article was published in 1796 in the *New York Weekly Magazine*. The anonymous author described the case of an unnamed French music teacher who suffered from a severe fever. After nearly two weeks of constant distress, a concert was performed at the patient's request. His symptoms reportedly disappeared during the performance but returned upon its conclusion. The music was repeated throughout the man's waking hours, resulting in the suspension of his illness. In two weeks' time, the music teacher recovered completely.

Both authors based their conclusions of the music's effectiveness on anecdotal, rather than scientific, evidence. Such claims lack credibility by today's standards, but these articles suggest that some practitioners during the eighteenth century were interested in using music in medical treatment. At that time, medical care was crude and often dangerous, so a gentle treatment like music therapy was likely welcomed by the general public, who often suffered at the hands of the unregulated medical profession (Heller 1987).

Literature from the Nineteenth Century

During the nineteenth century, several authors wrote about the use of music to treat physical and mental illness. Articles appeared in music journals, medical journals, psychiatric periodicals, and medical dissertations. Although these reports varied in length as well as quality, they supported the use of therapeutic music as an alternative or a supplement to traditional medical treatment.

The earliest documents produced during this period were dissertations written by two medical students, Edwin Atlee and Samuel Mathews, who attended the University of Pennsylvania. Atlee's work, entitled *An Inaugural Essay on the Influence of Music in the Cure of Diseases,* was completed in 1804. He cited literary, medical, and scholarly sources, including material from theorist Jean-Jacques Rousseau, physician and psychiatrist Benjamin Rush, poet John Armstrong, and the British musicologist Charles Burney, as well as personal experiences. The purpose of Atlee's brief dissertation was "to treat the effects produced on the mind by the impression of that certain modification of sound called music, which I hope to prove has a powerful influence upon the mind, and consequently on the body" (8). After defining important terms used in his text, he suggested that music has the ability to arouse and affect a variety of emotions, including joy and grief. The final part of Atlee's dissertation discussed the beneficial effects of music on a variety of mental and physical illnesses and described three cases in which he successfully treated patients with music. In one of his examples, he encouraged a client to resume playing the flute.

Samuel Mathews wrote *On the Effects of Music in Curing and Palliating Diseases* in 1806. His article was in some respects similar to Atlee's, but more sophisticated in its use of sources and in the amount of information presented to the reader. Mathews outlined the benefits of music in the treatment of diseases of the mind and body. For example, in order to alleviate depression, he recommended using music that matched the mood of the patient (today this is known as the iso principle), because "with the precaution, we may gradually raise the tunes from those we judge proper in the commencement [of a depressed state] to those of a more lively nature" (14). In addition to other citations, Mathews used the Bible to support his assertions, recounting the story of the therapeutic effects of David's harp playing on Saul's psychological difficulties.

The dissertations of Atlee and Mathews were strikingly similar in form, content, and physical appearance. Of the many sources they cited, no one person was relied on more heavily than physician/psychiatrist Benjamin Rush, who was a professor at the University of Pennsylvania and a strong advocate for the use of music to treat mental disease. Rush played a major role in creating interest in music therapy during the beginning of the nineteenth century and likely encouraged Atlee and Mathews to write on the topic (Carlson et al. 1981). Their dissertations made a unique contribution to music therapy during the early years of the nineteenth century.

Music Therapy in Nineteenth-Century Educational Institutions

The use of music therapy in educational institutions began in the nineteenth century. In 1832, the Perkins School for the Blind was founded in Boston by Dr. Samuel Gridley (Heller 1987). Perhaps, because of the urging of his wife Julia Ward Howe (who composed the lyrics to "Battle Hymn of the Republic"), Dr. Howe, the school's administrator, included music in the curriculum from the beginning. Dr. Howe was instrumental in engaging prominent Boston musicians to help establish ongoing music programs at the school. One of the first of these musicians was Lowell Mason, who taught at the school from 1832–36. He was responsible for teaching vocal music and piano lessons as well as other music activities. By the time Mason left the school, he had established a strong curriculum in music instruction, which is still in effect today (Darrow and Heller 1985).

There are other examples of music therapy in institutional settings during the mid-1800s. George Root, a music pupil and friend of Mason, taught at the New York School for the Blind from 1845 to 1850 (Carder 1972). During the 1840s, William Wolcott Turner and David Ely Bartlett developed a successful music program at the American Asylum for the Deaf, located in Hartford, Connecticut. One student, identified only as Miss Avery, successfully completed a difficult course of piano study. Turner and Bartlett reported her accomplishment in an article entitled "Music among the Deaf and Dumb," which appeared in the October 1848 issue of the *American Annals of the Deaf and Dumb* (Darrow and Heller 1985). Music programs were also developed for physically disabled students during the early to mid-1800s.

During this period when music therapy was being developed in educational settings, there was also renewed interest in its use as treatment for disease. Three unsigned articles (all entitled "Medical Powers of Music") appeared in *Musical Magazine* within a span of two months in 1840–41. These reports focused on the linkage of therapeutic music with history, philosophy, and religion, but added little in the way of new information. Much of the material in the articles came from British music historian Charles Burney, whose book, *A General History of Music,* was published in 1789. One prominent example was the story of King Philip V of Spain, who suffered from depression. During the late 1730s, the famous Italian baroque castrato Farinelli, who had retired to Spain, was summoned to Madrid to perform for King Philip. It was reported that the king was so moved by the singing of Farinelli that all signs of his chronic depression disappeared, thus assuring the singer lifelong gratitude from the Spanish monarch. The final article in the series cited stories from composers, writers, historians, and performers who had firsthand experience with the therapeutic effects of music (Heller 1987). Despite their questionable credibility, these articles indicated ongoing interest in music therapy during the first third of the nineteenth century.

The next substantial support for music therapy was in an 1874 article penned by physician James Whittaker. The article, entitled "Music as Medicine," was published in the Cincinnati *Clinic.* Whittaker cited an impressive number of American and European sources to support his theory that musical response was linked to physiological, psychological, and sociocultural attributes. Numerous examples were provided to support his belief in the power of music to influence mind and body. Whittaker concluded that the greatest effects from the use of music were on mild forms of mental illness, whereas the treatment of physical ailments and severe mental distress with music was temporary at best. A second article during that decade was published in the *Virginia Medical Monthly* in 1878. "Music as Mind Medicine" was an edited version of a piece that originally appeared in *The World,* a New York newspaper, dated March

6, 1878. The journal article, edited by Landon B. Edwards, described a series of experiments that took place at Blackwell's Island (now Roosevelt Island), an infamous facility for the care of New York City's indigent, insane citizens. These sessions were held to test "lunatics'" reactions to live music provided by instrumental and vocal soloists. The report began with introductory information about the purpose of the experiment and the people who participated. The principals included the distinguished American pianist, John Nelson Pattison, who was credited with initiating the project. Also taking part were New York City Charities Commissioner William Brennan, several physicians, and a number of New York City government officials. A large entourage of musicians also accompanied Pattison and the others to the hospital. The group included 40 members of D. L. Downing's Ninth Regiment Band and several vocalists from the New York Musicians Guild.

The musicians provided music for a large group of patients following a series of nine individual sessions. Pattison directed the individual sessions from a piano, while the doctors assisted by taking physiological data and recording each patient's reaction to the music. The government officials apparently were onlookers, although this was not specifically stated. The article reported that similar sessions had taken place on four previous occasions, about which no information has been located.

The music experiments on Blackwell's Island marked an unprecedented attempt to alleviate the suffering of a large group of mentally ill patients. The concerts and individual sessions were supported by authorities who were in a position to implement and maintain such programs, an occurrence not seen previously in the United States.

In 1882, a short article by another physician, George L. Beardsley, appeared in the *New England Medical Monthly.* "The Medical Uses of Music" reviewed the use of music in therapy, recounting several old, unsubstantiated stories probably extracted from Charles Burney's *A General History of Music.* In the second part of the article, Beardsley advocated the use of music to treat nervous and mental disorders. Unfortunately, he provided no specific examples, and his report did little to advance the practice of music therapy in the United States.

"The Influence of Music and Its Therapeutic Value," by physician Sebastian J. Wimmer, appeared in the *New York Medical Journal* on September 7, 1889. Like the Beardsley article, this report added little to existing knowledge about music therapy in the nineteenth century. Wimmer used dated concepts to prove music's worth as a therapeutic tool. For example, he promoted the idea that music could bring the body and mind into harmony. This idea had been useful during the previous century, when human physiology and neurology were just beginning to be explored. But by the late 1800s, neurology and psychiatry had become recognized specialties in medicine. Disease and injury to the brain were considered the primary causes of mental distress (Deutsch 1949). Wimmer, however, made no mention of new trends, such as the use of tranquilizing medications, in diagnosing and treating mental disease. He appeared to hold a fleeting interest in music therapy, adding a single, unimpressive contribution to the literature. During the final decade of the nineteenth century, two important papers appeared that provided strong support for music therapy in institutional settings and in private practice. In January 1892, George Alder Blumer's treatise, entitled "Music in Its Relation to the Mind," appeared in the *American Journal of Insanity.* Although the author recognized the therapeutic value of music, he did not support the extravagant claims made by others. Blumer believed that music was a part of moral treatment. The combination of art, reading, music, and physical education provided a well-rounded therapy program for mentally ill patients. Blumer held music in such high regard that he hired immigrant musicians to perform for the patients at Utica State Hospital in New York, where he served as chief executive officer. In fact, Blumer may have been the first person to establish an ongoing music program in an American hospital. He should be considered a pioneer in the music therapy movement in the United States.

James Leonard Corning, a prominent neurologist, made another innovative contribution to the advancement of music therapy practice in the late-nineteenth century. His article, entitled "The Use of Musical Vibrations before and during Sleep—Supplementary Employment of Chromatoscopic Figures—A Contribution to the Therapeutics of the Emotions," was published in the *Medical Record* in 1899. Corning's work represented the first controlled attempt to treat mental illness with music. He kept up-to-date with trends in psychology and neurology and used the information from both professions to fashion his unusual treatment procedures, which he called vibrative medicine.

Using an interesting array of equipment, Corning maintained a consistent environment for testing his patients' reactions to music. He presented music and visual images to his patients as they passed from presleep to sleep. Corning believed that during sleep, a person's thought processes became dormant, allowing the penetration of "musical vibrations" into the subconscious mind. Appropriate musical selections (classical music only) helped to transfer those pleasant images and emotions into the waking hours, which suppressed and eventually eliminated the morbid thoughts that plagued his patients. Corning's theories about the relationship between sleep, emotions, and health were based on assumptions that have not been validated by modern research. His work, however, was important, because it represented the first documented attempt to systematically record the effects of music on mental illness.

Throughout the nineteenth century, music therapy was championed by musicians, physicians, psychiatrists, and other individuals interested in promoting this unique form of therapy. However, these advocates worked independently of each other, so there was little overall growth in its use. During the final decade, articles about music therapy began to appear more frequently in popular and professional journals, and the public began to gain an awareness of the therapeutic possibilities (Davis 1987). This growth continued into the early years of the twentieth century.

Early Twentieth-Century Music Therapy

During the first years of the twentieth century, music therapy continued to gain support, although sporadically. Physicians, musicians, psychiatrists, and the general public presented their cases for music therapy in scientific publications, newspapers, and the popular press. Clinical and experimental research provided data to support therapists' contentions that music could be effective in a variety of settings. In addition, a number of short-lived organizations promoted music therapy programs in hospitals, especially for returning World War I and II veterans (Taylor 1981).

One of the most influential figures to advance the cause of music therapy during the first two decades of the twentieth century was Eva Vescelius. She promoted music therapy through numerous publications and the National Therapeutic Society of New York, which she founded in 1903. In *Music and Health,* a publication completed shortly before her death in 1917, she provided a fascinating view of music therapy based on both age-old and contemporary concepts of health and disease. Vescelius believed that the object of music therapy was to return the sick person's discordant vibrations to harmonious ones. She gave precise instructions for the treatment of fevers, insomnia, and other ailments with music.

Perhaps her most unique contribution was the publication of the short-lived journal *Music and Health.* Published in 1913, only three issues appeared in print. Each contained poems and articles by Vescelius and others on the therapeutic applications of music. Additionally, there were advertisements for a course in "musicotherapy" offered by Vescelius. After her death, her sister Louise carried on her work for a short period of time (Davis 1993).

The first course work in music therapy offered through a university was organized and taught by Margaret Anderton, an English-born pianist who had provided music therapy services to Canadian soldiers suffering from physical and mental disabilities during World War I. During 1919, she taught classes at New York City's Columbia University that prepared musicians for working in hospitals as therapists. She wrote, "it is the object of the course to cover the psychophysiological action of music and to provide practical training for therapeutic treatment under medical control" (*Literary Digest,* 1 March 1919, 59). Like Vescelius, she strongly believed that musicians should be thoroughly trained as therapists before working with patients.

Anderton advocated two principal ways to administer music therapy. For soldiers suffering from psychological conditions, the therapist should provide the music. For those afflicted with physical conditions, the patient should be responsible for producing the music, because it would help strengthen an injured arm or leg. She also favored the use of woodwind instruments (especially for psychological conditions) because, according to her research, the timbre produced healing effects (Taylor 1981).

Isa Maud Ilsen, a musician, nurse, and hospital executive, founded the National Association for Music in Hospitals in 1926. Previously, she had served as a teacher of musicotherapy at Columbia University with Margaret Anderton in 1919. She had also been director of hospital music in World War I reconstruction hospitals for the American Red Cross. Ilsen viewed music as a way to alleviate pain for surgical patients and those with physical ailments. Her 20 years as a hospital musician helped refine her theories concerning music therapy, and like Eva Vescelius, she viewed a healthy person as one who is in harmony (Ilsen 1926). Ilsen believed rhythm to be the vital therapeutic component in the music, although she believed that certain styles of music, such as jazz, were inappropriate for treatment.

Like other musicians and physicians during the first half of the twentieth century, Ilsen prescribed a specific treatment regimen, using primarily classical music for the relief of a variety of disorders. For severe insomnia, for example, she prescribed a "dose" of Schubert's *Ave Maria.* For terminal illness, she believed that Brahms waltzes or Sousa marches were appropriate. She sometimes used ethnic songs and instrumental music in making her selections, which would suggest some consideration of the patient's music preferences (*Literary Digest,* 23 August 1919, 26). Like many other early music therapists, she wanted hospitals to use qualified individuals to administer music therapy programs. Isa Maud Ilsen should be considered an important pioneer in the movement to promote music therapy in American hospitals (Boxberger 1962).

Like Ilsen and Anderton, Harriet Ayer Seymour worked with World War I veterans as a music therapist, gaining experience and insight into the therapeutic value of music. Inspired by the writings of Eva Vescelius, she published her own guide for the aspiring music therapist in 1920, entitled *What Music Can Do For You.* Over the next 25 years, she actively promoted music therapy through her writings and practical demonstrations. During the depression of the 1930s, she became involved in the Federal Music Project of the Works Progress Administration, which was an employment program implemented by the Roosevelt administration. Under her guidance, music programs were presented at numerous New York City hospitals and prisons. She conducted experiments to determine the effectiveness of certain types of music on physical and mental disorders (Davis 1997). Seymour founded the National Foundation for Music Therapy in 1941. As president, she presented lectures and taught classes, emphasizing music therapy techniques used with returning World War II veterans. Her career culminated with the 1944 publication of the first text outlining a course of study in music therapy (Boxberger 1962; Seymour and Garrett 1944).

An Instruction Course in the Use of Practice of Musical Therapy presented Seymour's ideas about the appropriate applications of music with a variety of clinical populations. Only brief consideration was given to specific techniques. Essentially, her therapeutic strategy was the same for all clients, consisting of a variety of light classical music selections and folk songs performed by a small group of musicians under the guidance of a lead therapist. According to Seymour, a successful therapeutic experience was achieved through a combination of the music and positive thought, or musical meditation. Because the book was crude in its appearance, organized in a confusing manner, and printed with errors in typesetting and spelling, it is unlikely that the book received wide distribution or use. Despite those shortcomings, Seymour may have used the text to help train some of the 500 music therapy students that she claimed to have worked with between 1941 and 1944 (Davis 1996).

Although the number of reports of music therapy activity in institutional settings increased dramatically during the first half of the twentieth century, music therapy was not widely accepted as a profession by the medical community. The attempts of Vescelius, Ilsen, and Seymour to establish permanent jobs in hospitals, prisons, and schools met with only partial success, probably because of limited support from physicians and hospital administrators (Davis 1993). Some doctors, however, actively promoted music therapy. In 1914, Dr. Evan O'Neill Kane, in a letter to the *Journal of the American Medical Association,* enthusiastically endorsed the use of the phonograph in the operating arena for the purposes of distracting and calming patients undergoing surgical procedures. The music was particularly important during the administration of anesthesia, because ". . . the phonograph talks, sings, or plays on, no matter how anxious, busy or abstracted the surgeon, anesthetist and assistants may be, and fills the ears of the perturbed patient with agreeable sounds and his mind with other thoughts than that of his present danger" (Kane, p. 1829).

In 1915, Dr. W. P. Burdick, who often worked with Kane in the operating room, reported in the *American Yearbook of Anesthesia and Analgesia* that the phonograph was being used not only in operating rooms, but also in wards as a diversion from discomfort and an aid to sleep. Burdick indicated that even the most serious cases improved while the music was playing and that 95 percent of his patients expressed interest in having the music as part of the healing process (Burdick 1915).

In 1920, Esther Gatewood further emphasized the use of music in the operating arena, especially during the administration of anesthesia. Like Kane and Burdick, Gatewood advocated patient-preferred music during surgical procedures but believed that it was important to initially match the music to the mood of the client, then to change the temperament of the patient by degree. Gatewood was describing the technique which would later be named the iso principle. This principle became more fully developed in the 1940s by Ira Altshuler (Taylor 1981).

As more reports appeared, the use of music spread from the operating room to other treatment areas. In 1929, Duke University included music for patients not only in operating and recovery areas, but also in wards for both children and adults. Every patient had access to radio reception through earphones or speakers located throughout the hospital. This development represented the first extensive commitment to music therapy by a major American hospital (Taylor 1981).

In 1930, J. A. McGlinn published an article that reviewed the side effects of anesthesia used in obstetric and gynecological procedures. McGlinn reported that music could effectively reduce patient anxiety during the administration of anesthesia without disrupting operating room routine. Specifically, he recognized four benefits of the music that was chosen to fit the mood of the patient: (1) it effectively masked the sounds in the operating room; (2) it engaged the attention of the patient under local or spinal anesthesia; (3) it relaxed operating room personnel, including nurses, doctors, and other assistants during the surgical procedure; and (4) it provided a source of entertainment for the custodial crews cleaning up after the operation. McGlinn also indicated a bias against jazz and "sentimental" music, believing that it had no place in the hospital (McGlinn 1930).

Dr. A. F. Erdman continued to champion the cause of music during surgical procedures in the 1930s. Like McGlinn, Erdman believed that music was effective in diverting the patient's attention from the impending operation. Instead of providing music for the entire staff, however, Erdman experimented with a Western Electric music reproducer and earphones, which allowed the patient to hear both the music and instructions from the surgeon. Preferences of the patient were considered when selecting the music prior to the surgical procedure (Erdman 1934).

Besides its use during surgical procedures, music therapy was also employed in hospital orthopedic and pediatric wards. Harriet Ayer Seymour, founder of the National Foundation for Music Therapy, prescribed specific styles of music for children suffering from ailments such as tuberculosis and physical disabilities. Later, music was successfully used by physicians including K. L. Pickerall and others in all phases of a patient's hospital stay, from admission to discharge. In addition to the reduction in anxiety provided by the music, Pickerall noted that medication levels were often reduced and that recovery time was shorter than with clients not receiving music (Taylor 1981).

Willem Van de Wall was another music therapy innovator noted chiefly for his contributions to the development of music therapy programs in mental hospitals and prisons between World War I and World War II. The Russell Sage Foundation, a philanthropic organization devoted to improving the human condition, provided financial support for his work. Grants led to the publication of a number of important books on music therapy, including a comprehensive work entitled *Music in Institutions,* published in 1936.

Van de Wall, like Anderton and Ilsen, lectured on music and health at Columbia University, from 1925 to 1932. He also served on the State of Pennsylvania's Bureau of Mental Health, where he was a field representative in charge of music and other therapeutic programs. This position was developed to improve conditions in Pennsylvania mental hospitals (Boxberger 1963). The first hospital music program developed by Van de Wall in the Commonwealth of Pennsylvania was at Allentown State Hospital for Mental Diseases during the late 1920s. In 1944, Van de Wall was appointed chairman of the Committee for the Use of Music in Hospitals, whose purpose was to oversee the progress of music therapy programs in psychiatric hospitals. Boxberger (1963) considered Willem Van de Wall one of the most important twentieth-century figures in the development of music therapy in hospitals and institutions.

Although substantial music therapy activity was recorded during the first four decades of the twentieth century, there was no trend toward its regular use. Despite support from such people as Van de Wall, Vescelius, Ilsen, and Seymour, music therapy had still not developed as an organized clinical profession (Boxberger 1962).

THE DEVELOPMENT OF THE MUSIC THERAPY PROFESSION

In the 1940s, the use of music in the treatment of psychiatric disorders became more widespread, partly because of a gradual change in treatment philosophy. Many therapists, including the eminent psychiatrist Karl Menninger, began to advocate a holistic treatment approach (one that incorporates a variety of treatment modalities). With this shift in philosophy and increased knowledge about its effective applications, music therapy finally became an accepted treatment modality in many hospitals. In addition, the belief that music was somehow "magic" was starting to be dispelled as hospitals and clinics began to sponsor scientific research in music therapy. Much of this effort can be attributed to Frances Paperte, founder of the Music Research Foundation in 1944, and later director of applied music at Walter Reed General Hospital located in Washington, D.C. (Rorke 1996).

During World War II, numerous organizations, including the Musicians Emergency Fund, the Hospitalized Veterans Music Service, Sigma Alpha Iota, Mu Phi Epsilon, and Delta Omicron, provided musicians to Veterans Administration hospitals and later to state institutions. These volunteers assisted hospital staff in organizing ongoing music programs for patients.

At that time, most music therapists were unpaid, part-time staff members who worked under the supervision of hospital personnel and lacked professional status.

Many people began to recognize that future growth of the profession would be predicated on effective leadership of trained music therapists. During the 1940s, institutions such as Michigan State University, the University of Kansas, Chicago Musical College, College of the Pacific, and Alverno College started programs to train music therapists at both the undergraduate and graduate levels (Boxberger 1962). Graduates of these programs comprised the first group of professionally trained music therapists, most of whom worked with persons who were mentally ill (Figure 2-1).

While music therapy training programs were being developed at a few colleges and universities, movement toward the formation of a national organization was also taking place. The Committee on Music in Therapy of the Music Teachers National Association (MTNA) presented programs during the late 1940s to educate musicians, physicians, psychiatrists, and others in the ways that therapeutic music could be used in schools and hospitals. Ray Green chaired an organizational committee to form a national music therapy association (Boxberger 1962). The first meeting of the new organization took place in June 1950. Attendees adopted a constitution, set goals, developed membership categories, and appointed a standing committee for research. The National Association for Music Therapy, Inc. (NAMT) was born. The first annual conference was held in conjunction with MTNA in Washington, D.C., during December of 1950. The years following the founding of NAMT focused on improving education and clinical training as well as establishing standards and procedures for the certification of music therapists. Professional publications also enhanced the credibility of the young organization. Monthly newsletters, annual publications, and quarterly periodicals preceded the establishment of the *Journal of Music Therapy (JMT)* in 1964. This journal, edited by William Sears, was (and still is) devoted to research efforts of music therapists.

FIGURE 2-1 Music therapy session with psychiatric clients c. 1958. Source: University of Kansas Archives

FIGURE 2-2 E. Thayer Gaston. Source: University of Kansas Archives

Probably the most important leader in the field of music therapy during the formative years of NAMT was E. Thayer Gaston (1901–71) (Figure 2-2). As chairman of the Music Education Department at the University of Kansas, he championed the cause of music therapy during the decades of the 40s, 50s, and 60s. In collaboration with the renowned Menninger Clinic, a facility in Topeka, Kansas, that specializes in the treatment of mental disorders, he established the first internship training site in the United States. In addition, Gaston started the first graduate music therapy program in the United States at the University of Kansas. His "insatiable thirst for knowledge, dedication to scholarship, and unquestioned integrity led to his preeminent position in this field, and many of his associates referred to him as the 'father of music therapy' " (Johnson 1981, 279).

Perhaps the most important action taken by NAMT during its early years was the establishment of the registered music therapist (RMT) credential. This designation was established in 1956 in conjunction with the National Association for Schools of Music (NASM), which served as the accrediting agency. The RMT credential provided assurance to employers that the therapist had met educational and clinical standards set by NAMT and National Association for Schools of Music (NASM).

As the number of RMTs increased, so did the types of populations served. During the early years of NAMT, music therapists worked primarily with psychiatric patients in large, state-supported institutions. By the mid-1960s, music therapists were also working with mentally retarded adults and children, physically disabled people, and sensory impaired individuals. By 1990, music therapy clients included elderly people in nursing homes, patients with medical conditions, and prisoners. During the final years of the twentieth century, music therapists continue to work with increasingly diverse clinical populations. In addition to the conditions listed above, significant numbers of music therapists are improving the lives of persons with Retts syndrome, AIDS, substance abuse, and terminal illness.

A second organization, the American Association for Music Therapy (AAMT), was established in 1971. Many of its purposes were similar to those of NAMT but differed in the way music therapists were trained academically and clinically (see Chapter 1). In January of 1998 the National Association for Music Therapy and American Association for Music Therapy merged to create a single organization, the American Music Therapy Association (AMTA).

Since the inception of NAMT in 1950 and AAMT in 1971, the profession of music therapy has continued to grow, with both organizations emphasizing high standards for education, clinical training, and clinical practice. In addition, publications have added to the development of the profession. *Music Therapy,* published annually by AAMT, began in 1980 and a second NAMT periodical, *Music Therapy Perspectives,* began publication in 1984. This semiannual journal provides information on music therapy techniques with specific populations. Since 1998, the *Journal of Music Therapy* and *Music Therapy Perspectives* have served as the two official journals of AMTA. In 1985, a board certification exam sponsored by both NAMT and AAMT was implemented to strengthen the credibility of the profession. In 1997, there were more than 3,600 NAMT members and 700 AAMT members in the United States working in diverse settings with a variety of disability groups. The music therapy profession is strong and viable and anticipates continued growth into the twenty-first century.

SUMMARY

The earliest references to the relationship between music and medicine are found in ancient preliterate cultures. In some of those societies, which exist in parts of the world today, an ill person was seen as a victim of an evil spell, and in others, as a sinner against a tribal god. Music was used extensively in healing rituals by "medicine men," either to appease the gods who had caused the illness or to drive away evil spirits from the patient's body.

Throughout the development of civilization, the relationship between music and healing has complemented the theory of disease prevalent at the time. This evolutionary process has included periods of magic, magico-religious, and rational interpretations of disease. By the sixth century B.C., rational medicine had almost completely replaced magical and religious treatment in Greece. For the first time in history, the study of health and disease was based on empirical evidence. The predominant theory at the time was that of the four cardinal humors developed during the time of Hippocrates.

During the Middle Ages, Christianity influenced attitudes toward sick people, who were viewed as neither inferior nor being punished for their sins. Hospitals were established to provide humanitarian care to persons with physical ailments, although the mentally ill population was still mistreated. The theory of the four cardinal humors was still predominant and provided the basis for the use of music in the treatment of disease.

Advances in anatomy, physiology, and clinical medicine during the Renaissance marked the beginning of the scientific approach to medicine. However, treatment of disease was still based upon the theories of the Greek physicians Galen and Hippocrates. Music was often used in combination with medicine and art to treat medical conditions and also as a preventive measure against mental and physical disorders.

During the Baroque era, the theory of the four cardinal humors continued to dominate but was joined by Kircher's theory of temperaments and affections. Music continued to be closely linked with medical practice. Music was used to treat physical ailments as before but also played an increasing role in the amelioration of mental disorders such as depression.

Music in the treatment of disease was still popular during the last few decades of the eighteenth century, but a shift was underway to a more scientific approach to medicine. This change was evident in Europe as well as in the United States. Accounts of music therapy in the United States first appeared during the late eighteenth century, as various physicians, musicians, and psychiatrists supported its use in the treatment of mental and physical disorders.

During the nineteenth and the first half of the twentieth centuries, music therapy was used regularly in hospitals and other institutions but almost always in conjunction with other therapies. The reports that appeared in books, periodicals, and newspapers persuaded early twentieth-century pioneers, such as Vescelius, Anderton, Ilsen, Van de Wall, and Seymour, to promote music therapy through personal crusades and organizations, which were, unfortunately, short lived. Researchers, such as Gatewood, Seymour, and Altshuler, attempted to study the reasons why music was effective in the treatment of certain physical and mental disorders; however, their efforts were overshadowed by the lack of trained music therapists and unsubstantiated claims of effectiveness that stunted the growth of the profession until collective research efforts and the establishment of undergraduate and graduate curricula began during the mid-1940s.

During World War II, music therapy was used primarily to boost the morale of returning veterans, but it was also used in the rehabilitation of leisure skills, socialization, and physical and emotional function. Most music therapists during this time served as volunteers under the supervision of doctors and other hospital staff.

With the formation of NAMT in 1950, and AAMT in 1971, professional recognition to the women and men working as music therapists was finally forthcoming. The development of a standardized curriculum, regular publications, an efficient administrative organization, and the merger of NAMT and AAMT to form the American Music Therapy Association in 1998, have all contributed to the growth of the profession. Today, music therapy is recognized as a strong, viable profession.

STUDY QUESTIONS

1 What is the concept of cause and treatment of disease in preliterate cultures?
2 Define and discuss the importance of the four cardinal humors in relationship to the ancient Greek concept of health and illness.
3 What part did music play in the treatment of disease during the Renaissance?

4 What was the importance of the unsigned article printed in *Columbia Magazine* in 1789?
5 Some of the prominent people in the mid-nineteenth century who established music therapy programs in institutional settings include ______________________________ .
6 Why were the music therapy experiments conducted on Blackwell's Island in 1878 considered important?
7 Describe the contributions of James L. Corning to music therapy.
8 Eva Vescelius was a music therapy pioneer in the early twentieth century who edited and published the first music therapy periodical in the United States. This journal was called ____________________ .
9 Who taught the first U.S. university courses in music therapy and where?
10 How was music used in the operating arena during the early part of the twentieth century?
11 What was the status of the music therapy profession during World War II?
12 Two periodicals published by the American Music Therapy Association include ____________________ and ____________________ .
13 What were the events of the late 1940s that led to the formation of NAMT?
14 Discuss the importance of the board certification (BC) in the music therapy profession.

REFERENCES

Atlee, E. A. 1804. *An inaugural essay on the influence of music in the cure of diseases.* Philadelphia: B. Graves, Printer.

Beardsley, G. L. 1882. The medical uses of music. *New England Medical Monthly* 2:214–216.

Blumer, G. A. 1892. Music in its relation to the mind. *American Journal of Insanity* 5:350–364.

Boxberger, R. 1962. Historical bases for the use of music in therapy. In *Music therapy 1961,* edited by E. H. Schneider, 125–166. Lawrence, KS: National Association for Music Therapy.

———. 1963. A historical study of the National Association for Music Therapy, Inc. In *Music Therapy 1962,* edited by E. H. Schneider, 133–197. Lawrence, KS: National Association for Music Therapy.

Burdick, W. P. 1915. The use of music during anesthesia and analgesia. In *The American yearbook of anesthesia and analgesia,* edited by F. H. McMechan. New York: Surgery Publishing.

Burton, R. 1651. *The anatomy of melancholy.* Oxford, England: Henry Cripps, Printer.

Carapetyan, A. 1948. Music and medicine in the Renaissance and in the 17th and 18th centuries. In *Music and medicine,* edited by D. M. Schullian and M. Schoen. New York: Wolff.

Carder, M. P. H. 1972. George Frederick Root, pioneer music educator: His contributions to mass instruction in music. Ph.D. diss., University of Maryland, College Park.

Carlson, E. T., J. L. Wollock, and P. S. Noel, eds. 1981. *Benjamin Rush's lectures on the mind.* Philadelphia: Philadelphia Philosophical Society. Columbia University to heal wounded by music. 1919. *Literary Digest* 60 (1 March): 59–62.

Corning, J. L. 1899. The use of musical vibrations before and during sleep—supplementary employment of chromatoscopic figures—a contribution to the therapeutics of the emotions. *Medical Record* 14:79–86.

Darrow, A. A., and G. N. Heller. 1985. Early advocates of music education for the hearing impaired: William Wolcott Turner and David Ely Bartlett. *Journal of Research in Music Education* 33:269–279.

Davis, W. B. 1985. An analysis of selected nineteenth-century music therapy literature. Ph.D. diss., University of Kansas, Lawrence, KS.

———. 1987. Music therapy in nineteenth-century America. *Journal of Music Therapy* 24:76–87.

———. 1993. Keeping the dream alive: Profiles of three early twentieth-century music therapists. *Journal of Music Therapy* 30:34–45.

———. 1996. An instruction course in the use and practice of musical therapy: The first handbook of music therapy clinical practice. *Journal of Music Therapy* 33:34–46.

———. 1997. Music therapy practice in New York City: A report from a panel of experts, March 17, 1937. *Journal of Music Therapy* 34:68–80.

Deutsch, A. 1949. *The mentally ill in America: A history of their care and treatment from colonial times.* 2d ed. New York: Columbia Press.

Edwards, L. B., ed. 1878. Music as mind medicine. *Virginia Medical Monthly* 4:920–923.

Erdman, A. F. 1934. The silent gramophone in local anesthesia and therapy. *Scientific American* 149:84.

Feder, E., and B. Feder. 1981. *The expressive arts therapies.* Englewood Cliffs, NJ: Prentice Hall.

Heller, G. N. 1987. Ideas, initiatives, and implementations: Music therapy in America, 1789–1848. *Journal of Music Therapy* 24:35–46.

Hodges, D. A., ed. 1980. *Handbook of music psychology.* Lawrence, KS: National Association for Music Therapy.

Ilsen, I. M. 1926. How music is used in hospitals. *Musician* 31:15, 30.

Johnson, R. E. 1981. E. Thayer Gaston: Leader in scientific thought on music in therapy and education. *Journal of Research in Music Education* 29:279–285.

Kane, E. O. 1914. The phonograph in the operating room. *Journal of the American Medical Association* 57:1829.

Mathews, S. J. 1806. *On the effects of music in curing and palliating diseases.* Philadelphia: Wagner.

McGlinn, J. A. 1930. Music in the operating room. *American Journal of Obstetrics and Gynecology* 20:678–683.

Medical powers of music. 1841. *The Musical Magazine; or, Repository of Musical Science, Literature and Intelligence* 55:45–47.

Merriam, A. P. 1964. *The anthropology of music.* Evanston, IL: Northwestern University Press.

Music physically considered. 1789. *Columbian Magazine* 111:90–93.

Musical prescriptions. 1919. *Literary Digest* 60 (23 August): 26.

Nettl, B. 1956. Aspects of primitive and folk music relevant to music therapy. In *Music therapy 1955,* edited by E. T. Gaston, 36–39. Lawrence, KS: Allen Press.

Remarkable cure of a fever by music: An attested fact. 1796. *New York Weekly Magazine* 11:44.

Rorke, M. A. 1996. Music and the wounded of World War II. *Journal of Music Therapy* 33:189–207.

Sachs, C. 1965. *The wellsprings of music.* New York: McGraw-Hill.

Seymour, H. A. 1920. *What music can do for you.* New York: Harper.

———, and E. E. Garrett. 1944. *An instruction course in the use and practice of musical therapy.* New York: National Foundation of Musical Therapy.

Sigerist, H. E. 1970. *Civilization and disease.* 3d ed. Chicago: University of Chicago Press.

Smith, B. 1978. Humanism and behaviorism in psychology: Theory and practice. *Journal of Humanistic Psychology* 18:27–36.

Stevenson, B., ed. 1967. *The home book of quotations: Classic and modern.* 10th ed. New York: Dodd, Mead.

Strunk, D. 1965. *Source readings in music history.* New York: Norton.

Taylor, D. B. 1981. Music in general hospital treatment from 1900 to 1950. *Journal of Music Therapy* 18:62–73.

Van de Wall, W. 1923. *Music in correctional institutions.* Albany, NY: Russell Sage Foundation.

———. 1936. *Music in institutions.* New York: Russell Sage Foundation.

Whittaker, J. T. 1874. Music as medicine. *The Clinic* 6:289–294.

Wimmer, S. J. 1889. The influence of music and its therapeutic value. *New York Medical Journal* 50:258–260.

Winner, E. 1982. *Invented worlds.* Cambridge, MA: Harvard University Press.

3

MUSIC: A HUMAN PHENOMENON AND THERAPEUTIC TOOL

Kate E. Gfeller

CHAPTER OUTLINE

Carol has gone to see her physician because she has a sore throat. After examining her, the doctor writes up a prescription for an antibiotic, which will kill the bacteria causing the infection. Had Carol's sore throat been the result of a virus rather than an infection, the physician would have recommended a different treatment regimen, because viruses do not respond to antibiotics as do bacterial infections. The physician's choice of treatment is based on scientific knowledge about human physiology, the causes of particular diseases, and the impact of specific medications and other treatments that have been tested through rigorous research and clinical trials.

Just as a physician should understand the effects of pharmaceuticals or surgical procedures, similarly, a professional music therapist should understand the influence of music and musical activity on physiological, psychological, and social functioning, and specific uses of music in a treatment regimen.

This chapter will focus on how humans respond to music throughout their life spans. Knowledge of human response to music forms an important foundation for therapeutic uses of music that will be presented in later chapters of this book.

HUMANS AS MUSICAL BEINGS

Humans and higher vertebrates of the animal kingdom are alike in many ways. Like humans, animals seek food and shelter, mate and form families, nurture their young, fight for territory, and even communicate through special vocalizations and body movements. One of the ways in which humans differ from animals, however, is through the creation of and purposeful involvement in music. This nonverbal form of communication is not necessary for survival, yet it is a prevalent part of everyday life and can be found in every culture known to humankind (Nettl 1956; Radocy and Boyle 1979).

For centuries, the power of music has been extolled in verse and song. Carlyle referred to music as "the speech of angels," and Martin Luther described music as an "art capable of affording peace and joy to the heart." Throughout recorded time, music has inspired comrades in battle, expressed social conscience and religious faith, elicited joyful dancing and play, and soothed fretful infants.

E. Thayer Gaston, an early leader in music therapy, describes music's power in the following way: "From a functional viewpoint, music is basically a means of communication. It is far more subtle than words. In fact, it is the wordless meaning of music that gives it potency and value. There would be no music and, perhaps, no need for it if it were possible to communicate verbally that which is easily communicated musically" (Gaston 1958, 143).

Nonverbal communication, then, often permits the demonstration of feelings and sentiments that need to be expressed for the sake of health. Music has always spoken for people and to people when words are inadequate (Gaston 1968).

"From the lullaby to the dirge"—these words suggest an important feature of music: the fact that music can be a valued art form from the first days of life through old age. This fact contributes to music's versatility and usefulness as an art form and a therapeutic medium.

MUSIC AS A LIFE-SPAN ACTIVITY

Youngsters are often told, When you get older, you can do that. Many enjoyable activities such as reading, riding a bike, drawing pictures, playing baseball, or conversing with friends require adequate mental or physical development for participation and are difficult or impossible for infants and very young children to do. In contrast, newborns all around the world have responded to the gentle lullabies or rhythmic nursery rhymes of caregivers. Music is a common part of everyday life for many infants and continues to be a prevalent art form throughout our lives. However, the manner in which we respond to, or create, music varies across the life span. In the following section, we will examine the musical development of children in light of physical, mental, social, and emotional growth.

Musical Development of Children

Musical, like nonmusical (i.e., walking or talking), skills emerge at somewhat different times from child to child; nevertheless, under normal circumstances, developmental milestones occur in a relatively predictable sequence. Although a number of existing theories describe the process of child development, probably the best known is that of Jean Piaget, a Swiss psychologist, who outlined four primary stages of child development: (1) sensorimotor, (2) preoperational, (3) concrete operations, and (4) formal operations. During each of these stages the child demonstrates a readiness for a particular level of mental, social, and motor ability. That is, at the outset of each of these stages, the normally developing child has matured physically (e.g., neurological and muscular development) to the point where he or she can perform the tasks characteristic of that stage. Development continues as the child interacts with the environment. For example, in order to take their first steps, toddlers must have adequate neuromuscular maturation to control their legs and trunk in purposeful movement. Recall the halting wobbly first steps of a toddler, often supported by the strong supportive arms of mom or dad. With repeated practice, those tiny muscles become stronger, and the child's steps become more sure and precise. As Piaget noted many years ago, developmental progress is the result of both physical maturation and interaction with the environment.

Although Piaget did not address musical development specifically in his writings, we know that musical response and involvement require a host of mental, motor, and social skills that have been documented by developmental psychologists. Researchers have studied musical milestones for each stage of child development, and participation in musical activity contributes to continued mental, social, and motor development.

Sensorimotor Development (Ages Newborn–2) During the sensorimotor stage of development, children learn about their environments through their senses and motor activity. For example, an infant initially learns about his or her mother through the sound of the mother's voice, scent, and touch. As motor skills develop, an infant begins to explore the immediate environment by grasping, mouthing objects, kicking, creeping, crawling, and other exploratory activities. For the child in this stage of development, music offers manifold opportunities for sensory stimulation and motor activity.

In the first days of existence, the infant will receive both sensory and motor stimulation as the parent rocks the baby, singing a lilting lullaby. Newborns are active listeners (Bayless and Ramsey 1982). Even though hearing is not fully developed at birth, young infants can discriminate one sound from another and seek out the source of the sound (McDonald and Simons 1989; Standley and Madsen 1990).

Infants as young as two days old will respond to fluctuations in a rhythmic beat (Spiegler 1967); babies of two months will fix attention on a singer or musical instrument. As the baby matures, he or she will respond with an expanding range of responses to musical sounds and objects. Musical bells or chimes can elicit smiles or wiggles from a three-month-old. During the first six months of life, children will seek out sensory stimulation and attend selectively to musical sound sources (Standley and Madsen 1990) such as lullabies, chants and rhymes, music boxes, rattles, and the musical inflection of the caregiver's voice. Bright-eyed babies coo with delight as they discover the silvery sound created as they kick the ankle bells on their booties.

Over the first year and a half, the child's listening skills evolve. Initially, the child will be able to discriminate musical dynamics (loud versus soft) and differences in timbre (i.e., environmental sounds and different types of musical instruments). Eventually, the ability to discriminate pitch and rhythm will evolve (Greenberg 1979; Moog 1976; Zimmerman 1971).

At the age of six months, gross physical response to music becomes more apparent. The infant of six months responds to music with generalized body movements. As physical maturation occurs, these movements eventually become purposeful arm and leg movements that occasionally synchronize briefly with an external beat (McDonald and Simons 1989). During this stage, the baby advances from reflexive to deliberate movements such as rolling over, sitting up, crawling, and eventually walking. Concurrently, the baby will learn to manipulate objects, including the shaking of rattles and the kicking of ankle bells, to musical sounds. The youngster bouncing on a parent's knee and clapping to the chant "Patty-Cake" is discovering the relationship of events in time through motor and tactile experiences. The toddler banging on pots and pans is learning about sound, shapes, and sizes. Increasing variety in motor activity occurs not only in the limbs and trunk, but also in the vocal mechanism. Vocal play and babbling (making repetitive sounds such as "buh, buh, buh" or "dadadadada") emerge between the ages of 12 to 18 months. These first babblings are important steps in developing motor control of the tongue, teeth, and lips. By 19 months, some melodic and rhythmic patterns appear in vocalization, followed by increasing use of spontaneous songs made up of short melodic intervals and flexible rhythmic patterns (Davidson et al. 1981). As children play in their cribs and sandboxes, the observant listener can hear short little melodic phrases that are paving the way for more sophisticated speech and songs.

Truly, the sensorimotor child is a musical child. Music as a sensory stimulation that promotes motor activity is an ideal medium for learning in these tender years. Music is a natural and enjoyable part of childhood and encompasses a range of responses including sensation, cognition, communication, socialization, and motor activity. Musical activities can be designed with the child's present developmental level in mind. Thus, it is a flexible and useful therapeutic and educational tool through which a child can practice and eventually master a host of important developmental tasks. Music functions as an excellent therapeutic medium for young infants and children (i.e., high-risk infants, hospitalized babies and toddlers, etc.), as well as for severely disabled persons who, despite an older age, are still functioning mentally at this initial level of development.

Preoperational Stage (Ages 2–7) The preoperational stage of development is characterized by rapid language and conceptual growth. The child can use words as symbols to represent objects and events in the environment rather than function solely through perceptual acts as is the case during the sensorimotor stage. For example, the child in the sensorimotor stage experiences the concepts of *fast* and *slow* by direct observation of, or participation in, events that exemplify these contrasting tempi (such as playing quickly and slowly on a drum). During the preoperational stage, the child can label these concepts with the words fast and slow and is no longer completely dependent upon physical involvement with the object or event for understanding. In music activities, the rapid development of language is apparent as the child learns to label musical objects and events, such as "big drums" and "little drums" or "loud music" and "soft music."

Burgeoning verbal communication is paralleled by increasing vocalization during music activities. In the earliest years of this developmental stage, the child may improvise short, melodic patterns, or join in on a few words of a song. For example, as the adult sings "Old MacDonald Had a Farm," the two- or three-year-old may join in on "e-I-e-I-o." More accurate imitation of pitch patterns and greater vocal involvement will occur as the child reaches ages four or five. Make-believe, action and story songs, and imitations are not only favorite singing experiences but also excellent opportunities for playful practice at communication (Barrickman 1989; Bayless and Ramsey 1982; McDonald and Simons 1989).

In addition to language growth, the preoperational stage of development is a time of increasing social awareness. In the first few years of this stage, children are very egocentric. In other words, they are unaware of others' points of view or needs. Children may play next to one another and be engaged in similar activities, but cooperation or interaction is rare. This type of playtime interaction is called *parallel play.* Around ages four or five, youngsters show increasing willingness to share and cooperate with their peers. Although still egocentric, children from ages four through six can be expected to follow directions, take turns, cooperate with others, and exhibit the other social amenities required for musical activities. Musical games such as "Farmer in the Dell" or "London Bridge" provide opportunities to practice and develop social skills.

Gradual motor development facilitates increasing coordination and a larger repertoire of movements (McDonald and Simons 1989). From ages two to four, toddlers may show brief moments of beat synchrony to rhythmic music. Beat competency, however, requires greater physical maturation, the rate of which varies from child to child. By age three or four, walking, galloping, and jumping can all be incorporated in musical games. Motor development is accompanied by increasing sophistication in spatial concepts, such as over, under, up, and down. Musical games such as the "Hokey Pokey," which require directed motor movement, encourage practice of these emerging spatial and motor skills. In the later years of the preoperational stage, normally developing children will master skipping and clapping to a beat.

Although children in the preoperational stage of development are no longer reliant solely upon sensory or motor experiences for understanding their world, activities with sensory and motor involvement are still valuable aids for learning (Gfeller 1990a; McDonald and Simons 1989) and form an important connection between direct experiences and symbolic representation. Many of the new language concepts, such as labeling of directions or size, are paired with visual aids or motor experiences in the educational setting.

As the individual matures through the preoperational stage of development, music continues to be an effective, enjoyable modality for learning. Music activities that require language, social cooperation, and physical activity promote practice and mastery of the skills that characterize this stage of development.

Concrete Operations (Ages 7–11) Around age seven, the normally developing child begins to understand her or his world in a new way. Youngsters in this developmental stage can think systematically and solve problems mentally as long as the situation is related to immediate reality (i.e., events common in their own experience). This ability to think logically helps the young musician learn musical notation and acquire concepts of rhythm and harmony. At this stage, children can sustain, or conserve, a melody or rhythm in their memories, despite distraction of harmony or competing melodies. For example, children can sustain a musical descant while other children sing another melody line.

The egocentrism of the preoperational child is giving way to a greater sense of community involvement. Social experiences outside the home, such as Boy Scouts, Brownies, and soccer, are valued events. Musical groups such as choirs and bands offer special opportunities for cooperation and group involvement.

By age seven, normally developing children have attained and refined their basic motor movements. Activities such as folk dances require sequencing of gross motor skills. Fine motor coordination is required for mastery of symphonic (string, woodwind, brass) and social instruments (guitar, autoharp).

For music therapy clients who are within the concrete operations stage of development, music acts effectively as a focal point for fostering social interaction and cooperation in groups. Furthermore, musical activities can provide ample opportunity for the development of motor functioning and for personal achievement and mastery of musical skills.

Formal Operations (Age 11–Adulthood) The most notable characteristic that distinguishes this stage of development is the ability to think abstractly. During the stage of concrete operations, children can think systematically and solve mental problems as long as the experience is related to their own world of events. However, in formal operations, people are able to grapple mentally with ideas outside their own realm of existence. For example, the young child of seven or eight may learn about world hunger from seeing the faces of starving children, or from missing his or her own lunch. The adolescent, however, can think about world hunger through abstract figures of crop production and population decline. Although the capacity to use abstract thinking is in place by junior high, formal thinking will be refined through a multitude of learning experiences throughout adulthood.

The Musical Adolescent

By adolescence, those children who have achieved formal operations have at their disposal a wide range of musical experiences. Some teenagers may participate in formal musical organizations such as choirs or drum and bugle corps. Others may start up their own informal musical groups, such as rock bands or jazz ensembles. However, playing music is not the only avenue of musical involvement. Teenagers spend many hours watching music videos or listening to musical recordings. Rock music, in particular, is an important part of teen culture, and music is often used as an outlet for feelings of rebellion and confusion that accompany this time of life (Brooks 1989). Because music is such an important part of adolescent culture, it can be an extremely powerful therapeutic tool for use with clients in this age group.

The Musical Adult

A small percentage of people develop musical skills to high levels of sophistication. These individuals become professional performers, music teachers, composers, and music therapists. Although the levels of musical involvement and skill vary greatly from adult to adult, music is a valued art form for many people. Musical listening brings beauty and enjoyment to life. Some adults find considerable satisfaction in avocational music activities, such as the church choir, civic band, or social dancing. As is the case with children, adults with no special musical talent or training can attain considerable enjoyment from listening to music. Our society spends large sums of money each year attending concerts, buying stereo equipment, and listening to recordings in order to bring music into our lives. All of these activities, whether active or passive, can contribute to a sense of community, enjoyment, and personal expression.

Older Adults In past years, some people assumed that musical enjoyment declines as we reach retirement. Old age is too often associated with senility, passivity, and indifference. Some researchers have suggested that as we reach old age, we disengage from the usual activities that filled our early and middle adult years. This theory, called disengagement theory, suggests that musical response and interest will decline as we age (Gibbons 1988). Research on the musical preferences, skills, and abilities of the elderly contradicts this notion.

It is true that hearing loss often accompanies the process of aging. Furthermore, research suggests that discrimination of small pitch changes or complex rhythm patterns may be more difficult for adults of age 65 or older (Gibbons 1982a, 1983). However, musical enjoyment does not necessarily decline during the years of retirement. In particular, older adults seem interested in music that was popular in their early years (Gibbons 1977). What is more, the tapping toes of the elderly as they listen to the big band music from their youth dispels the myth that older people like only quiet, sedate music.

Passive listening is not the only avenue for musical involvement during retirement years. According to Gibbons (1982b), many older adults express interest in singing and playing musical instruments. In fact, musical hobbies that were initiated during early childhood, may reemerge after the pressures of making a living subside (Larson 1983). As is the case with other age groups, preference for various styles of music will vary depending on the individual's past musical training and cultural background (Gilbert and Beal 1982; Lathom et al. 1982).

As we will learn in future chapters, music can be used therapeutically with older adults, including the elderly who are well and those with health problems. Music can be used to encourage social involvement and physical activities (i.e., music for social dancing or in sing-alongs) (Bright 1972; Palmer 1977). In addition, music can be used to express tender emotions. For example, some terminally ill adults may choose special songs to express their religious faith as they face their own mortality (Munro 1984).

In summary, music is an art form that is a valued part of our lives from infancy to our final days. The fact that music can be enjoyed by people of all ages contributes to its flexibility as a therapeutic tool. There are other ways in which music proves to be a flexible and usable art form. For example, music serves a wide variety of functions.

FUNCTIONS OF MUSIC

Scholars who study the lives of people around the world tell us that music is present in all known cultures. According to A. P. Merriam, "There is probably no other human cultural activity which is so all pervasive [as music] which reaches into, shapes, and often controls so much of human behavior" (Merriam 1964, 218).

If we think about the many ways in which music is used in our everyday lives, the list is almost endless. Music is heard on TV and radio, in places of business, at church, in schools, at sporting events, during concerts and dances, and at home, to name just a few. People spend millions of dollars annually on tape recordings, compact disc players, portable cassette players, tickets to concerts, and musical instruments. Music is enjoyed by young and old, rich and poor, male and female, and people from all walks of life.

Although the varied uses of music in society are too numerous to list, Merriam (1964) has attempted to classify the functions of, or broad purposes or reasons for, music in cultures around the world. He believes that the following 10 major functions exist in most cultures: (1) physical response, (2) communication, (3) emotional expression, (4) symbolic representation, (5) enforcement of conformity to social norms, (6) validation of social institutions and religious rituals, (7) contribution to the continuity and stability of culture, (8) contribution to the integration of society, (9) aesthetic enjoyment, (10) entertainment. We will next consider these functions.

Physical Response

It is easy to think of everyday examples of physical response to music: tapping toes to a good musical beat, bands marching to a drum cadence, dancing, clapping hands to a folk song. Not all physical response is so easy to see, however. Our bodies respond to musical stimuli in many covert ways as well, starting with the perception of music in the ear and auditory center of the brain.

Music as a Sensory Stimulus At its most basic level, music is a form of energy perceived by the auditory and tactile senses. Whether the sound source is a violin, piano, music box, or human voice in song, each musical source creates energy that causes the surrounding air molecules to move in patterns of greater (compression) or lesser (rarefaction) density. These patterns are known as sound waves (Figure 3-1). One of the biggest differences between music and other environmental noises is the fact that musical sound waves tend to be organized in a somewhat regular fashion over time. Structural qualities such as pitch, loudness, timbre, and harmony help the listener

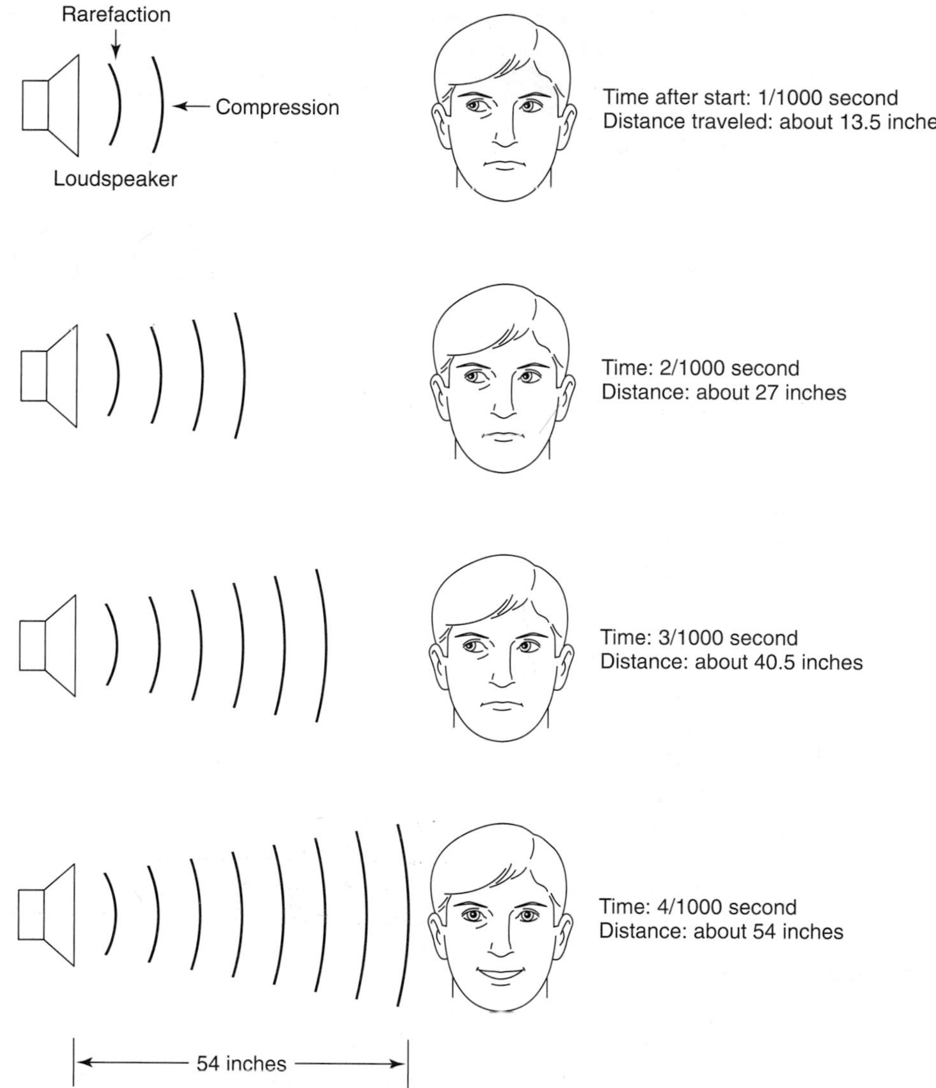

FIGURE 3-1 Progression of a sound wave from a loud speaker to a listener. Source: Theodore J. Glattke, "Sound and Hearing," in Hixon/Shriberg/Saxman, Introduction to Communication Disorders, © 1980, p. 102. Reprinted with permission of Prentice Hall, Inc., Englewood Cliffs, NJ.

organize the musical sounds into enjoyable and meaningful listening experiences. Sound waves are funneled into the ear canal to the tympanic membrane (eardrum), which in turn transmits this sound energy to other middle ear structures (Figure 3-2). There, three small bones, known as ossicles, conduct the sound waves to the inner ear, the cochlea. Sensory receptors for hearing, which are found within the cochlea, pick up information on the characteristics of the sound signal, such as frequency (pitch) and

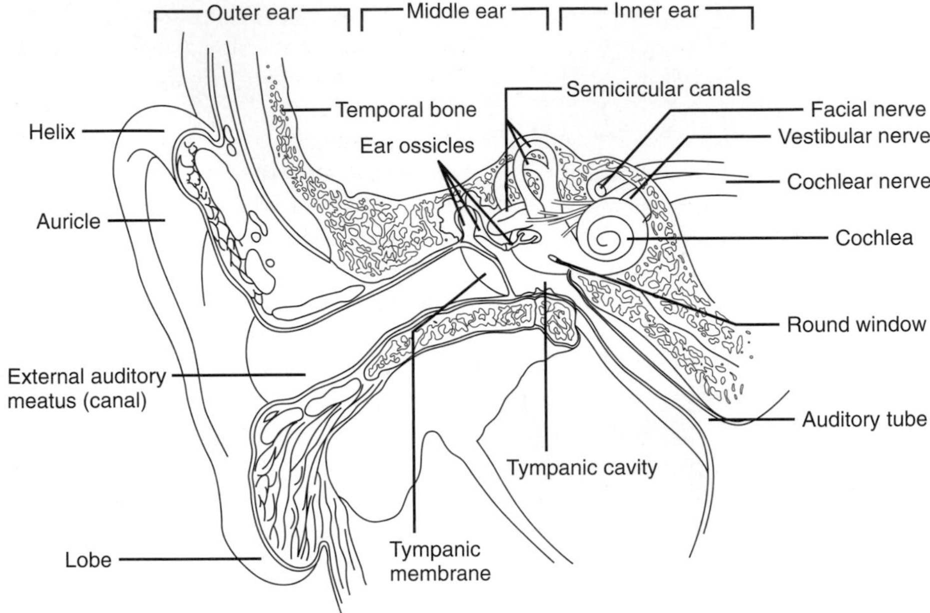

FIGURE 3-2 The ear. Note the external, middle, and inner ear. Source: From John W. Hole, Jr., Human Anatomy and Physiology, 5th ed. © 1990 Wm. C. Brown Publishers, Dubuque, Iowa. All rights reserved. Reprinted by permission.

magnitude (loudness). This information is then sent via the auditory nerve to the brain. The ear transmits the sound, but it is in the brain where the sound source takes on meaning. The brain perceives the physical organization of the melody, harmony, instrumentation, and other elements, and also interprets the music. For example, is the music of a familiar style? Is the music pretty? Does it sound sad, or bombastic, or irritating? No two people will interpret any given musical selection in exactly the same way because musical meaning is related to a whole host of factors such as past experiences, musical training, cultural perspective, and cognitive development. Musical response is a complex phenomenon that operates at a variety of functional levels (Gfeller 1990c).

Although the sense of hearing is that which comes to mind when we think of musical perception, sound waves are also perceived by the tactile sense, or sense of touch. For example, in your apartment or dorm room, you may feel the pulse of the rhythm from your neighbor's stereo in your chest cavity even if you cannot hear the tune. As the strings of a guitar are plucked, the wooden body of the guitar transmits the vibrations set up by the sound waves. Some sounds tend to be felt in the abdomen and chest; other frequencies resonate in the cranial bones. Because of this tactile transmission of music, even people with severe hearing loss can perceive musical stimuli.

Therapeutic Aspects of Sound At this most basic level, music as auditory and tactile stimulation can control attention and promote learning. In particular, if sound (auditory) stimuli are perceived as beautiful, novel, or interesting, they are more likely to garner attention. This has important implications for music therapy. For example, following a serious brain injury, some people may be unable to interact in many typical ways such as conversing or understanding complex instructions. Some of these same individuals, however, have shown alerting responses (i.e., blinking, smiling, making eye contact, tears, etc.) to attractive or familiar musical stimuli. In other words, the auditory and tactile stimulation of music can be a valuable tool in eliciting initial responses from patients who are unable at that point in time to respond in traditional verbal discourse.

Even adults with severe mental deficits who function at an intellectual level similar to infants can respond to music at this stimulus level. Engaging musical stimuli can capture the attention of severely disabled individuals who need encouragement to maintain attention with other people. In short, the auditory and vibrotactile qualities of music offer a very basic, yet attractive form of sensorimotor stimulation that can contribute to particular therapeutic objectives (Gfeller 1990c). Both Sears (1968) and Gaston (1968) attribute the therapeutic benefits of music to its structural properties, especially rhythm, which can assist the individual in self-organization and perceptual awareness.

The Effects of Music on Autonomic Responses For more than 100 years, scientists have been trying to find out how internal systems of the body, such as the circulatory or respiratory systems, respond to music (Thaut 1990). These internal and automatic functions are called autonomic responses, and are controlled by the autonomic nervous system. Scientists have studied the effects of various styles or tempi on body functions such as pulse rate, respiratory rate, blood pressure, and muscular tension. The bulk of studies on physical response to music support the notion that music influences physiological response. However, researchers have discovered a variety of responses to different kinds of music: No clear picture of specific types or direction of response exists (Dainow 1977; Thaut 1990). For example, we cannot say with certainty that all people will show an increase in heart rate if they hear Beethoven's Fifth Symphony and a decrease in heart rate to Brahm's "Lullaby."

Why is there so little agreement? In part, the outcomes of some of the research studies differ because the various scientists have used very different types of music, or because they measured body functions in inconsistent ways. But part of the difference stems from the fact that human beings in general show such a variety of physical responses to any given stimulus. Human beings are very complicated. Not all people will react to a happy or fearful situation with exactly the same physical response. People have very individual reactivity patterns to many types of stimuli, including music (Thaut 1990). In addition, music is a complex stimulus that rapidly changes over time and is perceived differently from one person to the next.

In summary, musical stimuli do elicit physiological responses within what Thaut (1990) describes as highly idiosyncratic response patterns, determined not only by the differing characteristics of the music, but also by the many variables within the individual. Although we cannot easily predict autonomic responses to music, we can speak with somewhat greater confidence about gross motor response to musical stimuli.

Rhythmic Auditory–Motor Integration Although the body of research concerning the role of auditory perception in motor learning is still relatively small, there are several basic ways in which a predictable and regularly recurring rhythmic signal is believed to facilitate temporal (doing movement at a particular time) muscular control of movement patterns (Thaut 1990): by (1) influencing the timing and readiness (called potentiation) of the nervous system, which in turn controls physical movement; and (2) assisting automatic movement by providing a cue for timing. In addition to motor readiness, music can have an impact on psychophysiological factors affecting motor performance, such as fatigue.

According to studies conducted by several scientists (Pal'tsev and El'ner 1967; Rossignol 1971; Rossignol and Jones 1976), sound primes the motor system by arousing the motor neurons in the spinal cord and thus sets the motor system in a state of heightened readiness and excitability. When sound is organized in repetitive rhythmic patterns, the priming effect begins to arouse the motor neurons and activates muscle patterns in a predictable time structure, thus creating a physiological auditory–motor entrainment effect; that is, the motor system tends to synchronize movement responses to the time structure of auditory rhythmic stimuli. This synchronization remains very stable, even when the rhythm changes (Thaut and Schauer 1997).

Recent research (Thaut and Miller 1994; Thaut et al. 1998) suggests that synchronization occurs in the following manner: after hearing one or two beat intervals, the brain very rapidly computes a representation of the duration of the beat interval, then the brain matches the duration of the movement to the beat interval, and after establishing a preferred comfortable timing between the beat and movement response, synchronization is maintained by matching the duration of the movement to the rhythmic beat interval. This has important implications for the use of rhythm to cue movement. Examples from everyday life come to mind: marching to a drum cadence, dancing to rhythmic music, or doing aerobic exercise to music that has a strong beat. In these sorts of situations, the person listening to the rhythmic beat can use the regularly recurring beat to help anticipate the correct speed of movement.

In addition to the effect of rhythm on readiness and timing, attention to a positive auditory stimulus can divert attention from physical discomfort or fatigue that can accompany motor activity and physical rehabilitation (Marteniuk 1976). This can assist with motor persistence.

Therapeutic Benefits As we will find in the section on orthopedic disabilities, the fact that rhythmic stimuli serve to enhance timing and readiness can be helpful for treatment programs such as gait rehabilitation or physical fitness programs. According to Gaston (1968), "the utilization of the unique potential of rhythm to energize and bring order" (v) is one of the primary ways in which music contributes to the therapeutic process.

Recent clinical research and studies regarding rhythmic perception suggest an important role for auditory rhythm in motor control and the rehabilitation of movement disorders, especially for gait in neurological disorders such as stroke (Thaut et al. 1993; Jeffery and Good 1995; Prassas et al. 1997) and Parkinson's disease (Miller et al. 1996; Mcintosh et al. 1997). Rhythmically cued movements have resulted in immediate improvements in motor performance as well as longer-term and stable therapeutic improvements over time (Thaut et al. 1996; Thaut et al. 1997).

In addition to enhancing timing and readiness, music can also help sustain muscular effort. For example, according to Marteniuk (1976), through the process of selective attention, an individual may pay more attention to the pleasant stimuli of enjoyable music than to the muscular fatigue that accompanies extended exercise. For many years, music therapists have also noted that doing physical movements in activities such as playing musical instruments can be highly motivating, thus reducing the drudgery of laborious and repetitive physical exercises (Staum 1983; Thaut 1990).

Therefore, the long recognized link between music and physical response can be exploited in a variety of ways in order to maintain or improve physical functioning. Music can be used (1) as tactile stimulation, (2) to stimulate motor readiness (i.e., in rhythmic gait or aerobic exercise), (3) as a structure for motor movements, and (4) as motivation or distraction to encourage persistence during labored or painful movement.

Physical response is only one of many ways in which we are affected by music. The next section will focus on music's function as a form of communication.

Music as Communication

Communication and Emotional Expression When we think of communication, we tend to think of words. For example, the letters c a d, when put together, bring to mind a sleazy womanizer who charms young naive ladies with flattery and promises. However, when we play the notes C A D on the piano, no specific meaning comes to mind. Musical symbols are abstract in nature and are not readily translatable (Kreitler and Kreitler 1972; Winner 1982). Yet music has long been considered a form of communication, for it is made up of a system of symbols through which people can express themselves (Berlyne 1971; Kreitler and Kreitler 1972).

Music has long been associated with emotional expression and, in fact, has even been called the "language of emotions" (Winner 1982). As a purveyor of emotions, music plays an important role in society, because it provides a vehicle for expression of ideas and emotions that are not easily expressed through ordinary discourse (Radocy and Boyle 1979). In some instances, such as times of sorrow or loss, we may find words inadequate for expressing our deepest feelings. In other instances, such as times of social protest, music is an acceptable way to express ideas that may be considered controversial or unacceptable if spoken. For example, teenagers or members of political groups have often used rock music as a vehicle for speaking out against the ills of society. Some have called this use of music to *let off steam* regarding social issues a *safety valve* function (Merriam 1964; Radocy and Boyle 1979).

Within a given culture, music alone conveys emotional content or mood (Gaston 1968; Merriam 1964; Radocy and Boyle 1979). But music, in conjunction with textual or visual information, can also intensify or alter the message found in the words or image (Galizio and Hendrick 1972; Gfeller et al. 1990; McFarland 1984; O'Brian and Willbanks 1978; Thayer and Levenson 1983; Wintle 1978). The extent to which music, a nonverbal language, can convey feelings and ideas can be illustrated by the use of music in sound tracks to movies and television programs. Film directors have long recognized the power of music to communicate. For example, in the days of silent pictures, much of the message of the movie was transmitted by the background music on the piano. As the train came closer and closer to the fair young maiden tied to the tracks, the music picked up in speed and power. Even today, with highly sophisticated cinematography and spoken dialogue, movie directors still rely on music to express the emotions behind the action. Love scenes are accompanied by the sweep of violins, and monsters are anticipated through the ominous thundering of discordant music. Closing your eyes during a horror movie is little consolation, because the background music alone can relay feelings of fear and impending doom.

Advertisements are another place in which music contributes to the meaning of the message. Notice the difference in the background music chosen to advertise a rugged Landrover Jeep compared with the music used on a commercial for a Mercedes Benz. Research has shown that music can be an effective form of communication for highlighting particular attributes of a product (Wintle 1978). To summarize, music as a form of communication can transmit nonverbal emotional messages, influence or reflect the mood of the listener, and can be used to intensify, amplify, or alter the meaning of imbedded textual or visual information (Gfeller 1990b; Gfeller et al. 1990).

Why is music so often used as an expression of emotion? Many scholars have attempted to answer this question over the past decades, and a variety of explanations have been proposed. Some have suggested that the *musical sound reminds us of or mirrors emotions and other nonmusical events in life* (Langer 1942). This is known as a *referential philosophy* of musical meaning. Others have suggested that the *meaning and resulting emotional expression are embodied, or found directly, in the musical structure itself.* This philosophy is known as *expressionism.* We will briefly examine these two points of view.

Music and Emotion

A Referentialist Point of View The term *referential* reflects the belief that the meaning in music arises from connections the listener makes between the music itself and some nonmusical object or event. For example, composers like Beethoven in his *Pastoral* (Sixth) Symphony used high-pitched trills on instruments such as the flute to imitate the sounds of birds. This musical reference brings to mind the pleasant sights, sounds, and smells of a walk through a sylvan glen. In contrast, the roll on a timpani drum might be used to connote the ominous sound of thunder or cannons of war. In addition to these more obvious imitations of nature or events, other structural qualities of music have been used to refer to nonmusical events or feelings. For example, depression, a feeling that often results in downcast facial expressions and slow, lethargic movement, might be represented musically through slow tempo or descending musical scales (Kreitler and Kreitler 1972). The imitation of nonmusical events or objects is called *iconicity.*

Iconicity is not the only mechanism through which music can refer to nonmusical events. *Association through contiguity* is another way in which music can refer to objects or events in life (Radocy and Boyle 1979). *This phenomenon occurs when a par-*

ticular musical selection or style of music has been paired with a specific event. The music alone can eventually elicit the same types of feelings that occurred as an event took place. For example, many of us have heard discordant music with shrill violins during frightening moments at a horror movie. As a result of this rather stereotypic use of music in horror movies, this musical style alone can evoke the "spine-tingling" feelings that we experienced as we watched an ax murderer or monster during the movie. On a more positive note, Sousa marches can evoke the feelings of excitement and team spirit associated with a football game.

Most of us can think of special songs or musical styles that bring back memories and feelings of past events. However, we can have an emotional response to music we have never heard before. Scholars of the expressionistic school of thought would argue that the true meaning in music is not reliant on extramusical references, but emerges from the structural qualities of the music itself. In other words, the emotional meaning of music is embodied in the music itself.

An Expressionistic Point of View From an *expressionistic* point of view, *music's value or meaning results from the musical sounds themselves and nothing more* (Radocy and Boyle 1979). It is the structural characteristics of the music itself, as opposed to extramusical associations, that excite feelings and emotions in the listener.

If the structural qualities of music can indeed evoke emotional response, how does this happen? Several people have proposed theories and conducted experiments to explain how emotions arise from musical experiences. One theory by psychologist Daniel Berlyne (1971) proposes that structural qualities of music, such as how complicated or simple or how familiar the composition is, contribute to emotional response. According to Berlyne's theory, we feel pleasurable feelings if the music is at an optimal, or ideal, level of complexity or familiarity. Music that is too complex or unfamiliar in style can leave the listener with a sense of confusion, chaos, and discomfort. In contrast, if music is too simple or has been heard again and again so that it lacks freshness, the listener may feel bored and unsatisfied.

This theory can be illustrated by considering the top 10 hits on the radio. When new songs are introduced on the radio, their style of music is often similar to many other popular songs, so some familiarity already exists. This familiarity helps people organize and make sense of what they are hearing. However, some songs attract particular attention because they contain novel and interesting elements, such as a unique beat or unusual lyrics.

But these top 10 hits will eventually drop from the top of the charts. Why? Because as they gain in popularity, radio disc jockeys tend to play them again and again—so often, in fact, that they lose some of that novelty or newness that attracted the listener in the first place. The rock hit at the top of the charts is, for that week, an example of a song that still contains the ideal balance between being unique and yet familiar. According to Berlyne, this balance arouses pleasant feelings in the listener.

Berlyne's theory (referred to as his *theory of arousal and hedonic value*) concerning emotional response to art such as music has been investigated through many research studies, and a number of experiments (Berlyne 1974; Gfeller et al. 1990; Gfeller and

Coffman 1990; Heyduk 1975) support this theory as plausible. Other theories of emotional response to music have been based not on experimental findings, but on philosophical inquiries in which the scholar has used logic to explain human response. Leonard Meyer's theory of expectations is one example. Meyer, a scholar of music, bases his beliefs about music and emotion on psychologist John Dewey's conflict theory of emotions. This theory states that emotions are aroused when a tendency to respond is arrested or inhibited (Meyer 1956). What does that mean? When we listen to music written in a familiar style, we often can anticipate what will come next. For example, imagine that someone plays the following notes on a piano: C, D, E, F, G, A, B, and then stops. Most people from Western cultures would be surprised because they expect to hear the scale completed with another note, C. This expectation of a completed major scale has been inhibited because the note was omitted. Some people may respond by actually singing the final note, some people may giggle, some people may show surprise on their faces. In short, the expectations of the listener are inhibited when the typical musical pattern is not completed, and an emotional response of surprise results.

This theory might also be illustrated by considering Haydn's *Surprise Symphony.* In this composition, the music proceeds along in a fairly predictable manner, when all of a sudden Haydn inserts an uncharacteristically loud chord. When people first hear this symphony, it often brings chortles or startled responses. According to Meyer's theory of expectations, these emotional responses are the result of inhibited or arrested expectations. It is the balance of the expected and unexpected within a composition that helps bring meaning and emotion to music.

Neurological Explanations Some researchers attribute emotional response to music to neurological changes in the brain (Goldstein 1980; Roederer 1982). Preliminary studies suggest that musical processing may take place, at least in part, in centers of the brain that are associated with emotional response, such as the limbic region of the brain. At present, research supporting this idea is just emerging. The brain is a very complex organ and still holds many mysteries, even for neurologists. But with increasingly sophisticated technologies that provide us with a better understanding of the brain, we should come to understand more thoroughly neurological explanations for affective or emotional responses to music.

Implications for Therapy Although many people would agree that music is linked with emotions, how does this relate to music's use in therapeutic settings? As we will discover in later chapters, many of the clients served in music therapy are struggling to express or cope with feelings in a healthy and appropriate way. For example, people with mental illness, or elderly persons facing impending death, may feel overwhelmed by sadness, a sense of isolation, anger, or other uncomfortable emotions. Rather than expressing their feelings directly, they may become withdrawn, or may even use aggressive ways such as attempting suicide or striking out at others if unable to express emotions and needs more directly.

Sometimes these same individuals who have difficulty expressing uncomfortable feelings verbally have found music a less threatening or alternative way to share emotions. Music as an outlet for expressing emotions has enormous potential as a therapeutic tool for clients with emotional upsets. As Gaston (1968) remarked, music can often express deep emotions when words no longer suffice.

Symbolic Representation

In addition to communicating emotional information, music conveys symbolic meaning. A symbol stands for or represents another thing, such as a cultural value or universal principle. For example, an artwork depicting a dove is not simply a picture of a bird with white feathers. Rather, the dove is often used to represent peace and harmony among people. Similarly, the opening motive of Beethoven's Fifth Symphony has often been perceived as a symbol of fate knocking at the door. According to Kreitler and Kreitler (1972), symbols expressed in art forms such as music may evoke sensations and feelings.

Musical symbols differ from culture to culture. Although many people describe music as the universal language, in actuality, no single style of music is meaningful to every culture. (Music does, however, has a certain universality in that it is an art form present within every culture known to us [Nettl 1956].) Rather, the traditions and beliefs of each culture influence musical creation and response. For example, in Western culture, much of our music has been organized around a series of half and whole tones that make up major and minor scales. We have often associated music based on a major scale with positive happy feelings, whereas music in a minor key often has connotations of melancholy or sadness. The dark, low timbre of an English horn may represent melancholy; the bright triadic outline of a trumpet fanfare would be more likely to connote triumph and exultation.

In contrast, music from India is organized around scalar patterns made up of smaller musical intervals, or semitones. For example, between our notes of C and D on the piano, an Indian scale may have several notes, not just one halftone (C#) in-between. An American listening to traditional Indian music for the first time will probably find it difficult to organize and understand the music because it is so different from his or her own culture's music. The American will also be at a loss to interpret the emotional sentiments expressed by the music.

In short, the symbols expressed in music operate within the context of a particular culture (Merriam 1964). Within any given culture, musical communication of mood and sentiments becomes somewhat standardized (Meyer 1956). These conventional symbolic uses of music connote a shared meaning to people with the same cultural background, and in so doing, act as an efficient purveyor of information. Each culture will represent feelings, cultural values, or other abstract ideals through its own musical symbols.

Implications for Therapy Because symbols can express information in a very powerful and efficient manner, musical symbols can be a useful tool for communication in therapeutic settings. However, it is crucial that the therapist is sensitive to the fact that symbols differ from one culture to the next. This is particularly important in work with diverse populations. The next section expands on the importance of music within a cultural context.

Music and Culture

Music and Social Values According to Merriam (1964), music reflects the values and behaviors of a given culture, such as sexual mores; the positions of men, women, and children in society; religious values; or work ethics. Songs of social control directly or indirectly inform members of society about proper behavior (Merriam 1964; Radocy and Boyle 1979), thus enforcing conformity to social norms. For example, during the initial stages of the Vietnam war, the government and many American citizens believed that this military effort was essential to protecting U.S. interests abroad. Song lyrics such as "One hundred men will fight today, but only three wear the green beret" (Green Berets are an exclusive group of highly trained soldiers) expressed the expectation that men in society should be brave in the face of battle and aggression. As the war dragged on, this conflict became increasingly controversial and the target of immense protest and political turmoil. These values were reflected in a host of songs such as "Give Peace a Chance," "The Cruel War Is Raging," and other antiwar ballads. These songs were as much a part of any political protest as any of the signs or rhetoric, and gave credence to the notion of peaceful resistance.

In addition to expressing appropriate behaviors and social norms, music has been used to validate social institutions and religious rituals. For example, our national anthem is sung at many major gatherings (i.e., sports events, school meetings, the dedication of buildings, etc.). Universities typically have a school fight song that describes the glories of the school. Most religions have a body of music that expresses the major tenets upon which the faith is founded. In some churches, for example, hymns and liturgy tell the creeds and legends of the church. These ritualized uses of music emphasize and transmit the most important attitudes and beliefs at the center of an organization or religion. As music enforces conformity to social norms and validates social institutions and religious rituals, cultural values and beliefs are shared among members of the community and transmitted from one generation to the next.

As Merriam (1964) points out, "few elements of culture are so diverse as is music in meeting human needs. Music allows emotional expression, gives aesthetic pleasure, entertains, communicates, elicits physical response, enforces conformity to social norms, and validates social institutions and religious rituals. [Therefore] it is clear that it contributes to the continuity and stability of culture" (Merriam 1964, 225).

Cultural Issues in the Therapeutic Process Because music is so commonly found in everyday life, it is easy to take for granted its power as a bearer of cultural values. However, we can no doubt all remember times when we joined our fellow humans in song for a religious or political event. "The Battle Hymn of the Republic," "Amazing Grace," and "We Shall Overcome" have buoyed our spirits and strengthened our resolve. As music therapists work with individuals who are struggling with pain or emotional distress, music as a bearer of culture can help support the individual in his or her quest for meaning and quality of life.

As we consider the power of music as a bearer of culture, it is important to realize, however, that each culture has its own musical heritage. Musical meaning is shaped not only by national citizenship, but by our membership in a variety of subcultures. Religious affiliation is a strong cultural context through which we perceive and interpret music. The hymn "Amazing Grace" may have great spiritual and sentimental value to a member of the Methodist church. In contrast, the complex, chromatic incantations of the rabbi will hold greater significance to people of Jewish heritage.

Our membership within a socioeconomic group can also affect our cultural perspective (Radocy and Boyle 1979). Several studies have shown preference for different styles of music based on income and formal education. For example, people in higher economic brackets tend to enjoy operas and symphonic works more than do blue-collar workers (Gilbert & Beal 1982; Lathom et al. 1982). In short, the value and meaning that we attribute to any given musical selection will be filtered through our own cultural context.

Is cultural context of any concern when using music toward a therapeutic purpose? Absolutely! The selection of musical stimuli for any intervention should take into account the cultural traditions of those clients involved. For example, a therapist may find that clients from a predominately Latino urban neighborhood along the Texas border are more comfortable with different styles of music than are Caucasian, blue-collar clients from the heart of Nashville, Tennessee. In short, no single style of music will be valued by all people, because music's ability to function depends on a commonality of experience with music in the appropriate functional context (Radocy and Boyle 1979).

Contributions to the Integration of Society According to Merriam (1964), music forms a solidarity point for social congregating, cooperation, and coordination. Consider the many musical events that require the combined efforts of many musicians toward a common goal: church choirs, community choruses, civic musicals, orchestras and bands, duets, trios, quartets, sing-alongs around a camp fire, bell choirs, bluegrass fiddlers at a square dance, jazz and rock groups—the list is almost endless. These musical activities call for a strong measure of cooperation because the extent to which the entire composition has merit depends on the contributions of each individual. The elements of rhythm, melody, and harmony require a level of order and structure created by the combined efforts of the group.

Social Integration as a Therapeutic Objective Although social integration may seem to be a natural by-product of everyday life, for many clients served by music therapists, social interaction is difficult or limited. For example, people with emotional disorders may demonstrate withdrawn or aggressive behaviors, which can prevent appropriate socialization. Other people, such as the elderly, may long for companionship and social opportunities, but may lack the physical strength or resources to initiate community involvement. For whatever reason, improved social interaction has been identified as an important goal in many music therapy settings.

Both Gaston (1968) and Sears (1968), early leaders in the professional development of music therapy, have noted the value of music as a tool in social integration. According to Gaston, music aids in "the establishment or reestablishment of interpersonal relationships" (1968, v). Because music activities often occur in groups, appropriately structured musical events can provide "experience in relating to others" (Sears 1968, 31). In fact, a perusal of research within music therapy journals over the past few decades indicates that improved socialization is a common goal in music therapy practice (Gfeller 1987).

Aesthetic Enjoyment and Entertainment

Another function of music identified by Merriam was that of aesthetic enjoyment. First, let's consider what this means. The word *aesthetics* refers to appreciation of the beautiful. According to philosophers, the value of an aesthetic object stems from its own intrinsic value as a thing of beauty rather than because it has a practical use or function. Therefore, when Merriam refers to music's function for aesthetic enjoyment, he is referring to the enrichment of culture through intrinsically beautiful and valuable music.

Music as entertainment refers to its use as amusement or diversion. Music for entertainment need not have lasting value as an art object but, rather, it helps people enjoy themselves or forget the cares of everyday life. For example, in the waiting room of the doctor's office or in an elevator, we often hear music that is intended to divert attention from the process of waiting. In a similar vein, some people play guitar or piano primarily for fun or to entertain others. In these instances, some of the music played may have artistic value, some may not. The major function of the music is enjoyment rather than artistic enrichment.

Some musical works are more representative of principles of aesthetics than entertainment. For example, Schoenberg's composition *A Survivor from Warsaw* tells the recollections of a prisoner in a concentration camp. This powerful composition is anything but amusing. Rather than acting as a diversion, this composition confronts the listener with the ugly realities of our history. The listener finds himself or herself feeling anxious and uncomfortable as the atrocities of the Nazi soldiers are recounted. Despite the dark and uncomfortable feelings it evokes, this composition has enormous aesthetic value as a meaningful work of art. It carries an important message about the human condition and will continue to express important messages as long as people are searching for ways to coexist with dignity and peace.

In contrast, some music is essentially entertaining and fun to hear, rather than functioning as an aesthetic art form. For example, the "bubble gum" music most beloved by junior high adolescents has a catchy beat that is perfect for dancing. These "come-and-go" hits are typically chosen for quick enjoyment rather than lasting value. Furthermore, the depth of artistic value and meaning could be debated.

Sometimes, music may have aesthetic value, yet may be entertaining as well. For example, many people would consider Mozart's opera, *The Magic Flute,* to be a work of true artistic value. The beautiful choruses and arias have taken their place among the great opera repertoire, and in the work the listener can find symbolic meaning concerning values of brotherhood and a better world. At the same time, the lavish scenery, amusing costumes, and comic elements in the opera are entertaining and enjoyable.

Implications for Music Therapy Music functions both as an aesthetic object and as entertainment in most cultures, and both functions fulfill important human needs. According to E. Thayer Gaston, the need for aesthetic expression and experience is essential to the development of humanness (Radocy and Boyle 1979). The involvement in a successful and fulfilling aesthetic experience can contribute to improved self-esteem through self-actualization (Gaston 1968). Similarly, the psychologist and philosopher Maslow (1970) maintains that aesthetic experience is crucial to a sense of personal worth or self-actualization, but follows prerequisite attainment of basic physiological needs.

As we will learn in later chapters, music therapists have long recognized that people with disabilities need and have the right to self-actualization and participation in aesthetic activities as part of the human experience (Nordoff and Robbins 1971; Ruud 1980). Thus, music as an aesthetic art form can contribute to the quality of life for many clients in music therapy. Although the use of music as entertainment may seem less noble or important than its use for aesthetic purposes, recreational music has its place in society and can even contribute to emotional and physical well-being. People often seek diversional activities to relieve tension after a difficult workday, or to take their minds off pressing personal matters. As a form of relaxation, diversional music can contribute to improved mental health and stress reduction. Sharing the fun of making music can also provide a focal point for group interaction and cooperation.

In conclusion, music is an important part of our lives, and functions in many different ways. Merriam's (1964) functions of music in society point out the breadth of roles that this art form plays in our everyday lives. At its most basic level, music is a form of sound energy that can stimulate the auditory or tactile senses. It can prime the nervous system for physical movement such as marching or dancing. Music is also a form of nonverbal communication exquisitely capable of expressing our deepest thoughts and most tender emotions. It is an art form that can bind us together toward a common resolve. Because music is such a flexible medium, it serves as a powerful tool for the professional music therapist in a variety of therapeutic objectives.

SUMMARY

There are many reasons why music can be used as a flexible and therapeutic tool. One advantage in using music is that some type of musical enjoyment or involvement is possible for people of any age. From the earliest days of infancy through old age, music can be appreciated by people both with and without formal musical training. Musical involvement will differ, however, depending on the level of development. Young children will experience music as a sensorimotor stimulus and can benefit from the direct experiences of making and listening to musical sounds. As the child grows older, participation in music as a social activity will become more and more common. In adulthood, music can be enjoyed through listening or direct participation, and as an individual or group member. Musical enjoyment can extend into the retirement years, offering a source of beauty and social involvement.

Another reason music can function so effectively for a variety of therapeutic purposes is the many uses of music in society. Merriam has outlined the following 10 functions of music: (1) physical response, (2) communication, (3) emotional expression, (4) symbolic representation, (5) enforcement of conformity to social norms, (6) validation of social institutions and religious rituals, (7) contribution to the continuity and stability of culture, (8) contribution to the integration of society, (9) aesthetic enjoyment, and (10) entertainment. Each of these functions has important implications for music therapy practice.

STUDY QUESTIONS

1 Describe the musical responses of a child in the sensorimotor stage of development.
2 What types of musical activities are engaging to a child in the preoperational stage of development?
3 Describe the musical capabilities of children who have reached the concrete operations stage of development.
4 What is the most notable cognitive characteristic of the formal operations stage of development?
5 How do the musical preferences and abilities of older adults compare to those of adults below the age of 65?
6 List Merriam's 10 functions of music in society, and give an everyday example that illustrates each one.
7 Compare and contrast the referentialist and expressionist views of music and emotions.
8 What does association through contiguity mean in the context of music and emotions?
9 Which psychologist believed that emotional responses to music resulted from the structural qualities (i.e., complexity, simplicity, etc.) of music?
10 What scholar is associated with the theory of expectations?
11 Is music a universal language? Explain your answer.
12 Compare and contrast the use of music for aesthetic purposes and for entertainment.
13 Describe our present research knowledge concerning the influence of music on autonomic responses.

REFERENCES

Barrickman, J. 1989. A developmental music therapy approach for preschool hospitalized children. *Music Therapy Perspectives* 7:10–16.

Bayless, K. M., and M. E. Ramsey. 1982. *Music, a way of life for the young child.* St. Louis, MO: Mosby.

Berlyne, D. E. 1971. *Aesthetics and psychobiology.* New York: Appleton-Century-Crofts.

———. 1974. *Studies in the new experimental aesthetics: Steps toward an objective psychology of aesthetic appreciation.* New York: Halsted Press.

Bright, R. 1972. *Music in geriatric care.* New York: St. Martin's Press.

Brooks, D. M. 1989. Music therapy enhances treatment with adolescents. *Music Therapy Perspectives,* 6:37–39.

Dainow, E. 1977. Physical effects and motor response to music. *Journal of Research in Music Education* 25:211–221.

Davidson, L., P. McKernon, and H. Gardner. 1981. The acquisition of song: A developmental approach. Documentary report of the Ann Arbor Symposium: National Symposium on the Applications of Psychology to the Teaching and Learning of Music. Reston, VA: Music Educators National Conference.

Galizio, M., and C. Hendrick. 1972. Effect of musical accompaniment on attitude: The guitar as a prop for persuasion. *Journal of Applied Social Psychology* 2:350–359.

Gaston, E. T. 1958. Music in therapy. In *Progress in psychotherapy,* edited by J. H. Masserman and J. L. Moreno, 142–148. New York: Grune and Stratton.

———, ed. 1968. *Music in therapy.* New York: Macmillan.

Gfeller, K. E. 1987. Music therapy theory and practice as reflected in research literature. *Journal of Music Therapy* 24:176–194.

———. 1990a. A cognitive-linguistic approach to language development for the preschool child with hearing impairment: Implications for music therapy practice. *Music Therapy Perspectives* 8:47–51.

———. 1990b. Music as communication. In *Music therapy in the treatment of adults with mental disorders,* edited by R. F. Unkefer, 50–62. New York: Schirmer.

———. 1990c. The function of aesthetic stimuli in the therapeutic process. In *Music therapy in the treatment of adults with mental disorders,* edited by R. F. Unkefer, 70–81. New York: Schirmer.

Gfeller, K. E., E. Asmus, E. Eckert, and M. Eckert. 1990. An investigation of musical stimuli on emotional response to verbal information. Paper presented at the Music Educators National Conference Research Session, Washington, DC.

Gfeller, K. E., and D. Coffman. 1990. An investigation of emotional response of trained musicians to verbal and musical information. Paper presented at the Music Educators National Conference Research Session, Washington, DC.

Gibbons, A. C. 1977. Popular music preferences of elderly people. *Journal of Music Therapy* 14:180–189.

———. 1982a. Music aptitude profile scores in a noninstitutionalized elderly population. *Journal of Research in Music Education* 30:23–29.

———. 1982b. Musical skill level self-evaluation in noninstitutionalized elderly. *Activities, Adaption, and Aging* 3:61-67.

———. 1983. Primary measures of music audiation scores in an institutionalized elderly population. *Journal of Music Therapy* 14:21–29.

———. 1988. A review of literature for music development/education and music therapy with the elderly. *Music Therapy Perspectives* 5:33–40.

Gilbert, J. P. 1977. Music therapy perspectives on death and dying. *Journal of Music Therapy* 14:165–171.

Gilbert, J. P., and M. Beal. 1982. Preferences of elderly individuals for selected music education experiences. *Journal of Research in Music Education* 30:247–253.

Goldstein, A. 1980. Thrills in response to music and other stimuli. *Physiological Psychology* 8:126–129.

Greenberg, M. 1979. *Your children need music.* Englewood Cliffs, NJ: Prentice Hall.

Heyduk, R. 1975. Rated preference for musical composition as it relates to complexity and exposure frequency. *Perception and Psychophysics* 17:84–91.

Jeffery, D. R., and D. C. Good. 1995. Rehabilitation of the stroke patient. *Current Opinion in Neurology* 8:62–68.

Kreitler, H., and S. Kreitler. 1972. *Psychology of the arts.* Durham, NC: Duke University Press.

Langer, S. 1942. *Philosophy in a new key.* New York: Mentor.

Larson, P. S. 1983. An exploratory study of lifelong musical interest and activity: Case studies of twelve retired adults. Ph.D. diss., Temple University. Philadelphia, PA. *Dissertation Abstracts International* 44: 100A.

Lathom, W., M. Peterson, and L. Havlicek. 1982. Musical preferences of older people attending nutritional sites. *Educational Gerontology: An International Bimonthly Journal* 8:155–165.

Marteniuk, R. G. 1976. *Information processing in motor skills.* New York: Holt, Rinehart and Winston.

Maslow, A. H. 1970. *Motivation and personality.* 2d ed. New York: Harper and Row.

McDonald, D. T., and G. M. Simons. 1989. *Musical growth and development.* New York: Schirmer.

McFarland, R. A. 1984. Effects of music upon emotional content of TAT stories. *Journal of Psychology* 116:227–234.

Mcintosh, G. C., S. H. Brown, R. R. Rice, and M. H. Thaut. 1997. Rhythmic auditory-motor facilitation of gait patterns in patients with parkinson's disease. *Journal of Neurology, Neurosurgery, and Psychiatry* 62:22–26.

Merriam, A. P. 1964. *The anthropology of music.* Evanston, IL: Northwestern University Press.

Meyer, L. B. 1956. *Emotion and meaning in music.* Chicago: University of Chicago Press.

Miller, R. A., M. H. Thaut, G. C. Mcintosh, and R. R. Rice. 1996. Components of emg symmetry and variability in Parkinsonian and healthy elderly gait. *Electroencephalography and Clinical Neurophysiology* 101:1–7.

Moog, H. 1976. The development of musical experience in children of preschool age. *Psychology of Music* 4:38–47.

Munro, S. 1984. *Music therapy in palliative/hospice care.* St. Louis, MO: Magnamusic-Baton.

Nettl, B. 1956. *Music in primitive cultures.* Cambridge, MA: Harvard University Press.

Nordoff, P., and C. Robbins. 1971. *Music therapy in special education.* New York: John Day.

O'Brian, M. P., and W. A. Willbanks. 1978. The effect of context on the perception of music. *Bulletin of the Psychonomic Society* 12:441–443.

Palmer, M. D. 1977. Music therapy in a comprehensive program of treatment and rehabilitation for the geriatric resident. *Journal of Music Therapy* 14:162–168.

Pal'tsev, Y. I., and A. M. El'ner. 1967. Change in the functional state of the segmental apparatus of the spinal chord under the influence of sound stimuli and its role in voluntary movements. *Biophysics* 12:1219–1226.

Prassas, S. G., M. H. Thaut, G. C. Macintosh, and R. R. Rice. 1997. Effect of auditory rhythmic cuing on gait kinematic parameters in hemiparetic stroke patients. *Gait and Posture* 6:218–223.

Radocy, R. E., and J. D. Boyle. 1979. *Psychological foundations of musical behavior.* Springfield, IL: Charles C Thomas.

Roederer, J. G. 1982. Physical and neuropsychological foundations of music. In *Music, mind, and brain,* edited by M. Clynes, 37–48. New York: Plenum Press.

Rossignol, S. 1971. Reaction of spinal motor neurons to musical sounds. *Proceedings XXV International Physics Congress IX.* Abstract 480.

Rossignol, S., and G. Jones. 1976. Audio-spinal influence in man studied by the H-reflex and its possible role on rhythmic movements synchronized to sound. *Electroencephalography and Clinical Neurophysiology* 41:83–92.

Ruud, E. 1980. *Music therapy and its relationship to current treatment theories.* St. Louis, MO: Magnamusic-Baton.

Sears, W. 1968. Processes in music therapy. In *Music in therapy,* edited by E. T. Gaston, 30–44. New York: Macmillan.

Spiegler, D. 1967. Factors involved in the development of prenatal rhythmic sensitivity. Ph.D. diss., West Virginia University, Morgantown, WV. *Dissertation Abstracts International* 28: 3886B.

Standley, J. M., and C. M. Madsen. 1990. Comparison of infant preferences and responses to auditory stimuli: Music, mother, and other female voice. *Journal of Music Therapy* 27:54–97.

Staum, M. 1983. Music and rhythmic stimuli in the rehabilitation of gait disorders. *Journal of Music Therapy* 20:69–87.

Thaut, M. H. 1990. Physiological and motor responses to music stimuli. In *Music therapy in the treatment of adults with mental disorders,* edited by R. F. Unkefer, 33–49. New York: Schirmer.

Thaut, M. H., G. C. Mcintosh, R. R. Rice, and S. G. Prassas. 1993. Effect of rhythmic cuing on temporal stride parameters and emg patterns in hemiparetic gait of stroke patients. *Journal of Neurologic Rehabilitation* 7:9–16.

Thaut, M. H., G. C. Mcintosh, R. R. Rice, R. A. Miller, J. Rathbun, and J. A. Brault. 1996. Rhythmic auditory stimulation in gait training with parkinson's disease patients. *Movement Disorders* 11:193–200.

Thaut, M. H., G. C. Mcintosh, and R. R. Rice. 1997. Rhythmic facilitation of gait training in hemiparetic stroke rehabilitation. *Journal of Neurological Sciences* 151:207–212.

Thaut, M. H., and R. A. Miller. 1994. Multiple synchronization strategies in tracking of rhythmic auditory stimulation. *Proceedings of the Society for Neuroscience.* 146:11.

Thaut, M. H., R. A. Miller, and M. L. Schauer. 1998. Multiple synchronization strategies in rhythmic sensorimotor tasks: phase vs. period corrections. *Biological Cybernetics.* In press.

Thaut, M. H., and M. L. Schauer. 1997. Weakly coupled oscillators in rhythmic motor synchronization. *Proceedings of the Society for Neuroscience* 298:20.

Thayer, J. F., and R. W. Levenson. 1983. Effects of music on psychophysiological responses to a stressful film. *Psychomusicology* 3:44–52.

Winner, E. 1982. *Invented worlds.* Cambridge, MA: Harvard University Press.

Wintle, R. R. 1978. Emotional impact of music on television commercials. Unpublished Ph.D. diss., University of Nebraska, Lincoln.

Zimmerman, M. P. 1971. *Musical characteristics of children.* Reston, VA: Music Educators National Conference.

PART TWO

POPULATIONS SERVED BY MUSIC THERAPISTS

4

MUSIC THERAPY FOR MENTALLY RETARDED CHILDREN AND ADULTS

William B. Davis

CHAPTER OUTLINE

School mornings at 10-year-old Jimmy's house are much like those for many families. After awakening, there are dressing and grooming chores to complete, breakfast to eat, and preparations to make for a full day at school. There are, however, differences in how these tasks are carried out, because Jimmy is mentally retarded. Although he is 10, he must have assistance with dressing, toileting, and feeding. Jimmy is educated in a special-education classroom at the public school that his brothers and sisters attend. He learns preacademic skills, such as the identification of basic colors, words, and numbers. He also learns social skills and works on communication and language arts skills. Jimmy requires help with gross and fine motor skills, so he visits an occupational therapist twice a week. He also works with a speech pathologist, a school psychologist, and a music therapist on a regular basis. Jimmy, like millions of other children and adults who are mentally retarded, exhibits developmental delays in language acquisition, cognitive abilities, motor skills, and social adaptation.

A BRIEF HISTORICAL PERSPECTIVE

A brief overview of past attitudes toward mental retardation enables us to better understand the current climate. With such a historical perspective, we can appreciate the various approaches to caring for a population that has been successful—and not so successful—over time.

Not too many decades ago, people with mental retardation were a very poorly treated segment of American society. Scorned, segregated, persecuted, and punished sometimes to death, these individuals were not given the chance to learn and contribute to society. Times have changed and, today, many mentally retarded people lead productive lives.

Before the eighteenth century, mental retardation was not considered a serious problem in any culture, because people with moderate or mild retardation usually functioned well in the predominantly agrarian culture of the time. Individuals with severe/profound retardation were likely to die from natural causes; those who survived but could not contribute to the productivity of society were often killed (Drew et al. 1996).

The move to improve care and treatment of persons with mental retardation began during the nineteenth century in France and Switzerland, then spread to the rest of

Europe and, finally, to the United States. Two Frenchmen—Jean Itard, a physician, and Edouard Seguin, an educator—developed programs to teach social, academic, language, and gross and fine motor skills to adults and children with mental retardation (Sheerenberger 1983). During the late 1800s, Seguin introduced his educational concepts to American institutions. Some of his ideas are still in use today, including a multidisciplinary approach to teaching, small class sizes, and the use of well-trained teachers. Seguin also advocated the use of music to teach listening skills and speech and to develop gross and fine motor skills. Because of his influence, many nineteenth-century schools for mentally retarded students used pianos and rhythm instruments to augment traditional teaching techniques (Kraft 1963).

Since 1900, the quality of education for individuals with mental retardation has continued to improve, albeit unevenly at times. Educational settings have ranged from large state-supported institutions to, more recently, small group homes and public school classrooms.

From the middle of the nineteenth century, music therapy has played an important role in the treatment of mental retardation in both institutional and educational settings. In this chapter, we will define mental retardation, learn about its causes, discuss teaching strategies, and learn how music therapy can be used in the habilitation of these individuals.

DEFINITION OF MENTAL RETARDATION

"Mental retardation is a concept that has meaning in personal, social and behavioral contexts. The various ways social scientists have classified and defined mental retardation over the years emphasize how the concept of mental retardation has changed. As perceptions have changed, understanding and acceptance have been significantly affected" (Drew et al. 1996, 54).

According to Thomas (1996), few other disciplines have had as much difficulty formulating a definition that is agreeable to professionals in the field. Diverse disciplines, such as medicine, education, law, sociology, and psychology have developed their own definitions to reflect a specific point of view. The most widely used and accepted definition was developed by the American Association on Mental Retardation (AAMR) (Drew et al. 1996). The AAMR definition of mental retardation states: "Mental retardation refers to substantial limitations in present functioning. It is characterized by significantly subaverage intellectual functioning existing concurrently with related limitations in two or more of the following applicable skill areas: communications, self-care, home living, social skills, community use, self-direction, health and safety, functional academics, leisure, and work. Mental retardation manifests before age 18" (AAMR 1992, 1).

There are three primary components within the AAMR definition of mental retardation: subaverage intellectual functioning, adaptive skill deficits, and onset prior to age 18. Let us look at those three areas in more detail.

1 Mental retardation is characterized by significantly subaverage intellectual functioning. Intellectual (or cognitive) functioning is usually determined from an intelligence quotient (IQ) test. On the Stanford-Binet Intelligence Scale, an IQ level below 70–75 signifies a deficit in intellectual functioning. This figure will vary slightly depending upon the psychometric scale used. When compared with peers of average or higher intelligence, adults and children with mental retardation are less likely to remember information, use abstract concepts, display logical reasoning, and make good decisions (Dunn and Fait 1989).

2 Mental retardation exists concurrently with related limitations in two or more of the following applicable skill areas: communication, self-care, home living, social skills, community use, self-direction, health and safety, functional academics, leisure and work. In other words, subaverage intelligence by itself is not sufficient for a diagnosis of mental retardation; adaptive skill deficits must also be present. This part of the definition was added following observations that some adults and children functioned well in life despite deficits in intelligence.

Evans (1990) defined adaptive skill as "The ability to change one's behavior to suit the demands of a situation" (34). Social expectations vary with age. During the first few years of life, mental retardation may manifest itself through significant delays in communication skills, self-help skills (the ability to care for personal needs), and sensorimotor activities (delays in crawling and walking). In adolescence, deficits in interpersonal relationships may indicate retardation. During adulthood, mental retardation may be apparent by the inability to hold a job or act in a socially responsible manner. Individuals with the most serious difficulties adapting to the norms and values of society must usually be cared for in an institution (Dunn and Fait 1989).

3 Mental retardation manifests before the age of 18. In most Western societies, 18 marks the age of adulthood. It should be noted that this portion of the definition has been criticized because mental retardation sometimes does not manifest until after age 18. A number of experts believe that the definition should be expanded to include adults with mental retardation who are in need of services such as vocational training. Public schools frequently use the age of 18 (and sometimes age 21) to terminate public education for students with mental retardation (Thomas 1996).

ASSESSMENT OF MENTAL RETARDATION

Historically, the assessment of persons with mental retardation was achieved through the use of standardized psychometric tests designed to measure intelligence, adaptive skills, educational achievement, and other facets of development (Hickson et al. 1995). Today, the prevailing concept of assessment has been enlarged to include the acquirement of knowledge from informal sources such as the home and school classroom.

The AAMR identifies four important considerations when assessing an individual for mental retardation:

1 The individual's cultural background, primary language, communication requirements, and behaviors must be considered. Not considering important factors such as the person's culture and primary language may render an assessment invalid and lead to an incorrect diagnosis.

2 The individual's intellectual and adaptive functioning must be assessed within the complexity requirements of his or her environment. Thus, a person with mental retardation who lives in a complex environment such as an urban area will have to negotiate a myriad of social and safety issues, whereas the same person living in a more predictable environment may function more independently.

3 An individual will likely exhibit strengths in some adaptive skills and deficits in others. A person with mental retardation will frequently display competence in one or more adaptive skill areas. For example, a person may have strengths in social and motor functioning while showing deficits in communication.

4 Most individuals with mental retardation can improve their adaptive skills over time with appropriate supports and services. In some situations, however, the goal may be to preserve the current functioning level or slow regression (AAMR 1992, 1).

CLASSIFICATION OF MENTAL RETARDATION

After a person has been diagnosed with mental retardation, the next step is to ascertain the level of severity. Classification is an attempt to sort individuals with mental retardation into categories on the basis of ability and/or achievement. Classification systems for mental retardation have varied over time much as definitions have. Until recently, most classification systems focused on two important criteria: severity and cause of the disability. The current edition of the *Diagnostic and Statistical Manual* (*DSM IV* 1994) uses IQ ranges as well as descriptors such as mild, moderate, severe, and profound to describe the severity of disability and level of adaptive behavior (see Table 4-1).

Mild Mental Retardation

A person with mild retardation has the capacity to learn basic math, reading, and writing skills up to about the sixth-grade level. These individuals are capable of living independently in the community but may need assistance and support when confronted with extraordinary social or vocational stress. They can usually become economically independent or semi-independent.

Children with mild retardation, sometimes referred to as "educable," are often mainstreamed (integrated into regular classrooms) in the public schools (Hickson et al. 1995). Most individuals with mild retardation appear physically normal and may not manifest signs of mental retardation until they enter school and fail to keep pace with their age-mates' academic progress (Brantley 1988). This category comprises approximately 35 percent of those defined as mentally retarded (*DSM IV* 1994).

TABLE 4-1 MENTAL RETARDATION DESCRIPTORS

Mild mental retardation: IQ level from 50–55 to 70
Moderate mental retardation: IQ level of 35–40 to 50–55
Severe mental retardation: IQ level 20–25 to 35–40
Profound mental retardation: IQ levels below 20 or 25
Mental retardation, severity unspecified: Intelligence not testable by available methods

Source: Diagnostic and Statistical Manual, 1994.

Moderate Mental Retardation

People who are moderately retarded are capable of learning functional academic skills up to about the second grade level, including basic reading proficiency, simple number concepts, and limited verbal communication skills. These individuals can learn self-help skills to meet their basic needs, such as toileting, dressing, and feeding. They can develop satisfactory interpersonal relationships with family members, friends, and acquaintances. Adults with moderate retardation may work in a supervised work setting, such as a sheltered workshop, which prepares persons with mental retardation for employment outside the institutional setting or, in some cases, provides permanent jobs within the institution (Brantley 1988; Drew et al. 1996).

Despite their abilities, however, adults with moderate retardation and children require supervision and economic support throughout their lives. Today, small residential group homes provide this support and supervision while simultaneously allowing residents to gain a measure of social and economic independence.

Children with moderate retardation, sometimes referred to as "trainable," are normally found in segregated classrooms within the public school setting. Along with intellectual deficits, they may exhibit secondary disabilities, such as speech and language disorders, neurological problems (cerebral palsy), sensory impairments (deafness and/or blindness), and poor eating and dental practices (Dunn and Fait 1989). This group makes up approximately 10 percent of the total population with mental retardation (*DSM IV* 1994).

Severe and Profound Mental Retardation

In addition to subnormal intelligence, many individuals with severe/profound retardation suffer from medical conditions that delay or completely arrest development of social skills. The approximately 4 percent to 6 percent of people with mental retardation who fall in this category also exhibit the disabilities described above, but with more frequency and severity (*DSM IV* 1994). In addition, musculoskeletal defects (malformed limbs), and debilitating emotional and psychiatric problems often accompany severe/profound retardation. Although many of the individuals in this category are able to attain some level of social competence in a highly structured, supervised setting, all need lifelong care and treatment.

Children with severe/profound retardation are sometimes placed in segregated public school classrooms but also may be educated within the residential institutional setting. The curriculum focuses on self-care skills (eating, dressing, and toileting) and rudimentary verbal and nonverbal communication skills (Brantlcy 1988).

A six-year-old child with mild or moderate retardation has a life expectancy comparable to that of a normal child. For children with severe or profound retardation, however, average life expectancy is significantly less, although some individuals will live to the age of 70 or 80. It is likely that this group will live longer in the future because of advances in medical treatment and care. This change will present challenges to both caregivers and policy makers to provide for the care of increasing numbers of elderly persons with mental retardation.

Mental Retardation, Severity Unspecified

The diagnosis of mental retardation, severity unspecified, is used when there is a high probability of mental retardation, but the person cannot be tested by available methods, such as standardized intelligence tests. People who would fall into this category would include one who is too disabled or uncooperative to be assessed, or an infant who cannot be tested by available psychometric tests, such as the Bayley Scales of Infant Development or the Cattell Infant Intelligence Scales. Generally, the younger the age of the person to be assessed, the more difficult it is to establish a diagnosis of mental retardation, with the exception of those who are profoundly impaired (*DSM IV* 1994).

AAMR CLASSIFICATION APPROACH

Mental retardation has been classified by the AAMR from a different perspective than that of the *DSM IV* and other approaches that have used IQ as the primary basis for classification. The AAMR system eliminated severity levels (mild, moderate, severe, and profound) and uses a single diagnostic code. A person is therefore diagnosed as either having or not having mental retardation based on subaverage intellectual functioning, adaptive behavior deficits in two or more of the skill areas listed previously, and age of onset (Luckasson et al. 1992). Differentiation is based on the level of support that the person with mental retardation needs.

Support levels from the most to least intrusive are: (1) pervasive, (2) extensive, (3) limited, and (4) intermittent. Pervasive and extensive supports are defined as continuous, extremely intrusive services that often extend beyond the school environment to vocational and home settings. Persons with profound and severe mental retardation often need pervasive or extensive support characterized by a high level of involvement by family, teachers, and medical personnel. Limited and intermittent supports involve less intrusive services and fewer support staff. Individuals with mild or moderate mental retardation usually fall into this category.

The intent is to provide an appropriate level of support for each individual that optimizes his or her functional level. It requires that the interdisciplinary team provide a pertinent and comprehensive assessment and treatment plan (Thomas 1996; Drew et al. 1996). A diagnosis of mental retardation under the AAMR system may therefore result in statements such as: (1) Bob is a person who is mentally retarded and needs extensive supports in functional academics, and (2) Jane is a person who is mentally retarded and needs intermittent supports in social skills, communication, and self-direction (Jones 1996).

CAUSES OF MENTAL RETARDATION 

The time before and shortly after birth are extremely critical to the health and well-being of a child who is at the mercy of his or her environment. There are a number of conditions that can damage the brain and cause mental retardation before or during birth or during childhood. Over 300 causes have been identified, but in about 30 percent to 40 percent of mental retardation cases, the etiology (cause) cannot be determined (*DSM IV* 1994).

In 1992 the AAMR identified a number of risk factors associated with the development of mental retardation. These include biomedical, social, behavioral, and educational factors. Biomedical factors comprise conditions caused by genetic disorders and poor nutrition; social factors relate to the quantity and quality of sensory stimulation that an infant receives from caregivers; behavioral factors include engaging in risky activities (driving recklessly, for example) and substance abuse by the mother; and educational factors encompass the quantity and quality of educational supports that aid in the development of cognitive and adaptive skills (Jones 1996). Mental retardation may be caused before birth (prenatal), during birth (perinatal), or after birth (postnatal).

Prenatal causes of mental retardation include chromosomal abnormalities and genetic errors. Disorders such as Down's syndrome or fragile X syndrome (two of the leading causes of mental retardation) are caused by changes in the number or structure of specific chromosomes. Phenylketonuria (PKU) is a genetic metabolic disorder that causes severe brain damage because of the body's inability to break down a chemical called phenylalanine. Drugs or toxic substances, such as alcohol or cocaine, ingested by a pregnant woman can lead to mental deficiency in her child. Other disorders in this category include tumors of the brain, the central or peripheral nervous system, or other organ systems. These conditions, many of which are hereditary, manifest in the postnatal period.

Neurofibromatosis, also known as von Recklinghausen's disease, is an inherited disorder of the nervous system and skin that also falls into this category. Mental deficiency can also be caused by the failure of the mother to maintain a balanced diet during pregnancy.

Perinatal causes of mental retardation include abnormal labor and delivery (premature, breech, multiple births), situations in which the infant's brain is deprived of oxygen (anoxia), and infections (meningitis, herpes, aids). Low or excessive birth weight are additional examples of perinatal conditions that can cause delayed cognitive development.

Whooping cough, chicken pox, and measles are examples of postnatal conditions that can, in a small number of cases, lead to meningitis or encephalitis, which can cause mental retardation. Other postnatal causes include injuries to the head, near drowning, or ingestion of lead, mercury, or other poisonous substance that damages the brain and/or nervous system.

It has been shown that most mental retardation with a known cause is due to adverse social and economic conditions. Numerous studies have confirmed the connection between poverty and mental retardation. Poor living conditions, malnutrition, inadequate prenatal and postnatal medical care, and dysfunctional family situations have all been linked to mental deficiency (Jacobson and Mulick 1996). In addition teenagers, women over the age of 35, undernourished or obese women, and women with diabetes or a history of genetic disorders have a higher risk of bearing a child with a gestational disorder leading to mental retardation.

In recent years, the number of cases of mental retardation has been reduced through aggressive improvements in prenatal care and in the ability to assess newborn babies for risk factors for mental retardation. With earlier identification of high-risk infants, interventions are initiated earlier, which leads to prevention of mental retardation in some cases.

PREVENTION OF MENTAL RETARDATION

Although advances have been made in the prevention of mental retardation through basic and applied research, progress has been slow. We will briefly examine progress in the three categories of prevention: primary, secondary, and tertiary.

Primary Prevention

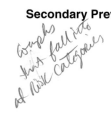

Specific prenatal care strategies reduce the risk of giving birth to a child who is mentally retarded. Proper prenatal care, which begins before pregnancy, is the best method of reducing that risk. The prospective mother should refrain from consuming alcohol, tobacco, drugs, and other toxic substances. Chronic medical conditions, such as diabetes, heart disease, and high blood pressure, also present a potential danger to the fetus. Such conditions should be monitored throughout pregnancy.

Teenage mothers, women over the age of 35, and mothers who have given birth multiple times are also considered at high risk, because they have a higher than normal probability of giving birth to a low-birth-weight infant. Babies weighing less than 1,500 grams have a high mortality rate, and those children who survive are likely to be mentally retarded. Proper nutrition plays a major role in reducing the number of premature and underweight infants born to women of all ages. This, in turn, can help reduce the number of children born with mental retardation and other disabling conditions (Drew et al. 1996; Brantley 1988).

Secondary Prevention

Secondary prevention is based on identifying potential parents with a high probability of having a child with mental retardation. Recent advances in prenatal diagnostic techniques, such as amniocentesis and ultrasound, have made it possible to detect genetic abnormalities, metabolic errors, and inherited conditions that might lead to mental retardation.

Testing for prenatal birth defects is justified under the following circumstances: advanced age of the mother or father (35 and 55, respectively), a family history of an inherited disorder (such as Down's syndrome or fragile X syndrome), a record of miscarriage or infertility, a history of inborn malformations in the parents or a previous child, a chronic medical condition in the mother that requires medication or x-ray treatment, or parents who are close biological relatives.

The sophistication in prenatal diagnosis and treatment techniques continues to grow. In the future, intrauterine surgical techniques to reduce the problems related to hydrocephaly, modification in the mother's diet to reduce the baby's probability of metabolic disorders, and drugs that positively influence fetal development will decrease the birthrate of infants who are mentally retarded (Brantley 1988).

Tertiary Prevention

Tertiary prevention seeks to minimize the long-term effects of mental retardation in children. Research has indicated that infant stimulation programs and early education programs have helped children with mental disabilities achieve gains in communication skills, social abilities, and academic competence. Due to the overwhelming evidence in favor of early intervention for mental retardation, federal legislation PL 99-457, which went into effect in 1990, requires educational services for disabled children between the ages of three and five. There are also financial provisions in this legislation to assist families in providing services for their disabled children as young as one day old. These and other programs, such as the interdisciplinary programs of the University Affiliated Facilities and Head Start, are crucial in minimizing the effects of mental retardation and maximizing each individual's potential (Hickson et al. 1995; Dunn and Fait 1989).

Although important research into the prevention of mental retardation continues at the primary, secondary, and tertiary levels, progress is slow. There is still much to be learned before we can assure the birth of a healthy child.

DEVELOPMENTAL PROFILES OF PERSONS WHO ARE MENTALLY RETARDED

Just as the normal population displays individual variations in the developmental timetable, so does the mentally retarded population. However, there are similarities among mentally retarded individuals in the way they develop language skills, adapt socially and emotionally, acquire physical skills, and process information. In this section, we will examine some of these characteristics.

Cognitive Development

Limited cognitive ability is the most evident characteristic of children who are mentally disabled. Basically, they learn in the same developmental sequence as their nonretarded peers, except at a slower pace with less retention of information. Rate of information acquisition and retention is related to the severity of retardation. Severely and profoundly retarded individuals acquire and retain less information than their mildly and moderately retarded peers. Other learning characteristics include a short attention span, the inability to use abstract concepts, and difficulty generalizing information to other settings (Thomas 1996; Dunn and Fait 1989).

How do mentally retarded people think and process information? It is not enough to know what their learning difficulties are. We must also have an awareness of how they think, because it affects the teaching strategies used in the classroom and in therapy sessions. Information processing can be divided into three operations:

Reception: The perception of a visual, aural, or other sensory stimulus.

Central processing: The categorization of the incoming stimulus using memory, reasoning, and evaluation.

Expression: The ability to select an appropriate response to the incoming stimuli from a variety of choices.

According to Kirk, Gallagher, and Anastasiow (1993), these steps are controlled by executive function, which is the process governing the moment-to-moment decisions that a person makes each day. Each decision is based on several factors, including the information received from a stimulus (reception), the ability to classify the stimulus (central processing), and finally, the choice of response from an assortment of possibilities (expression). Expression leads to feedback for the individual from the initial stimulus. The information provided by the feedback becomes the new stimulus, to which the person then reacts by reapplying the three information-processing steps.

The following example will help clarify how the information-processing model works. A young girl is walking down the sidewalk. A man approaching from the other direction is the stimulus. She becomes aware of the man's presence (reception). The girl does not recognize the man. She remembers that her parents and teachers have urged her to be cautious around strangers (central processing). The girl's behavioral choices include walking away from the man, walking toward him to speak with him, or ignoring him. She decides to walk away from the man (expression).

This model can be used to identify cognitive problems in mentally retarded individuals. Cognitive deficits can occur in any or all of the three stages of information processing or in the executive function process. People with mental disabilities are often unable to attend to relevant stimuli, organize information, and choose an appropriate response. For example, if a mentally retarded girl were in the situation described above, she might not remember what her teachers and parents have told her about talking to strangers and therefore might not exercise due caution. Thus, her ability to make the best decision might be compromised because of her mental retardation.

Another cognitive problem experienced by mentally retarded people is the inability to correctly categorize information. For example, a normal 10-year-old child has little difficulty classifying eagles, robins, and sparrows as birds, whereas Jimmy, our 10-year-old mentally retarded boy introduced at the beginning of this chapter, has difficulty making that connection.

Mentally retarded individuals often have difficulty retaining information, which interferes with generalization, the ability to take information learned in one setting (such as a classroom) and apply it to a different setting (in the home). Teachers, parents, and therapists must work closely together on similar goals so the client has a chance to practice what he or she has learned in a variety of situations.

Language Acquisition

The ability to use language effectively is vital for success in our complex society. For mentally retarded people, the characteristic delay in language development is perhaps the most incapacitating aspect of the disability (Thomas 1996).

Most researchers agree that the rate and quality of language acquisition is dependent upon cognitive development. As you have learned, cognitive ability develops slowly in mentally retarded individuals, which, in turn, impedes the development of language (Kirk et al. 1993).

In normal children, most preverbal forms of communication (babbling, cooing) are replaced by two- or three-word phrases by the twentieth month of life. By the beginning of the third year, pronouns are incorporated into the child's speech, and by the age of four, most children are able to ask questions, manipulate words, and, in general (many parents would agree!), talk incessantly. At age five, meandering speech patterns have been replaced by more concise language skills (Baroff 1986).

Mentally retarded children follow the normal sequence of language development but generally exhibit lags in language acquisition based upon the severity of retardation. Severely and profoundly retarded individuals have much more difficulty developing language skills than do their mildly and moderately retarded peers.

Mentally retarded people nearly always exhibit deficiencies in language. As mentioned above, language deficits hamper cognitive, social, and emotional growth. Even a mildly retarded child exhibits language patterns markedly different from those exhibited by a normal peer. Quantity is diminished, content is deficient, and language structure is rudimentary. As the severity of retardation increases, language development is even more impaired because of the potential of neurological damage to the language areas of the brain. Such impairment makes speech impossible for some individuals. Other conditions can also negatively influence language development. Children with Down's syndrome, for example, have a high incidence of mild hearing loss that is difficult to detect (Kirk et al. 1993) but can contribute to delayed language skills.

Physical and Motor Development

Most mentally retarded children exhibit problems with physical fitness, gross and fine motor control, posture, and stamina. Conditions that frequently accompany mental retardation, such as cerebral palsy, spina bifida, and epilepsy, can also hinder or even prohibit development of physical and motor skills.

Studies have shown that mentally disabled persons perform at a level lower than that of their normal peers on physical tasks requiring strength, endurance, coordination, running speed, flexibility, and reaction time (Thomas 1996; Bruininks 1974; Rarick 1973). Their average rate of achievement is two to four years behind, but some mildly and moderately retarded persons perform at a level comparable to their normal age-mates.

It has been suggested that many of the problems in motor performance of mildly and moderately retarded children might be due to a lack of problem-solving skills and failure to understand the assignment, both cognitive tasks, rather than inherent deficits in motor planning and execution. In addition, severely and profoundly retarded individuals frequently suffer from damage to the motor cortex and spinal column (Drew et al. 1996; Dunn and Fait 1989).

Certain groups of adults and children, such as those with Down's syndrome, exhibit unique physical problems. Many are short and obese and often exhibit hypotonia, or lack of muscle tone. Frequent respiratory infections, heart defects, and a type of misalignment of the upper spinal column called atlantoaxial instability are also common among this population. The therapist or teacher must be aware of the presence of these medical conditions and make appropriate adjustments.

Social and Emotional Characteristics

Mentally retarded adults and children often display maladaptive behaviors that interfere with learning and interacting appropriately. Some behaviors, such as short attention span, low frustration tolerance, hyperactivity, and fighting, can result from the person's repeated failure to learn in the classroom and in other settings rather than from the mental retardation. Other problems arise from relationships with normal peers. The development of self-esteem and social patterns occurs during a child's early years through play behavior. A mentally retarded child may be rejected by peers, or because of limited intellectual ability, may have little or no interest in play. The resulting lack of experience and quality interaction with normal role models can lead to poor self-esteem. In addition, a delay in language acquisition significantly interferes with social adaptation (Jones, 1996).

The environment also influences social skills development. Many institutionalized adults and children who are mentally retarded display gross maladaptive behaviors, perhaps from a combination of inadequate attention, poor training, and stress due to lack of privacy. A trend toward deinstitutionalization of people with mental retardation began during the late 1960s. Many residents moved out of large state-supported institutions into small group homes, often located in residential areas. Usually housing no more than eight residents per home, these facilities provide a more normalized setting in which to learn the skills necessary to function at school, in a work setting, and in the community. In many cases, especially for residents with mild and moderate retardation, these homes have positively influenced self-esteem by reducing failure, providing positive, consistent role models, and creating a more homelike environment (Baroff 1986; Dunn and Fait 1989; Kirk et al. 1993).

EDUCATIONAL PLACEMENT OF CHILDREN WITH MENTAL RETARDATION

Until the passage of PL 94-142 (Education for All Handicapped Children Act) in 1975, children who were mentally retarded were usually educated in an environment segregated from nondisabled peers, often in institutional settings. The 1975 law was the result of years of litigation dealing with discrimination against children with disabilities. For the first time in United States history, all school-age children were entitled to a free and appropriate education. In 1990 Congress passed PL 101-476, the Individuals with Disabilities Education Act (IDEA), which strengthened the earlier law. Specifically, IDEA requires:

Nondiscriminatory and multidisciplinary assessment
An individual education program (IEP)
Parental involvement
Education in the least restrictive environment

According to Drew and colleagues (1996) about 5 million American children between the ages of 3 and 21 with disabilities were educated under IDEA. About 500,000 of these students have mental retardation.

The role of the individualized education plan (IEP) in a disabled child's rehabilitation program is extremely important. IDEA mandates that an individual program plan be developed for every child who has a disability (including mental retardation) and is enrolled in a public school. This written plan includes an assessment of the child's strengths and weaknesses, concrete goals and objectives, the names of the people administering the program, and a process for evaluation. The classroom placement of a student with mental retardation depends primarily on his or her level of intellectual and social functioning. Some children with mild and moderate retardation are mainstreamed into regular classrooms with their normal peers, but they may require special services. Frequently, remedial help is provided for reading, math, speech, motor development, and psychological needs. This assistance is usually provided in a special resource room, which is staffed and equipped to help students who are mentally retarded with their particular difficulties (Hickson et al. 1995; Thomas, 1996).

Students with more severe disabilities also attend public schools but are assigned full time to a special classroom designed for their more demanding needs. A specially trained teacher usually works with small groups of students on preacademic skills, personal grooming, safety, and social skills. Education in a residential institution is reserved for those who need a more highly structured setting, including many students with severe and profound retardation as well as children with mild and moderate retardation who also have severe emotional or behavioral disturbances. Students in this setting learn personal care skills, such as eating, dressing, toileting, safety, and fundamental communication. Children with mental retardation who have emotional or severe maladaptive behaviors also receive therapy for these difficulties.

EDUCATIONAL STRATEGIES USED WITH PERSONS WHO HAVE MENTAL RETARDATION

Persons with mental retardation can learn when given the opportunity and appropriate educational program. It should be pointed out, however, that the curriculum for students with mental retardation has met with mixed results because of the heterogeneity of the population.

According to Kirk, Gallagher, and Anastasiow (1993), one of the most important educational goals for a student with mental retardation is to eliminate behaviors that interfere with the learning process and social skills development. It is not surprising, therefore, that schools and institutions stress the acquisition of social skills. Three other areas are important in instructional programs for children who have mild and moderate retardation: (1) academic skills (reading, writing, and math); (2) communication skills (verbal and, if indicated, nonverbal techniques, such as signing); and (3) prevocational and vocational training (cooperation, on-task behavior, promptness, dependability, and specific job skills). Achieving social competence is also the primary objective for students with severe and profound retardation. Other goals usually focus on communication, safety, and personal grooming skills. Two primary teaching strategies for achieving these goals are behavior modification techniques and task analysis.

It is important to consider four sequential learning strategies when selecting educational materials: acquisition, proficiency, maintenance, and generalization (Hickson et al. 1995). Acquisition pertains to the learning of new skills, proficiency relates to the mastery of skills, maintenance concerns the successful use of a skill over time, and generalization refers to the use of a learned strategy in an unfamiliar setting.

Task Analysis

One approach to teaching the acquisition, proficiency, maintenance, and generalization of skill in children and adults who are mentally retarded is called task analysis. This method of breaking down a task into smaller steps is an effective way for an adult or child with mental retardation to learn a skill that might ordinarily prove difficult. For example, a child brushing his or her teeth must pick up the toothbrush, open the tube of toothpaste, apply the right amount of toothpaste, and use proper brushing techniques. In task analysis, these steps are learned one at a time until the entire sequence is mastered. This approach can be used to teach dressing, feeding, toileting, and prevocational skills (Baroff 1986; Hickson et al. 1995; Kirk et al. 1993).

Behavior Modification Techniques

Behavior modification based on the principles of B. F. Skinner is widely used and has been successful in reducing maladaptive behaviors and improving social skills (Davis et al. 1983; Madsen 1981; Sulzer-Azaroff and Mayer 1977). We will briefly examine four behavior modification techniques: positive reinforcement, differential reinforcement, time out, and contingent social reinforcement.

Positive Reinforcement The most preferred way to increase a desirable behavior, such as punctuality or reading, is through the use of positive reinforcement. Immediately after the student demonstrates the appropriate response, he or she receives a desired reward. The reward can be a smile, a hug, a pat on the back, a piece of candy, a chance to listen to favorite music, or many other things. When positive reinforcement appropriate to each individual child is applied in a systematic manner, the student is likely to repeat the desired behavior. Note the difference between positive reinforcement and a bribe; the reward in positive reinforcement is given only after the desired response has occurred.

Differential Reinforcement This technique both rewards appropriate behavior and ignores undesirable behavior, such as verbal aggression. Therapy that ignores an undesirable behavior and then reinforces a corresponding desired behavior leads to extinction of the ignored behavior and to an increase in the desired response. This strategy is widely used for inappropriate attention-seeking behaviors, such as talking out of turn, tantrums, and out-of-seat behavior.

Time Out Although there are variations of time out, the most common method is to remove the person from a setting that is usually reinforcing, such as the dinner table or the music therapy session, for a brief period of time. Once rules have been introduced, time out has been effective in decreasing tantrums, hostile behavior, and other inappropriate conduct.

Contingent Social Reinforcement A token system can be very effective in shaping behavior. Students earn tokens or other concrete items, such as stickers or pennies, for demonstrating desired, or target, behaviors. Tokens can then be used to "purchase" a desirable item or activity, such as extra recess time, an ice-cream cone, a toy, or an opportunity to listen to music (Baroff 1986; Kirk et al. 1993; Sulzer-Azaroff and Mayer 1977). Taking away tokens for undesirable behavior tends to increase the effectiveness of this technique.

Behavior modification techniques work. They can be used to improve academic, social, and language skills of mentally retarded children and adults. They can help create a structure conducive to learning. These techniques, however, are not without controversy. Opposition may arise when behavior modification is used to control behavior without that person's knowledge or consent. The use of any therapeutic modality, including behavior modification, is subject to legal guidelines and professional ethics that generally require informed consent. Many persons with mental retardation are incapable of informed consent, so the responsibility shifts to a parent or guardian.

Another criticism is that behavior modification techniques focus on overt (observable) behaviors and ignore feelings and attitudes. An approach called cognitive behavior modification attempts to overcome this limitation by including self-reinforcement and self-evaluation in the therapeutic process. This strategy works well with students who have mild and moderate retardation and who have the capacity to deal with emotions, but it is less effective with people who are more severely retarded because of their limited cognitive and language abilities (Kirk et al. 1993).

Children and adults with mental retardation present a challenge to families, educators, and therapists because of the complex nature of their disorder. We have learned that a deficit in cognitive functioning is only one of the diagnostic criteria for mental retardation; social competence is perhaps a more important indicator of a person's ability to function within society. The main goal, therefore, for persons with mental retardation is to achieve social competence, which involves the progressive development of language, self-help, safety, preacademic, academic, prevocational, and vocational skills. The music therapist can be an integral team member in this effort.

MUSIC THERAPY WITH THE MENTALLY RETARDED

In the United States, the use of music therapy in the treatment of mental retardation dates back to the middle of the nineteenth century. During this time, a few private and public schools used pianos, guitars, and rhythm instruments to assist in the development of language, motor skills, and social competence. Public training schools for the "feebleminded" in Massachusetts, Illinois, Pennsylvania, Ohio, and Kentucky included music as an integral element of their curriculum. Private facilities, most of which were located in urban areas on the East Coast, were attended by the few children whose parents could afford specialized training (Kraft 1963).

By the turn of the twentieth century, most state institutions were terribly overcrowded. Individuals with mental retardation were condemned to a life of custodial care in these overcrowded institutions, where little, if any, training (including music therapy) was provided. Conditions gradually improved over the years, and by the 1950s, the use of music therapy with clients who were mentally retarded was regularly reported in the literature (Brewer 1955; Isern 1959; Loven 1957; Peterson 1952;

Wendelin 1953). Music therapists noted that music elicited affective (emotional) responses and improved memory, communication, and social and motor skills, even in the lowest functioning individuals.

The decade of the 1960s brought about significant improvements in the treatment of mental retardation. First, a shift in government policy led to increased funding for state institutions. New programs were developed to teach residents personal care, social, motor, and language skills. Music therapy became an integral part of many residential treatment programs during this time. Second, the quantity and quality of music therapy research literature improved, which further strengthened the rationale for its inclusion in treatment programs (Reynolds 1982). Third, the medical model of mental retardation, which viewed the condition as a disease without a cure, was gradually replaced with the developmental model, which emphasized the acquisition of social, preacademic and academic, motor, and language skills (Coates 1987). Music therapy was considered an important component of the developmental process.

Behavior modification techniques emerged in the late 1960s in conjunction with music to reinforce a variety of skills and behaviors. Music was found to be a potent stimulus that improved social behavior (Davis et al. 1983; Garwood 1988; Hauck and Martin 1970; Jorgenson 1971; McCarty et al. 1978; Reid et al. 1975; Steele 1968), language skills (Michel and May 1974; Seybold 1971; Talkington and Hall 1970; Walker 1972), academic achievement (Eisenstein 1976; Holloway 1980; Madsen and Forsythe 1975; Miller et al. 1974), and motor skills (Holloway 1980; James et al. 1985; Moore and Mathenius 1987; Wolfe 1980). Behavioral techniques incorporating music are still widely used to train and educate individuals who are retarded, including the most severely disabled.

Until 1975, most children with mental retardation lived in residential institutions, which provided for their educational as well as other needs. However, there were a few public school classrooms that offered music and other special services to noninstitutionalized students with disabilities. Unfortunately, these students were segregated from their normal peers and achieved minimal academic progress. Passage of the Education for All Handicapped Children Act (PL 94-142) in 1975 (later strengthened by the passage of IDEA—the Individuals with Disabilities Act of 1990) dramatically changed the educational process of children with disabilities between the ages of 3 and 21. This law mandated that all children with disabilities have access to a free, appropriate public education. PL 94-142 was the catalyst for the subsequent proliferation of community services for the mentally retarded population, including education, housing, and job opportunities. Many children previously confined to residential institutions were placed in foster homes, small group homes, or with their natural parents (Coates 1987). In addition to opening new doors for individuals with mental retardation, the law provided new employment opportunities for music therapists.

For many years, music therapists have observed that adults and children with mental retardation often respond more positively to music than to other educational and therapeutic strategies (Atterbury 1990; Boxhill 1985; Goll 1994; Howery 1968; Lathom 1980; Standley and Hughes 1996). In fact, the use of music therapy with clients who are mentally retarded has grown faster than with any other population. Today, about 6 percent of all registered music therapists work with clients who are mentally retarded in such settings as residential institutions, intermediate care facilities, public and private schools, and private practice (NAMT 1997).

MUSIC THERAPY GOALS

Music therapy goals for persons with mental retardation can be grouped into five categories: (1) a strategy for improving social and emotional behavior, (2) a means of improving motor skills, (3) a tool for improving communication, (4) an aid in teaching preacademic and academic skills, and (5) a leisure activity (Atterbury 1990; Boxhill 1985; Carter 1982; Coates 1987; Edenfield and Hughes 1991; Graham and Beer 1980; Lathom 1980; Michel 1979). Because the needs of individuals with mental retardation vary, treatment strategies must be individualized, even though most music therapy occurs in groups.

Music Therapy to Improve Social and Emotional Behavior

Persons with mental retardation often have problems acquiring appropriate social skills. Structured music therapy activities that incorporate movement, songs, and rhythmic activities provide a stimulating environment in which social behaviors can be learned. Because of the group nature of music therapy sessions, experiences can be structured to promote cooperation, sharing, taking turns, and learning appropriate ways to greet people. For example, a "hello song" teaches names of group members, a proper greeting (e.g., shaking hands), and taking turns. The pleasure of participating in musical activities is a powerful reinforcer and usually captures the client's attention and cooperation.

Inappropriate behaviors, such as talking out of turn, verbal or physical aggression, and out-of-seat behavior, are a problem for many people who are retarded. Because participating in music therapy is enjoyable for most clients, inappropriate behaviors can often be reduced or even completely eliminated. A skilled music therapist combines a pleasurable music activity, such as performing on instruments, listening or moving to music, singing, or creating music, with positive reinforcement to increase cooperative behavior (Lathom 1980).

Music Therapy to Improve Motor Skills

The development of motor skills is highly correlated with learning (Boxhill 1985; Cratty 1974). Music, because it is time ordered (must be continued without interruption to complete an idea), is an ideal stimulus to help coordinate movement. All movements involve the central nervous system, which arouses and controls muscular activity. This highly complex system is immature at birth. In normal infants, it matures rapidly, and by the age of six most children are capable of complex motor skills, such as hopping, galloping, and skipping. In individuals with mental retardation, however, the central nervous system develops slowly or incompletely. Voluntary control of movement can be difficult or impossible. Movement activities allow the client to explore the environment, and development of motor skills creates a foundation for learning. Music and movement activities, therefore, are a vital part of a music therapy program for persons with mental retardation (Figure 4-1).

Individuals who are mildly or moderately retarded can generally learn complex gross and fine motor skills, although at a less sophisticated level than their normal peers. Clients with severe and profound retardation, on the other hand, usually have difficulty mastering even basic movements, because of physical and cognitive limita-

FIGURE 4-1 Using music therapy to improve gross motor function in a mentally retarded child. © Mike Vogl, Poudre Valley Hospital

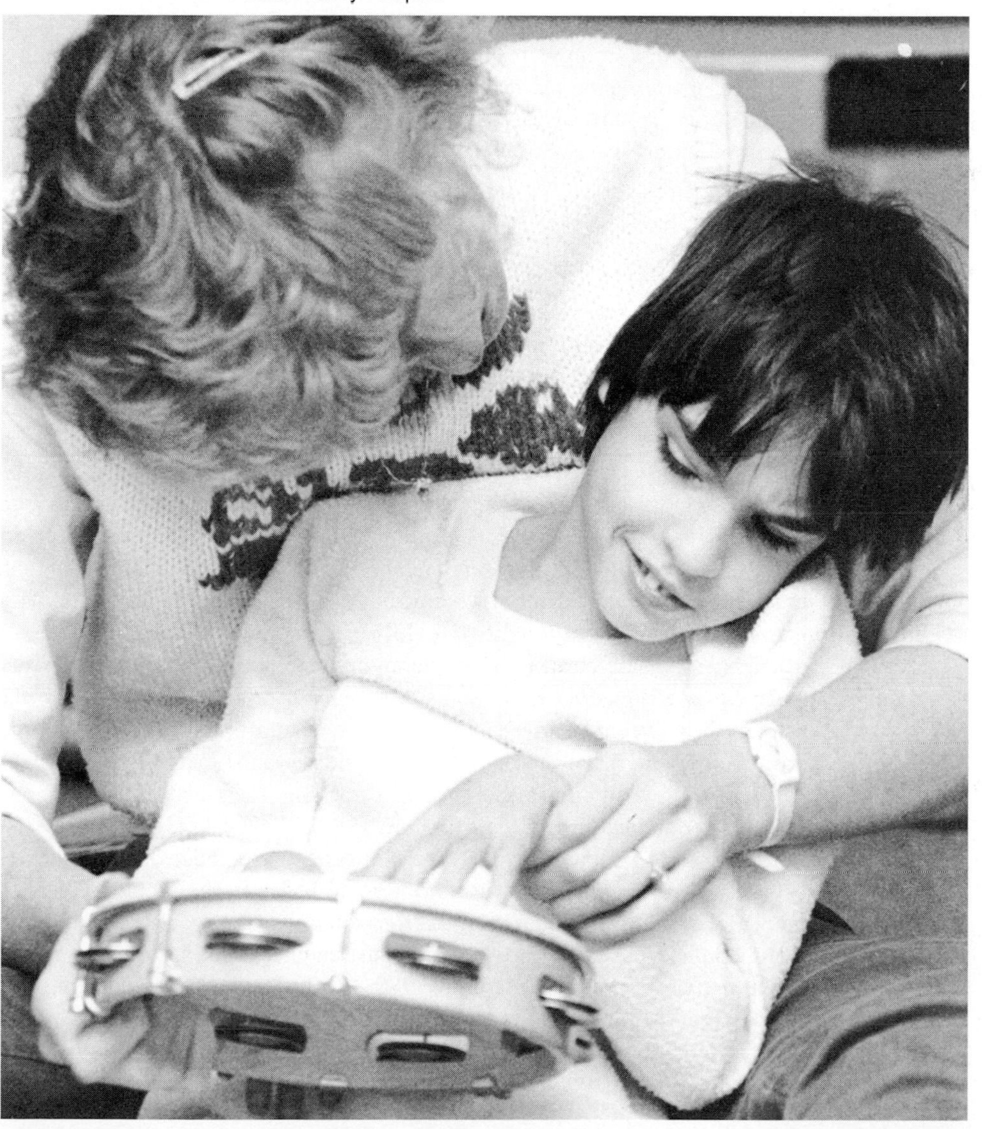

tions. Nonetheless, music therapy activities that promote movement enable these individuals to interact more fully with the environment. Movement activities can range from very simple tasks, such as nodding the head or tapping a foot to a simple beat, to complex motor tasks, like the steps of an intricate folk dance (Lathom 1980).

The rhythmic element of music provides structure and motivation that helps clients learn to walk, run, hop, skip, and gallop. In turn, these skills are associated with improvements in body image, balance, locomotion, agility, flexibility, strength, laterality (side-to-side movement), directionality (up/down, right/left, back/forth movement), and general learning. Initially, attempts to move rhythmically are more important than successes. As the client becomes more comfortable with movement, the therapist encourages him or her to coordinate movements with the music. Gross motor activities, such as folk dancing, strengthen large muscles and help develop coordination, agility, and balance. Instrumental activities, such as playing the piano, guitar, or autoharp, promote fine motor control, which can contribute to improvements in such activities as writing and drawing (Boxhill 1985; Lathom 1980; Moore and Mathenius 1987).

Music Therapy to Improve Communication Skills

As we learned earlier, one of the most incapacitating problems for a person with mental retardation is the limited ability to communicate. Whereas an individual with moderate or mild retardation will likely develop functional speech, a client who is severely/profoundly retarded must develop a nonverbal means of communication, such as basic sign language or a communication board with pictures of important objects in the environment (Atterbury 1990). Music is an ideal tool for teaching communication skills, because the therapist can use melody, rhythm, tempo, pitch, dynamics, and lyrics to develop expressive language (the ability to send messages verbally or nonverbally), receptive language (the ability to understand messages), and the ability to follow directions. In addition, music activities can help improve vocal range, pitch discrimination, articulation, and vocal quality (Boxhill 1985; Grant 1989).

Auditory awareness, or the perception of sounds in the environment, is a necessary skill for language comprehension. Individuals with mental retardation often lack the ability to distinguish between meaningful and irrelevant aural stimuli; thus, they are unable to grasp the communicated message. The music therapist can help "fine-tune" the auditory system by devising music exercises for tracking, locating, identifying, and discriminating among sounds (Grant 1989; Lathom 1980).

A music therapy session should include many language experiences, by using age-appropriate songs with some repetition of melodies and lyrics (to help clients remember important material) and by emphasizing the important words in each song. It is important for the therapist to speak clearly, use simple sentences, and allow the client a sufficient length of time to respond (Lathom 1980). To further enhance learning, the use of visual cues is recommended. For example, songs and activities about Thanksgiving can include pictures of a turkey, Pilgrims, Native Americans, and other appropriate symbols.

Music Therapy to Improve Preacademic Skills

Certain behaviors must be present before learning can take place, including a sufficient attention span, the ability to follow directions, and eye contact. We will examine how music can be helpful in developing these fundamental skills, often lacking in individuals with mental retardation.

Attention Span Many people who are mentally retarded have difficulty focusing on a simple task because of their inability to filter out irrelevant stimuli and attend to important directions. Using aural, visual, tactile, and other sensory cues, the therapist can help improve the attention of poor learners by providing structure and motivation. For example, a group musical activity may require a client to wait for a musical cue, such as the beat of a drum, before playing his or her part. The success of the activity will depend, in part, on the ability to play at the right time. The therapist can increase attention span by gradually lengthening the client's waiting time (Atterbury 1990).

Following Directions Effective learning requires the ability to follow simple commands. Activities to develop this skill focus on sequencing directions into one-, two-, or three-step commands. For example, a client first learns to follow one-step directions, such as, "Stand up." Once proficient, a two-step sequence is introduced, such as, "Stand up, then pick up the tambourine." An example of a three-step direction is, "Stand up, pick up the tambourine, and give it to Bob." Music activities with directions in the lyrics are effective in helping clients learn a sequence of directions.

Eye Contact The inability to initiate and maintain eye contact interferes with the development of attention span and the ability to communicate. Many important messages are conveyed nonverbally and are therefore missed if eye contact has not been established (Lathom 1980). Interesting music activities help the therapist attain eye contact with the client. The duration of eye contact can then be systematically lengthened using behavior modification and other techniques.

Music Therapy to Improve Academic Skills

Music activities can be used to teach academic concepts, such as identifying colors and shapes (object classification); grouping objects by size, number, or attribute (seriation); learning up/down and in/out (spatial relationships); and recognizing the differences between first, second, and last (temporal relationships). As an illustration, colors can be taught through the use of different-colored instruments, and high/low can be conveyed with musical pitches (Gfeller 1990).

Individuals with mental retardation often have difficulty with short-term memory, the ability to recall information shortly after it has been presented. Music can help clients remember important academic information. For example, an enjoyable, familiar melody paired with learned information is an effective way to improve retention. Multisensory activities, which involve the presentation of material in two or more sensory modalities, also improve the ability to retain short-term information. For example, pictures of animals could be used with the song "going to the zoo." In addition, music to enhance information retention needs frequent repetition and a relatively slow tempo.

Music as a Leisure Activity

Without appropriate training, free time for persons with mental retardation can be meaningless (DiGiammarino 1990; 1994). Music therapy can help individuals with mental retardation develop leisure skills. During the early years of community integration, clients learned to work in a vocational setting, interact in a socially appropriate manner, and care for their basic needs. However, many of these people had no idea how to use their free time at the end of the workday, during weekends, and on holidays. Many newly deinstitutionalized people engaged in activities, such as petty crimes or substance abuse, that resulted in their return to the institution.

The music therapist can encourage the leisure-time use of music in several ways. Clients can learn how to operate a stereo system and how to purchase or use the library to borrow prerecorded music. They can join community music groups or attend concerts. Learning to play a musical instrument can be another means of leisure gratification (Coates 1987; Howery 1968). The therapist may need to help the client adapt instruments or audio equipment to his or her special needs. Additionally, the music therapist should become familiar with resources in the community where the client will be living and make appropriate contacts for him or her. For example, is there a music teacher willing to provide piano lessons to a student who is mentally retarded? What types of concert opportunities are available? Is there a church choir or civic music group for the client to join? Music as a meaningful leisure activity may help promote a successful community adjustment for the person with mental retardation.

SUMMARY

Mental retardation, characterized by deficits in intelligence and adaptive skills, affects millions of adults and children. Educational and community placement depends on the ability to adapt to societal demands. In this discussion, we identified four classifications of mental retardation: (1) mild, (2) moderate, (3) severe/profound, and (4) severity unspecified. Mental retardation can be caused by genetic and metabolic disorders, toxic agents, environmental factors, trauma, infections, or injury, but most cases are of unknown etiology.

Mental retardation is characterized by problems in four areas: (1) cognitive development, (2) physical/motor development, (3) language acquisition, and (4) social/emotional development. The severity of these problems is the primary determinant of residential and educational placement. Preferred educational strategies for students with mental retardation include behavior modification techniques and task analysis.

For many years, music has been an important component of treatment for mental retardation. Music therapists working with this population individualize treatment goals according to five broad categories:

1 As a strategy for improving social and emotional behavior. Therapeutic music experiences can be structured to promote appropriate and/or minimize inappropriate behaviors.

2 As a means of improving motor skills. Music and movement activities can help develop motor skills and enhance the ability to learn.

3 As a tool for improving communication skills. Music therapy experiences can promote language development and improve vocal production.

4 As an aid in teaching preacademic and academic skills. Well-planned therapeutic music experiences can help teach basic skills, such as attending, following directions, and maintaining eye contact, as well as more difficult concepts.

5 As a leisure activity. Music therapists can help individuals with mental retardation incorporate meaningful musical activities into their leisure time, by listening, or performing, or both.

STUDY QUESTIONS

1 The three components in the AAMR's definition of mental retardation include ________, ________, and ________.

2 Mental retardation can be divided into four categories according to the level of mental retardation. List the four categories, then discuss the differences among them.

3 List at least five causes of mental retardation.

4 Progress is being made in the prevention of mental retardation. Name, then define, the three categories of prevention discussed.

5 What types of cognitive deficits are you likely to find in a person who is severely/profoundly mentally retarded?

6 Why are social skills stressed in the education of persons with mental retardation?

7 List, then define, three behavior modification strategies used to help persons with mental retardation learn.

8 Why is music an effective strategy to help persons with mental retardation learn?

9 Three important music therapy goals developed for persons with mental retardation include ________, ________, and ________.

10 What is PL 101-476, and what impact does this law have on the education of children with disabilities?

REFERENCES

American Association of Mental Retardation (AAMR). 1992. *Mental retardation: definition, classification, and systems of supports.* 9th ed. Washington, DC: American Association of Mental Retardation.

Atterbury, B. W. 1990. *Mainstreaming exceptional learners in music.* Englewood Cliffs, NJ: Prentice Hall.

Baroff, G. S. 1986. *Mental retardation: Nature, cause, and management.* 2d ed. Washington, DC: Hemisphere.

Boxhill, E. H. 1985. *Music therapy for the developmentally disabled.* Rockville, MD: Aspen Systems.

Brantley, D. 1988. *Understanding mental retardation.* Springfield, IL: Charles C Thomas.

Brewer, J. E. 1955. Music therapy for the mentally deficient. In *Music therapy 1954,* edited by E. T. Gaston, 113–116. Lawrence, KS: Allen Press.

Bruininks, R. 1974. Physical and motor development in retarded persons. In *International review of research in mental retardation,* edited by N. R. Ellis, 209–261. New York: Academic Press.

Carter, S. A. 1982. *Music therapy for handicapped children: Mentally retarded.* Lawrence, KS: National Association for Music Therapy.

Coates, P. 1987. "Is it functional?" A question for music therapists who work with the institutionalized mentally retarded. *Journal of Music Therapy* 24:170–175.

Cratty, B. J. 1974. *Motor activity and the education of retardates.* 2d ed. Philadelphia: Lea and Febiger.

Davis, W. B., N. A. Wieseler, and T. E. Hanzel. 1983. Reduction of rumination and out-of-seat behavior and generalization of treatment effects using a nonintrusive method. *Journal of Music Therapy* 20:115–131.

Diagnostic and statistical manual of mental disorders (DSM IV). 1994. Washington, DC: American Psychiatric Association.

DiGiammarino, M. 1990. Functional music skills of persons with mental retardation. *Journal of Music Therapy* 27:209–220.

———. 1994. Functional music leisure skills for individuals with mental retardation. *Music Therapy Perspectives* 12:15–19.

Drew, C. J., M. L. Hardman, and D. R. Logan. 1996. *Mental Retardation: A life cycle approach.* 6th ed. Englewood Cliffs, NJ: Prentice Hall

Dunn, J., and H. Fait. 1989. *Special physical education: Adapted, individualized, developmental.* 6th ed. Dubuque, IA: William C. Brown.

Edenfield, T. N., and J. E. Hughes. 1991. The relationship of a choral music curriculum to the development of singing ability in secondary students with Down's syndrome. *Music Therapy Perspective* 9:52–55.

Eisenstein, S. R. A. 1976. A successive approximation procedure for learning music symbol names. *Journal of Music Therapy* 13:173–179.

Evans, I. M. 1990. Testing and diagnosis: A review and evaluation. In *Critical issues in the lives of people with severe disabilities,* edited by L. H. Meyer, C. A. Peck, and L. Brown. Baltimore: Brookes.

Garwood, E. C. 1988. The effect of contingent music in combination with a bell pad on enuresis of a mentally retarded adult. *Journal of Music Therapy* 25:103–109.

Gfeller, K. E. 1990. A cognitive-linguistic approach to language development for the preschool child with hearing impairment: Implications for music therapy practice. *Music Therapy Perspectives* 8:47–51.

Goll, H. 1994. *Special education music therapy with persons who have severe/profound retardation.* Frankfort, Germany: Peter Lang.

Graham, R. M., and A. S. Beer. 1980. *Teaching music to the exceptional child.* Englewood Cliffs, NJ: Prentice Hall.

Grant, R. E. 1989. Music therapy guidelines for developmentally disabled children. *Music Therapy Perspectives* 6:18–22.

Hauck, L. P., and P. L. Martin. 1970. Music as a reinforcer in patient-controlled duration of time-out. *Journal of Music Therapy* 7:43–53.

Hickson, L., L. S. Blackman, and E. M. Rice. 1995. *Mental retardation: Foundations of educational programming.* Boston: Allyn and Bacon.

Holloway, M. S. 1980. A comparison of passive and active music reinforcement to increase preacademic and motor skills in severely retarded children and adolescents. *Journal of Music Therapy* 17:58–69.

Howery, B. I. 1968. Music therapy for mentally retarded children and adults. In *Music therapy 1968,* edited by E. Thayer Gaston, 47–55. New York: Macmillan.

Isern, B. 1959. The influence of music on the memory of mentally retarded children. In *Music therapy 1958,* edited by E. H. Schneider, 162–165. Lawrence, KS: Allen Press.

Jacobson, J. W., and J. A. Mulick, eds. 1996. *Manual of diagnosis and professional practice in mental retardation.* Washington DC: American Psychological Association.

James, M. R., A. L. Weaver, P. D. Clemens, and G. A. Plaster. 1985. Influence of paired auditory and vestibular stimulation on levels of motor skill development in a mentally retarded population. *Journal of Music Therapy* 22:22–34.

Jones, C. J. 1996. *An introduction to the nature and needs of students with mild disabilities.* Springfield, IL: Charles C Thomas.

Jorgenson, H. 1971. Effects of contingent preferred music in reducing two stereotyped behaviors of a profoundly retarded child. *Journal of Music Therapy* 8:139–145.

Kirk, S. A., J. J. Gallagher, and N. J. Anastasiow. 1993. *Educating exceptional children.* 7th ed. Boston: Houghton Mifflin.

Kraft, I. 1963. Music for the feebleminded in nineteenth-century America. *Journal of Research in Music Education* 11:119–122.

Lathom, W. 1980. *Role of music therapy in the education of handicapped children and youth.* Lawrence, KS: National Association for Music Therapy.

Loven, M. A. 1957. Value of music therapy for mentally retarded children. In *Music therapy 1956,* edited by E. T. Gaston, 165–174. Lawrence, KS: Allen Press.

Luckasson, R., ed. 1992. *Mental retardation: Definition, classification, and systems of supports.* 9th ed. Washington, DC: American Association on Mental Retardation.

Madsen, C. K. 1981. *Music therapy: A behavioral guide for the mentally retarded.* Lawrence, KS: National Association for Music Therapy.

Madsen, C. K., and J. L. Forsythe. 1975. Effect of contingent music listening on increases of mathematical responses. In *Research behavior in the classroom,* edited by C. K. Madsen, R. D. Greer, and C. H. Madsen, Jr. New York: Columbia University, Teachers College Press.

McCarty, B. C., C. T. McElfresh, S. V. Rice, and S. J. Wilson. 1978. The effect of contingent background music on inappropriate bus behavior. *Journal of Music Therapy* 15:150–156.

Michel, D. E. 1979. *Music therapy: An introduction to therapy and special education through music.* 2d ed. Springfield, IL: Charles C Thomas.

Michel, D. E., and N. H. May. 1974. The development of music therapy procedures with speech and language disorders. *Journal of Music Therapy* 11:74–80.

Miller, D. M., L. Dorow, and R. D. Greer. 1974. The contingent use of music and art for improving arithmetic scores. *Journal of Music Therapy* 11:57–64.

Moore, R., and L. Mathenius. 1987. The effects of modeling, reinforcement, and tempo on imitative rhythmic responses of moderately retarded adolescents. *Journal of Music Therapy* 24:160–169.

National Association for Music Therapy (NAMT). 1997. *1997 Membership directory.* Silver Spring, MD: National Association for Music Therapy.

Peterson, E. D. 1952. Music to aid the mentally handicapped. In *Music therapy 1951,* edited by E. G. Gilliland, 19–21. Lawrence, KS: Allen Press.

Rarick, G. L. 1973. Motor performance of mentally retarded children. In *Physical activity: Human growth and development,* edited by G. L. Rarick, 225–256. New York: Academic Press.

Reid, D. H., B. K. Hill, R. J. Rawers, and C. A. Montegar. 1975. The use of contingent music in teaching social skills to a nonverbal, hyperactive boy. *Journal of Music Therapy* 12:2–18.

Reynolds, B. J. 1982. Music therapy literature related to mental retardation. In *Music therapy for handicapped children: Mentally retarded,* edited by S. A. Carter, 43–56. Lawrence, KS: National Association for Music Therapy.

Seybold, C. K. 1971. The value and use of music activities in the treatment of speech-delayed children. *Journal of Music Therapy* 8:102–110.

Sheerenberger, R. C. 1983. *A history of mental retardation.* Baltimore: Brookes.

Standely, J. M., and J. E. Hughes. 1996. Documenting appropriate objectives and benefits of a music therapy program for early intervention: A behavioral analysis. *Music Therapy Perspectives* 14: 87–94.

Steele, A. L. 1968. Programmed use of music to alter uncooperative problem behavior. *Journal of Music Therapy* 5:103–107.

Sulzer-Azaroff, G., and G. R. Mayer. 1977. *Applying behavior analysis procedures with children and youth.* New York: Holt, Rinehart and Winston.

Talkington, L. W., and S. M. Hall. 1970. A musical application of Premack's hypothesis to low verbal retardates. *Journal of Music Therapy* 7:95–99.

Thomas, G. E. 1996. *Teaching students with mental retardation.* Englewood Cliffs, NJ: Merrill.

Walker, J. B. 1972. The use of music as an aid in developing functional speech in the institutionalized mentally retarded. *Journal of Music Therapy* 9:1–12.

Wendelin, A. 1953. Instrumental music for the mentally retarded. In *Music therapy 1952,* edited by E. G. Gilliland, 133–138. Lawrence, KS: Allen Press.

Wolfe, D. E. 1980. The effect of automated interrupted music on head posturing of cerebral palsied individuals. *Journal of Music Therapy* 17:184–206.

5

MUSIC THERAPY IN THE TREATMENT OF MENTAL DISORDERS

Kate E. Gfeller
Michael H. Thaut

CHAPTER OUTLINE

The words *psychiatric* or *mental disorders* bring to mind different things to different people. Some people might think about the psychopathic killer depicted in a horror movie. Others might consider people who are morose and suicidal to have mental problems. Still others have suggested that eccentric bag ladies, wearing bizarre clothing and hording items in a shopping cart, are actually undiagnosed victims of mental illness. Although many people would agree that the aforementioned behaviors are odd, and possibly the result of mental disorders, other similar behaviors may be considered acceptable by society. For example, a Marine in hand-to-hand combat in World War II killed others, but his behaviors are thought to be heroic. Tears and sadness, when expressed by a grieving widow, are considered normal, even healthy. Refugees of political turmoil may have no alternative but to wear tattered, ill-fitting clothing and to carry their belongings on their backs, but their disheveled appearance is attributed to political circumstance rather than to mental illness. How do society and, in particular, mental health professionals, determine which behaviors are "normal" and which constitute mental illness?

The concept and classification of mental disorders have been redefined many times and will be subject to ongoing debate. However, within each culture, there is a range of acceptable behavior for particular situations. For example, there are unspoken as well as clearly articulated views regarding how one should act in a variety of circumstances. The kind of behavior that is appropriate in church differs from that suited to a playground or football field. Some actions, such as killing, are considered illegal within everyday life, but are condoned on the field of battle. Thus, social mores will, to a greater or lesser extent, determine what constitutes acceptable or normal behavior.

At what point is a behavior considered inappropriate enough to be considered a psychiatric disorder? The assignment of a diagnosis of emotional or behavioral disorder is often related to the (1) *frequency,* (2) *duration,* and (3) *intensity* with which a behavior occurs, as well as the circumstances surrounding the behavior. For example, it is not unusual for an individual to experience fluctuations in mood. Every once in a while, a healthy individual will feel discouraged or depressed by events such as the loss of a loved one or failure in school or business. However, if bouts of depression occur quite frequently, last for months on end (duration), and are of such severity (intensity) that the individual is unable to function, or even attempts suicide, this same emotion may be considered maladaptive. In short, a wide range of behaviors are considered acceptable, but when some of the same behaviors become disruptive or overwhelming, they are considered symptoms of a psychiatric disorder.

Psychiatric disorders can occur at almost any age. Affected individuals may demonstrate disturbances in mood and thinking, perception of reality, and ability to relate to other persons. They may also suffer from excessive fears, panic, and obsessive or compulsive behaviors. Other problems such as eating disorders, substance abuse, and organic illnesses (a deterioration of brain function) are also considered psychiatric disorders.

A major attempt to collect and organize data to describe and diagnose psychiatric disorders objectively occurred with the 1980 publication of the *Diagnostic and Statistical Manual of Mental Disorders (DSM III).* This important work systematically organized and categorized the many forms of mental illness into a uniform system. Since 1980, several revisions of this manual have been published as mental health professionals learn more about the causes and characteristics of various disorders. The *Diagnostic and Statistical Manual of Mental Disorders IV (DSM IV),* published in 1994, is the most recent version of this important diagnostic tool. The following section of this chapter presents a brief introduction to some of the major psychiatric disorders as listed in the *DSM IV.* This survey of major disorders will be followed by an overview of several prominent approaches to psychiatric treatment and various ways that music therapy can be used in the treatment of mental illness.

AN INTRODUCTION TO SEVERAL MAJOR PSYCHIATRIC DISORDERS

Schizophrenia

Susan is a 28-year-old woman who is living at home with her parents and is currently receiving Social Security disability checks because she has been unable to sustain gainful employment over the past eight years. Susan's early childhood seemed unremarkable, but during her first year at college, her parents noticed a personality change. Susan seemed aloof and uncomfortable with others. At times, she expressed fears that other people were against her, or trying to "get her," despite the lack of any real evidence. As her condition deteriorated over a period of months, even her grooming and ability to take care of herself deteriorated. She was often so preoccupied that she failed to carry out simple tasks of daily living, such as grocery shopping or making the bed. Susan's parents were concerned, of course; but it was not until she started to talk about aliens from other planets speaking to her over the radio that they realized Susan needed psychiatric help. An evaluation of Susan's behavior by a psychiatrist confirmed their suspicion that Susan had a psychiatric disorder. The psychiatrist told them that Susan has schizophrenia, and recommended for Susan hospitalization where she would be treated with medications and milieu therapy (a structured environment consisting of a host of supportive therapies such as counseling, vocational rehabilitation, and other forms of therapy).

What Is Schizophrenia? **Schizophrenia** is a serious mental disorder in which the individual experiences profound alterations in thinking, sensory perception, affect (emotional expression), and behavior. According to the *DSM IV,* in order to be diagnosed with schizophrenia, a person must exhibit two or more of the following symptoms for a significant period of time: delusions, hallucinations, disorganized or incoherent speech, very disorganized or catatonic behavior, or symptoms such as lack of facial expression, little or no speech, or extreme social withdrawal. Schizophrenia usually involves impairment in more than one area of functioning and there are usually multiple symptoms (Wilson et al. 1996). Two people may be diagnosed as having schizophrenia, but they may experience different symptoms. During some phases of the illness, these behaviors will reach psychotic proportions, which means the patient will suffer from a complete loss of contact with reality and self-perception (Scully 1985). The most common misconception about this disease is that it means "split personality," which in fact is another disorder called multiple personality (Andreasen 1984). In actuality, the term *schizophrenia* refers to the "splitting of the mind," meaning disturbances in thinking, feeling, and actions.

Approximately 1 percent of the population develops schizophrenia during their lifetime. Although this is a small proportion of the population, the impact of this illness is tremendous. Schizophrenia tends to have a very negative impact on behavior and can be chronic in nature. People diagnosed with schizophrenia are the major users of psychiatric hospital beds in the United States (Wilson et al. 1996).

According to the *DSM IV* (1994), there are several clinical symptoms typically exhibited by individuals with schizophrenia (at least two of the following):

1 ***Delusions:*** False beliefs that lack any basis in reality and are maintained by the patient despite evidence that they are false. These include delusions of being persecuted, delusions of grandeur (e.g., believing that you are a famous person, such as Elvis Presley or Jesus Christ), delusions of control (e.g., thinking that an alien force is controlling one's behavior), and delusions of romance (false belief that someone is in love with you, such as John Hinckley's belief that Jodi Foster loved him).

2 *Hallucinations:* Sensory experiences that occur in the absence of actual environmental stimulation, such as hearing voices, or seeing things that don't exist.

3 *Disorganized speech:* Shifting from one topic to another with no natural transitions, or responding to questions in a tangential way. The speech often seems illogical or incoherent. At its most severe, such disorganized speech can make effective communication nearly impossible.

4 *Grossly disorganized behavior or catatonic behavior:* The inability to organize even basic activities of everyday life or, in the case of catatonic behavior, marked abnormality in motor behavior, such as a long fixed posture.

5 *Negative symptoms:* Deficits in facial affect, poverty of speech, or the inability to begin and sustain goal-directed activity. (*DSM IV* 1994; Wilson et al. 1996).

There are several types of schizophrenia, each characterized by particular and predominant symptoms. *Catatonic type* schizophrenics are characterized by unusual patterns of motor activity such as rigid, statuelike postures. *Disorganized type* is characterized by verbal incoherence and grossly disorganized behavior. *Paranoid type* is characterized by preoccupation with delusions, such as the unfounded belief that one is being persecuted. *Undifferentiated type* is characterized by psychotic symptoms, such as illogical thoughts. However, the individuals in this category do not meet all the specific criteria for other subtypes. *Residual type* refers to persons who no longer display gross thought disorders such as hallucinations or delusions, but there is still limited affect and little motivation (*DSM IV* 1994).

What Causes Schizophrenia? The onset of schizophrenia usually occurs in late adolescence or early adulthood. The symptoms, which continue for at least six months, result in considerable disruption in social and occupational functioning. The course of the illness can vary. Some individuals will recover fully after one or two active psychotic episodes. Some individuals will intermittently require hospitalization throughout a lifetime, but will have long periods of relatively normal and independent functioning. Unfortunately, there is a proportion of this population that does not respond to current treatment. The illness is chronic, and everyday functioning is greatly impaired.

A variety of biological, psychological, and social factors are believed to contribute to the development of schizophrenia. Biological factors cited in research include genetic factors, brain dysfunction, and biochemical abnormalities. Psychological factors include family dysfunction and communication abnormalities. Social factors that place persons at risk for schizophrenia include low education and income. Most experts believe that biological factors cause schizophrenia, and that some people have a genetic predisposition to the disease. However, environmental factors (e.g., periods of stress or major transitions at work or in one's personal life) may contribute to the development of the disease in those predisposed to the illness (Wilson et al. 1996).

How Is Schizophrenia Treated? One of the most significant changes in the treatment of schizophrenia has been the development of antipsychotic medications in this century. These medications, which help to normalize neurological processes, have transformed the lives of many psychotic individuals who were once exiled to lifelong residency in the back wards of institutions. Although these medications do not cure the disease, they can reduce or eliminate the very debilitating symptoms such as delusions or hallucinations in some individuals. However, some people develop serious side effects as a result of medications, and other people show limited or no improvement.

Other treatments that have helped schizophrenics to cope with the negative effects of the disease are various forms of psychosocial therapies (Smeltekop and Houghton 1990). Many clinical studies show that pharmacological treatment by itself may be less efficient than a combination of medication and individual and group therapy. Psychosocial therapies are carried out in individual or group settings. A stable therapeutic relationship between client and therapist as well as a stable work and home environment can help the client cope with the illness and can promote maximization of the client's behavioral strengths and changes in maladaptive behavior patterns.

Therapeutic experiences may help the clients test the reality of their perceptions in a supportive environment. Techniques may be taught to diminish anxiety and induce relaxation. Uplifting mood experiences may help the clients experience positive feeling states and find motivation to cope with their lives. The structure of a daily schedule of therapy and activities *(milieu therapy)* may make reality more predictable and less threatening for the client. The therapist functions as an outside personality who supports, strengthens, and guides the disturbed personality of the client. This function includes teaching the client to deal with everyday problems, such as personal hygiene, paying bills, trying to live independently, and taking medication (Smeltekop and Houghton 1990).

Mood Disorders

Bryan is a 25-year-old salesperson who was recently admitted to the hospital by his wife, who complained about his crazy spending sprees and grandiose ideas for his hardware business. In particular, within a period of just a few days, he had purchased a fleet of white limousines, a yacht, and 100 paisley tuxedo jackets, all for the purpose of throwing a party for his business associates at which he planned to entertain the group by playing the trombone. All of these actions were carried out, despite the fact that his business assets are quite modest as is his musical talent. Bryan's wife also recounted to the psychiatrist that Bryan often stays up day and night and that he seems to have boundless energy. The energy would be fine if he spent it wisely, but instead, he comes up with harebrained schemes about buying a fleet of jets to transport hardware all around the globe. Bryan's psychiatrist tells Bryan that he suffers from a mood disorder, and that he is currently having a manic episode.

What Are Mood Disorders? **Mood disorders** are a class of mental disorders characterized primarily by disturbance in mood, such as depression or extreme elation (Wilson et al. 1996). Because most mood disorders tend to come and go over time (episodic), the *DSM IV* (1994) organizes the diagnostic section about mood disorders around different kinds of mood episodes that occur. Episodes are discrete periods of time during which a person has a number of specific symptoms that reflect a marked change from previous functioning (Wilson et al. 1996). The marked change in functioning can be a period of depression and diminished interest *(depressive episode),* or a period of unusually elevated mood, which is referred to as a *manic episode.*

During a depressive episode, the person has a persistent depressed mood (most of the day and nearly every day), and several other symptoms, such as diminished interest in activities that are generally enjoyable, changes in appetite or weight, changes in sleep patterns, agitation or lack of energy, feelings of worthlessness, difficulty concentrating and thinking clearly, and thoughts of suicide (*DSM IV* 1994). The symptoms may develop at a time of personal crisis (such as the loss of a spouse, or a divorce), but people can also feel depressed for no apparent reason.

During a manic episode, people may have decreased need for sleep, their thoughts may race, and they may be extremely talkative. They may engage in wild spending sprees or take on unrealistic projects. For example, the vignette about Bryan includes extravagant purchases of yachts and paisley tuxedos, and an unrealistic appraisal of his own skill as a musician. These are all characteristic of a manic episode.

A combination of episodes and other features (e.g., the course or outcome of the disorder) together make up a mood disorder. For example, in November, Donna started feeling very blue and discouraged. This feeling of depression lasted for about four months. Around mid-March, she started to feel like "her old self" again. She continued to feel just fine for about eight months. Then around the end of October, she started having those same blue feelings that she had felt the previous fall. This pattern of depressive episodes and periods of normalcy make up one types of mood disorder, which is called a *recurrent major depressive disorder.* Donna's pattern of recurring depressive episodes is only one of many types of mood disorders. Another common type of mood disorder, *bipolar disorder,* is characterized by one or more *manic, mixed* (that is mood episodes characterized by alternation between depressive and manic episodes), or *hypomanic* (a milder version of a manic episode) episodes. Bryan, in our opening vignette, has a bipolar disorder. Under the general category, mood disorders, different sequential patterns of episodes, and differences in severity of symptoms are described by different specific types of mood disorders (e.g., major depressive disorder, bipolar disorder, etc.).

However, all have in common as a primary feature significant changes in mood that occur with enough frequency, duration, and intensity to be considered maladaptive (*DSM IV* 1994).

What Causes Mood Disorders? Major depression is a common disorder. Some studies of disease prevalence (i.e., what percentage of the population has a particular disorder) indicate that at least 12 percent of men and 21 percent of women have experienced at least one bout of depression in their lifetime (Wilson et al. 1996). Sometimes mood disorders occur in conjunction with other disorders, such as anxiety or substance abuse. There are a variety of factors that are believed to contribute to mood disorders. Biological models of depression have predominated the mental health field for over 30 years (Wilson et al. 1996). Two major areas of investigation are (1) *genetic studies* and (2) *neurobiochemical factors*. According to genetic theories, people inherit a predisposition to the development of neurobiochemical dysfunction that causes depression (Wilson et al. 1996). Studies of neurobiochemical factors indicate that depression can result from abnormalities in the neurotransmitters (chemical messengers in the brain) and hormonal abnormalities. Other factors that are associated with depression include loss in close relationships, disturbances in self-esteem, negative outlook on life, and interpersonal problems. It is not clear, however, exactly how these factors are related to depression. Some may contribute to the development or maintenance of a depression, whereas others may be an effect of depression.

How Are Mood Disorders Treated? Nowadays, there are a variety of medications that can treat depression or manic episodes effectively. Several types of antide pressants exist which act on either the neurotransmitters or endocrine system. Lithium is a medication that is quite effective for treating bipolar disorders. For severely depressed persons who do not respond to medication and who are in acute danger of harming themselves, electroconvulsive therapy (ECT) remains an effective treatment choice (Andreasen 1984; Wilson et al. 1996). Psychotherapy is often a useful component of treatment for mood disorders. The form of therapy varies depending on those factors believed to contribute to the disorder and the particular needs of the individual. In some instances, supportive guidance and counseling can be helpful and all that is needed. Cognitive therapy techniques, on the other hand, are used to alter faulty perceptions of reality, which are thought to contribute to depression. Some patients require more in-depth therapy in which unresolved or unconscious conflicts, problems, or relationships are explored (Goodwin and Guze 1979). In many instances, an intervention may include a combination of medication and various types of psychotherapy.

Personality Disorders

Nancy is a 22-year-old checkout clerk at the local discount store. Nancy will tell you, however, that this job is just temporary, for she anticipates that she will soon be spotted by a talent agent who will notice her beauty and charm. Some of her coworkers, however, find Nancy's charm a bit tiresome: She often takes extra coffee breaks so that she can "fix her face," assuming that the others can take care of the store. After all, she needs to look her best. When confronted by the manager about her extra breaks, Nancy walks off in a huff, baffled by the manager's lack of sensitivity to her talents and charm. As customers go through the checkout line, Nancy often engages them in conversation about her own appearance—her new haircut, her nice skin, or her future as a model. Nancy is the sort of person who wears thin the patience of others and tends to have unsatisfying relationships. She has what is called a narcissistic personality disorder.

What Are Personality Disorders? When we are asked to describe someone's personality, we often think about particular traits or characteristics that are rather stable. For example, we might describe some people as having an outgoing and talkative personality. Others might be described as shy or introverted. Some people tend to be a bit crabby or cynical. However, most people can modify their behavior to some extent in order to successfully navigate the requirements of each day.

In the case of a personality disorder, the individual exhibits personality traits that are so extreme and so inflexible that they are distressing to the individual and cause difficulties in school, work, and interpersonal relationships (Wilson et al. 1996). According to the *DSM IV* (1994), there is an enduring pattern of internal experience (such as thoughts or beliefs) and behavior that is markedly different from the expectations of one's culture. These differences can include deviation in (1) cognition, or how people perceive and interpret themselves, others, and events; (2) affectivity, meaning the range, intensity, and appropriateness of emotional responses; (3) interpersonal functioning; or (4) impulse control. These traits are inflexible and appear across a broad range of situations, tend to interfere with social and occupational functioning, and tend to be stable, that is, of long duration (*DSM IV* 1994).

There are a number of different types of personality disorders, but they can be categorized into three clusters, based on descriptive similarities (*DSM IV* 1994; Wilson et al. 1996). The first cluster, cluster A, includes personality disorders in which the individuals seem *odd or eccentric.* The specific personality disorders within this cluster include (1) *paranoid personality disorder,* (2) *schizoid personality disorder,* and (3) *schizotypal personality disorders.* The names of these disorders sound very much like the terms used in another classification, schizophrenia. Although there are some features of the disorder that resemble schizophrenia, there are very important differences. For example, as is the case with schizophrenics, people with personality disorders within cluster A tend to be reclusive or uncomfortable in interpersonal relationships. Some may be suspicious of others (as in the case of paranoid schizophrenia), or may have odd or eccentric behaviors. However, people who have schizophrenia have intermittent episodes of psychosis during which they are out of touch with reality and their eccentric thoughts and behaviors can be so debilitating that they require hospitalization and antipsychotic medication.

In contrast, people with personality disorders (cluster A) have enduring personality traits (rather than intermittent episodes) such as reclusiveness or suspiciousness. However, their odd behaviors cannot be attributed to psychosis as is the case in schizophrenia. These individuals have not totally lost contact with reality. The town eccentric, or someone we might informally describe as a hermit might have a personality disorder. This sort of person may never seek or be referred for psychiatric treatment because the behaviors may not interfere so drastically with everyday functioning to precipitate some type of intervention.

The second cluster, cluster B, includes personality disorders characterized by *dramatic, emotional, and erratic personalities* (*DSM IV* 1994; Wilson et al. 1996). For example, Nancy, the checkout clerk at the beginning of this section, fits within this category. Four specific diagnoses fit within this cluster: *antisocial, borderline, histrionic,* and *narcissistic personality disorders.* Each of these diagnoses has specific characteristics. For example, an antisocial person often violates the rights of others, whereas a narcissistic person has extreme need for admiration.

The third cluster, cluster C, includes personality disorders characterized by anxiety or fearfulness (*DSM IV* 1994; Wilson et al. 1996). The diagnoses in this cluster include *avoidant, dependent, and obsessive-compulsive personality disorders.* Each of these diagnoses has characteristic behaviors. For example, someone with dependent personality disorder has an excessive need to be taken care of and tends to be submissive and clinging. Someone who has an obsessive-compulsive personality disorder tends to be preoccupied with orderliness and control.

What Causes Personality Disorders? Personality disorders are fairly common. According to Wilson and associates about 10 percent to 13 percent of the population will exhibit a personality disorder within their lifetimes. It is also common for a personality disorder to occur in conjunction with another psychological problem, such as depression, substance abuse, or an eating disorder to name just a few. This can make diagnosis and treatment complicated. Because personality itself is considered a combination of biological temperament and developed character (Wilson et al. 1996), many researchers consider that both hereditary and environmental factors are important in the development of personality disorders. However, it is difficult to specify the particular factors in each case and how the interaction of those factors contributed to the disorder.

How Are Personality Disorders Treated? Because a personality disorder is comprised of an enduring personality trait, change is difficult to attain. Few personality disorder types, especially from the odd and eccentric class, seek treatment of their own volition. When seen by professionals, they are often treated in outpatient settings. Clients may seek outpatient treatment in order to complain about problems in their lives. They often lack insight regarding their own limitations, frequently projecting blame onto others. This lack of insight makes therapeutic progress difficult to achieve (Scully 1985). They will complain about problems in their lives, mood disturbances, or physical illness, but fail to recognize their own contributions to the problems.

Because of the enduring pattern of maladaptive behavior and the lack of insight often observed in these diagnoses, individuals with these disorders may benefit little from many traditional forms of treatment. The use of psychoanalysis (with the goal of effecting fundamental changes in the personality structure) has long been a treatment of choice for personality disorders (Corey 1996; Wilson et al. 1996), but this form of therapy typically requires an extended commitment of time and financial resources in order to achieve positive change. Counseling techniques that facilitate changes in cognition, behavior, or social interaction are now being used with greater frequency (Wilson et al. 1996). Pharmacology (medication) has been used to reduce the negative impact of various symptoms, such as depression, anxiety, impulsiveness, or cognitive distortions, but these medications do not change the fundamental personality traits per se. Consequently, it is common to pair psychotherapy with pharmacological approaches (Wilson et al. 1996).

Anxiety Disorders

Carrie is a computer programmer for a large insurance company. She is bright, capable, and well liked by her friends. However, her daily trip to the office has become a source of anxiety since the company moved its offices last month to the 23d floor of a high-rise building. Carrie has a phobic reaction to elevators. When she starts to anticipate taking the elevator, she feels intense anxiety and fear. Although she knows her fears are silly, she has at times even avoided the elevator by taking the stairs. She tells her friends that she is using stair climbing as aerobic exercise but knows all too well that her actions are irrational. Carrie suffers from an anxiety disorder called specific phobia.

What Are Anxiety Disorders? The **anxiety disorders** are a group of diagnoses (see Table 5-1) that are characterized by unrealistic or excessive anxiety, panic attacks, or avoidance behavior. The term, *anxiety,* in psychological terms, is a blending of thoughts and feelings in which the person feels lack of control and inability to predict potentially aversive life events. According to the *DMS IV* (1994), there are two particular types of symptoms that often occur within the context of many of the anxiety disorders: *panic attacks* and *agoraphobia.* A panic attack is a discrete occurrence of sudden and intense feelings of apprehension, fearfulness, or terror. These feelings may be accompanied by physical symptoms such as shortness of breath, palpitations, or a feeling of losing control. This kind of feeling would seem quite normal if it occurred in the face of a life-threatening event, such as an accident or assault. However, this sort of terror and apprehension can result for no apparent reason. Agoraphobia is anxiety about or avoidance of places or situations in which help might not be available should some embarrassing or incapacitating event occur (such as being outside the home alone, being in a crowd, traveling on public transportation, etc.). As is the case with a panic attack, the degree of fear or negative response is disproportionate to the threat posed by the stressor (i.e., standing in a line at the bank, being on a bridge, etc.).

The anxiety disorders are the most common type of psychiatric disorder in the United States (Wilson et al. 1996). Table 5-1 lists the specific diagnoses within the general classification of anxiety disorders, and the most prominent symptoms associated with each diagnosis (*DSM IV* 1994).

What Causes Anxiety Disorders? Until recently, anxiety was considered a psychological response to some deep-seated conflict or external stress. This is consistent

Table 5-1 SPECIFIC DISORDERS WITHIN THE CLASSIFICATION, ANXIETY DISORDER

A *Panic disorder without agoraphobia:* Characterized by recurrent and unexpected panic attacks that cause persistent concern. No history of agoraphobia.
B *Panic disorder with agoraphobia:* Characterized by recurrent and unexpected panic attacks and agoraphobia.
C *Agoraphobia without history of panic disorder:* Characterized by agoraphobia and paniclike symptoms, without a history of panic attacks.
D *Specific phobia:* Characterized by excessive fear provoked by a feared object or situation, which often leads to avoidance behavior.
E *Social phobia:* Characterized by excessive anxiety provoked by certain types of performance or social situations, which can lead to avoidance behavior.
F *Obsessive-compulsive disorder:* Characterized by obsessions (recurring thoughts, images, or impulses that cause anxiety or distress) or compulsions (repeated and stereotyped behaviors, such as hand washing or locking doors, that have no useful purpose).
G *Generalized anxiety disorder:* Characterized by general anxiety that persists for at least six months, and cannot be attributed to any particular situation or event that might cause anxiety. The intensity of the anxiety, as well as duration is enough to interfere with everyday functioning.
H *Posttraumatic stress disorder:* Caused by exposure to a traumatic event (such as combat or assault) which the individual later reexperiences through memories, dreams, and associated images and events.

with a psychodynamic view of anxiety. The cognitive-behavioral view of anxiety is that anxiety is a learned response to aversive or stressful situations that are beyond an individual's ability to cope. However, recent research suggests that particular biochemical processes in the brain may be responsible for the feelings and physical symptoms that accompany anxiety or panic. Further, some people may be biologically predisposed to anxiety states (Scully 1985; Wilson et al. 1996).

How Are Anxiety Disorders Treated? Because treatment of a disorder is usually related to the therapist's perspective on the cause of the illness, and because there are a range of symptoms and causes associated with particular disorders, there are a variety of treatments prescribed for an individual with an anxiety disorder. Traditional psychotherapy focuses on deep-seated conflicts, though recent studies show little effectiveness of psychotherapy with some anxiety disorders (Wilson et al. 1996). Cognitive behavior therapy, which focuses on changing catastrophic thoughts that activate anxiety, has proven successful with many of the anxiety disorders. For example, the individual may be taught techniques to reduce the fear response by using special relaxation techniques during gradual exposure to the fearful stimulus (Corey 1996). Successful use of pharmacological treatments suggests a link between some forms of anxiety and biological factors. Drugs have been successful, for example, in the reduction of panic disorder and obsessive-compulsive disorder (Scully 1985). A combination of cognitive behavior and pharmacological therapy has helped many people with anxiety disorders.

OTHER PSYCHIATRIC DISORDERS

Although the aforementioned disorders are considered some of the major disorders treated in psychiatry (Andreasen 1984), there are many other types of mental disorders frequently seen in psychiatric treatment. You will learn about other types of mental disorders in psychology courses and more advanced music therapy classes.

As can be seen, different emotional disorders have very different symptoms, and may result from different causes. Some disorders are brief in duration; others are chronic. Some disorders are more disruptive to everyday functioning than are others. Therefore, the treatment of choice varies from one disorder to the next. For example, if there is a biochemical basis to the disease, most likely, the psychiatrist will want to prescribe a medication to relieve the negative symptoms. Sometimes medications do not fully address the negative symptoms, so the individual must also learn to cope with the illness through psychological and social forms of therapy and support.

If some type of psychological or environmental stressor is the culprit, then counseling, changes in lifestyle, or modification to the environment can be the primary intervention. However, because stressors can have a negative impact on biological functioning, the psychiatrist (a medical doctor who specializes in emotional disorders) may wish to prescribe medication as well as counseling. In short, the sorts of interventions recommended will depend on the type of disorder and its cause. In the following section of this chapter, we will discuss some of the prominent treatment philosophies found in current psychiatric treatment. Then we will describe how music therapy interventions can contribute to each of these treatment approaches.

PHILOSOPHICAL ORIENTATIONS TO PSYCHIATRIC TREATMENT

There are many different philosophical orientations to psychiatric treatment. Several of the existing models commonly used are (1) *psychodynamic,* (2) *behavioral,* (3) *cognitive,* (4) *humanistic,* and (5) *biomedical* (Corey 1996; Ruud 1980; Unkefer 1990). Let's briefly review each of these, and the implications of each philosophy for music therapy treatment.

Psychodynamic Model

The psychodynamic model of treatment is based on theories initially developed by Sigmund Freud (Corey 1996). This model attributes emotional problems to the existence of internal conflicts that have resulted from negative events and conflictual relationships, many of which occurred during early childhood. The role of the therapist is to help the client become more aware of unconscious conflicts, relating these to present anxieties. In this model, emotional health is achieved by making unconscious drives and conflicts conscious, and by strengthening the ego or sense of self. Thus, behavior is less a response to instinctual urges and more a reaction to the events of reality (Corey 1996; Ruud 1980; Unkefer 1990).

Although Freud himself never addressed the use of music in therapy, some of Freud's followers have discussed the therapeutic nature of music. According to Ruud (1980), music is used as a therapeutic tool within this model in several ways: (1) *music as a nonverbal form of expression can be used to explore unconscious materials,* (2) *music can be used as an outlet for expressing hostile or unacceptable urges (sublimation),* and (3) *through involvement in successful musical participation, the client can experience a sense of mastery and control that contribute to improved self-worth and strengthening of the ego.*

Musical activities such as improvisation or guided imagery (using music to evoke images) may be used to explore unconscious material (Blake and Bishop 1994; Bonny 1994; Goldberg 1989; Nolan 1994; Warja 1994; Wheeler 1983). The individual may play music on an instrument as an alternative expression for uncomfortable or conflictual thoughts and feelings (Ruud 1980). For example, perhaps a person is feeling very hostile and angry toward someone. Rather than expressing those feelings through verbal or physical aggression, the person plays the piano very loudly and physically. The socially inappropriate feelings are thus sublimated by substituting an acceptable action, namely, playing the piano. Toward the objective of an increased sense of mastery, the music therapist selects musical tasks (such as learning a new musical instrument, or reviving old musical skills) that provide a realistic challenge for the client. Through this process, the individual has a sense of control over his or her own actions and develops increased self-worth (Ruud 1980).

The techniques used in psychodynamic music therapy are typically reconstructive, that is, result in major changes in the personality structure. Therefore these techniques require specialized professional training beyond the undergraduate music therapy degree (Bonny 1994; Wheeler 1983). Furthermore, because reconstructive therapy typically requires extended time for meaningful change, the client must be willing to commit extensive personal energy and financial resources. Some people argue that the necessary financial and personal commitment is unrealistic, or that some people (especially low-functioning or nonverbal clients) may realize minimal benefits from this model (Corey 1996; Wilson et al. 1996). In addition, some therapists are uncomfortable with the basic philosophical views of the psychodynamic model. One model that has developed in reaction to psychodynamic philosophy is the behavioral model of therapy (Corey 1996).

Behavioral Model

This philosophical model is commonly associated with psychologists such as B. F. Skinner, Joseph Wolpe, and Hans Eyseneck. Behaviorists (therapists and psychologists who are primarily behavioral in philosophical orientation) believe that human behavior is learned (Corey 1996; Hall 1971). Not only do we learn our ABCs and other academic information, but we learn how to relate to others, how to behave in different situations (e.g., how to act in church as opposed to how to act at a football game), and how to express our feelings. We learn through a process of reinforcement (reward). If we receive some type of reward for something we do, it is likely that we will repeat this behavior. For example, one of the early sounds that infants produce is "ma-ma." As the infant makes this sound, often the mother's face and voice will express great enthusiasm. "Oh, listen, Don! Allison said 'ma-ma'! See, she knows her mother!" The baby reacts positively to the mother's excitement; furthermore, the young child also delights in the sound of her own voice. Subsequently, Allison has been amply rewarded and will probably try that same sound again. Principles of reinforcement can be effective with adults as well. For example, at work, we are generally rewarded for doing our job by receiving a paycheck. If, for some reason, our paycheck stopped coming, it is unlikely that most people would choose to stay at that same job. These are only two examples of the many ways in which reinforcement is used to change or direct behavior.

Both of the examples above illustrate the use of reinforcement to increase desired actions. Sometimes, we inadvertently reinforce undesirable behaviors, too. For example, at bedtime, many children resist the idea of giving up their playtime to go to sleep. Sometimes children will cry, scream, or ask for more stories, water, or other forms of attention.

> If three-year-old Jason does not get his way upon the first verbal request, he may decide to get Mom's attention by crying or screaming. It is not unusual for a parent to succumb to the child's screams, allowing another story or an extra glass of water in order to stop the loud wailing. When this happens, the child discovers that by screaming, he may get his way. As a result, Jason is more likely to scream the next time he wants to stay up longer.

In much the same way that Jason's screaming behavior was learned, more serious behaviors such as physical aggressiveness, antisocial acts, and other characteristics of mental disorders can be learned through reinforcement. For example, an adolescent from a poor home environment may get little attention in the form of love and nurturing from mom and dad; however, the same teenager may gain the admiration of peers for having an expensive tape recorder that he shoplifted from a store. In short, the reinforcement for the antisocial behavior may be strong enough, especially in the face of a poor family environment, to encourage future illegal acts.

The fundamental role of the therapist in the behavioral model is to create an environment in which positive, desirable behaviors are rewarded, and to reduce negative behaviors by eliminating any reinforcement of those actions (Corey 1996). In order to do this, the therapist, sometimes in conjunction with the client, will evaluate the client's present behavior. Problem behaviors are identified, and the extent to which they occur is noted (see Chapter 10 on clinical assessment). Then the therapist and the client talk about how they think these behaviors should be changed. For example, if a little child is easily distracted, it may be important to decrease the number of times that the child looks away from the therapist during an activity. Concurrently, the therapist will wish to increase the amount of time that the child actually participates in a purposeful activity (Hall 1971).

There are many ways in which different professionals on a treatment team might approach behavioral goals. One key is finding a reinforcement that is truly meaningful to the particular client. Some people respond well to praise. Some people may prefer free time playing a favorite game. Some people find food very reinforcing. There are many different things that can be used as reinforcement in a behavioral program (Hall 1971). In addition to using some of the aforementioned rewards, one of the special tools that music therapists may use for reinforcement is music itself. Because music is a beautiful sound, and music activity can be a great deal of fun, it can be used as a reward to help change behavior in the desired direction (Lathom and Eagle 1984).

> The therapist may reward Sarah, a distractable child for making eye contact by playing Sarah's favorite song or musical instrument. As Sarah makes eye contact, the music therapist might ring a beautiful bell near her own face, both reinforcing eye contact and drawing attention toward the therapist's face.

At this level, music functions as an engaging and rewarding sensory stimulation.

With more mature or higher functioning clients, more complex and sophisticated music activities might be used as a reward. For example, many teenagers are attracted to guitar music, because rock music is an important part of adolescent culture (Paul 1982).

> When Jerry, a behaviorally disordered adolescent, demonstrates appropriate behavior on his treatment program, he may be rewarded by a guitar lesson with the music therapist.

Behavioral therapy can be used to change a wide variety of behaviors, including antisocial behaviors, muscular tension, poor social skills, underdeveloped communication, phobias (unrealistic fears), passive or unproductive ways of relating to others, to name just a few. Behavioral therapy is very flexible and can be used with clients of all ages and with a variety of functional levels (Corey 1996). However, not all therapists are fully convinced that behavioral therapy is the best way to improve mental health. Some psychologists believe that behavioral theories explain only partially or inadequately many types of human behavior. Furthermore, some therapists are concerned that the external behavior may be changed, but that beliefs that sustain the problem remain (Corey 1996). Therefore, some therapists align themselves more closely with a philosophy that emphasizes internal thoughts or meaning of events as they influence mood or behavior.

Cognitive Model

A number of therapeutic models fit within the general group of cognitive therapy: Ellis's rational emotive therapy (RET), Maultsby's rational behavior therapy, Beck's cognitive therapy, Meichenbaum's cognitive behavior modification, Glasser's reality therapy, and Berne's transactional analysis (TA). Although these different approaches vary in some ways, all share the basic premise that emotional and behavioral disorders spring from dysfunctional thinking about oneself and the world (Corey 1996; Unkefer 1990). Rather than emphasizing the importance of early childhood events on personality development (as does the psychodynamic model), or the impact of reinforcement on learning (as does behavioral therapy), the cognitive model emphasizes the importance of cognitive (mental) processes as determinants of behavior. Irrational thinking creates stress and feelings of inadequacy. Therefore, the treatment goal is to identify and then alter maladaptive thoughts.

> Janna holds the belief that she should excel in all things. Because no one person can humanly expect to achieve excellence in all endeavors, this would be considered an irrational thought. In her quest to feel adequate (which to Janna, means being excellent at all things), Janna pressures herself to get a grade of A on all her tests in all her classes, to have a perfect figure, to win all her tennis matches, to always look beautifully groomed, and to be liked by everyone.

Imagine the kind of stress and feelings of dissatisfaction that would accompany this kind of internally generated pressure.

The cognitive therapist acts as a guide to help the client realize and confront irrational thoughts and then adopt new and healthy responses. For example, Janna may start to feel hopeless or very anxious as a result of her belief that she must achieve perfection. After the therapist has established a working relationship with Janna, she would guide her in the following steps: (1) *help her become aware of this belief,* (2) *confront its irrational nature,* (3) *identify experiences in life during which this irrational belief system has been at work,* and (4) *take steps toward altering her behaviors* (Corey 1996).

> In music therapy, the therapist might use the lyrics and musical content of songs in group or individual therapy to help explore beliefs and the subsequent emotions produced as a result of disordered thinking (Bryant 1987; Maultsby 1977). For example, the singer Billy Joel once recorded a song entitled "Pressure" that portrays the buildup that occurs when people try to accomplish more than is humanly possible. Perhaps the music therapist would involve Janna in a group therapy discussion, using the lyrics of the song "Pressure" as a focal point for interaction (Plach 1980). Hopefully, Janna will have increased self-awareness and insights into her irrational thoughts and how they result in unhealthy behaviors.

Humanistic Model

There are a number of therapy models that might be considered humanistic, including existential therapy (associated with Rollo May), person-centered therapy (associated with Carl Rogers), and Gestalt therapy (associated with Fritz Perls). With all of these approaches, the basic premise is that emotional disorders result when an individual fails to establish personal fulfillment and meaning in her or his life. One central concept is called *self-actualization,* which the humanistic thinker, Abraham Maslow, described as moving beyond basic human needs (food, shelter, basic economic security) and living a life that is rich with meaning and a sense of well-being. In humanistic therapies, the therapist's relationship with the client is extremely important. Genuine and unconditional positive regard for the individual as well as empathy for the perspective and feelings of the client are essential to therapy. Therefore, it is important that the music therapist develop a supportive relationship with the client, based on genuine caring and respect for the client as a person. This relationship helps the client feel secure enough to move beyond defensiveness or mental and emotional blocks, and confront the most fundamental questions concerning the personal meaning of life.

In this type of therapy, the relationship between the therapist and client is probably more important than any individual techniques (Corey 1996). However, the music therapist will use music activities (whether they are music-based discussions or active music making such as improvisation) as one vehicle through which the relationship can be built, and through which the clients can achieve insights about their own life.

Some music therapists emphasize that access to the aesthetic beauty of music can, in and of itself, contribute to the quality of life. For example, Nordoff and Robbins (1971) maintain that music can help *lift* the person with disabilities out of his or her limitations in terms of self-actualization and personal fulfillment (Ruud 1980). The music therapist who works within a humanistic model uses music experiences to help the client achieve quality of life and a sense of meaning.

The humanistic model places great emphasis on the inherent capabilities of clients to control their own lives and to make good decisions for themselves. In contrast, the biomedical model emphasizes the impact of biological processes on human behavior, some of which are beyond the control of the individual.

Biomedical Model

The biomedical model attributes emotional and behavioral disturbances to biological factors such as biochemical imbalances, genetic problems, or physical illnesses such as infections (Andreasen 1984; Unkefer 1990; Wilson et al. 1996). Recent technological advances have made it possible to identify biological changes that accompany some types of mental illness, for example, schizophrenia. Special x-ray technology that allows physicians to view brain tissue has demonstrated clear physical differences in the brains of some chronic schizophrenics. Furthermore, chemical analyses of various body fluids show different proportions of important chemicals that help control mental stability (Andreasen 1984).

Although some physically based disorders can be clearly attributed to biological origins such as genetic predisposition, in some cases it is difficult to determine the etiology of the mental disorder. For example, although we know that physical changes (i.e., change in appetite, lethargy, poor sleep patterns) may accompany depression, the question remains whether the biological change occurred first and actually brought on the depression, or whether environmental stressors actually precipitated subsequent physical changes. Consider some examples in everyday life that illustrate the close relationship between our feelings and our physical well-being. When some people have extended stress, they may develop a skin rash or increased acne. Some people complain of increased heartburn or a racing heart. In fact, the mind and the body work together closely in reaction to the environment (Andreasen 1984).

Some disorders believed to have biological origins are treated primarily through pharmacological means (medication) or through special types of treatments (such as electroconvulsive therapy) (Andreasen 1984). In other instances, particularly where environmental stressors are believed to be a factor, changes in the environment or behavioral response to the stressor may be used in conjunction with or in lieu of medication (Hanser 1985; Unkefer 1990; Wilson et al. 1996). For example, depression or anxiety related to stressors might be treated through a program of muscle relaxation training (Byrnes 1996) .

Neil, a business executive for a large corporation, has been feeling immense pressure at work and subsequent feelings of anxiety and depression. His treatment team has recommended, in addition to psychotherapy, relaxation training. The music therapist may assist Neil in relaxation response by selecting appropriate musical stimuli for use during relaxation training sessions. Because Neil also indicated in his admission interview that he used to enjoy playing in a jazz ensemble, the music therapist might explore with Neil the possibility of reviving music as a positive leisure-time skill.

In addition to assisting with relaxation training, the music therapist may work with clients who are on medication for the primary symptoms of a disorder, but who still need additional support in order to return to a normal life. For example, some clients with serious, chronic disorders such as schizophrenia may respond only partially to medication. Even with medication, some patients may need a structured milieu and some assistance in developing more appropriate interpersonal skills (Unkefer 1990). Some clients may also need to rebuild self-esteem and confidence following a major emotional upheaval before they return to their everyday responsibilities. Music therapists can provide music activities that offer varying levels of structure, and that require lesser or greater response difficulty. Within the context of music therapy activities, clients can practice and role-play social interaction, maintaining good reality orientation, following through on requests, appropriate expression of feelings, and other important behaviors.

Eclectic Model

Although these philosophical models may all seem very different, in actuality many of them share some common features. Furthermore, many therapists would argue that no existing model is effective for all clients in all situations. Therefore, although a particular therapist or clinical setting may favor one model or another (e.g., some clinics use primarily behavioral models), more often, therapy teams will draw from a variety of models, integrating the benefits of several approaches in order to serve a particular client's needs. This is called an *eclectic model* (Corey 1996).

Within the psychiatric setting, the music therapist must take into consideration the philosophical model of treatment recommended for each client. By cooperating with the rest of the treatment team (e.g., psychiatrists, psychologists, and social workers) on the treatment approach, the client will benefit from a more cohesive and coordinated treatment program. However, the music therapist's approach differs in an important way. Rather than relying primarily on verbal therapy and medication to elicit change, the music therapist draws from a host of musical experiences to facilitate emotional and behavioral change. The following section provides a brief overview of different types of music therapy interventions.

CLINICAL USES OF MUSIC THERAPY IN THE PSYCHIATRIC SETTING

Clinical uses of music therapy in the psychiatric setting vary as greatly as does the clientele itself. As was discussed earlier in this chapter, psychiatric disorders can result from maladaptive aspects of the personality structure, environmental stresses, biochemical problems, or genetic predisposition. Symptoms can range from social withdrawal to aggression, or from euphoria to depression. Some clients may have poor reality orientation; others may be fully cognizant of their present circumstances. Some disorders are short in duration, some recur intermittently, and others tend to be chronic in nature. Furthermore, emotional disorders can span a wide age range, with some problems first appearing in childhood; other problems may be more likely to occur primarily in adulthood. Given this variance among clientele, how does a music therapist select interventions that are suitable for individual treatment programs?

In part, the fact that music can be used in a wide range of treatment programs is due to its flexibility as an art form. Music can be meaningful to a wide range of ages and can fulfill numerous functions within society (see Chapter 3). Structurally, music varies greatly in style and complexity. Consider the difference between the nursery song "The Itsy-Bitsy Spider," the country-western song "The Gambler," and Beethoven's Fifth Symphony. Almost everyone can find some type of music that is enjoyable and interesting. This wide range in style and complexity contributes to music's accessibility. Further, people can be involved in music in so many different ways. They can listen and respond to music with thoughts and feelings, compose music, play music, and move to music (Unkefer 1990). Music can stand alone as a satisfying art form, or it can be paired with words, with visual art, dance, or drama. Music can be a part of a very emotional or aesthetic experience, a catalyst for fun and entertainment, or a stimulus that promotes relaxation. Think of the many ways that people engage in musical activities in everyday life. The following section outlines some of the ways that music is used as a therapeutic intervention with psychiatric clients.

Different Uses of Music in Therapy

As has been discussed previously, one of the real strengths of music as a therapeutic tool is its flexibility. Music exists in a wide range of styles and complexities. Furthermore, it can be enjoyed passively by listening or through direct involvement in music making. Music can be enjoyed by people with little or no training as well as by individuals with extensive musical background. It can be enjoyed as a separate artistic entity or in conjunction with lyrics, with dance, or as a part of visual stimuli (i.e., background music at movies). Music can be enjoyed privately or shared in groups. All these characteristics make music a flexible therapeutic medium through which personal growth and behavioral change can occur.

Listening and Responding to Music As we noted in Chapter 3, music can arouse in people emotions and thoughts. Sometimes, people describe music as sounding like a particular feeling. For example, someone might describe music as sounding mournful, or perhaps happy. Some music may bring to mind particular thoughts. For example, a song might remind us of a prior event in our lives. Because music is an emotional language that elicits thoughts and feelings, it can be a powerful tool toward increasing emotional expression and self-awareness.

> John, a client in music therapy, has gone through a devastating series of personal losses throughout his lifetime. As a child, his father abandoned the family. Later, his mother became ill and died while he was in high school. In his adolescence and young adulthood, he found it difficult to meet and establish a comfortable relationship with women. Hal, the music therapist, decided to focus today's group therapy session on the topic of relationships, and he started the group discussion with Simon and Garfunkel's classic song, "I Am a Rock," which describes a person who is afraid to get close to others for fear of being hurt. After the song is finished, John tells Hal that he feels just like the singer, that he, too, is afraid to get close for fear that the person will abandon him, and he'll get hurt all over again. The rest of the group then offers Hal feedback and support.

As this example illustrates, a music therapist can use the emotional language of music to help clients become more aware of their feelings and thoughts, or to promote discussion, social interaction, or insights (Unkefer 1990). In the example above, music is used in conjunction with verbal forms of psychotherapy.

When using music as a part of psychotherapy, a therapist uses a number of steps in order to facilitate therapeutic change. Although there are various approaches to group therapy and leadership, often, the therapist will begin a group session with introductory activities that introduce the basic rules of the group, and that help them feel comfortable and safe within the group. During this initial period of acclimation, the therapist can also assess the current moods and functional levels of group members, and group members can contribute input regarding the goals and direction that the group will take.

After an initial warm-up period, the therapist will select musical stimuli and activities that facilitate emotional response and personal insights or motivate desirable behavioral changes. For example, through the musical experience, the client may relive feelings of anxiety. The therapist helps the client reflect on those feelings, and then helps the client make connections between the feelings experienced in the session and in real-life situations. The client, with the help of the therapist and other group members, can begin to formulate concrete plans of therapeutic change in response to what was learned during the session. For an example of a session structure for music psychotherapy, the reader is referred to the Appendix.

Playing and Composing Music Music therapists are trained to help even people with no musical training to sing, play instruments, or compose music. The act of playing music can include improvisation, where members of the group make up music and interact with one another. In other cases, music performing will consist of the playing of precomposed works. Sometimes, music performing will focus around the creation of a new composition by an individual or a group of clients (Ficken 1976). Adaptive teaching techniques and specially arranged musical compositions can facilitate participation by people with a wide range of skills and functional levels.

Music making includes both *process-* and *product-oriented* music activities. Process orientation means that the actual interactions and behaviors that occur while making music are the primary focus of therapy (Unkefer 1990). Often, clients will exhibit the same sorts of behaviors (both healthy and maladaptive) that they show in other aspects of their lives. For example, during group singing, a shy and withdrawn client may find it very difficult to take the initiative to select a favorite song. The client may also feel quite self-conscious, thus finding it difficult to actually stay with the group from beginning to end. In contrast, a client who is in a manic episode may be expansive and dominate the group. Within the music making activity, the therapist encourages each client to try more healthy and adaptive behaviors, and sets limits to maladaptive behaviors. Healthy interaction and on-task behaviors are the predominant objectives in this type of activity.

Product-orientated activities focus primarily on the creation of an end product, such as the completion of a musical composition, or the performance of a newly mastered song (Unkefer 1990). Because many clients have very poor self-esteem or feel inept or like failures, the sense of accomplishment and improved self-esteem that accompanies this event is a desirable therapeutic outcome.

Moving to Music Music and dance or movement have been paired throughout history. Movement can be a powerful tool for personal expression or to enhance self-awareness. For example, a group of clients may transform the lyrics of the song "You'll Never Walk Alone" into expressive movement. In addition, more structured types of social dances can be used to promote appropriate social interaction and active participation. In some instances, music can be used to promote physical exercises, as in an aerobics class. In each of these instances, music acts as a stimulus to movement whether it is a supportive activity such as folk dance, or an insight-oriented activity such as expressive movement (Unkefer 1990).

Music Combined with Other Expressive Arts Music can be paired effectively not only with movement and dance, but also with visual and written arts. Musical stimuli can act as a catalyst for expression of thoughts and feelings in an art or literary medium. For example, in group therapy, clients may cooperate to draw a picture and write a poem that reflects the music heard in a recording of Debussy's *Afternoon of a Faun.* This activity has at least two therapeutic objectives. First, individuals in this group are encouraged to express themselves through an artistic medium. Second, the group members must cooperate with one another, solving problems and working out interpersonal differences in order to create a final product. The qualities of the music, whether the music is rhythmic and brisk, or quiet and contemplative, will help generate ideas and structure the visual and literary art (Plach 1980; Unkefer 1990).

Music for Recreation and Enjoyment People often assume that therapy consists entirely of somber, thought-provoking events. However, in actuality, many clients also benefit from opportunities to relax and have fun, especially in structured social events (Plach 1980; Unkefer 1990). For example, some high-functioning business executives may suffer primarily from an inability to unwind and enjoy themselves. Recreation may be as valuable for some low-functioning, psychotic individuals who have difficulty organizing their own thoughts and actions enough to participate effectively in leisure-time events. Some chemically dependent clients may have spent a good proportion of their free time getting "high" on drugs. Following detoxification, these individuals may need appropriate leisure-time skills to fill those now-empty hours.

In these, and other instances, music activities can provide a healthy individual or group focus for personal enjoyment and fun. Playing music with friends is a perfect example. Learning to play the guitar or piano can be an enjoyable and rewarding pastime. Playing games such as "Name That Tune" or "Musical Bingo" can add much-needed leisure to a life filled with problems and social isolation.

Music and Relaxation In music therapy sessions, music is used to promote relaxation not so much in the incidental manner that may occur during leisure hours, but rather to the provision of structured techniques that promote mental and physical relaxation. For example, music can be introduced along with various types of muscle relaxation training in order to promote physical relaxation (Hanser 1985). With enough training, sometimes, even the sound of a particular musical selection that has been used consistently in relaxation training can trigger a relaxation response. Music can also be used to evoke images in a process called *music imagery.* For example, the music therapist may select an instrumental piece that tends to remind listeners of ethereal events or the peacefulness of a meadow. These images can help the client reduce tension and focus on positive thoughts and feelings (Scartelli 1989). On a more superficial level, listening to favorite music of a relaxing nature can temporarily distract the client from a barrage of anxious thoughts and feelings.

The previous uses of music therapy techniques should not be interpreted as a "cookbook" for how to do music therapy. Rather, it provides an overview of different ways in which music can be used as a therapeutic tool. The effectiveness of the activity or musical stimulus requires appropriate application and implementation. The best potential activity can be a disaster if used with the wrong client, or if the activity is not effectively facilitated. Successful implementation of an activity requires the sensitivity and knowledge of an adequately trained professional. In addition, the selection of intervention should be based on the treatment needs of the individual and group as determined in assessment. One important consideration is the present functional level of the client. The following section will provide an overview of music therapy interventions broken down by levels of group therapy, based on the client's functional level and need.

LEVELS OF GROUP THERAPY BASED ON THE CLIENT'S FUNCTIONAL LEVEL

As the aforementioned discussions on diagnostic categories suggest, clients with emotional or behavioral disorders demonstrate a wide range of characteristics and function more or less effectively in everyday life. For example, people having psychotic episodes may be confused about who and where they are (poor reality orientation) and have difficulty with even the most basic self-help skills (i.e., eating or dressing). In contrast, some individuals, while possibly suffering from a change in mood, may be fully cognizant of reality and capable of personal insights concerning their own problems (*DSM IV* 1994; Unkefer 1990; Wilson et al. 1996).

Furthermore, the extent to which the individual's functioning is impaired will vary across the course of treatment. In the first few days following admission to a hospital, a client with a biologically based disorder may be confused and have difficulty doing even simple tasks. After several days of successful pharmacotherapy and a structured milieu of individual and group therapy, the same individual may be lucid and readily able to follow through on daily responsibilities.

Wheeler (1983) has proposed three levels of clinical practice in music therapy in order to meet the widely divergent needs of psychiatric clients: (1) *supportive, activity-oriented music therapy,* (2) *reeducative, insight- and-process-oriented music therapy,* and (3) *reconstructive, analytically and catharsis-oriented music therapy.*

Supportive, Activity-Oriented Music Therapy

On this level, the music therapist designs activities that promote healthy behavior and foster participation. The music activity requires active involvement and awareness of the here and now (Unkefer 1990; Wheeler 1983). The types of activities used at this level may appear similar to those initiated informally in everyday life, such as group singing, playing musical instruments, or musical games.

There are, however, some important differences. These activities are carefully structured by the therapist in order to maximize participation by clients who may vary greatly in functional level and musical ability. For example, clients who are disoriented, withdrawn, or anxious may have difficulty initiating or sustaining even the simplest interactions and involvement with others. The music therapist can design the activity so that these types of individuals can experience some level of success and appropriate participation in a social event. This level of activity may also be appropriate for some individuals who, as a result of an acute emotional problem, may be temporarily functioning at a lower level than usual. Even higher-functioning clients can benefit from leisure skills that can be developed during activity-oriented sessions.

There are a number of therapeutic objectives that can be realized in activity-oriented music therapy: (1) *improved social interaction and awareness of others;* (2) *maintainance of reality orientation, or awareness of the here and now;* (3) *diversion from neurotic concerns or obsessions;* (4) *appropriate and successful involvement in a group activity;* (5) *impulsive behavior control;* and (6) *healthy use of leisure time* (Unkefer 1990; Wheeler 1983). Let us consider one example of an activity-oriented music therapy session.

Patricia's music therapy clients tend to have chronic mental illness, and often have difficulty with concentration, simple social interaction, and completing a task. Today, she has chosen the song, "My Favorite Things" from *The Sound of Music* to start her session. First, she puts up a chart with the words to the song, and plays the guitar as the group sings the song. After singing the song as a group, she asks each group member to turn to his or her neighbor and ask that person about his or her fa-

> vorite kind of music, favorite sport, and favorite season of the year. After a few minutes, Patricia puts up a copy of the song, "My Favorite Things," but there are words missing from the song. Patricia asks each member to share one of the favorite things that the neighbor talked about, then she puts the ideas into the song. Finally, the group sings their own version of "My Favorite Things," which now includes their own ideas, rather than "raindrops and roses and whiskers on kittens" as occurs in the original song. From time to time, during this session, various group members were very reluctant to participate or had difficulty staying with the group. Other people made comments that might seem odd or irrelevant to the topic at hand. Patricia encouraged or redirected each person in keeping with the treatment team's therapy plan.

Although this looks basically like a fun sing-along, much more is going on. The participants in this group have serious mental disorders that interfere with their concentration, with talking to others, or with completing even simple tasks (Unkefer 1990; Wilson et al. 1996). During this activity, Patricia first encourages purposeful participation in a structured, reality-oriented task by getting the clients involved in group singing. Then, she facilitates appropriate social interaction on a reality-based topic of favorite things. The structure of a simple topic can assist withdrawn or psychotic individuals to interact more effectively. As she filled in the new lyrics to the song, Patricia helped the clients contribute ideas related to the topic of favorite things.

During supportive group therapy, the therapist may reflect back to the client when a negative behavior occurs (such as interrupting others, talking about things unrelated to the group discussion, failing to comply with instructions, etc.), and help the client try healthy alternatives. However, at this level of intervention, the therapist usually does not delve into the reason for maladaptive behaviors. That type of intervention is more likely to occur at the next level of treatment: *reeducative, insight- and process-oriented music therapy.*

Reeducative, Insight- and Process-Oriented Music Therapy

At this level, active involvement is still important, but there is greater emphasis on verbal reflection and processing about interpersonal relationships and emotions. Therefore, activities are designed that foster (1) *identification and expression of feelings,* (2) *problem solving,* (3) *awareness of one's own behaviors,* and (4) *facilitation of behavioral changes.* At this level, the client is capable of gaining insights into feelings and behaviors, and reorganizing values and behavioral patterns (Unkefer 1990; Wheeler 1983). How is music used at this level? Let's consider one example.

> Patricia has a weekly outpatient group for clients who no longer need hospitalization, but who still need some ongoing support and therapy at this stage in their treatment. Patricia starts the session with what appears to be a sing-along. Each group member receives a song book with many popular songs. If Patricia were planning this activity for lower-functioning clients, she might simply ask each client to pick a song to sing with the rest of the group. The objective would be appropriate group participation. However, at the reeducative level, she will set higher

expectations. For this group, she has asked each client to pick one song that best expresses how she or he feels today. After the group sing the songs together, then Patricia encourages each client to share how the song reflects her or his feelings, what events have possibly contributed to those feelings, and in the case of negative emotions, to explore possible coping strategies.

This level of therapy generally requires that the clients are well oriented to reality and are able to communicate with others more than superficially. Within this sample activity, the therapist may ask the clients to (1) identify one feeling that they have, (2) share that feeling with the group, and (3) try to determine one event that has possibly contributed to that feeling. Although the therapist may facilitate awareness of and insights regarding emotions or behaviors, at this level the focus still tends to be on present events rather than unconscious conflicts that may contribute to emotional distress. That sort of in-depth probing occurs at the next level: *reconstructive, analytically and catharsis-oriented music therapy.*

Reconstructive, Analytically and Catharsis-Oriented Music Therapy

On this level, music activities are used to uncover, relive, or resolve subconscious conflicts, such as traumas experienced as far back as early childhood, that continue to hamper personality development (Corey 1996).

Steven, an adult male of 40 years of age, may have difficulty interacting comfortably with women. According to Steven's psychotherapist, this difficulty might be attributed to his relationship with his mother who was a punitive, intimidating woman. In outpatient music therapy, Patricia chooses activities for Steven that elicit images or feelings associated with the client's present or past. Through the process of bringing unconscious feelings and conflicts (i.e., Steven's feelings of frustration and hostility toward his mother) to conscious awareness, the client can achieve the insights necessary to work out maladaptive behaviors and anxieties (Corey 1996; Ruud 1980; Unkefer 1990; Wheeler 1983). Thus, the neurotic elements of the client's behavior can actually be restructured to reduce dysfunctional behavior. For example, Steven may, as a result of therapy, feel less intimidated when he interacts with women.

The music therapist who provides reconstructive therapy requires advanced training and supervision (Unkefer 1990; Wheeler 1983). The patient who engages in this level of treatment needs to have good reality orientation and a high level of motivation for personal change. In reconstructive therapy, music is often used to help elicit images or reconstruct past conflicts. For example, many people have heard music and described it as reminding them of a scene (i.e., a peaceful meadow, or a thunderstorm), or as representative of different kinds of emotions. The music therapist selects music that is particularly effective at eliciting images. Another type of activity often used at this level is improvisation (Unkefer 1990; Wheeler 1983). Through the process of interacting with musical instruments, the client may nonverbally express feelings or act out relationships with significant people from the past.

The client's diagnosis, the philosophical approach of the treatment team, and the level of psychosocial functioning and therapeutic need are all important considerations in designing an appropriate intervention (Unkefer 1990). It is also important to consider the maturational development, chronological age, and cultural background of the clients.

DEVELOPMENTAL AND CULTURAL CONSIDERATIONS

In addition to accommodating the functional level of the client and the philosophical orientation of the client's treatment program, the therapist must adjust for the chronological and developmental age of the client as well. As children develop from infancy to young adulthood, they change rapidly in terms of cognitive, communicative, social, and emotional development. However, sometimes normal patterns of development can be delayed or disrupted in the case of an emotional impairment. For example, young children with emotional disorders are typically less sophisticated in their ability to verbalize problems and anxieties. They may also lack impulse control or have difficulty organizing their actions (Friedlander 1994).

Musical activities are a natural part of childhood and can be tailored to suit the abilities and needs of children at all stages of development. Thus music is a wonderful therapeutic tool for children. The music therapist may select activities that reduce verbal requirements (Friedlander 1994) but emphasize the use of movement, art, and active music making. Puppets, toys, and other children's games may be incorporated into therapy interventions.

A music therapist working with adolescents is likely to draw heavily on music from the rock music genre, because that style of music is such an important part of adolescent culture (Brooks 1989). With maturity, adults tend to develop a range of preferred styles such as classical, popular, rock, and jazz. The music therapist working with elderly clients will need to address the musical tastes as well as some of the unique physical and psychosocial changes that occur as a result of the aging process (Corey and Corey 1987).

It is also important for the music therapist to consider the cultural background of individual clients. For example, a client who is Muslim, and grew up in the Middle East may find no particular emotional satisfaction from a song such as "Amazing Grace," which has particular meaning to many Christians who grew up in America. Furthermore, there are important cultural differences with regard to values and acceptable behaviors that require consideration. For example, making direct eye contact is a sign of positive self-esteem and good social skills in some cultures. In others, direct eye contact with an elder or with a stranger can be considered inappropriate. These cultural differences must be incorporated into treatment objectives (Brooks 1989).

CHANGES IN HEALTH CARE DELIVERY: SHORT-TERM CARE

The manner in which psychiatric treatment is provided has changed dramatically over the past few decades. For many years, people with chronic psychiatric disorders such as schizophrenia or chronic mood disorders spent much of their lives in remote institutions. Music therapists helped enhance the quality of life and maximize on-task functioning by establishing hospital bands, orchestras, and choirs. After the discovery of antipsychotic medications, many people with severe and chronic mental illnesses were able to function more normally, but may have required intermittent hospitalization for several weeks or months.

In the past decade, in response to more effective pharmacological treatments and changes in health care policy (Sarafino 1997), hospitalization for a mental disorder is likely to be quite short in duration. An individual may be admitted to a hospital because of a severe psychotic episode or in response to a suicide attempt. However, the person may be hospitalized only long enough for a psychiatric evaluation, to stabilize the behavior of the individual through pharmacological treatment and milieu therapy, and to plan an outpatient treatment protocol, such as individual psychotherapy or group therapy at a community mental health drop-in center.

The emphasis on short-term hospitalization has changed the manner in which music therapy is delivered. Music therapists are more likely to provide activities that help stabilize the behaviors of the individual (supportive, activity-oriented therapy) while the client is hospitalized. A music therapist may provide reeducative or reconstructive music therapy programming for higher functioning clients who attend outpatient therapy.

In short, there are no simple formulas for selecting music therapy activities. The music therapist needs to consider each client's diagnosis; his or her developmental level, chronological age, and cultural background; the philosophical approach of the treatment team; the level of functioning; and the therapeutic needs of the client attending music therapy. Often, participants in group therapy will represent a variety of diagnoses, age levels, functional abilities, and cultural backgrounds. That poses an interesting challenge for the therapist, who must find ways to accommodate each client's needs within a single session. Given these complexities, music therapists need considerable training both in basic therapeutic interaction as well as specific uses of music in order to best meet the needs of clients with mental disorders.

SUMMARY

Psychiatric disorders are manifested in a variety of ways. The first part of this chapter discussed the classification of psychiatric disorders that included schizophrenia, mood disorders, personality disorders, anxiety disorders, and other classifications. Psychiatric symptoms can be observed at all ages with many different aspects of a person's personality functioning afflicted, including thinking, feeling, perception of reality, and the ability to master the tasks of daily life. Also, we have seen that most psychiatric illnesses consist of different phases in which symptoms may be amplified or may be more moderate, allowing the patient to lead a nearly normal life.

Many advances have been made in the last 30 years toward an understanding of the causes of mental illness and the development of better treatment methods in pharmacological and psychosocial therapies. Music therapy is one of the therapies frequently used to eliminate or reduce the impact of maladaptive behaviors. Music therapists serve children and adults with mental disorders. Because music is a flexible art form that appeals to many people, it has great potential as a treatment tool with widely divergent therapeutic needs. Music will be used in different ways, however, depending on the functional level of the client.

Music therapy can act as a supportive, activity-oriented therapy, as a reeducative, insight-oriented therapy, or as a reconstructive, analytic tool. In addition to being adapted for the different functional levels of clients, music therapy interventions should also reflect the philosophical orientation of the treatment. Five commonly used treatment models in psychiatric care include: psychodynamic, behavioral, cognitive, humanistic, and biomedical models of treatment.

Music therapy can take a variety of forms, including listening and responding to music, playing and composing music, music and movement, music combined with expressive arts, recreational music, and music and relaxation. The application of various interventions should be adapted for the chronological and developmental age of the client. In addition, it should be based on information gathered in a music therapy assessment and from other existing information found in the client's records.

STUDY QUESTIONS

1 What are the major diagnostic features of schizophrenia?
2 What are the two most prominent theories about what causes schizophrenia? Major mood disorders?
3 Describe the different types of schizophrenic illness.
4 Describe different treatment approaches to schizophrenia.
5 What are the diagnostic classifications of mood disorders?
6 What is the definition of a personality disorder?
7 What are the diagnostic classifications of anxiety disorder? Which treatment approach works best with which disorder type?
8 List three factors believed to contribute to anxiety disorders.
9 List the three levels of therapy described by Wheeler.
10 Briefly summarize the basic philosophy behind psychodynamic therapy, behavioral therapy, cognitive therapy, humanistic therapy, and biomedical models of treatment. Identify the major leaders associated with each philosophy.
11 Give an example of how music therapy might be used in each of the philosophical approaches listed in 10.

REFERENCES

Andreasen, N. 1984. *The broken brain.* New York: Harper and Row.

Blake, R., and S. Bishop. 1994. Bonny method of guided imagery and music (GIM) in the treatment of posttraumatic stress disorder with adults in the psychiatric setting. *Music Therapy Perspectives* 12:125–129.

Bonny, H. 1994. Twenty-one years later: A GIM update. *Music Therapy Perspectives* 12(2): 70–74.

Brooks, D. 1989. Music therapy enhances treatment with adolescents. *Music Therapy Perspectives* 6:37–39.

Bryant, D. 1987. A cognitive approach to therapy through music. *Journal of Music Therapy* 24:27–34.

Byrnes, S. R. 1996. The effect of audio, video, and paired audio-video stimuli on the experience of stress. *Journal of Music Therapy* 33:248–260.

Corey, G. 1996. *Theory and practice of counseling and psychotherapy.* 5th ed. Pacific Grove, CA: Brooks/Cole.

Corey, M., and G. Corey. 1987. *Groups: Process and practice.* 3d ed. Monterey, CA: Brooks/Cole.

Diagnostic and statistical manual of mental disorders (DSM IV). 1994. Washington, DC: American Psychiatric Association.

Ficken, T. 1976. The use of songwriting in a psychiatric setting. *Journal of Music Therapy* 13:163–172.

Friedlander, L. H. 1994. Group music psychotherapy in an inpatient psychiatric setting for children: A developmental approach. *Music Therapy Perspectives* 12:92–97.

Goldberg, F. S. 1989. Music psychotherapy in acute psychiatric inpatient and private practice settings. *Music Therapy Perspectives* 6:40–43.

Goodwin, D., and S. Guze. 1979. *Psychiatric diagnosis.* New York: Oxford University Press.

Hall, V. 1971. *Managing behavior.* Vol. 2. Lawrence, KS: H & H Enterprises.

Hanser, S. 1985. Music therapy and stress reduction research. *Journal of Music Therapy* 22:193–203.

Lathom, W., and C. Eagle. 1984. *Music therapy for handicapped children.* Vol. 2. Lawrence, KS: Meseraull Printing.

Maultsby, M. 1977. Combining music therapy and rational behavior therapy. *Journal of Music Therapy* 14:89–97.

Nolan, P. 1994. The therapeutic response in improvisational music therapy: What goes on inside? *Music Therapy Perspectives* 12:84–91.

Nordoff, P., and C. Robbins. 1971. Music therapy in special education. New York: John Day.

Paul, D. 1982. *Music therapy for handicapped children: Emotionally disturbed.* Washington, DC: National Association for Music Therapy.

Plach, T. 1980. *The creative use of music in group therapy.* Springfield, IL: Charles C Thomas.

Ruud, E. 1980. *Music therapy and its relationship to current treatment theories.* St. Louis, MO: Magnamusic-Baton.

Sarafino, E. 1997. *Heath psychology: Biopsychosocial interactions.* 3d ed. New York: Wiley.

Scartelli, J. P. 1989. *Music and self-management methods.* St. Louis, MO: Magnamusic-Baton.

Scully, J. H. 1985. *Psychiatry.* New York: Wiley.

Smeltekop, R., and B. Houghton. 1990. Music therapy and psychopharmacology. In *Music therapy in the treatment of adults with mental disorders,* edited by R. F. Unkefer, 109–125. New York: Schirmer.

Unkefer, R., ed. 1990. *Music therapy in the treatment of adults with mental disorders.* New York: Schirmer.

Warja, M. 1994. Sounds of music through the spiraling path of individuation: A Jungian approach to music psychotherapy. *Music Therapy Perspectives* 12:75–83.

Wheeler, B. 1983. A psychotherapeutic classification of music therapy practices: A continuum of procedures. *Music Therapy Perspectives* 1:8–16.

Wilson, G. T., P. E. Nathan, K. D. O'Leary, and L. A. Clark. 1996. *Abnormal psychology: Integrating perspectives.* Boston: Allyn and Bacon.

6

MUSIC THERAPY AND ELDERLY POPULATIONS

William B. Davis

CHAPTER OUTLINE

Aging seems like a simple concept to define. We know, for example, that the aging process produces observable changes, such as wrinkled skin, stooped posture, graying hair, and, often, memory loss. However, it must be viewed from a psychosocial perspective as well. Growing old is a complex developmental process that involves the interaction of physical, psychological, and social factors (Birren and Bengsten 1988; Posner 1995).

This chapter will introduce you to the rapidly growing profession of gerontology, the demographics of aging, prominent theories and characteristics of aging, and disorders associated with aging. The final portion of this chapter considers how music therapy is used in rehabilitation programs for the elderly population.

GERONTOLOGY: THE STUDY OF AGING

Over the past 30 years, gerontology has been among the fastest growing scientific disciplines. It can be defined as "the scientific study of the phenomena of aging, involving the processes of aging and senescence, and including the related problems and achievements of older people" (Spence 1989, 1). A gerontologist is a person who specializes in one or more aspects of aging. Prominent areas of study include medicine, psychology, sociology, occupational therapy, recreation therapy, physical therapy, nursing, and music therapy. In fact, the study of aging should be multidisciplinary, drawing upon research findings and experiences of many different disciplines.

The term **geriatrics** is sometimes used interchangeably (but erroneously) with **gerontology**. Geriatrics is a medical subspecialty concerned with the care of elderly patients and treatment of their medical problems; thus, it is more limited in scope than gerontology (Papalia et al. 1996; Spence 1989). **Senescence,** another term frequently encountered in discussions of aging, describes the universal and inevitable decline in the efficiency of body systems. It is a normal aspect of aging and not considered dysfunctional. Senescence is slow and progresses at various rates in different people. It leads to a decrease in energy, eventual organ-system failure, and ultimately, death. On a more positive note, there are strategies to compensate for senescence that allow elderly persons to live satisfying, useful lives (Cunningham and Brookbank 1988; Rybash et al. 1995; Spence 1989).

THE GRAYING OF AMERICA

The number and proportion of people in the United States over the age of 65 have grown steadily during the twentieth century. This growth has fostered increased awareness of the unique problems associated with aging as well as an interest in working with elderly people (Papalia et al. 1996; Spence 1989). In 1900, a little more than three million people, or slightly more than 4 percent of the U.S. population, were over the age of 65. By 1940, that number had increased threefold to more that nine million people, or 6.8 percent. In 1991, more than 12.5 percent of the population was over the age of 65 (31.8 million people). It is estimated that the percentage of elderly Americans will be 13 percent by the year 2000 and more than 21 percent by 2030 (Papalia et al. 1996).

One factor contributing to the rising proportion of elderly people is increased longevity. For example, a man born in 1900 had a life expectancy of 46.3 years; a woman born during this time could expect to live an average of 48.3 years. By 1985, the life expectancy for men had increased to 71.3, whereas women born during 1985 can expect to live an average of 78.3 years (Longino et al. 1990). Increase in life expectancy can be attributed to several factors, including improvements in health care and changes in lifestyle (exercise, dietary modifications, and reduced use of tobacco products). Today it is not uncommon for people in this country to live to the age of 80, or 90, or even 100. In fact, the fastest-growing segment of our population are those individuals who are 85 years and older (Lewis 1989; Rybash et al. 1995).

As you can see, there has been and will continue to be a trend toward a large elderly population in our society, which could be beneficial to individuals in those age groups. There is strength in numbers, and this group can wield considerable economic, political, and social clout. This growth, however, presents a challenge to society, because the elderly population requires increased medical, social, and psychological services. Elderly people comprise nearly 13 percent of our population, but account for about 33 percent of our total health care expenditures (Posner 1995). In addition, this growth implies the need for specialized social and leisure activities for elderly individuals (Rabin 1989; Spence 1989).

BIOPHYSICAL THEORIES OF AGING

Three basic types of aging have been identified: primary, secondary, and tertiary aging. Primary aging is the systematic, genetically determined decline in the efficiency of organ systems in the body. The rate of primary aging varies from person to person and cannot be altered. Stress, trauma, and disease contribute to secondary aging; tertiary aging refers to changes that occur rapidly in the very old person. The overall rate at which an individual grows old is determined by primary, secondary, and tertiary aging factors (Birren and Schaie 1996; Lewis 1989).

We know that aging is primarily a biological process that is influenced by psychosocial and environmental factors, but our understanding of how and why we age is limited. There are numerous theories that attempt to explain this universal phenomenon, including six described below (Cunningham and Brookbank 1988; Davis 1986; Papalia et al. 1996; Saxon and Etten 1987; Thorson 1995).

Free-Radical Theory

This theory states that an increase in free-radical chemical molecules (which are by-products of normal cell activity) alter normal cell activity, cause chromosomal changes, and alter collagen (a protein that provides the elasticity in connective tissues of the body). It is believed that environmental pollution and oxidation of fats, proteins, and carbohydrates cause these changes. Papalia and associates (1996) stated that most of the data supporting this theory are circumstantial and do not confirm whether damage from free radicals is a cause or a result of aging.

Stress-Adaptation Theory

This theory holds that an accumulation of internal and external stressors (physical, psychological, and social) eventually damages the structures of the body. Such damage can be reduced through lifestyle modifications, including changes in exercise and eating habits and use of stress-reduction techniques.

Wear and Tear Theory

This early, simplistic theory states that the organism eventually "wears out" from overuse and damage to the body. This theory ignores the fact that the body has a remarkable capacity to repair itself and that increased use of some systems (muscles, for examples) actually strengthens the body.

Genetic Programming Theory

This theory, developed by Leonard Hayflick, states that each human cell is capable of a finite number of cell divisions, after which it dies. Each cell, then, has its own biological clock programmed to self-destruct after a set period of time. Research has shown that reduction in body temperature and changes in diet can postpone cell division but does not change the number of divisions programmed into each cell.

DNA–RNA Theory

This theory holds that metabolism becomes less efficient as one ages because of changes in the deoxyribonucleic acid (DNA) molecule. The DNA errors are then transmitted to the RNA molecules (ribonucleic acid), which in turn produce faulty enzymes that alter normal metabolic processes.

Immunologic Theory

According to this theory, the immune system essentially cannibalizes itself with age. This results in normal cells being attacked and destroyed by the immune system. In addition, B-cells (those that protect against viral and bacterial invasion) and T-cells (those that protect against alien tissue, such as tumors) lose their effectiveness with age. This may help explain why elderly individuals frequently develop chronic diseases.

These are only a few of the theories that attempt to explain the complex process of biological aging. Together, they answer some questions about the mechanisms of aging, but also raise other questions about the role of genetics, nutrition, environment, metabolism, and immune factors.

GENERAL BIOPHYSICAL ASPECTS OF AGING

There are universal characteristics of aging that occur in everyone. Aging may be viewed as an ongoing process that begins at conception and ultimately ends with death. At about the age of 40, a person starts to show physical signs of the aging process, such as a decrease in stamina and strength, the appearance of a few wrinkles or gray hair, and changes in weight and body composition. It is important to note that these characteristics do not appear at the same age for all people (Whitbourne 1996).

In addition, cellular, molecular, and organ functions become less efficient with age. This decreases the older person's ability to maintain homeostasis, or stability of chemical and physical states within the body. For example, the ability to govern blood chemistry and pulse rate declines with advancing years, which eventually contributes to dysfunction of the skeletal, muscular, nervous, and sensory systems (Spence 1989; Weiner et al. 1987).

SPECIFIC BIOPHYSICAL ASPECTS OF AGING

In addition to general biophysical changes that occur with age, every body system undergoes its own aging process. This portion of the chapter focuses on some of the changes that occur in the following systems: (1) central nervous system, (2) sensory system, (3) musculoskeletal system, (4) cardiovascular system, (5) pulmonary/respiratory system, (6) digestive system, (7) genitourinary system, and (8) endocrine system.

Central Nervous System

The central nervous system, which is the communication center of the body, includes the spinal cord and the brain. Over time, the brain exhibits changes in tissue, electrochemical function, and memory and cognition (Menks, in Davis and Kirkland 1986). Neurons are not regenerated when they die, so there is a steady loss of brain tissue that begins in childhood and progresses throughout a person's lifetime. By the age of 90, this loss represents 10 percent to 12 percent of original brain weight. Rather than being spread evenly throughout the brain, this loss is generally confined to the cerebral cortex (the area responsible for thought, memory, and other sophisticated cognitive processes) and those areas that control auditory, visual, and sensorimotor functions. The reduction in neurons may lead to problems with short-term memory, motor coordination, endurance, strength, gait, and the ability to learn new information. Vision and hearing acuity may also be compromised (Cunningham and Brookbank 1988; Whitbourne 1996). Changes in electrochemical activity in the brain may cause a decrease in reflex strength and an increase in reflex response time (Gambert 1987; Lewis 1985; Spence 1989).

On a more positive note, research has shown that the brain can continue to function at a high level into old age. It continues to create new neural connections in the presence of an interesting and challenging environment (Papalia et al. 1996).

Sensory System

The senses of taste, smell, sight, hearing, balance, pain, and touch are all involved in accumulating information about the environment. As we age, the efficiency of these important sensory modalities diminishes.

With advancing age, there is a decreased ability to perceive salty, sweet, sour, and bitter tastes. This loss of gustation is due to a reduction in the number of taste buds and a decline in the volume of saliva. It can decrease an elderly person's interest in food and in eating, which, in turn, can lead to malnutrition and weight loss (Cunningham and Brookbank 1989; Gambert 1987).

It is also believed that olfactory ability (sense of smell) declines after middle age. The loss of olfactory cells may result from the aging process or destruction from prolonged inhalation of substances such as tobacco or gas fumes. Research has shown that the threshold for perceiving most odors decreases with age (Spence 1989).

Typical changes in the eye that occur during the aging process include a slight reduction in its size, deterioration of cells within the eye, a decrease in blood flow to the eye, and a loss of fat and elastic tissue around the eye. In addition, the cornea becomes less spherical, a condition known as astigmatism, and peripheral vision is reduced. These changes occur over a long period of time and, in some individuals, impair vision (Birren and Schaie 1996).

Around the age of 40, a gradual loss of hearing begins. By the age of 75 about 50 percent of the population suffer noticeable hearing impairment, which can create feelings of frustration and isolation. Females, in general, have better hearing acuity than males and develop losses in audition later in life (Lewis 1989; Spence 1989).

Most age-related changes that affect hearing occur within the inner ear. An important exception, however, is the accumulation of earwax within the meatus (ear canal). The wax tends to dry out as a person ages and becomes difficult to remove. If not periodically eliminated, the wax can cause a hearing loss in low frequencies, which can impede the understanding of speech. Thinning of the tympanic membrane (eardrum) and ossification of the three bones in the middle ear (malleus, incus, and stapes) may also occur. This, however, will only slightly impair the transfer of sound vibrations to the inner ear and does little to affect hearing.

The vestibulocochlear nerve is a structure located in the inner ear that serves a dual function. The cochlea is involved in hearing, and the vestibular structure governs balance and equilibrium. In people over the age of 45, there is a degeneration of fibers in both areas. This can result in hearing loss as well as problems with balance. Falls are a significant problem for elderly people, because their brittle bones break easily (Spence 1989).

The sensation of pain is a warning that something in the internal or external environment is causing damage to the body. Most pain receptors are located near the surface of the skin or in muscles, tendons, joints, connective tissue, or organs. Some research has shown a decline in the ability to perceive pain as one grows older. Other studies have concluded that pain sensitivity increases with age; still other investigations have suggested little or no changes in the pain threshold between younger and older persons (Papalia et al. 1996).

Receptors for warmth and cold are also located near the surface of the skin. As people age, there is a diminished ability to sustain constant body temperature and cope with extreme changes in temperature. Even under normal conditions, some older persons develop hypothermia, a condition in which body temperature drops significantly below normal (95 degrees Fahrenheit and below). Comfort can often be achieved by adding or removing layers of clothing (Lewis 1989; Papalia et al. 1996).

Musculoskeletal System

The spinal column becomes less flexible and more compressed with age because of the deterioration of the disks that protect vertebrae from damage. Stooped posture is caused by calcification (hardening) of the ligaments and pliant fibers in the spinal column. Changes in the jaw, especially in the mandibular joint, and loss of teeth can result in speaking and eating problems. Bones lose mass and flexibility with age, leading to brittle bones that are easily fractured. The loss of calcium in bones is a common age-related phenomenon affecting women especially. By the time a woman reaches the age of 70, she may have lost as much as 30 percent of the calcium from her skeletal system. In some cases, estrogen and calcium therapy have been effective in slowing the loss of calcium for both women and men (Cunningham and Brookbank 1988; Lewis 1989).

Muscle strength begins to decline between the ages of 40 and 50. Muscle mass and elasticity decrease, and intracellular fat increases. This results in decreased strength and endurance, as well as the need for a longer recovery period between activities. These changes in muscle composition and activity can also alter posture, slightly reduce height, and impair gross and fine motor control (Spence 1989; Whitbourne 1996).

The skin, hair, and nails also undergo a number of changes with age. Skin loses elasticity, which leads to wrinkling and increases the length of time for wounds to heal. Hair may fall out (more common in men than women) or turn gray. Fingernails and toenails become brittle, discolored, and tough. They grow more slowly and sometimes split into layers (Cunningham and Brookbank 1988; Lewis 1989).

Cardiovascular System

There are few changes in blood chemistry or composition as one ages. Blood volume remains constant until about the age of 80, when it decreases slightly. Reduced bone marrow production causes the rate of blood cell formation to decrease somewhat with age, but it is usually not a problem unless there is extensive bleeding.

Heart size of elderly people generally remains about the same as in middle age, but it may decrease slightly because of reduced muscle mass. Other structural changes include an increase in fat deposits around the heart, a thickening of the heart valves, and changes in thickness of the endocardium (lining of the heart). Blood pressure tends to increase, and reduced oxygen delivery to the muscles may limit muscular activity.

Blood vessels also show changes with age, including a reduction in the elasticity of the walls. The internal diameter of arteries may decrease because of deposits of lipids (fats), and the walls of the veins may thicken. Both can contribute to increased blood pressure (Lewis 1989; Papalia et al. 1996; Spence 1989).

Pulmonary/Respiratory System

There is a noticeable decrease in the efficiency of the pulmonary/respiratory system as one grows older. A result is increased vulnerability to respiratory diseases, such as emphysema. Structural changes in the chest wall, reduced elasticity of the lungs, rigidity of the trachea, bronchii, and thorax, and alterations in posture occur with age. When these changes are combined with those of the circulatory and muscular systems, there is reduced ability to obtain and transfer oxygen to the blood. This can cause fatigue and lead to decreased activity.

Digestive System

Normally, the digestive system functions well in older individuals. Relatively minor problems include heartburn, indigestion, loss of appetite, and constipation. Cancer of the colon or other areas of the digestive tract are more serious disorders.

Structural changes that can occur include the loss of teeth, gum disease, and a reduction in saliva output, which can make chewing and swallowing difficult. In the stomach and intestines, the secretion of fewer enzymes may interfere with digestion. The large intestine becomes prone to diverticulitis (inflammation). Research has shown that the liver, pancreas, and gall bladder maintain normal levels of function in most elderly people (Whitbourne 1996).

Because of decreased physical activity, weight loss, and reduced metabolism, elderly individuals use less energy and thus require fewer calories per day. However, nutritional requirements remain virtually unchanged. It is important that an older person's diet include adequate vitamins, minerals, carbohydrates, proteins, and fats (Lewis 1989).

Genitourinary System

The urinary system is composed of two kidneys that manufacture urine, the ureters that transport urine to the bladder, and the urethra, which carries the urine outside the body. With age, a number of changes occur in the system, which lead to decreased blood flow to the kidneys and decreased strength and elasticity of the muscles in the bladder and urethra. The capacity of the bladder is reduced and necessitates more frequent trips to the bathroom (Lewis 1989; Spence 1989).

Endocrine System

The pituitary, thyroid, parathyroids, adrenals, and gonads comprise the main glands of the endocrine system. This system releases hormones to regulate metabolic activity and works in harmony with the nervous system to maintain homeostasis within the body.

As a person ages, there is generally little or no change in the ability of the endocrine system to maintain a balanced state. Sometimes there is increased glucose (sugar) intolerance, which may lead to elevated blood sugar. Reduced production of hormones by the immune system may lower resistance to disease (Whitbourne 1996).

AGE-RELATED DISORDERS

The presence of chronic disease is not uncommon in elderly people, and frequently, two or more conditions may be present at the same time. Despite medical advances that have reduced the incidence or impact of many debilitating conditions, chronic disease continues to be a major problem for this population. This section will discuss some of the psychological and physical age-related disorders found in elderly people.

Psychological Disorders

It has been estimated that up to 25 percent of people over the age of 75 develop some type of psychological problem (Lewis 1989). Disorders in this category include depression, paranoid conditions, substance abuse, anxiety disorders, and dementia (Papalia et al. 1996). Because we discussed these conditions in detail in Chapter 5, we will present only a brief summary on how each disorder relates to the elderly population.

Depression The incidence of depression increases with advancing age, with estimates that 20 percent to 45 percent of people over the age of 65 suffer from this condition. In fact, the highest suicide rate occurs in white males over the age of 80 (Lewis 1989). Symptoms of depression include sleep disturbance, loss of self-esteem, chronic fatigue, inability to concentrate, irritability, and social withdrawal. Other characteristics include thought disturbances, deteriorating interpersonal relationships, and a sense of helplessness. Depression in elderly people can be exacerbated by situational factors, including the loss of spouse, relatives, and close friends, displacement from home, and the loss of vitality and ability to do mental and physical tasks that were once routine. Fortunately, depression can usually be treated effectively with medication and psychotherapy.

Paranoid States As we learned earlier, paranoia is a psychotic state marked by delusions and disturbances in thought, mood, and personality. In older people, it can be caused by sensory loss, isolation, or physical illness.

Substance Abuse In general, elderly people are more sensitive to medications, such as painkillers and tranquilizers. Incorrect dosage or prolonged use of prescription (or nonprescription) medicines can lead to a substance abuse problem. Whereas some individuals have a long-standing history of substance abuse, others may develop the problem after turning to alcohol or drugs in an attempt to alleviate loneliness or depression. Substance abuse often leads to nutritional deficiencies, because the person may not maintain proper eating habits.

Anxiety Disorders Debilitating anxiety symptoms often accompany depression and organic disorders. This condition is usually temporary, triggered by apprehension about physical illness, relocation, isolation, or institutionalization. Symptoms include feelings of dread, confusion, episodes of crying, sleep disorders, and feelings of helplessness.

Dementia **Dementia** is an illness characterized by multiple cognitive deficits and includes over a dozen similar conditions that have different causes. Dementia may be caused by one or more conditions, such as Alzheimer's disease, substance abuse, Parkinson's disease, or cardiovascular disease. Dementia may have a sudden onset or occur very gradually. Symptoms include the loss of ability to learn new information, remember previously learned information, or both. Impairment in areas such as speech, writing, gross and fine motor skills, recognition of familiar objects or people, personal hygiene, financial matters, and social skills are common. Dementia is more prevalent in older adults with the rate doubling about every five years after the age of 75 (Papalia et al. 1996). The following section describes some common causes of dementia.

Alzheimer's Disease Dementia of the Alzheimer's type is considered to be one of the most devastating diseases of middle and old age (Corain et al. 1993). This disease is the fourth leading cause of death among the elderly in the United States, affecting about four million American adults and claiming an estimated 100,000 lives each year. It is the most frequent cause of severe cognitive dysfunction in elderly adults over the age of 65. When initially described by Alois Alzheimer in 1907, the disease was thought to be a rare occurrence, but today it is considered the primary cause of dementia. Prevalence estimates range from 2 percent to 10 percent of those over the age of 65 and from 13 percent up to 50 percent of those individuals 85 and older (Papalia et al. 1996).

Alzheimer's disease causes a steady, gradual decline in cognitive function because of structural changes in the brain. Early symptoms include lapses in judgment, decline in personal hygiene, bizarre thought patterns, changes in personality, disorientation to time and place, anxiety, depression, and general deterioration in overall functioning. In the final stages, the disorder is characterized by the inability to recognize loved ones and by the loss of speech. Alzheimer's disease is always fatal, with death occurring anywhere from 3 to 20 or more years after onset with the average between 4 and 8 years (McNeil 1995).

At this time, the cause of Alzheimer's disease remains unknown, but theories include a genetic link, abnormal protein deposits in the brain, and environmental factors. Diagnosis of the disease is complicated and usually made only after other conditions (such as brain tumors, metabolic disorders, alcoholism, or infections) have been ruled out. To date, autopsy is the only way to confirm the diagnosis. Brains affected by Alzheimer's disease exhibit neurofibrillary tangles (damaged proteins in the outer layer of nerve cells in the brain) and neuritic plaques (degenerated nerve endings) in areas of the brain responsible for memory and other cognitive functions. Extensive neurological and psychiatric evaluations can help eliminate other conditions (Cutler and Sramek 1996).

Vascular Dementia This condition, which is sometimes referred to as multi-infarct dementia, is caused by restricted blood flow to the brain. This results in a series of ministrokes to very small areas of the brain. Affected cells are damaged but do not die, except in cases where there has been complete blockage. Symptoms include impaired motor coordination, speech, and memory (Cutler and Sramek 1996).

Huntington's Disease **Huntington's disease** is a hereditary disorder that usually manifests during middle age. Symptoms include involuntary movements of the limbs and facial muscles. A personality change and diminished intellectual function are also common. As the disease progresses, dementia becomes probable. Like Alzheimer's disease, Huntington's is always fatal.

Creutzfeldt-Jakob Disease A rare and fatal disorder of the brain, Creutzfeldt-Jakob disease is most likely caused by a virus. Behavioral symptoms include a decline in intellectual function and difficulty in coordinating movements. Once diagnosed, death usually comes within a year or two.

Pick's Disease **Pick's disease** is a rare disorder that mimics Alzheimer's disease, except without physical deterioration of the brain. Changes in personality and behavior usually occur before memory loss in Pick's disease, whereas the opposite is true for Alzheimer's disease.

Physical Disorders

In this section, we examine age-related physical disorders. Many people who are elderly will suffer from two or more of these conditions simultaneously.

Disorders of the Central Nervous System Most pathological conditions affecting human behavior involve the nervous system. Two common neurological disorders associated with aging include Parkinson's disease and tardive dyskinesia.

Parkinson's Disease This disease is a degenerative disorder of the central nervous system that usually develops after the age of 50. It is characterized by involuntary contractures of the skeletal muscles, resulting in tremors and muscle rigidity. Other symptoms of this chronic and progressive condition include slow and slurred speech, shuffling gait, drooling, and loss of control of facial muscles. There is no known cause, but the drug, L-Dopa, is effective in controlling most symptoms. Intellectual functioning is usually not impaired until later stages of the disease (Cutler and Sramek 1996).

Tardive Dyskinesia This increasingly common neurological disorder is a side effect of taking certain medications over a prolonged period of time. It is marked by involuntary facial grimaces, movement of the arms and legs, rocking motions, and bizarre lip and tongue movements. It is usually irreversible, but symptoms can be reduced by taking other medications, discontinuing or reducing levels of antidepressants, antihistamines, L-Dopa, and some antipsychotic drugs (Saxon and Etten 1987).

Musculoskeletal Disorders Elderly individuals can develop pathological conditions associated with changes in muscular function and bone mass and structure.

Myasthenia Gravis Myasthenia Gravis is a progressive condition that can occur at any age but is more common in older persons. It is characterized by diffuse weakness of the muscles because of a malfunction of the immune system (Spence 1989).

Early symptoms of muscle weakness occur around the face and eventually impair speech, chewing, and swallowing. Treatment consists of drug therapy, including steroids and anticholinesterase therapy.

Osteoarthritis This common form of arthritis in people over the age of 50 is characterized by inflammation of the joints, cartilage covering, and bone. It causes stiffness, swelling, and pain, which makes movement difficult. During early stages of the disease, the joints in the hands are most often affected, with later involvement of the hips, knees, spine, and shoulders. These changes are irreversible, so treatment consists of managing pain and maintaining flexibility. In severe cases, surgery may be performed to replace the joint (Saxon and Etton 1987).

Osteoporosis Osteoporosis is a common condition that especially affects postmenopausal women (present in about 25 percent of women over the age of 60). Bones lose mass, become brittle, and are easily fractured. Most frequently affected are the bones in the wrist, hip, and femur (thigh bone). Posture can also be affected by osteoporosis. The cause of the condition is unknown, but contributing factors include estrogen deficiency, calcium deficiency, vitamin D deficiency, lack of exercise, and decreased capability of the body to absorb calcium. Exercise, proper posture, estrogen replacement therapy, vitamin supplements, and calcium are frequently used to reduce the seriousness of osteoporosis (Gambert 1987; Papalia et al. 1996).

Disorders of the Blood, Heart, and Circulatory System Age-related diseases of the blood, heart, and circulatory system include coronary heart disease, arteriosclerosis, myocardial infarction, angina pectoris, cerebral vascular accident, and hypertension (Papalia et al. 1996; Spence 1989).

Coronary Heart Disease Also called atherosclerosis, coronary heart disease results from blockage of the coronary artery because of a buildup of fibrofatty plaques. Plaques stick to the walls of the artery, eventually narrowing the passageway so that the flow of blood is severely restricted, which can result in a heart attack.

Arteriosclerosis Hardening and thickening of the arteries, or **arteriosclerosis,** is a major cause of irreversible brain damage. These changes increase the resistance of blood flow through the carotid and coronary arteries, which results in decreased blood flow and/or higher blood pressure. Lack of blood to the brain causes tissue death, which leads to mental and/or physical impairment.

Myocardial Infarction (MI) Myocardial infarction, also called a heart attack, occurs when blockage of an artery interferes with blood supply to the heart. Symptoms include chest pain, decreased blood pressure, difficulty breathing, and a weak pulse. Although sometimes mistaken for heartburn or indigestion, MI is very serious and can lead to heart failure and death.

Angina Pectoris The primary symptom of angina pectoris is chest pain, which is due to the heart muscle not receiving adequate oxygen. The excruciating pain usually radiates from the chest down the left arm. Other symptoms include a feeling of suffocation and gastrointestinal distress. Medication, such as nitroglycerin, and stress reduction programs are used to alleviate the symptoms of angina pectoris.

Cerebrovascular Accident (CVA) Commonly referred to as a stroke, a CVA occurs when blood flow to the brain is restricted, or when a blood vessel in the brain ruptures (an aneurism). As with arteriosclerosis, the resultant lack of oxygen to brain cells causes them to die, leaving permanent brain damage. The specific effects of a stroke are determined by extent and location of damage. Affected areas can include speech, memory, vision, motor skills, or personality. CVA can cause paralysis or death.

Hypertension Chronic hypertension (consistently elevated blood pressure) is common in elderly persons and is associated with arteriosclerosis. Symptoms are often undetected until there is damage to the heart, kidneys, brain, or other body systems. Treatment includes medication, stress reduction, changes in diet, and exercise.

Age-Related Sensory Dysfunction Humans gather information about their environment through the senses. Changes in the ability to perceive, interpret, and respond to stimuli can affect social interaction, impair safety, and reduce independence. The most common age-related dysfunctions of vision, audition, and balance in the elderly include the following conditions.

Presbyopia Presbyopia is a normal decline in visual acuity affecting a person's ability to read fine print and focus on objects up close. Caused by loss of elasticity and flexibility in the lens, presbyopia first appears between the ages of 35 and 50. The condition is usually corrected with glasses or contact lenses.

Glaucoma This disease of the eye progresses slowly, often without noticeable symptoms. Caused by excessive accumulation of fluid within the eye, it is a leading cause of blindness in the elderly population. Excess fluid causes increased pressure, which can permanently damage the retina and optic nerve. Treatment with medication and laser surgery can return the pressure to normal levels.

Cataracts Cataracts are the most common age-related dysfunction of the eye, caused by clouding of the lens. As a result, vision becomes increasingly dim and distorted. Surgery to replace the lens is the best treatment.

Macular Degeneration This disorder is marked by degeneration of the part of the eye responsible for fine vision (the macula). Reduced blood flow results in gradual loss of central vision. Total blindness does not usually occur, and a person will often retain peripheral vision (Saxon and Etten 1987).

Presbyacusis The most common age-related dysfunction of hearing, presbyacusis is an abnormal physiological deterioration of the auditory system. Higher frequencies are first affected, usually at a relatively young age. This is followed by a decrease in the ability to hear lower frequencies, which is more serious because it affects the ability to understand speech.

Tinnitus Ringing in the ear, or tinnitus, is a common complaint of elderly individuals. Marked by buzzing, roaring, or ringing, it often occurs in conjunction with a conductive or sensorineural hearing loss (discussed in Chapter 9). Tinnitus can also be caused by excessive earwax, damage to the tympanic membrane (eardrum), or fluid in the middle ear (Lewis 1985).

Dizziness Dizziness is a pathological condition associated with balance and equilibrium. There are many causes, but a frequent one is inflammation of the vestibular mechanism located in the inner ear. Dizziness can cause loss of balance and disorientation, and therefore create insecurity when walking. Elderly people often compensate by altering the way they walk to provide extra stability (Cunningham and Brookbank 1988).

Disorders of the Respiratory System Many respiratory problems associated with aging are caused by cumulative exposure to environmental hazards, such as smoking, air pollution, or chemical fumes.

Emphysema Emphysema is a disease of the lungs that is caused by long-term exposure to pollutants such as tobacco smoke and air pollution, or by chronic respiratory infections. It develops gradually and results in the lungs' inability to ventilate efficiently. This puts stress on the heart, which must work harder to adequately oxygenate the blood. Persons with emphysema often die from heart failure (Papalia et al. 1996).

Bronchitis Bronchitis is caused by a bacterial infection or by consistent exposure to environmental hazards. Inflammation of the bronchii interferes with the flow of oxygen in and out of the lungs. This results in excess production of mucus, which can block air passages and cause chronic coughing (Lewis 1985; Spence 1989).

Disorders of the Gastrointestinal System Common diseases that affect the digestive system in older people include ulcers, cancer of the stomach, throat, mouth, and intestines, and diverticulitis (Spence 1989).

Gastritis and Ulcers Gastritis is an inflammation of the lining of the stomach and can be a precursor to the development of gastric ulcers, the most common form of ulcers in the elderly. Symptoms include pain in the upper abdomen, significant weight loss, and dehydration. Complications from bleeding become more frequent with age and cause more than half of all deaths attributed to ulcers. Treatment involves the use of medication during early stages and surgery for the most severe cases.

Cancer The incidence of cancer of the esophagus, intestines, stomach, liver, gall bladder, or pancreas all increase with age. Symptoms are often vague, so the disease may not be diagnosed until it has spread to other organs. Chemotherapy, radiation, and surgery are the treatments of choice for cancer.

Diverticulitis After the age of 50, it is not uncommon for bulges (called diverticula) to appear in the intestines. These pockets are created by weaknesses in the abdominal wall. If the areas become inflamed, diverticulitis is the result. Symptoms include pain, nausea, and change in bowel habits. Treatment includes diet modification for mild cases or surgery for more advanced forms of the disease.

Disorders of the Genitourinary System Problems sometimes noted in the elderly population include urinary tract infections (cystitis and pyelonephritis), uremia, and cancer of the prostate gland and bladder (Gambert 1987; Spence 1989).

Cystitis Cystitis, or inflammation of the bladder, occurs more frequently in women. Symptoms include frequent urination, burning sensation during urination, and, sometimes, blood in the urine. Antibiotics are used to treat the disease.

Pyelonephritis Pyelonephritis is caused by bacteria that invades the urinary tract. This serious disease can lead to kidney failure if not identified and treated in an expedient manner. Older men are the most likely candidates for the disease, although elderly women are also susceptible. Symptoms include fever, chills, pain around the kidneys, low vitality, and weight loss. This disorder is treated with antibiotics.

Disorders of the Endocrine System The most common age-related dysfunction of the endocrine system is diabetes mellitus.

Diabetes Older people are more likely to contract maturity-onset (rather than juvenile-onset) diabetes. In general, diabetes is the result of insufficient amounts of insulin being produced by the pancreas. Elderly individuals who are overweight are likely candidates for diabetes. The condition can often be treated with diet, exercise, medication, and weight reduction, but chronic diabetes can lead to ulcers of the skin, weight loss, glaucoma, cataracts, and circulation problems (Spence 1989).

As we noted at the beginning of this chapter, the scientific study of aging is a twentieth-century phenomenon. Only within the past 25 or 30 years have gerontologists begun to discover the normal and pathological changes that occur in the body with age. In most activities, older people do not function as efficiently as they did during their younger years, and things seem to go wrong with their bodies with greater frequency. However, these physiological deviations are only one aspect of the aging process. In the next part of this chapter we discuss the psychological and social influences that impact aging.

PSYCHOSOCIAL THEORIES OF AGING

A number of theories attempt to describe and predict the social behavior of elderly people. In this section, several of these theories will be presented and briefly discussed.

Disengagement Theory

This controversial theory of aging was based on research conducted by E. Cummings and W. E. Henry during the early 1960s. These investigators suggested that elderly individuals voluntarily disengage from society, both psychologically and socially. At the same time, the society in which they live withdraws from them. This mutual disassociation results in predictable changes in vocational, social, and financial status. Disengagement has been criticized by many gerontologists, especially the implication that it is unavoidable and universal (Watts 1980). Recently, Cummings and Henry have modified the theory to suggest that disengagement may be an indication of depression and, therefore, not a normal part of aging. It is now generally accepted that not all elderly people reduce their societal roles and that those who do may suffer from depression (Davis 1986; Thorson 1995).

Activity Theory

Activity theory, also developed during the 1960s, was proposed by R. Havighurst and colleagues. Its basic principle is that people who age most successfully are those who stay active and involved. Life satisfaction, defined as having a positive view of life and gaining satisfaction in the activities of daily life, is an important concept of this theory. However, as with disengagement theory, the activity theory is not universally accepted, because not all individuals successfully adapt to the physical, social, and psychological changes that occur during aging. Thus, an active, satisfying lifestyle is more likely for those individuals who are physically and mentally healthy and have adequate financial resources. Disengagement and activity theories may be viewed as complementary. Some elderly individuals withdraw and reduce the number and quality of their social contacts, whereas others maintain and seek an active lifestyle (Davis 1986; Thorson 1995).

Person–Environment Transactional Perspective

The person–environment transactional perspective theory recognizes the importance of the interaction of the older person with his or her environment and stresses the idea of continuous growth throughout the life cycle. According to Schwartz (1974), healthy self-esteem and the ability to cope with numerous losses are necessary components of successful aging. By effectively structuring the social and physical environment, the individual can continue to live a productive and satisfying life (Lewis 1989).

Subcultural Theory

Subcultural theory was developed by Butler and Lewis during the early 1980s. It states that the elderly population is a distinct subgroup of society, with a unique set of norms, feelings, and attitudes best understood by the aging individual. Butler and Lewis stress the importance of communication among members of the elderly population. In rehabilitation settings, for example, older volunteers and therapists can be effective in establishing relationships and communication with elderly patients (Lewis 1985).

Although it is difficult to make generalizations about the elderly population, a number of prevalent characteristics can provide a framework for our discussion about important psychological and social issues. We know, for example, that people over the age of 65 constitute a rapidly growing segment of our society that requires increased medical, social, and psychological services (Spence 1989). Elderly people tend to shift toward jobs with reduced physical requirements and increased supervisory or leadership components. These and other general traits influence how society addresses the special needs of this group.

PSYCHOSOCIAL ISSUES OF AGING

There is little doubt that our society idealizes youth and discounts much of the experience, wisdom, and knowledge that the elderly population has to offer. Older people are often treated differently simply because of their age. Discrimination against elderly people is called ageism. Negative attitudes can begin in early childhood (Thorson 1995). For example, older adults are often portrayed as insignificant or as a representation of evil or ugliness in children's literature (Leitner 1983). We hear an older person described as "over-the-hill," "old fool," or "old maid." With some exceptions, older people are often portrayed negatively in movies, television, or music. The Beatles song, "When I'm Sixty-Four," for example, even though musically upbeat, describes aging as an unpleasant process.

The emphasis of contemporary American society is on maintaining youthful beauty. We are bombarded with advertisements for hair dyes, wrinkle creams, and vitamins to keep us looking young. Cosmetic surgery is a booming business. The message is clear:

The physical effects of aging are undesirable and should be avoided at all costs. It is interesting to note that many other cultures hold their elderly members in esteem and an older person is looked to for wisdom and guidance.

Socioeconomic Issues

Major economic and social changes occur in people's lives as they grow older. For example, the transition into old age is marked, for many people, by retirement, reduced income, changes in social status, loss of responsibility, and, often, a decline in health (Posner 1995).

Retirement Retirement is a twentieth-century phenomenon. In the past 20 years, there has been a tremendous increase in the number of older Americans no longer working. This growth has been due to increased longevity and retirement incentives, financial and otherwise. According to Cunningham and Brookbank (1988), there were fewer than 100,000 persons earning Social Security benefits in 1940, and few private pension programs even existed. Today, an estimated 21 million people receive Social Security payments, and an additional 7 million individuals collect private retirement benefits.

Because people are retiring earlier and living longer, changes in daily activity patterns must be made to compensate for vocational losses. Those who have planned ahead for retirement are more likely to make a successful adjustment. Changes that frequently accompany retirement include reduced financial resources and the need to identify a new role. In addition, older people frequently experience losses (death of spouse or friends, children leaving home, etc.). Preparation for these events helps lessen their effects and prevents the feelings of depression and isolation associated with retirement (Papalia et al. 1996).

Health Care As a person ages, the risk of contracting a major illness increases. Health insurance is a major cornerstone of economic security during retirement years. Medicare and Medicaid are two government-sponsored programs that pay medical benefits. Medicare, available to 90 percent of those aged 65 and over, covers a substantial portion of the costs of acute medical care. Private insurance plans are available to supplement Medicare coverage. Medicaid, available to those who meet low-income eligibility requirements, also provides coverage for acute care but primarily benefits elderly people by paying for long-term care. Commercial insurance plans that cover long-term care are prohibitively expensive for most of the elderly population. With the likelihood of catastrophic illness increasing with age, preretirement planning is important to assure adequate medical coverage. Unfortunately, many elderly individuals are underinsured, which places them at risk of economic ruin in the event of a major illness (Thorson 1995).

The good news is that the majority of elderly people are healthy. In fact, since the mid-1960s, there has been little or no increase in the proportion of the elderly population that is institutionalized in nursing homes, psychiatric hospitals, prisons, and facilities for the mentally retarded. Two factors helping maintain the status quo in nursing home utilization are the growth in outreach services designed to help older people avoid institutional placement and an increase in wellness programs for this population. Research has shown that age-related decline of some physiological processes can be modified through exercise programs. For example, cardiovascular fitness and muscular function can be improved by aerobic conditioning. Exercises such as walking and water aerobics are being promoted as relaxation techniques that can help reduce the use of medication (Cunningham and Brookbank 1988).

Housing Suitable housing for an elderly person is an important consideration in encouraging self-sufficiency. Housing choices depend on many factors, including cost, suitability, and proximity to medical care. Approximately 65 percent of all elderly people live in their own homes, and 5 percent reside in nursing homes (Cunningham and Brookbank 1988; Lewis 1989). Other options include assisted living facilities, retirement communities, retirement hotels, boarding homes, and the homes of adult children. One type of setting, a life care community, provides a continuum of care that includes social programs, meals, cleaning, and skilled nursing care should it become necessary (Papalia et al. 1996; Thorson 1995). It should be noted, however, that life care communities are expensive. People without adequate financial resources are likely to reside in boarding homes, retirement hotels, or other types of subsidized housing.

Institutionalization It is estimated that approximately 1.77 million people reside in 16,388 nursing homes in the United States (Thorson 1995). The median age of nursing home residents is 81. About 1.4 percent are 65 to 74, and 6.8 percent of this population is 75 to 84. The largest group (21.6 percent) of nursing-home patients is 85 and older. Women outnumber men about three to one. More than half of all nursing home residents are impoverished, although they may not have been before entering the nursing home. Many nursing home patients suffer from at least one chronic physical or mental disability, such as arthritis, Alzheimer's disease, and visual or hearing impairments (Lipson and Pattee 1989).

Changes associated with aging present a challenge to a person's psychosocial wellbeing even under the best of circumstances. The changes that elderly people in nursing homes experience can be devastating. Nursing homes are designed to provide continuous medical care and social experiences for those individuals with severe physical and/or cognitive disabilities. They generally maintain a restrictive, regimented environment that is not unlike that of other institutional settings, such as psychiatric hospitals or prisons.

Institutional living is usually not conducive to encouraging individuality. The *good* resident is one who conforms to the rules and does not make too many demands. People who are elderly and confined to nursing homes frequently suffer a loss of individuality and diminished self-worth. Maintaining or improving self-esteem, a major goal for therapists in this setting, is difficult because of the lack of trained staff to carry out esteem-building activities (Kohut et al. 1987). Loss of self-worth can lead to depression, which is the most common psychological problem found in the institutionalized elderly population (Cunningham and Brookbank 1988; Papalia et al. 1996).

Privacy is at a premium in nursing homes. Residents are under continual supervision by staff but, paradoxically, many are deprived of meaningful social contact and feel isolated. In addition, the ability to make personal choices is often severely limited in nursing homes. For example, residents have little input into the activities or menus planned for the upcoming week. Lack of choice is one component of the dehumanization often felt by elderly people living in nursing homes (Weiner et al. 1987).

Finally, there is the belief that a nursing home is a place to wait for death. It is no wonder that many of the residents feel depressed, isolated, and socially aloof from one another and from the staff.

The combined effects of the factors that led to placement in a nursing home and the situational characteristics of institutional living often result in physical, mental, and emotional deterioration. Deficits include disorientation, poor short-term memory, emotional instability, passiveness, loss of physical functioning, and unsatisfactory social relationships. Fortunately, there are a number of rehabilitation strategies, including music therapy, that can be used to improve the quality of life of aging persons confined to nursing homes and other institutional environments.

MUSIC THERAPY WITH THE INSTITUTIONALIZED ELDERLY POPULATION

Music therapy has been used successfully for many years in rehabilitation programs for the elderly, especially those persons confined to nursing homes. By providing sensory stimulation, music therapy enhances quality of life and helps prevent or slow mental and physical deterioration. Music is a stimulus that can be adapted to the client's needs and reach patients in ways other modalities cannot (Strick 1997). According to McClosky (1985), "music is effective therapeutically because it is the most social of all the arts and it is precisely the social aspects of life that are affected through mental illness and old age" (73).

Therapeutic music can make an impersonal environment (such as that of a nursing home) less intimidating, improve social interaction, and diminish feelings of isolation (Bright 1972; Clair 1996). The following list of goals demonstrates the wide range of potential music therapy benefits for residents of nursing homes:

1 Increase upper/lower extremity strength, mobility, and range of motion (Cotter 1959; Olson 1984; Weideman 1986)

2 Promote social interaction (Bright 1972; Clair 1996; Johnson 1990; Lipe 1991; Lord and Gardner 1993; Pollock and Namazi 1992; Roskam 1993; Wylie 1990)

3 Stimulate long term-memory (Johnson 1990; Wylie 1990)

4 Improve short-term memory and other cognitive abilities (reduce confusion, improve retention of information) (Johnson 1990; Prickett and Moore 1991; Reigler 1980)

5 Improve reality orientation (Bumanis and Yoder 1987; Smith-Marchese 1994; Reigler 1980)

6 Improve self-esteem (Bright 1972; Clair 1996; Johnson 1990; McClosky, 1985)

7 Promote relaxation/reduce stress (Bright 1972; Clair 1996; Johnson 1990; McClosky 1985)

8 Improve verbal skills (Cotter 1959; Johnson 1990)

9 Improve personal hygiene (Kurz 1960)

10 Strengthen sensory training (Wolfe 1983)

11 Improve communication skills (Redinbaugh 1988)

12 Reduce maladaptive behavior (Bright 1972; Clair 1996; Gibbons 1984, 1988)

13 Enhance reminiscence (Bright 1972; Byrne 1982; Johnson 1990; Olson 1984; Wylie 1990)

14 Improve motor and verbal behaviors in Alzheimer's patients (Clair 1996; Millard and Smith 1989)

15 Maintain levels of participation in Alzheimer's patients (Brotons and Pickett-Cooper 1994; Clair and Bernstein 1990; Millard and Smith 1989)

16 Decrease wandering (Fitzgerald-Cloutier 1993; Groene 1993)

17 Assist in recalling information (Lipe 1995; Smith 1986; Sambandham and Schirm 1995; Depperschmidt 1992; Prickett and Moore 1991; Aldridge and Aldridge 1992)

18 Reduce agitation (Brotons and Pickett-Cooper 1996; Clair 1996; Goddaer and Abraham 1994; Gerdner and Swanson 1993)

Music is also used to assist in the important area of assessment with the elderly population. Using different media, such as movement, instrumental and vocal improvisation, structured performance and music listening, the therapist can identify a person's capabilities and limitations in communication (verbal and nonverbal), affect, attention, behavior, sensory motor perception, and memory (long- and short-term). Other areas that can be assessed using music are motivation, gross and fine motor skills, and reality orientation (Aldridge and Aldridge 1992; Glynn 1992; Lipe 1995; Santeramo 1997). An individual's music preferences, abilities, and skills can also be determined during the assessment process. Once the client's strengths, needs, and preferences have been assessed, the therapist develops an appropriate music therapy treatment program.

Myths, Misconceptions, and Preferences

An effective music therapy program for elderly, institutionalized clients includes the opportunity for creating and performing music. According to Gibbons (1988), however, many music therapy programs for the elderly have not been designed to develop musical skills or to take advantage of musical skills acquired earlier in life. Reasons for this oversight include the notions that older people are physically and mentally unable to master the skills necessary for musical development, have no desire to learn new tasks, or have little interest in creating music. Fortunately, research is helping discredit these myths. For example, Clair (1996) and Gibbons (1982, 1983b) demonstrated that older people not only have the inherent capacity to develop music skills, but also the ability to maintain those skills throughout life, even if confined to a nursing home and suffering physical and cognitive limitations.

Another widely held belief is that vocal range and the ability to aurally discriminate changes in rhythm and melodic line diminish with age. Gibbons has demonstrated that elderly people are capable of aurally discriminating simple rhythms and melodies that avoid half-step intervals. She also noted that, with practice, older clients can become competent musicians (Gibbons 1983a). Still another misconception is that elderly persons prefer activities that require little or no interaction with the therapist or peers. The evidence suggests, however, that elderly adults are interested in singing, performing, composing, dancing/movement, and learning about music (Brotons and Pickett-Cooper 1994; Clair 1996; Gibbons 1982, 1984; Hanson et al. 1996). Palmer (1977) also encourages the active involvement of mentally or physically impaired nursing home residents in music activities. She notes that music therapy can be an important part of a resident's social, emotional, and physical rehabilitation.

In addition, there is the idea that older individuals like only religious music or music from the turn of the century (Gibbons 1988), but research has shown otherwise. Gibbons (1977) found that older people enjoy music from their young adult years (ages 18 to 25), but also appreciate music of other styles and periods. Religious music, folk tunes, and country and jazz music are also popular among elderly individuals (Gilbert and Beal 1982; Hanson et al. 1996; Jonas 1991). The style of preferred music can be determined by simply asking the client or family members (if the client is nonverbal) or by watching reactions to the music (Clair 1996).

Another common belief is that elderly people prefer slow, quiet (sedative) music to more upbeat, lively music (stimulative). In Gibbons' 1977 study cited earlier, she found that elderly clients enjoy stimulative music as much or more than quiet music. This finding does not suggest that a music therapist should never use sedative music, but rather that both types are appropriate. Finally, vocal range of elderly clients has also been of concern to researchers. Greenwald and Salzberg (1979) determined that most older persons have a functional range of about one octave, which is adequate to sing many melodies. However, the therapist should modify melodic lines if the range falls consistently below A-sharp below middle C or higher than G above middle C. With practice, vocal range can be improved (Clair 1996).

For persons with dementia, Brotons and Pickett-Cooper (1994) found that singing, instrument playing, and movement activities, along with musical games, were preferred over composing and improvisation. All these findings are important for the therapist who wants to create an appropriate music therapy approach for each client.

Approaches to Music Therapy

In this section, we will explore music therapy approaches appropriate for elderly clients of various functioning levels. The techniques presented first are generally more effective with clients with mild to moderate levels of impairment, whereas the latter approaches are designed for individuals who are severely limited in cognitive and physical abilities.

Remotivation **Remotivation** is a technique to stimulate thinking and verbal interaction and to improve social skills. Clients who are apathetic about their situation but who have verbal skills and an awareness of their immediate environment are good candidates for this program. Remotivation is most effective in small groups, using activities that are short and highly structured. Topics selected for discussion are objective and noncontroversial, usually focusing on subjects relevant to the client's past or current situation. For example, the therapist may lead a discussion about current events, art, or music. Props, such as newspaper clippings, photographs, clothing, or music, are used to stimulate discussion (Figure 6-1) (Weiner et al. 1987).

Music is an effective component of many remotivation programs (Bright 1972; Gibbons 1988). It can provide motivation, create a mood, or introduce a specific topic. For example, if the discussion centers on World War II, music of that era can be used to help set the mood, trigger memories, and stimulate discussion.

Reality Orientation **Reality orientation** uses repetition of information to reeducate clients who may be disoriented and confused (e.g., may not remember information concerning time of day, place of residence, or names of people) but are still aware of their surroundings. The goals of reality orientation are to provide the client with accurate, consistent information about his or her environment, reduce the effects of institutionalization, improve self-awareness, and increase independence.

Reality orientation incorporates the use of clocks, calendars, and a reality orientation board (which contains such information as the year, month, day of week, weather conditions, and upcoming holidays) to help clients remember important information about the environment (Bright 1972). As in remotivation, reality orientation is most often done in a group setting. This technique works best with people who suffer from temporary or fluctuating confusion because of stroke, brain trauma, or vascular dementia. Reality orientation is less effective with clients suffering from irreversible

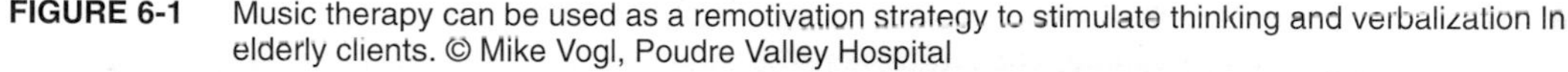

FIGURE 6-1 Music therapy can be used as a remotivation strategy to stimulate thinking and verbalization in elderly clients. © Mike Vogl, Poudre Valley Hospital

brain disorders, such as Alzheimer's disease (Bumanis and Yoder 1987; Kohut et al. 1987; Weiner et al. 1987).

Music therapy is an effective stimulus that can encourage and motivate elderly people to participate in reality orientation programs. Reigler (1980) compared a reality orientation program that did not use music with one that did. At the end of eight weeks, the group using music improved cognitive functioning significantly; clients could recall names, day of the week, and place of residence.

In another study, Bumanis and Yoder (1987) tested the effects of a music and dance program on elderly clients who were confused, disoriented, and suffering from memory loss. Results, although not statistically significant, showed that the music/movement group improved in alertness, enthusiasm, and social and emotional adjustment. Researchers noted that it took about six months of reality orientation training to achieve lasting changes in behavior.

Reminiscence **Reminiscence** is defined as the structured review of past life events and experiences (Butler 1963; Wylie 1990). It has become an important therapeutic tool with clients who are appropriate candidates for reality orientation or remotivation therapy (Kohut et al. 1987; Weiner et al. 1987). This technique is effective in individual therapy as well as in groups (Bright 1972; Byrne 1982; Karras 1987; Kartman 1980; Palmer 1977; Price 1983; Vickers 1983). Reminiscence, which at one time was considered dangerous to a person's mental health, is now viewed as a useful tool to help elderly people put their lives in perspective. Butler (1963) noted that a review of the past is a widespread, normal occurrence that could potentially be a helpful tool in adjusting to old age, particularly in resolving grief and dealing with stress.

As a therapeutic intervention, structured reminiscence can be used to increase socialization, improve interpersonal interactions, and strengthen self-esteem (Butler 1963; Price 1983). There is satisfaction in recalling past life events and sharing them with people who lived through the same times and events. In addition, reminiscence may help provide meaning in a person's life by reminding him or her of past activities and accomplishments.

Photographs, clothing, movies, magazines, and antiques can help foster reminiscence. Music can also be a powerful tool to facilitate the process (Bright 1972; Clair 1996; Karras 1983; Wylie 1990). For example, music can play an important role in setting the appropriate mood for a discussion about jobs, weddings, or other important life events. Music can also serve as the central theme for discussion. By using particular styles or time periods, the therapist can focus on the client's experience with music and how it influenced his or her life. Historical events can also be introduced with music. For example, songs of World War II can trigger memories about that era (Figure 6-2).

Sensory Training A therapeutic approach with elderly clients who are severely impaired is sensory training. This technique uses simple, structured activities to stimulate the client's visual, aural, tactile, and, sometimes, gustatory and olfactory senses. The major goal of sensory training is to restore contact with the environment by providing activities to improve social, physical, and psychological functioning. Sensory tech-

FIGURE 6-2 Using music therapy to facilitate reminiscence in an elderly person. © Mike Vogl, Poudre Valley Hospital

niques can be helpful with clients functioning at any level, but are most often used with the most severely regressed elderly individuals (those who are unresponsive, nonverbal, and withdrawn, and who have lost the ability to interact with their surroundings).

Sensory training can be divided into two levels. The first level is designed for the lowest-functioning patients. These clients have extremely short attention spans and deficits in gross and fine motor coordination. Communication skills can also be minimal, so it is often necessary to accept simple verbal or nonverbal responses from clients. Goals include improved body awareness, gross and fine motor skills, and social interaction.

Effective music therapy experiences for level I sensory training programs must be concrete, structured, and uncomplicated (Olson 1984; Wolf 1983; Clair 1996). The music therapist often uses passive activities (those that require very little verbal or physical response from the client), such as listening to music or participating in passive movement activities, in which the therapist physically manipulates a part of the client's body, such as an arm or a leg, to improve function. Activities are short, and the therapist asks few questions and uses concise directions, such as, "Move your arm up and down." Verbal responses are not necessarily required at this level, and clients who have a sensory deficit, such as a hearing or visual impairment, can also benefit from these therapeutic music experiences.

In some cases, an individual may progress to the second level of sensory training, in which music therapy experiences are used to further improve body awareness, attention span, memory, and motor function. Level II requires more social interaction, and clients are encouraged to take a more active role in their treatments. Nevertheless, the music therapist still uses simple, predictable, and highly structured activities with these individuals.

Other Music Therapy Considerations

As a word of caution, many clients suffering from progressive disorders, such as Alzheimer's disease, will not improve significantly and will eventually regress. Although this can be discouraging for the therapist, it is important to remember that he or she can make a difference in the client's quality of life. Therefore, it is important that even the most regressed clients be provided with music therapy services. Music therapy techniques provide effective, safe, and enjoyable ways for these individuals to relieve social isolation, improve communication, and increase motor function (Clair 1996). In this section, we will examine a few of the many programming possibilities.

Handheld percussion and mallet instruments (small drums, tambourines, maracas, xylophones, and glockenspiels) can be effectively used even with participants who function at very low levels. With clients that still have the capacity to speak, singing can provide a wonderful emotional and social outlet if the music is selected with care (pitch not too high, tempo not too fast, volume not too soft or loud). Hanson and colleagues (1996) found that movement activities requiring a high level of involvement (such as dancing) can be used across all functioning levels, and Clair and associates (1993) demonstrated that dancing can be used to help married couples rekindle emotional feelings even after the ability to sing and speak has diminished.

The presentation of music to severely regressed clients, whether live or recorded, can evoke desirable behaviors, including vocal responses, eye contact, motor responses, and affective behavior (smiling, crying). Clair and colleagues (1995) found that unaccompanied songs were particularly effective with persons affected by late-stage dementia. Other useful music experiences involve simple rhythmic activities using handheld drums and dancing. As dementia progresses, rhythmic and singing experiences must be drastically simplified (e.g., substituting humming for singing or letting the client create an original rhythm rather than try to imitate a predetermined pattern) (Hanson et al. 1996).

In later stages of Alzheimer's disease, severely regressed patients may not recognize place, time, or even the familiar face of a loved one. Attempts to communicate verbally with a client may be met with verbal and/or physical abuse. Validation therapy, developed by Feil (1993), can be an effective way to communicate and interact with this type of individual. This approach is to accept the person as he or she is, be an empathetic listener, and try to understand his or her point of view. Validation therapy can help the therapist understand and interpret important feelings. It is a reliable way to help disoriented people reduce stress and aggression, and to restore a sense of worth and well-being. Although we have identified some important uses of music in the treatment of the institutionalized elderly population, much remains to be done. As the number of older people increases in future years, rehabilitation techniques must keep pace. As Gibbons noted, "the role of music, music development, and music therapy is not clear. It can be defined only by careful research, integrated with competent practice, which are both based on sound theoretical constructs" (1988, 39).

SUMMARY

Aging is a lifelong developmental process that begins at conception and ends, ultimately, in death. Because of increased longevity and a surge in population, the United

States is experiencing explosive growth in the proportion of elderly people. This increase presents a challenge to gerontologists and society because of the increased medical, social, and psychological services required by this population.

Aging is marked by changes in functional capacity and structural modifications affecting virtually every system in the body, but the rate at which those changes occur varies among individuals because of genetic and environmental factors. As we grow older we are less efficient at physical and some cognitive tasks, and the body is more susceptible to age-related diseases. We experience psychosocial changes as well, related to roles, relationships, income, status, and activity patterns.

We distinguished between normal aging and age-related dysfunctions. Certain conditions, such as Alzheimer's disease and disorders of the circulatory system, are considered to be age-related diseases, whereas reduced vision and hearing are universal features of aging and not considered pathological.

Elderly people who are institutionalized have a unique set of problems and needs. Music therapy can be an effective means of rehabilitation for these clients in helping them maintain or improve physical, mental, and psychological functions. Research has shown that, as a group, elderly people have both the interest and ability to develop their music skills. A good music therapy program contains opportunities not only to listen to music, but also to create, perform, and move to music if clients are physically and cognitively capable.

Four music therapy approaches used with elderly persons confined to institutional environments were discussed. Remotivation techniques encourage clients to become interested in their environment. Reality orientation uses repetitive information to help clients organize their environment. Music can be used in remotivation and reality orientation groups to introduce topics, create a mood, and stimulate discussion. Reminiscence, the structured review of past life events and experiences, was the third approach discussed. Research has shown music to be a powerful tool that can evoke memories and assist in the recall of past events. Finally, sensory training uses music as an aural stimulus to help orient severely regressed clients to the immediate environment.

STUDY QUESTIONS

1. Three major developmental processes involved in aging include ______________, ______________, and ______________.
2. Distinguish among primary, secondary, and tertiary aging.
3. What are the limitations of the biophysical theories presented in this chapter?
4. What are some of the changes that occur in the sensory system as a person ages?
5. What factors play a part in increasing the incidence of depression among the elderly?
6. Three early symptoms of Alzheimer's disease include ______________, ______________, and ______________.
7. Define vascular dementia.
8. What is the disengagement theory and why is it controversial?
9. What impact does institutionalization have on elderly persons?
10. List at least seven music therapy goals often used with institutionalized elderly.
11. According to Gibbons, why has musical development in the elderly been neglected?
12. List, then discuss, the importance or remotivation, reality orientation, reminiscence, and sensory training in music therapy programs for the elderly.

REFERENCES

Aldridge, D., and G. Aldridge. 1992. Two epistemologies: Music therapy and medicine in the treatment of dementia. *The arts in psychotherapy* 19:243–255.

Birren, J. E., and V. L. Bengsten, eds. 1988. *Emergent theories of aging.* New York: Springer.

Birren, J. E., and W. K. Schaie, eds. 1996. *Handbook of the psychology of aging.* 4th ed. San Diego: Academic Press.

Bright, R. 1972. *Music in geriatric care.* Miami, FL: Belwin-Mills.

Brotons, M., and P. Pickett-Cooper. 1994. Preferences of Alzheimer's disease patients for music activities: Singing, instruments, dance/movement, games, and composition/improvisation. *Journal of Music Therapy* 31:220–233.

———. 1996. The effects of music therapy intervention on agitation behaviors of Alzheimer's disease patients. *Journal of Music Therapy* 33:2–18.

Bumanis, A., and J. W. Yoder. 1987. Music and dance: Tools for reality orientation. *Activities, Adaptation, and Aging* 10:25–33.

Butler, R. N. 1963. The life review: An interpretation of reminiscence in the aged. *Psychiatry* 26:65–76.

Byrne, L. A. 1982. Music therapy and reminiscence: A case study. *Clinical Gerontologist* 1:76–77.

Clair, A. A. 1996. *Therapeutic uses of music with older adults.* Baltimore: Health Professions Press.

Clair, A. A., and B. Bernstein. 1990. A comparison of singing, vibrotactile and nonvibrotactile instrumental playing responses in severely regressed persons with dementia of the Alzheimer's type. *Journal of Music Therapy* 27:119–125.

Clair, A. A., B. Bernstein, and G. Johnson. 1995. Rhythm characteristics in persons diagnosed with dementia, including those with probable Alzheimer's type. *Journal of Music Therapy* 32:113–131.

Clair, A. A., S. Tebb, and B. Bernstein. 1993. The effects of a socialization and music therapy intervention on self-esteem and loneliness in spouse caregivers of those diagnosed with dementia of the Alzheimer's type: A pilot study. *American Journal of Alzheimer's Disease and Related Disorders and Research* (January/February):24–32.

Corain, B., K. Iqbal, M. Nicolini, B. Winblad, H. Wishiewski, and P. Zatta, eds. 1993. *Alzheimer's disease: Advances in clinical and basic research.* West Sussex, England: Wiley.

Cotter, V. W. 1959. Effects of the use of music on the behavior of geriatric patients. Master's thesis, University of Kansas, Lawrence.

Cunningham, W. R., and J. W. Brookbank. 1988. *Gerontology: The psychology, biology, and sociology of aging.* New York: Harper and Row.

Cutler, N. R., and J. J. Sramek. 1996. *Understanding Alzheimer's disease.* Jackson: University Press of Mississippi.

Davis, L. J. 1986. Gerontology in theory and practice. In *The role of occupational therapy with the elderly,* edited by L. J. Davis and M. Kirkland, 29–39. Rockville, MD: American Occupational Therapy Association.

Depperschmidt, K. A. 1992. Musical mnemonics as an aid to memory in patients with dementia of the Alzheimer's type. Unpublished master's thesis. Colorado State University, Fort Collins, CO.

Feil, N. 1993. *The validation breakthrough: Simple techniques for communicating with people with "Alzheimer's-type dementia."* Baltimore: Health Professions Press.

Fitzgerald-Cloutier, M. L. 1993. The use of music to decrease wandering: An alternative to restraints. *Music Therapy Perspectives* 11:32–36.

Gambert, S. R., ed. 1987. *Handbook of geriatrics.* New York: Plenum Medical.

Gerdner, L. A., and E. A. Swanson. 1993. Effects on individualized music on confused and agitated elderly patients. *Archives of Psychiatric Nursing* 7:284–291.

Gibbons, A. C. 1977. Popular music preferences of elderly persons. *Journal of Music Therapy* 14:180–189.

———. 1982. Musical skill level self-evaluation in a noninstitutionalized, elderly population. *Activities, Adaptation, and Aging* 3:61–67.

———. 1983a. Item analysis of the primary measures of music audiation in elderly care–home residents. *Journal of Music Therapy* 20:201–210.

———. 1983b. Primary measures of music audiation in an institutionalized elderly population. *Journal of Music Therapy* 20:21–29.

———. 1984. A program for noninstitutionalized, mature adults: A description. *Activities, Adaptation, and Aging* 6:71–80.

———. 1988. A review of literature for music development/education and music therapy with the elderly. *Music Therapy Perspectives* 5:33–40.

Gilbert, J. P., and M. R. Beal. 1982. Preferences of elderly individuals for selected music education experiences. *Journal of Research in Music Education* 30:247–253.

Glynn, N. J. 1992. The music therapy assessment tool in Alzheimer's patients. *Journal of Gerontological Nursing* 18:3–9.

Goddaer, J., and I. L. Abraham. 1994. Effects of relaxing music on agitation during meals among nursing home residents with severe cognitive impairment. *Archives of Psychiatric Nursing* 8:150–158.

Greenwald, M. A., and R. S. Salzberg. 1979. Vocal range assessment of geriatric clients. *Journal of Music Therapy* 16:172–179.

Groene, R. W. 1993. Effectiveness of music therapy: Intervention with individuals having senile dementia of the Alzheimer's type. *Journal of Music Therapy* 30:138–157.

Hanson, N., K. Gfeller, G. Woodworth, E. A. Swanson, and L. Garland. 1996. A comparison of the effectiveness of differing types and difficulty of music activities in programming for older adults with Alzheimer's disease and related disorders. *Journal of Music Therapy* 33:93–123.

Johnson, S. 1990. Personal communication.

Jonas, J. L. 1991. Preferences of elderly music listeners residing in nursing homes for art music, traditional jazz, popular music of today, and country music. *Journal of Music Therapy* 28:149–160.

Karras, B. 1987. Music and reminiscences: For group and individuals. *Activities, Adaptation, and Aging* 10:79–91.

Kartman, L. L. 1980. The power of music with patients in a nursing home. *Activities, Adaptation, and Aging* 1:9–17.

Kohut, S., J. J. Kohut, and J. J. Fleishman. 1987. *Reality orientation for the elderly.* 3d ed. Oradell, NJ: Medical Economics Books.

Kurz, C. E. 1960. The effects of a planned music program on the day hall sound and personal appearance of geriatric patients. Master's thesis, University of Kansas, Lawrence.

Leitner, M. J. 1983. The representation of aging in pop/rock music in the 1960s and '70s. *Activities, Adaptation, and Aging* 3:49–53.

Lewis, C. B. 1985. *Aging: The health care challenge.* Philadelphia: F. A. Davis.

Lewis, S. C. 1989. *Elder care in occupational therapy.* Thorofare, NJ: Slack.

Lipe, A. 1991. Using music therapy to enhance the quality of life in a client with Alzheimer's dementia: A case study. *Music Therapy Perspectives* 9:102–105.

———. 1995. The use of music performance tasks in the assessment of cognitive functioning among older adults with dementia. *Journal of Music Therapy* 32:137–151.

Longino, C. F., B. J. Soldo, and K. G. Manton. 1990. Demography of aging in the United States. In *Gerontology: perspectives and issues,* edited by K. F. Ferraro, 19–41. New York: Springer.

Lord, T. R., and J. E. Gardner. 1993. Effects of music on Alzheimer's patients. *Perceptual and Motor Skills* 76:451–455.

McClosky, L. J. 1985. Music and the frail elderly. *Activities, Adaptation, and Aging* 7:73–75.

McNeil, C. 1995. Alzheimer's disease: Unraveling the mystery (NIH publication no. 95-3782). Bethesda MD: National Institutes of Health.

Menks, F. 1986. Anatomical and physiological changes in late adulthood. In *The role of occupational therapy with the elderly,* edited by L. J. Davis and M. Kirkland, 41–48. Rockville, MD: American Occupational Therapy Association.

Millard, K. O., and J. M. Smith. 1989. The influence of group singing therapy on the behavior of Alzheimer's disease patients. *Journal of Music Therapy* 26:58–70.

Olson, B. K. 1984. Player-piano music as therapy for the elderly. *Journal of Music Therapy* 21:35–45.

Palmer, M. D. 1977. Music therapy in a comprehensive program of treatment and rehabilitation for the geriatric resident. *Journal of Music Therapy* 14:190–197.

Papalia, D. E., C. J. Camp, and R. D. Feldman. 1996. *Adult development and Aging.* New York: McGraw-Hill.

Pollock N., and K. Namazi. 1992. The effect of music participation on the social behavior of Alzheimer's patients. *Journal of Music Therapy* 29:54–67.

Posner, R. A. 1995. *Aging and Old Age.* Chicago: University of Chicago Press.

Price, C. 1983. Heritage: A program design for reminiscence. *Activities, Adaptation, and Aging* 3:47–52.

Prickett, C. A., and R. S. Moore. 1991. The effects of music to aid memory of Alzheimer's patients. *Journal of Music Therapy* 28:102–110.

Rabin, D. L. 1989. Characteristics of the elderly population. In *Clinical aspects of aging,* edited by W. Reichel, 487–494. Baltimore: Williams and Wilkins.

Redinbaugh, E. M. 1988. The use of music therapy in developing a communication system in a withdrawn, depressed older adult resident: A case study. *Music Therapy Perspectives* 5:82–85.

Reigler, J. 1980. Comparison of a reality orientation program for geriatric patients with and without music. *Journal of Music Therapy* 17:26–33.

Roskam, K. S. 1993. *Feeling the sound: The influence of music on behavior.* San Francisco: San Francisco Press.

Rybash, J. M., P. A. Roodin, and W. J. Hoyer. 1995. *Adult development and aging.* 3d ed. Madison, WI: Brown and Benchmark.

Sambandham, M., and V. Schirm. 1995. Music as a nursing intervention for residents with Alzheimer's disease in long-term care. *Geriatric Nursing* 16:79–83.

Santeramo, B. 1997. The influence of music versus no music on agitation behaviors of Alzheimer's patients. Master's thesis, Colorado State University. Fort Collins, CO.

Saxon, S. V., and M. J. Etten. 1987. *Physical changes and aging.* New York: Tiresias Press.

Schwartz, A. N. 1974. A transactional view of the aging process. In *Professional obligations and approaches to the aged,* edited by A. N. Schwartz and I. Mensh, 4–26. Springfield, IL: Charles C Thomas.

Smith, G. H. 1986. A comparison of the effects of three treatment interventions on cognitive functioning of Alzheimer's patients. *Music Therapy* 64:41–56.

Smith-Marchese, K. 1994. The effects of participatory music on the reality orientation and sociability of Alzheimer's residents in a long-term-care facility. *Activities, Adaptation, and Aging* 18:41–55.

Spence, A. P. 1989. *Biology of human aging.* Englewood Cliffs, NJ: Prentice Hall.

Strick, E. 1997. The use of tactile stimulation in music to influence agitated behaviors in Alzheimer's dementia. Master's thesis, Colorado State University. Fort Collins, CO.

Thorson, J. A. 1995. *Aging in a changing society.* Belmont, CA: Wadsworth.

Vickers, W. D. 1983. Project looking back: A structured reminiscence experience. *Activities, Adaptation, and Aging* 3:31–37.

Watts, T. D. 1980. Theories of aging: The difference in orientations. *Journal of Music Therapy* 17:84–89.

Weideman, D. A. 1986. Effect of reminiscence and music on movement participation level of elderly care–home residents. Master's thesis, University of Kansas, Lawrence.

Weiner, M. B., A. J. Brok, and A. M. Snadowsky. 1987. *Working with the aged.* 2d ed. Norwalk, CT: Appleton-Century-Crofts.

Whitbourne, S. K. 1996. *The aging individual.* New York: Springer.

Wolfe, J. R. 1983. The use of music in a group sensory training programs for regressed geriatric patients. *Activities, Adaptation, and Aging* 3:49–62.

Wylie, M. E. 1990. A comparison of the effects of old familiar songs, antique objects, historical summaries, and general questions on the reminiscence of nursing-home residents. *Journal of Music Therapy* 27:2–12.

7

MUSIC THERAPY FOR CHILDREN WITH PHYSICAL DISABILITIES

Michael H. Thaut

CHAPTER OUTLINE

Emotional Skills
Musical Skills

Physically disabling conditions in children and adults encompass a wide variety of disorders with different causes and consequences for the afflicted person. The common problem, however, for all conditions discussed in this chapter is an interference with a person's physical abilities. Conditions that impede physical functioning are defined in various ways and include such terms as orthopedically handicapped, crippled, physically impaired, or physically handicapped. These terms are often used interchangeably. Because most rehabilitation efforts are usually utilized as early as possible, this chapter will emphasize pediatric rehabilitation for children.

Physically disabling conditions can be described according to a person's locomotor abilities (ability to walk). They can also be described as congenital and/or chronic and acquired and/or acute conditions (Sherrill 1981).

Congenital and/or chronic conditions are caused by birth defects. When bodily or functional abnormalities are present at birth they are called congenital. When they appear later in life but are genetically caused, they are called chronic. The most common conditions in this category are cerebral palsy, muscular dystrophies, spina bifida, clubfoot, congenital dislocation of the hip, arthrogryposis, juvenile rheumatoid arthritis, dwarfism, and osteogenesis imperfecta.

Acquired and/or acute conditions result from three different causes: trauma, disease, or disorders of growth and development (osteochondroses) (Sherrill 1981). These conditions encompass thermal injuries (burns), spinal cord injuries (traumatic paraplegia and quadriplegia), acquired amputations, and poliomyelitis.

It is important to realize that physically disabled children often suffer from multiple impairments. The trauma or defect that damages the human nervous system, be it congenital or acquired, rarely affects just one isolated area, but is often widespread and thus impairs more than one function. We often see physical impairment in conjunction with intellectual deficits, speech impairment, or sensory impairments such as blindness or deafness. For example, a cerebral palsy child also may be mentally retarded or may have impaired vision or speech. The opposite case, however, may also be found. A child could be very severely involved physically with a condition such as osteogenesis imperfecta but could have normal intellectual capacities. It is a challenge for the professional caregiver to create an environment for multiply disabled children in which their weaknesses are compensated for and their abilities are strengthened.

PHYSICALLY DISABLING CONDITIONS

Cerebral Palsy

Cerebral palsy is a nonprogressive disorder of movement and posture that is caused by damage to the motor areas of the brain. About 85 percent to 90 percent of such brain damage occurs during pregnancy or birth. Cerebral palsy from such early causes is termed congenital. Injuries to the brain during childhood account for the other 10 percent to 15 percent of cerebral palsy cases that are termed acquired (Bleck and Nagel 1982). Over 750,000 persons in the United States have been diagnosed as cerebral palsied, one-third of whom are under 21 years of age. According to Bleck and Nagel, 7 out of every 1,000 children are born with cerebral palsy. Many of the milder cases, approximately one out of those seven, do not require special treatment.

One common way to classify cerebral palsy is by motor abnormality. It is important to recognize in this context that motor abnormalities in cerebral palsy depend on the type of lesion. In spastic lesions, the pyramidal system in the central nervous system has been damaged. In pure athetoid lesions only the extrapyramidal system is involved. Important to note is that the central control system is damaged in cerebral palsy. The peripheral nervous system and muscles are intact (Gage 1989). Based on the type of lesion, functional movements may show different abnormalities. Understanding the different impairments associated with different lesions is essential to design effective treatment programs (Malherbe et al. 1992). Specifically in gait, several typical features, such as impaired balance, reflex patterns used to ambulate, abnormal muscle tone, imbalance between muscle groups, and loss of selective muscle control, have been well analyzed and described (Sutherland et al. 1993).

Seven types of cerebral palsy are commonly described:

Spasticity In spastic cerebral palsy, the muscles of the arms and legs are tight and contract strongly when one attempts to stretch or move suddenly. Several important muscle reflexes are also disturbed, which leads to abnormal movement patterns and posture. As the child grows older the contracted muscles become shorter, and deformities of the limbs, pelvis, and spine can occur.

Athetosis The athetoid child shows involuntary, purposeless movements of the limbs. In addition, purposeful movements are contorted.

Rigidity Rigidity is a more severe form of spasticity.

Ataxia Children with ataxia walk slowly, with a swaying trunk, with feet apart and arms held up to maintain balance. Ataxia refers to a lack of balance, a lack of sense of position in space, and uncoordinated movement.

Tremor This condition refers to a shakiness of limbs, especially when the person tries to move the limb. Tremor in a resting limb is unlikely to be observed.

Mixed Type Children with this condition usually have both spasticity and athetosis. Also, tremor and ataxia may be seen mixed in with other conditions.

Atonia This is a condition of no or very flaccid muscle tone, which may be seen in infants. Atonia will usually develop into athetosis.

Another way to categorize cerebral palsy conditions is according to limb involvement. The most common conditions are:

1 Monoplegia—one limb involved
2 Hemiplegia—upper and lower limb on one side of the body
3 Paraplegia—lower limbs only
4 Diplegia—major involvement of lower limbs and only minor involvement of upper limbs
5 Triplegia—involvement of three limbs, usually both lower limbs and one upper limb
6 Quadriplegia—major involvement of all four limbs

Almost all cerebral palsied children have multiple disabilities. Approximately 50 percent to 60 percent are mentally retarded, and about the same percentage have visual impairments. Between 5 percent and 8 percent have hearing loss. Approximately one-third have seizures at some time in their lives. Most of these children need some form of speech therapy. Learning disabilities are also very common, often accentuated by hyperactivity, distractibility, lack of concentration, and poor attention span.

Muscular Dystrophies

Muscular dystrophy is a progressive weakness of all muscles in the body, which can be attributed to a degeneration of muscle cells and their replacement by fat and fibrous tissue. The most common type of progressive muscular dystrophy is the Duchenne type. Its onset is usually before the age of 3, but symptoms may appear as late as age 10 or 11. The disease is genetically encoded. Inheritance patterns can be demonstrated in family histories. Approximately 250,000 persons suffer from muscular dystrophies in the United States.

Early signs of the disease include awkward and clumsy movements, poor posture, and tiptoeing. Muscle weakness develops from the feet upward to the legs, hips, abdomen, shoulders, and arms. Hands, neck, and face are affected later. In Duchenne-type muscular dystrophy, the course of the illness becomes progressively worse. Most children are wheelchair bound by age 10. Death occurs usually in the late teens. The disease itself is not fatal; however, secondary complications, such as heart failure due to a weakened heart muscle, or overwhelming lung infection because of weakness of the muscles involved in breathing, are the usual cause of death.

Spina Bifida

Spina bifida is an open defect in the spinal column caused by abnormal fetal development. It is the most seriously disabling condition in children. The incidence per 1,000 births ranges from 1.1 to 4.2 (Sherrill 1981). Spina bifida is caused by a failure of the back arches of the vertebra to close before birth. In Spina bifida occulta, the bony defect is covered by skin but there is no outpouching of the spinal cord. Few, if any, problems are associated with spina bifida occulta.

There are other forms of this disorder that are serious. Meningocele is a condition in which the meninges (spinal cord covering) protrude through the opening at the back of the spinal column. The most serious condition is called myelomeningocele, in which the spinal cord and the meninges develop outside the body.

There are many disabilities associated with spina bifida. The higher the location of the defect along the spinal column, the greater the likelihood that paralysis of the trunk and pelvis will manifest, which results in the inability to walk independently. Defects in the lowermost parts of the back may permit walking with crutches and leg braces. Many children have bony deformities, such as dislocation of the hip, clubfoot, turned-in feet, and so forth. Again, depending on the location of the defect, loss of skin sensation is a common problem. Paralysis of the bladder and the muscles involved in urination is present in all children with this condition; bowel paralysis is present in some children. In 90 percent of all children with spina bifida, hydrocephalus (water on the brain) occurs, which is caused by an increased amount of cerebrospinal fluid in the brain. Hydrocephalus is frequently associated with mental retardation. Medical attention to the problems of spina bifida, for example, neurosurgery to close the defect in the spinal column, orthopedic surgery to correct bone deformities, or urinalysis to control bladder function, has helped to improve the quality of life of the affected child. However, most children with spina bifida will need extended care throughout their lives.

Clubfoot

According to Sherrill (1981) congenital clubfoot is the most common of all congenital orthopedic disabilities, with an incidence of about 1 in every 700 births. The entire foot is inverted, with the heel drawn up, and the forefoot bent inward (adducted). Clubfoot varies in degrees of severity. Casting, bracing, splinting, and surgery can often correct the condition.

Congenital Dislocation of the Hip

Congenital dislocation of the hip is caused by an abnormal fetal development of the hip bones. It can be so mild that it is not detected until the child begins to walk. Corrective treatment includes surgery, casting, and splinting. In most instances the child will spend extended periods of time immobilized and hospitalized in casts or splints.

Arthrogryposis

Arthrogryposis is a congenital disease in which affected children are born with rigidly fixed and stiff joints and weak muscles. For example, shoulders may be turned in, elbows are straightened, and wrists are flexed and turned inward. Lower extremities are also frequently affected. Joints are often larger and have a loss of motion. The spinal cord sometimes is curved (scoliosis). Children with this disease may or may not be able to walk. However, within their limited mobility and movement awkwardness they can function well and have no pain associated with their deformities.

Juvenile Rheumatoid Arthritis

Juvenile rheumatoid arthritis is a disease that affects children, usually before the age of 11, with two peaks of incidence between the ages of 2 and 4, and between 8 and 11.

Girls are affected by this disease three to five times more often than boys. The specific cause for this disease is unclear. It appears that the inflammation of joints is a result of abnormal antibodies attacking normal body tissue. However, it is unknown why these antibodies appear. Unlike adult arthritis, most children sufferers will be free from active disease within 10 years after onset.

One or more joints will be inflamed during the disease. Some forms of disease are also associated with fever and skin rashes. Acute episodes of joint inflammations are usually extremely painful and may last from a few days to several weeks. The affected joints are swollen, discolored, and tender. Knees, ankles, feet, wrists, hands, shoulders, elbows, and hips can be affected.

Dwarfism

Dwarfism is a congenital condition that is due to abnormal skeletal development and is characterized by retarded physical growth, which is more than three standard deviations from the mean for the age group. Most dwarfs have relatively normal trunks and heads with disproportionately short arms and legs. Their physical mobility is rarely restricted other than by height, and their intelligence is normal or above average.

Osteogenesis Imperfecta

The common term for osteogenesis imperfecta (OI) is brittle bone disease. It is an inherited condition that affects males and females equally. The disorder, which can be present at birth or develop later, is characterized by weak bones and short limbs that deform easily because of repetitive fractures and healing in deformed positions. The joints are excessively mobile because of greater elasticity of muscle tissue and skin. Independent walking ability is rarely attained by children or adults. Children with OI have normal intelligence and achieve well academically. However, physical activities are severely restricted.

Thermal Injuries

Thermal injuries can be caused by fire, chemicals, electricity, radiation, and prolonged contact with extreme degrees of hot or cold liquids (Sherrill 1981). Thermal injuries are evaluated by extent and degree. The extent of damage to the body is evaluated by the total surface area affected by the injury. Degree is determined in three categories. First-degree burns affect only the outer layer of the skin and will heal quickly, although they appear red and are sensitive to touch. Second-degree burns destroy the outer skin layer and produce severe scarring. They expose nerve endings and are, therefore, very painful. However, second-degree burns can heal spontaneously over several weeks. Third-degree burns involve all skin layers and may involve muscles, tendons, and bones. The affected areas are white and dry and feel like leather. Because nerve endings are destroyed, initially no pain is present. Third-degree burns require skin grafting and prolonged hospitalization. Treatment involves bathing in special solutions, removal of dead skin tissue, dressing changes, and surgical procedures, including skin grafting.

Most treatment procedures associated with thermal injuries are very painful. Especially for younger children, these procedures can have an emotionally traumatizing effect. After hospitalization, long periods of rehabilitation are often necessary. Inevitably, scar tissue will form, which is very sensitive to sunlight. Also, layers of thick scar tissue will restrict the range of motion of joints. Braces, splints, and supportive bandages or masks are used to restrict the growth of scar tissue. One of the most difficult problems for burn victims to cope with is the deformed physical appearance, which sets them apart from other persons.

Spinal Cord Injuries

Severe spinal cord injuries result in different types of paralysis of parts of the body, categorized as paraplegia or quadriplegia. Paraplegia refers to paralysis of the lower part of the body, including motion and sensation. Quadriplegia refers to paralysis of all four limbs. Although these conditions can be caused by congenital abnormalities, more common in rehabilitation settings are traumatic injuries. Frequent causes are motor vehicle accidents, sports accidents, bullet wounds, or injuries from falling from a height. The paralysis is caused by an interruption of the nerve pathways going from the brain to the involved limb via the spinal cord. The higher in the spinal cord the injury occurs the more severe the resulting paralysis will be. Nerve pathways in the spinal cord that are completely destroyed will not regenerate and cannot be repaired by current medical techniques. Thus, the paralysis will be permanent. Handling of the patient and immediate start of emergency care after the trauma may be critical to the outcome of the injury. Any incomplete nerve damage may still be repairable if emergency procedures can start early.

In rehabilitation the major emphasis should be on the patient's psychological status in regard to morale, motivation, and attitude to an altered quality of life. Emotional, social, and occupational changes in an injured person's life can be severe. Supportive counseling, emotional support from family, friends, and peers, and adaptive techniques to facilitate activities of daily living and occupational endeavors are necessary.

Acquired Amputations

Most elective amputations in children occur between 12 and 21 years of age. Most common causes for traumatic amputations are motor vehicle accidents, farm accidents, power tool accidents, and gunshot injuries. Other causes for amputations include cancer, infections, bone tumors, or vascular conditions like gangrene.

The loss of a limb in elective amputation is one of the most psychologically traumatizing disabilities a child can experience. Any rehabilitation plan for an amputee child includes strong psychological support for both the child and the family. The main goal for treatment of an amputee child is to enable him or her to develop and grow as normally as possible and enjoy a meaningful quality of life. One of the major aspects of amputee rehabilitation is the use of prosthetic devices as artificial limbs. Today, prosthesis fitting occurs usually within 30 days after the amputation because of advances in surgical techniques. Training in the use of prostheses should include functional activities of daily living as well as leisure and recreational activities as much as possible.

Poliomyelitis

Poliomyelitis is a viral infection that attacks the motor cells in the spinal cord. The virus enters through the intestinal tract, travels through the bloodstream, and settles in the motor cells of the spinal cord. The virus may cause only inflammation and swelling of the cells, in which case full recovery can take place. In severe cases the motor cells are destroyed, and irreversible muscle paralysis will occur. At the onset of the infection, fever, painful muscle spasms, and muscle stiffness occur. After the acute phase, muscle function will return to normal or muscular paralysis will persist. A complete diagnosis of the extent of permanent damage should be made 18 months after onset of the infection.

Affected children will, for the most part, have moderate to severe paralysis of the lower limbs and, at times, the trunk. Also, spinal curvature (scoliosis) and joint deformities may develop because of muscle weakness. Rehabilitation includes strength training for weakened muscles, the use of braces to support weakened joints, and the use of crutches and wheelchairs for mobility. Poliomyelitis affects only the neuromuscular system. Other bodily functions and intellectual capacities are unaffected. Although poliomyelitis still exists today, cases have become rare in developed countries since the introduction of vaccines.

MUSIC THERAPY WITH THE PHYSICALLY DISABLED: AN OUTLINE

Settings

The music therapist will encounter physically disabled children in a variety of settings. Because of the mainstreaming laws in this country (PL 94-142), most physically disabled children will be part of an educational setting, be it a mainstreamed classroom with normal and disabled children, a special classroom in a normal school setting, or a school for children with special needs. Other settings in which music therapists work with these children include hospital outpatient programs, developmental centers, group homes, or preschool programs. Jellison (1988) provides a comprehensive research survey on the effectiveness of music therapy methods with disabled children in various settings.

Background Knowledge

In order to work efficiently with the physically disabled child, the music therapist must be thoroughly familiar with the particular disabling condition. Each condition has a different cause, diagnosis, and treatment requirements (Toombs-Rudenberg 1982). For example, conditions such as cerebral palsy require specific knowledge of handling techniques. The music therapist who works with physically disabled persons will need to know how to position a physically involved child on the floor, in a chair, or in a wheelchair, to support and allow for the best range of movement possible or to avoid reinforcing detrimental postures, reflexes, and motions. The music therapist also needs to be familiar with techniques for transferring children from a bed to a chair, or from a lying into a sitting position.

Another important consideration is the developmental course and diagnosis of the condition. Is the impairment a progressive illness that will get worse over time? If this is the case, what level of functioning can the therapist realistically expect from the child at a given stage of the illness? Understanding of the diagnosis of a particular condition will give the music therapist the knowledge of what areas of behavior are affected and what level of functioning can be expected from the child.

Another important area of knowledge for the music therapist includes the steps and progressions of normal development in the areas of motor, social, emotional, and cognitive behavior. Research has shown very clearly that the development of disabled children follows the same progressions as that of normal children. They will, however, develop at a slower pace or their development may be arrested at a certain level (Cratty 1975). This knowledge is very important for the formulation of appropriate treatment goals in order to move the child, in a developmentally meaningful and attainable way, to higher levels of functioning.

The Interdisciplinary Team Member

From the foregoing discussion, it is quite obvious that the music therapist must be thoroughly familiar with the developmental, psychological, and medical information that pertains to each disabling condition. This background of knowledge is also necessary for the music therapist to function efficiently as a member of an interdisciplinary treatment team, be it as a staff member in a special education program or as a therapist on a hospital staff.

Goals

The music therapist pursues three different types of goals in working with physically disabled children: educational, rehabilitative, and developmental.

Educational Goals Educational goals focus on the academic development of the child, which also includes social, emotional, and physical skill development. Music therapy goals are closely linked to the educational planning for the child, usually in a special education setting. The music therapist uses music activities and related experiences in speech, movement, and other creative arts media, such as drama or visual arts, to support and enhance educational concepts. Examples would be background music to enhance attention span and cognitive learning; songs and chants to teach academic concepts, for example, multiplication tables or knowledge about the world, music group activities to teach social skills, playing instruments to enhance motor skills, and musical activities such as singing and chanting or performing musical dramas to enhance communication skills.

Rehabilitative Goals Rehabilitative goals focus on remedial or compensatory therapy for physical deficits, such as the use of muscles for movement, posture, and respiration, or sensory perception in the auditory, visual, and tactile modes. Other therapeutic efforts may be directed toward disorders of speech, for example, aphasic or apraxic conditions, or problems with speech fluency or proper use of voice. The music therapist works on rehabilitative goals usually in an inpatient or outpatient hospital setting.

Developmental Goals Developmental goals focus on enhancing normal development of a child by enriching his or her life with as many normal social, emotional, and sensorimotor experiences through music as possible. The music therapist develops musical activities that utilize any existing functional ability in the child to provide rewarding recreational and leisure experiences. In other words, the music therapist uses music to enrich and *normalize* the quality of life for a disabled child as much as possible. For example, it may be possible to teach a child to play a musical instrument, using adaptive devices, or to integrate him or her into an orchestra, band, choir, or musical theater group.

Some settings for physically disabled children with expanded resources will enable music therapists to integrate educational, rehabilitative, and developmental goals in their work. An integrated approach usually has a positive motivational effect on the child because it diminishes the feeling of being a patient or of suffering from deficits that need special treatment.

MUSIC THERAPY IN THE TREATMENT OF PHYSICAL DISORDERS

As we have discussed, the goals of music therapy with physically disabled children can be divided into three major categories: educational goals, rehabilitative goals, and developmental goals. Within each of these goal areas, we can further divide music therapy interventions according to specific behaviors or skills that should be addressed in the treatment program. Six treatment areas for music therapy interventions are recommended: motor skills, communication skills, cognitive skills, social skills, emotional skills, and musical skills.

Motor Skills

Music therapy offers a wide variety of therapeutic music techniques and experiences to improve the motoric function of a physically disabled child. Common goals in this area are strengthening of muscles, increasing range of motion, exercising coordination and balance, training functional motor activities, enforcing proper muscular positioning, and mobility and gait training. Techniques can be divided into two approaches: movement to music and movement through music.

In the first approach, music is used as an accompaniment to guide and structure motor activities. Soothing music with low volume levels may be used to help muscle relaxation with conditions of muscle stiffness and spasticity. Rhythmic stimuli may be used very efficiently as pacemakers or timekeepers to structure proper timing and spatial coordination, anticipation, and rhythmicity in movement (Thaut 1985). Rhythmic musical stimuli can also influence muscle activity. Muscles can become more active and can work more efficiently when movement is synchronized with rhythm. A specific discussion of the effect of rhythmic synchronization on movement is provided in Chapter 11 (Music Therapy in Neurological Rehabilitation). Instrumental music or songs can be used to structure and pace arm and hand training, for example, during reaching and grasping exercises. Rhythmic stimuli can facilitate gait training very effectively (Thaut et al. 1998). Rhythmic intention is a technique utilizing rhythmic speech or counting to help children with cerebral palsy practice functional, goal-oriented motor tasks (Cotton 1974). Music and sound are used successfully to provide auditory feedback during movement training (Flodmark 1986; Talbot and Junkala 1981; Walmsley et al. 1981).

All music therapy techniques using movement to music can be categorized as either addressing intrinsically rhythmic movements such as gait, or as cuing broad ranges of functional movements that usually consist of single discrete motions. Rhythmic auditory stimulation (RAS) is a technique to facilitate rhythmic movement, especially gait. Patterned sensory enhancement (PSE) uses temporal, visual–spatial, and dynamic patterns in music to create structures for cuing discrete movements or longer movement sequences during functional tasks or exercises, especially during hand and arm training. Detailed discussions of RAS and PSE are provided in Chapter 11.

In the second approach, playing musical instruments provides an excellent resource for exercising muscles and improving gross and fine motor skills. This technique is called therapeutic instrumental music playing (TIMP). A detailed discussion of TIMP is given in Chapter 11. Musical instruments can be selected to meet the physical needs and abilities of physically disabled children. Playing musical instruments can help improve range of motion, strengthen muscles, increase respiratory functions, and exercise coordination of limbs and manual dexterity. Instruments can also be set up in a way to enforce proper body positioning. Musical instruments are highly motivational and efficient tools in physical rehabilitation. However, they must be selected and adapted properly to fulfill their functions.

Clark and Chadwick (1980) have written a comprehensive guide for the clinical adaptation of musical instruments for disabled populations. Elliot (1982) has provided an indepth manual in which the physical requirements (positioning, involved muscle groups, range of motion) to play musical instruments are assessed in great detail for many instruments. This guide allows the therapist to match specific instruments with specific physical abilities as well as select instruments for specific motoric goals in therapy.

Communication Skills

Music therapy techniques can serve goals in therapy for communication skills in three ways.

First, musical activities and experiences can be good motivators and facilitators to encourage children to communicate, be it verbally or nonverbally. Singing, chanting, the combination of music and plays, or just being involved in a rewarding musical activity with others, can encourage or motivate the child to engage in communication.

Second, music can serve as an efficient reward to encourage and reinforce communication behavior. The child can be rewarded for asking an appropriate question by being given the opportunity to play a musical instrument or listen to a favorite song.

Third, there are several speech therapy techniques that use musical materials to remediate speech deficiencies. Techniques based on melodic intonation therapy and the stimulation approach (see Chapter 11 for details) are used to work with aphasic or dyspraxic children.

Rhythmic techniques have also shown success in the treatment of some individuals affected by the fluency disorders of stuttering and cluttering. Stutterers may increase their fluency by speaking rhythmically or by using strong melodic inflections. Some clutterers may be able to slow down their rapid and unintelligible utterances by using similar techniques. In cases of voice disorders, vocal exercises may help to remediate abnormal pitch, loudness, timbre, breathing, and prosody of speech.

Cognitive Skills

Musical materials may enhance cognitive learning processes in the physically disabled child. Music can be used very efficiently as motivating stimulus, reinforcement, and reward for learning efforts. Educational/instructional songs, chants, or activities that combine speech, movement, and music can facilitate, clarify, and illustrate the acquisition of academic information. The melodic and rhythmic structure of songs can also serve well as a memory aid for song contents that emphasize academic concepts. Just think of songs about the alphabet or body parts, rhymes and chants that recite historical dates, computational tables, and so on. Music as background stimulus for the learning environment can promote heightened attention and reduce anxiety. Some theories suggest that information learned in a particular mood or associated with an emotional stimulus will be recalled more easily when the previous mood or stimulus is present in the recall situation (Bower 1981). Thus, music as mood stimulus, provided in the learning environment, may be used to facilitate efficient memory recall.

Social Skills

The physically disabled child is often severely restricted in his or her participation in social activities that require physical mobility. Social activities of children, however, are very commonly built around movement activities. Being left out of these activities will keep the child away from significant experiences of social learning that are fundamental for a healthy personality development. Health professionals, teachers, and parents, therefore, are faced with the challenge of finding activities that integrate the physically disabled child into social experiences.

Meaningful and enjoyable participation in musical group activities can take place on various levels of physical or intellectual abilities. Group singing or instrumental ensembles can be arranged to bring together ambulatory and wheelchair-bound children, children with skilled or impaired usage of hands and fingers, with or without sensory impairments, and engage them in social interaction through music.

Excellent resources for adaptive devices and proper selection of musical instruments according to physical ability are the books by Elliot (1982), Clark and Chadwick (1980), and the monograph series on music therapy for disabled children by the National Association for Music Therapy (Lathom and Eagle 1982).

Emotional Skills

Physically disabled children have the same need for healthy emotional development and opportunities to express their feelings as do normal children. Because of the experiences of their disabilities, these children may actually have an increased need to cope with feelings, such as grief, depression, or loneliness. Compounding their emotional needs, their physical limitations may prevent them from using some of the more common channels to express feelings.

Music therapy can play an eminent role in satisfying emotional needs. Music is a strong and rewarding affective medium. Access to musical experiences can be provided on many different levels of sensory, physical, and intellectual ability. Thus, the music therapist is well equipped to work for the child's emotional development and also to offer help in coping with emotional problems associated with the child's disability.

Musical Skills

As part of an overall strategy to normalize a physically disabled child's life, the development of special talents and recreational and leisure skills is very essential. By using proper resources for the selection of instruments and adaptive devices as referenced in the section on social skills, therapists can help these children achieve musically. Musical skill development will normalize the child's life by facilitating performance-oriented success experiences and providing the emotional, cognitive, social, and physical rewards of aesthetic musical training.

SUMMARY

In this chapter we have presented an overview of physically disabling conditions in children. We have also introduced you to treatment areas, goals, and clinical methods the music therapist uses when working with these children.

Physically disabling conditions can be categorized as ambulatory or nonambulatory. Furthermore, they can be distinguished as congenital and/or chronic or acquired and/or acute. The congenital and/or chronic conditions discussed in this chapter are cerebral palsy, muscular dystrophies, spina bifida, clubfoot, congenital dislocation of the hip, arthrogryposis, juvenile rheumatoid arthritis, dwarfism, and osteogenesis imperfecta. The acquired and/or acute conditions discussed are thermal injuries, spinal cord injuries, acquired amputations, and poliomyelitis.

Many physically disabled children suffer from multiple disabilities, affecting also intellectual and sensory functions. Music therapists encounter these children in special education settings, hospital programs, developmental centers, group homes, and preschool programs.

Music therapists pursue three different types of treatment goals with physically disabled children: educational goals, rehabilitative goals, and developmental goals. Within each of these large goal areas, music therapists use music-based methods to work on motor skills, communication skills, cognitive skills, social skills, emotional skills, and musical skills.

STUDY QUESTIONS

1. What are the different ways you can describe and categorize physically disabling conditions in children?
2. What different types of goals can the music therapist set with physically disabled children?
3. Describe the main features of physically disabling conditions according to the categories you answered under study question 1.
4. What are the six skill areas music therapists focus on developing with physically disabled children?
5. List three methods a music therapist uses to work on motor rehabilitation and motor skill development with musical stimuli.
6. List three methods the music therapist uses to work on communication skills with musical stimuli.
7. Why is music a particularly efficient medium to provide rewarding social and emotional experiences for physically disabled children?

REFERENCES

Bleck, E., and D. Nagel, eds. 1982. *Physically handicapped children: A medical atlas for teachers.* New York: Grune and Stratton.

Bower, G. H. 1981. Mood and memory. *American Psychologist* 36:129–148.

Clark, C., and D. Chadwick. 1980. *Clinically adapted instruments for the multiply handicapped.* St. Louis, MO: Magnamusic-Baton.

Cotton, E. 1974. Improvement in motor function with the use of conductive education. *Developmental Medicine and Child Neurology* 16:637–643.

Cratty, B. 1975. *Remedial motor activity for children.* Philadelphia: Lea and Febiger.

Elliot, B. 1982. *Guide to the selection of musical instruments with respect to physical ability and disability.* St. Louis, MO: Magnamusic-Baton.

Flodmark, A. 1986. Augmented auditory feedback as an aid in gait training of the cerebral-palsied child. *Developmental Medicine and Child Neurology* 28:147–155.

Gage, J. R. 1989. An overview of normal and cerebral palsy gait. *Neurosurgery: State of the Art Reviews* 4:379–401.

Jellison, J. 1988. A content analysis of music research with handicapped children (1975–1986): Applications in special education. In *Effectiveness of music therapy procedures: Documentation of research and clinical practice,* edited by C. E. Furman, 223–284. Washington DC: National Association for Music Therapy.

Lathom, W., and C. Eagle. 1982. *Music therapy for handicapped children,* Project Music Monograph Series. Washington DC: National Association for Music Therapy.

Sherrill, C. 1981. *Adapted physical education and recreation: A multidisciplinary approach.* Dubuque, IA: William C. Brown.

Sutherland, D. H., and J. R. Davids. 1993. Common gait abnormalities of the knee in cerebral palsy. *Clinical Orthopaedics and Related Research* 288:139–147.

Talbot, M. L., and J. Junkala. 1981. The effects of auditorally augmented feedback on the eye-hand coordination of students with cerebral palsy. *American Journal of Occupational Therapy* 35:525–528.

Thaut, M. H. 1985. The use of auditory rhythm and rhythmic speech to aid temporal muscular control in children with gross motor dysfunction. *Journal of Music Therapy* 22:108–128.

Thaut, M. L., C. P. Hurt, D. Dragon, and G. C. McIntosh. 1998. Rhythmic entrainment of gait patterns in children with cerebral palsy. *Developmental Medicine and Child Neurology,* in press.

Toombs-Rudenberg, M. 1982. Music therapy for handicapped children: Orthopedically handicapped. In *Music therapy for handicapped children,* edited by W. Lathom and C. Eagle, Project Music Monograph Series. Washington DC: National Association for Music Therapy.

8

MUSIC THERAPY WITH AUTISTIC CHILDREN

Michael H. Thaut

CHAPTER OUTLINE

Autism is a severe and incapacitating developmental disorder afflicting about 4 in every 10,000 children. Three to four times more common in boys than girls, the lifelong chronic disorder becomes apparent within the first 30 months of life. Two-thirds of all autistic children remain severely disabled and require custodial care throughout their lives (*DSM IV* 1994). In this chapter, we will define autism, learn about the conditions that cause this disability, and discover how music therapy can be included in the treatment of autistic individuals.

DEFINITION AND DIAGNOSIS

Autism as a distinct developmental disorder was first identified by Kanner (1943), a psychiatrist at Johns Hopkins University. He described a group of children who were relatively normal in physical appearance but who exhibited severely disturbed behavior patterns that included extreme social aloofness or aloneness, lack of emotional responsiveness, avoidance of eye contact, failure to respond to auditory or visual stimulation, lack of language development or failure to use language adequately for communication, excessive attachment to objects, and preoccupation with ritualistic, repetitive, and obsessive behaviors. Because the symptoms were present in early infancy, Kanner coined the term *infantile autism* to describe the condition.

Since that time, the definition and diagnostic criteria of autism have been interpreted and elaborated upon by many researchers (Donnellan 1985). Recognizing the need for standardized and generally agreed upon diagnostic criteria, the National Society for Autistic Children has suggested a behavioral definition of autism (1978). According to this definition, the disorder is manifested through severe disturbances in four areas: (1) developmental rates and/or sequences; (2) responses to sensory stimuli; (3) speech, language, and cognitive capacities; and (4) capacities to relate to people, events, and objects. These features must be apparent before 30 months of age in order to make a diagnosis of autism. The latest diagnostic criteria are included in the *DSM IV* (1994) which introduces the term *autistic disorder.* According to the *DSM IV,* delayed or abnormal functions in at least one of the following three areas have to be present before the age of three: social interaction, language for social communication, and symbolic or imaginative play.

Developmental Rates

Disturbances in the rate or the sequence of physical, cognitive, or socioemotional development may occur in specific areas, whereas other skills may appear normal for the child's age. For example, although his or her interactional skills may be extremely disturbed, the autistic child may show isolated areas of ability, such as in rote memory, fine motor skills, spatial perception, or musical skills.

Response to Sensory Stimuli

Disturbance in responses to sensory stimuli is usually exhibited through two symptoms: (1) faulty sensory modulation and (2) stereotyped, repetitive self-stimulation behaviors. Faulty sensory modulation is characterized by under- or overresponsiveness to sensory input, such as touch, light, sound, or pain. For example, the child may overreact with a startle reflex or tantrum to the sound of a dropped pencil but may be oblivious to a loud siren. Self-stimulatory behaviors typically include suspending or spinning objects before the eyes, vocalizing vowels in a repetitive and meaningless manner, flapping the hands, rocking, mouthing objects, or manipulating the fingers in front of the eyes. These behaviors seem to serve no apparent purpose other than to create sensory input. Disturbed responses to sensory stimuli are most pronounced in young autistic children, especially between two and four years of age, when these behaviors are observed with at least the same frequency as disturbances in relating to people, events, and objects.

Communication Disorders

Autistic children have severe disturbances in their communication skills. They often display complete absence of the ability or willingness to communicate either verbally or nonverbally. Some children may be mute or may occasionally babble. If they use spoken language, it may lack meaning. For example, they may have echolalic speech, in which previously heard words or phrases are repeated without any intent to convey meaning. Research shows that about half of all autistic children never gain useful language abilities (Rutter 1979). If language skills are developed, there are marked differences between autistic speech and normal speech. Autistic speech is characterized by (1) lack of social imitation (e.g., waving and saying "bye-bye"), (2) failure to use verbs in sentences, and/or (3) pronoun reversal (e.g., saying "you" instead of "I"). Even in higher-functioning children, language development rarely progresses beyond the stage of labeling or requesting items and will nearly always be characterized by syntactic problems, limited vocabulary and semantic concepts, and poor intonation patterns (Wing 1976).

Rutter (1979) stressed that the autistic child's ability to understand spoken language is always impaired. He or she may be able to follow simple one-step directions in a familiar social context when aided by physical cuing, but will fail to carry out instructions that, for example, include several ideas or steps or lack an assisting gesture.

Typically, autistic children also lack gesture or mime when trying to make their needs known. They seldom point to desired objects and will instead lead the caregiver by the wrist or forearm to the desired item or place. Acquisition of functional language by the age of five years is considered a crucial positive predictor of further social and intellectual development.

Cognitive Deficits

The nature and boundaries of cognitive deficits in autistic children have not yet been fully learned. In early clinical observations, autistic children were often suspected to have high intelligence that was masked by their symptoms (Kanner 1943). Now investigators generally agree that approximately 70 percent of autistic individuals are mentally retarded (IQ less than 70) and 40 percent have IQs less than 50 (Piven and Folstein 1994). Rutter (1979) points out that a child may be both autistic and developmentally disabled, just as he or she may be both autistic and highly intelligent. In general, cognitive deficits due to autism include limited ability to use abstract thinking, difficulties making sense of auditory or visual information, and problems sequencing events and organizing information in a useful or meaningful fashion (Rutter 1988; Hermelin and O'Conner 1970; Wing 1979).

Socioemotional Skills

Severe disturbance in the ability to relate to other people has been viewed as the primary feature of autism for many years. Most early theories of causes and methods of treatment for autism centered around this social aloofness, withdrawal, and emotional unresponsiveness. Although impaired social and emotional development remains a strong diagnostic criterion for autism, it is no longer viewed as the cause.

Four main symptoms characterize the autistic child's disturbed behavior in relating to people, objects, and events (Trevarthen et al. 1998). First, the child shows a profound failure to relate to other people, which is often apparent at birth. For example, the child may fail to smile during social greetings, or may even reject parental affection and nurturing. The autistic child may seem oblivious and be unresponsive to people in the environment, showing, for example, no distress when the mother leaves the room. The child may ignore the attempts of others to interact, such as another child offering toys. One of the most striking features of an autistic child's behavior is the lack of eye contact with people.

Second, autistic children often show disturbed emotional behaviors, characterized as either inappropriate or having no effect. They may exhibit prolonged temper tantrums without apparent cause, or they may laugh or giggle for no apparent reason. Facial and postural expressions likely will not show appropriate emotional responsiveness to environmental stimuli. For example, neither fear when crossing a busy street nor happiness when being hugged or praised will be displayed.

Third, autistic children nearly always fail to develop age-appropriate play behavior. They may ignore toys in favor of manipulating other objects (e.g., spinning a lamp shade or flicking a light switch on and off repeatedly), or toys may be used in an abnormal manner. An autistic child may chew on an object, use it to hit himself or herself, or flap it in front of his or her eyes. He or she may stack or sort objects in a repetitive pattern. Social play patterns with peers rarely develop in the autistic child.

Fourth, autistic children show an obsessive preoccupation with maintaining ritualistic behaviors in their daily routines and sameness in the physical environment. Small changes, like moving the dining room table to a different corner or changing the bedtime routine, may result in a tantrum. Many severe disruptions in the ability to relate to people, objects, and events change in intensity over time. Some extreme behaviors may lessen or subside. Social aloofness, however, usually conspicuously remains (Wing 1979).

ETIOLOGY

When autism was first recognized as a distinct disorder, psychiatrists attributed it to an early emotional trauma or to faulty parenting. The unusual array of symptoms (i.e., the relatively normal physical appearance and the presence of some highly developed isolated skills coupled with the extreme emotional unresponsiveness, social aloofness, and inability to use language) led many researchers to explain autism as the result of an emotional trauma in very early childhood. However, because no consistent patterns of social or emotional history emerged in these children, the explanation gave way to other etiological considerations.

Since the 1960s, accumulated research evidence strongly suggests that autism is a developmental disorder of brain function that is manifested in a variety of perceptual, cognitive, and motor disturbances (Baumann and Kemper 1994). According to Ornitz (1974), perceptual and motor disturbances are fundamental to the etiology of autism; all other abnormal behaviors can be explained as consequences of distorted sensory input. His theory states that faulty sensory modulation leads to perceptual inconstancy, that is, alternating hypo- and hypersensitivity to sensory stimuli, which prevents the autistic child from developing a stable representation of his or her environment. For example, a distorted perception of the environment might cause an autistic child's inattention to relevant social and emotional stimuli, which may account for lack of eye contact and failure to understand cognitive concepts and the meaning of daily events.

Several other pathological factors in autistic children have been identified, but the results of research studies are conflicting and hold true only for some groups of autistic children. Structural abnormalities in brain hemispheric functions have been found in about one-fourth of autistic individuals (Ornitz 1987). However, more recently, results from brain imaging studies using advanced imaging technology strongly suggest that the only consistent abnormalities in the brains of autistic individuals are confined to the limbic system and cerebellar circuits (Baumann and Kemper 1994). Researchers investigating deviances in language, memory, and general sensory and cognitive information processing are especially interested in these findings, because of the important involvement of limbic and cerebellar structures and circuits in these functions (Baumann and Kemper 1994).

Despite the current view that autism is caused by pathoneurophysiological brain dysfunction, postmortem examinations of autistic individuals' brains have not revealed any consistent neuropathology, and biochemical investigations have failed to show consistent neurotransmitter abnormalities. Additionally, diseases such as congenital rubella, toxemia, neonatal anoxia, and infantile spasms may be implicated as the cause in some autistic conditions (Ornitz 1987). In spite of a greatly increased amount of information about the neurobiology of autism, no comprehensive theory exists as of yet to explain the various findings within one causal model. At this time, no single cause can account for the etiology of autistic disorder, although there is mounting evidence for autism as a developmental brain disorder of prenatal origin.

DIFFERENTIAL DIAGNOSIS

The inability to find one cause of autism has contributed to the difficulty in diagnosing this condition. Furthermore, some of the behaviors found in autistic children are similar to those of other childhood disorders, so correct diagnosis can be a challenge. However, the ability to identify an autistic child is necessary for setting up specific and beneficial treatment and educational interventions.

Autism can be differentiated from mental retardation by the unevenness of developmental delays. Whereas mentally retarded individuals will have fairly uniform developmental deficits across all areas of behavior, autistic children will often exhibit isolated areas of "splinter skills" (e.g., rote memory, attraction to music, or mechanical skills).

Autism is commonly distinguished from childhood schizophrenia in two ways: (1) symptoms of autism must be observable by 30 months of age, whereas the onset of childhood schizophrenia is considerably later (5 to 12 years of age); and (2) schizophrenic children show a higher level of language skills than autistic children, whose communication abilities are severely impaired.

Because irregular responses to sensory stimuli are at the core of an autistic child's disturbances, he or she may initially be labeled as deaf, mute, or blind. However, the sensory pathways and sensory processing centers in the brain show normal functioning in autism, and sensory and primary language disorders do not manifest the high response variability (over- and underresponsiveness) to sensory stimuli that autism does. One of the new diagnostic criteria included in the *DSM IV* for the first time separates autistic disorder from Rett's syndrome, a childhood disintegrative disorder, and Asperger's syndrome as different diagnostic diseases.

TREATMENT

Treatment for autism has historically reflected the diagnostic and etiological theories prevalent at the time. Infantile autism, initially thought to be a psychiatric disorder, was at first treated exclusively with psychiatric interventions. Poor parenting, especially the lack of bonding between mother and child because of emotional rejection and other psychological trauma, was the focus of treatment. By 1956, however, Kanner and Eisenberg recognized that psychotherapy yielded only small positive results on the course of the disorder. Many different treatment concepts and models have since been developed and tried.

Because research in the last 25 years has focused on autism as a developmental disorder based on brain dysfunction, treatment has shifted toward programs that provide educational, linguistic, cognitive, and behavioral training. Studies in England (Bartak and Rutter 1973; Rutter and Bartak 1973) showed that over a three- and one-half-year time period, autistic children made more gains in educational, linguistic, cognitive, and behavioral skills from a highly structured, didactic, educational approach than from psychiatric treatment.

The shift away from treating autistic children within the psychiatric medical model to educating them in an educational or developmental environment received strong support in the United States in 1974 through the passage of Public Law 94-142. This law prescribes that all disabled children be educated in the least restrictive environment. Today, autistic children are found in both special and regular classrooms of the public school system as well as in developmental centers for special populations, which incorporate a broad range of medical and psychological services in addition to educational disciplines. Trevarthen and colleagues (1998) advocate an educational approach that provides a well-directed structure for learning, yet takes into account the individual needs of each child. This approach is supported by many recent research findings showing that autistic children, in spite of their considerable difficulties, have the basic capacity for differentiated attending, perceiving, and communicating behavior as well as for the development of affective behavior and attachment to other people. The educational/developmental approach has also changed the parents' role in the treatment process. In earlier times, parental involvement was often viewed as a potentially disturbing factor, but now, professionals seek to establish a working partnership with parents as standard practice. Parents are often trained in educational and behavioral management techniques.

Educational Curricula

Many different educational programs have been developed for autistic children in the last 20 years. A survey of the curricula reveals five primary areas of emphasis (Thaut 1980):

Social–Behavioral Skills These skills (1) decrease attention-interrupting behaviors, such as motility disturbances, self-stimulation, and temper tantrums; and (2) foster cooperative play, social interaction, control over own behavior, and peer relationships.

Independent Living and Self-Help Skills The child learns toileting, eating, dressing, hygiene, and safety skills.

Sensorimotor Development Sensorimotor development promotes the development of fine and gross motor skills, sensory integration and sensory perception in different modalities, body image, imitation skills, and tolerance of physical contact.

Cognitive Development Cognitive development increases skills in reading, spelling, basic math concepts, matching, memory, and de- and encoding basic symbols.

Language Development Usually the main focus of educational efforts. Develop receptive (understanding speech of others) and expressive (ability to express verbally one's own ideas) language skills, imitate speech sequences, and learn alternative forms of communication (i.e., sign language or picture systems) if necessary.

In addition, most educational/developmental programs for autistic children incorporate some form of cognitive and/or behavioral approach to therapy and learning. Currently, such approaches seem to offer the most broadly accepted, well-developed, and effective interventions for autism. Cognitive approaches emphasize the acquisition of skills of daily living and cognitive competence, mostly in the areas of behavioral independence, language, and communication. Currently, one of the most widely used, best-researched, and validated systems in this area is the TEACCH program developed at the University of North Carolina, Chapel Hill (Schopler and Mesibov 1984). Behavioral methods include basic positive and negative reinforcement procedures as well as more complex methods, such as relaxation and covert conditioning procedures that focus on behavioral self-control (Groden and Baron 1988). Lansing and Schopler (1978) summarized behavioral treatment of autistic children as a sequence of five steps: (1) decide on a relevant task, (2) analyze the child's functional behavior, (3) break the task down into a logical sequence or learning steps with gradually increasing complexity, (4) structure the child's responses and environmental stimuli, and (5) monitor progress and alter the training approach if necessary.

The learning process in an autistic child is consistently hampered by perceptual problems, such as lack of concentration, fluctuating attention, fading eye contact, and preoccupation with ritualistic behaviors. Therefore, it is suggested that a professional working with these children emphasize (1) insistence on eye contact, (2) frequent recall of attention, (3) repetition of instructions in consistent wording until an appropriate effort to respond has been made, and (4) encouragement of perseverance during performance (Thaut 1983). There is general agreement that interventions should start as early as possible.

MUSICAL RESPONSES OF AUTISTIC CHILDREN

Unusual sensitivity and attention to music is frequently mentioned in the literature on autistic children. The distinguished researcher Bernard Rimland even listed unusual musical capabilities as a diagnostic criterion for autism (1964). A brief review of some of the reports about the musical behavior of autistic children will illustrate this point.

In 1953, Sherwin noted pronounced reactions to music in a case study with autistic boys. All demonstrated strong melodic memory, recognition of classical music selections, and strong interest in playing the piano, singing, and listening to music.

In observing 12 autistic children over two years, Pronovost (1961) found heightened response and interest in musical sounds as compared with other environmental stimuli. Frith (1972) analyzed and compared spontaneously produced tone (using a xylophone) and color sequences (using flash cards) of autistic children and found that those using a musical modality were more complex and varied.

O'Connell (1974) reported exceptional ability in piano performance in an otherwise very low-functioning autistic boy. Blackstock (1978) carried out a study in which autistic and normal children were given a listening choice between verbal and musical selections. He found that normal children showed no preference, whereas the autistic children preferred music.

In an experiment by Applebaum and associates (1979), autistic children performed as well as or better than age-matched normal children on imitation of individual or a series of tones delivered by voice, piano, and synthesizer. Koegel and colleagues (1982) mentioned music as an efficient motivator and modality for enabling autistic children to learn nonmusical material and emphasized its use as positive sensory reinforcement in decreasing self-stimulation behaviors.

Thaut (1987) showed a significant preference in autistic boys for auditory–musical stimuli (listening to childrens' songs) over visual stimuli (watching slides of zoo animals), in contrast with normal children, who preferred watching the slides. In a related study, a group of autistic boys, age-matched normal boys, and developmentally disabled individuals were asked to improvise melodies on a xylophone (Thaut 1988). Through musical analysis, the melodies of the autistic boys were shown to be very similar to those of normal boys but distinctly different in many categories from the improvisations of the developmentally disabled persons. Differences in musical responses between developmentally disabled children with and without a concurrent diagnosis of autism were also investigated by Hairston (1990).

Three conclusions may be drawn regarding the musical responses of autistic persons:

1 Many autistic children perform unusually well in musical areas in comparison with most other areas of their behavior, as well as in comparison with many normal children.

2 Many autistic children respond more frequently and appropriately to music than to other auditory stimuli.

3 Little is known about the reasons for the musical responsiveness of autistic children. However, the most promising explanation may lie in the knowledge of brain dysfunction and perceptual processes of autistic children.

MUSIC THERAPY WITH AUTISTIC CHILDREN

The fact that music is an engaging stimulus for autistic children, and that many can participate successfully in music activities, contributes to music therapy's value in the treatment of autism. A number of studies have substantiated the benefits of musical stimuli or music therapy methods with autistic children.

Studies by Goldstein (1964), Stevens and Clark (1969), Mahlberg (1973), Hollander and Juhrs (1974), Saperston (1973), Schmidt and Edwards (1976), and Warwick (1995) have shown improved social behavior and interpersonal relationships as a result of music therapy treatment. Enhanced motor coordination or body image has also been reported (Goldstein 1964; Mahlberg 1973; Saperston 1973). In addition, several therapists have reported improved communication behavior (Edgerton 1994) and language skills as a result of music therapy interventions (Litchman 1976; Mahlberg 1973; Saperston 1973).

These and other studies reveal that music therapy for autistic children commonly focuses on the following areas:

1 Improve fine and gross motor coordination.
2 Increase attention span.
3 Develop body awareness.
4 Develop concept of self.
5 Develop social skills.
6 Develop verbal and nonverbal communication.
7 Facilitate learning of basic academic and preacademic concepts.
8 Interrupt and alter ritualistic, repetitive behavior patterns.
9 Reduce anxiety, temper tantrums, and hyperactivity.
10 Train sensory perception and sensorimotor integration (auditory, visual, tactile, kinesthetic).

The following techniques have been used to accomplish these goals:

1 Vocalization exercises (singing single or combinations of vowels, consonants, with proper inflection and breath support)

2 Singing and chanting, often accompanied by body percussion

3 Movement, including dance, creative movement, rhythmic exercises, and imitation techniques

4 Musical games

5 Instrument performance, using imitation or improvisation techniques in both groups and one-to-one settings

6 Music listening

The discussion that follows illustrates the steps of a music therapy process with an autistic child in four different treatment areas: (1) language development, (2) social and emotional development, (3) cognitive (preacademic) concept development, and (4) sensorimotor development.

Language Development

Establishment of Communicative Intent On this level, the therapist should facilitate and support the desire or necessity for the child to communicate. Techniques may include offering musical interaction (e.g., question and answer or imitative) on the drum or metallophone, accompanying the child's movements or habitual sounds (crying, laughing) on the piano, or singing an action song to the child and cuing the proper physical responses.

Action–Song Interaction Once the child understands communicative intentions and responses, chants or songs that integrate rhythm, body percussion, and vocalization can be introduced. The lyrics to these songs should include instructions or directions for active physical and vocal responses from the child.

Oral Motor Exercises Playing wind instruments and performing oral motor–imitation exercises of the articulators help strengthen awareness and functional use of the lips, tongue, jaws, and teeth.

Gross Motor Imitation—Oral Motor Imitation—Oral Vocal Motor Imitation This is a particularly efficient sequence of techniques to use once the autistic child has developed perceptual and imitative skills. First, the name of a body part (arm) may be introduced while moving that part. Next, the child works on oral motor positions of the articulators for that word ("a" and "m"). Finally, the child is asked to move the body part in an imitation exercise and simultaneously sound out as many letters of the word as possible. Some children may be able to say "arm" while moving, whereas others may say only "a" or "m."

Intonation Shaping If some speech has been acquired by the autistic child, various activities may be implemented to remediate intonation problems or facilitate fluency. Vocal improvisation on vowel and consonant combinations as well as improvisation on organum chord progressions to stimulate or shape vocal expressions may assist in improving the prosodic features of speech. Sustaining sounds on wind instruments may also help to stabilize and encourage vocal production, and intoning combined with graphic notations may assist in refining speech inflection. Breathing exercises can improve vocal strength, exercise laryngeal function, and refine oral motor function.

Social and Emotional Development

Music as Mediating Object Because autistic children often reject or ignore others' attempts at social interaction, an attractive object relation (e.g., a musical instrument) may provide a point of mutual contact between therapist and child. Although freedom of exploration should be encouraged, the perceptual problems of autistic children necessitate the therapist's careful selection and structured use of the instrument to minimize sensory overload, motility rituals, and potentially destructive behavior.

Building Relationships through Musical Interactions Piano accompaniment can be added to the previous technique to heighten the child's awareness of the therapist's presence. Gradually, the therapist can encourage physical contact, for example, holding the child's hand and moving to music or leading him or her to a particular instrument. Eventually, the therapist should assume more leadership in each activity, such as leading the child's hands in a keyboard activity or body percussion exercise.

Social Learning through Musical Interactions At this level, the emphasis is on music therapy experiences that place specific demands on the child's social responses within musical interaction activities. Musical exercises are structured so that the child learns particular responses within a social context, for example, musical interactions that feature changing dynamics, different tempos, rests, movement, and question-and-answer or imitative forms. Percussion and keyboard instruments are effective in these activities.

Emotional Learning through Music Expressive musical exercises are helpful in eliciting and shaping affective responses in the autistic child, who may learn to express emotions by associating different types of music with different feeling states. This learning process may be facilitated by activities that use body language, verbal labeling of mood states, or matching music to visual depictions of emotion.

Learning to Be a Group Member through Music Musical activities easily lend themselves to group formation and interaction goals. Through group singing, movement and dance, and instrument playing, autistic children can learn to tolerate the presence of and physical contact with others, distinguish between self and others, and practice social behaviors. Holding hands when moving together, facing each other in a circle, playing instruments together, and listening to each other are all major accomplishments in the social and emotional growth of autistic children.

Cognitive (Preacademic) Concept Development

Music as a Carrier of Nonmusical Information Songs and chants are useful in teaching skills and concepts to autistic children in an educational or developmental setting. For example, spatial concepts, math and language concepts, body image, world facts, and self-help skills can all be integrated into the lyrics of songs. Because many autistic children are attracted to music, a musical setting may motivate, facilitate attention and perception, and enhance memorization of the information.

Music in the Learning Environment Educational studies (Hollander and Juhrs 1974; Litchman 1976) have shown that alternating music listening with periods of instructional learning can reduce aggressive behaviors and preoccupation with ritualistic, self-stimulation behaviors as well as strengthen attention span and on-task behavior in autistic children.

Music as a Reinforcement of Learning Musical activities, both listening and playing, have been shown to be efficient reinforcers for the learning of nonmusical information by autistic children.

Musical Activities for Specific Learning Concepts

Labeling Concepts Follow single- or multistep directions; identify musical objects by (1) pointing, (2) playing, (3) recognizing different sounds, (4) recognizing different shapes, and (5) recognizing different instruments by name.

Number Concepts Respond correctly to quantitative prompts, for example, "How many?" or "Give me one, two . . ."; add and subtract numbers by building scales with tone bars, and so forth.

Color Concepts Identify colors by using different-colored instruments, color-coded tone bars, or colored graphic notations of the music.

Matching Concepts Match colors, shapes, or names of musical instruments with word cards, picture cards, hand signs, or verbal responses.

Form Perception Order and complete tone scales on bars, bells, and so on, of different sizes; build geometric shapes with drums or chime bars.

Decoding/Encoding Symbols Interpret graphic notations of music that incorporate colors and geometric shapes.

Auditory Memory Imitate single tones and progress to longer sequences; identify the sound of a hidden musical instrument or locate its source.

Auditory–Motor Memory Learn chants with various body percussion accompaniments; recall the chant from movement cues and vice versa.

Sensorimotor Development

Sensory Integration The autistic child learns to relate and integrate auditory, visual, and tactile stimuli through manual exploration of musical instruments. The appropriate use of hands and fingers may also be introduced at this level.

Sensory Reinforcement to Decrease Self-Stimulation Behavior The autistic child's preoccupation with self-stimulation behaviors is frequently of major concern to the therapist or educator. Many researchers believe it is perpetuated by the sensory feedback received while self-stimulating. Studies have shown that the introduction of a rewarding and pleasant substitute such as music may cause a reduction in meaningless and repetitive self-stimulating behaviors (Koegel et al. 1982). However, when considering the use of music as a substitute stimulus, the reactivity of each child must be considered. If he or she is hyporeactive (underaroused), extra sensory input may be quite helpful. However, if the child is paradoxically hyporeactive (withdrawing because of previous overarousal), sensory input of less intensity is needed. Conversely, the sensory input needs must be similarly assessed for hyperreactive and paradoxical hyperreactivity states (Nelson et al. 1984).

Sensorimotor Integration Physical contact with the therapist should begin at the earliest possible level to prepare the child for specific developmental movement activities. Incorporate exercises to improve body resistance, such as positioning the child on the floor and exerting gentle and rhythmic pressure on the arms, hands, or feet. Movement to music facilitates the integration and coordination of movement to auditory cues. For example, the child may learn to move when the music plays and to stop moving when the music stops. The therapist can guide movements by matching them with a musical accompaniment, for example, trills for turns, melodic runs for running, melodic leaps for hopping, or expanding chord textures for spreading arms and legs.

Imitation Exercises Imitation exercises to music can work to refine body and movement awareness through (1) stretching; (2) extending limbs; (3) stepping backward, forward, and laterally; (4) moving arms up, down, and uni-, bi-, ipsi-, and cross-laterally; and (5) crossing the body midline. These activities can be expanded to include visuomotor exercises with musical instruments. For example, various arrangements of tone bars may be used in different sequencing tasks.

Sensorimotor Coordination On this level, the autistic child should practice more complex patterns of motor activity primarily through the playing of percussion instruments. These exercises can be easily integrated into a musical context wherein the child performs with others and thus learns to integrate motor skills with sensory input that is meaningful and purposeful. For example, the child can learn to differentiate tempos, loudness levels, rhythm patterns, melodies, and accompaniments and adjust his or her motor skills accordingly. In addition, musical (especially rhythmic) accompaniments efficiently assist in the development of motor skills, such as running, hopping, skipping, and galloping. Musical–rhythmic movement games are particularly useful at this level.

SUMMARY

This chapter has presented an overview of autistic disorder as a childhood disorder as well as of music therapy as a treatment modality for autistic children.

Autism is a severely incapacitating lifelong developmental disorder that has to be present before the age of three years in order to be diagnosed as autism (*DSM IV* 1994). One behavioral definition describes autistic disturbances in four areas: (1) developmental rates; (2) responses to sensory stimuli; (3) speech, language, and cognitive capacities; and (4) ability to relate to people, objects, and events.

Autism is considered a developmental disorder based on some form of brain dysfunction. Although several research findings and associated theories have been brought forward in regard to neurophysiological disturbances or neuroanatomical abnormalities, no conclusive single cause for autism has been identified.

The most commonly accepted treatment approach for autistic children is the educational/developmental approach. Most programs for autistic children incorporate some form of behavioral therapy in their treatment interventions.

Research has shown over many decades that music can be a perceptually engaging and attractive stimulus for autistic children. Several studies have documented music therapy as a successful treatment modality, using this perceptual advantage to engage the child in social, emotional, cognitive, and sensorimotor learning activities. The final section of this chapter gave a detailed account of important treatment areas and associated methods in music therapy for autistic children.

STUDY QUESTIONS

1. Two major diagnostic disturbances in an autistic child's behavior include __________ and __________.
2. Theories on the causes of autism have changed over the past 30 years. What is the current view on the nature and etiology of autism?
3. What is the most accepted treatment approach to helping autistic children?
4. What are some of the major research findings on the musical behaviors of autistic children?
5. What are some of the treatment goals and respective clinical methods in music therapy for autism?
6. Why is music a beneficial stimulus to engage the autistic child in social and emotional interaction?
7. List treatment sequences and appropriate methods in music therapy for each of the four treatment areas detailed in the final section of this chapter.

REFERENCES

Applebaum, E., A. Egel, R. Koegel, and B. Imhoff. 1979. Measuring musical abilities of autistic children. *Journal of Autism and Developmental Disorders* 9:279–285.

Bartak, L., and M. Rutter. 1973. Special education treatment of autistic children: A comparative study. I. Design of study and characteristics of units. *Journal of Child Psychology and Psychiatry* 14:161–179.

Baumann M. L., and T. L. Kemper. 1994. Neuroanatomic observations of the brain in autism. In *The neurobiology of autism,* edited by M. L. Bauman and T. L. Kemper, 119–145. Baltimore: Johns Hopkins University Press.

Blackstock, E. G. 1978. Cerebral asymmetry and the development of early infantile autism. *Journal of Autism and Childhood Schizophrenia* 8:339–353.

Diagnostic and Statistical Manual of Mental Disorders IV (DSM IV). 1994. Washington, DC: American Psychiatric Association.

Donnellan, A., ed. 1985. *Classic readings in autism.* New York: Teachers College Press, Columbia University.

Edgerton, C. 1994. The effect of improvisational music therapy on the communication behaviors of autistic children. *Journal of Music Therapy* 31:31–62.

Frith, U. 1972. Cognitive mechanisms in autism: Experiments with color and tone sequence production. *Journal of Autism and Childhood Schizophrenia* 2:160–173.

Goldstein, C. 1964. Music and creative arts therapy for an autistic child. *Journal of Music Therapy* 1:135–138.

Groden, G., and M. G. Baron, eds. 1988. *Autism: Strategies for change.* New York: Gardner Press.

Hairston, M. J. 1990. Analyses of responses of mentally retarded autistic children and mentally retarded nonautistic children to art therapy and music therapy. *Journal of Music Therapy* 27:137–150.

Hermelin, B., and N. O'Connor. 1970. *Psychological experiments with autistic children.* Oxford: Pergamon Press.

Hollander, F. M., and P. D. Juhrs. 1974. Orff-Schulwerk, an effective treatment tool with autistic children. *Journal of Music Therapy* 11:1–12.

Kanner, L. 1943. Autistic disturbances of affective contact. *Nervous Child* 2:217–250.

Kanner, L., and L. Eisenberg. 1956. Early infantile autism. *American Journal of Orthopsychiatry* 26:556–566.

Koegel, R. L., A. Rincover, and A. L. Egel. 1982. *Educating and understanding autistic children.* San Diego: College Hill.

Lansing, M., and E. Schopler. 1978. Individualized education: A public school model. In *Autism: A reappraisal of concepts and treatment,* edited by M. Rutter and E. Schopler, 439–452. New York: Plenum Press.

Litchman, M. D. 1976. The use of music in establishing a learning environment for language instruction with autistic children. Ph.D. diss., State University of New York at Buffalo. *Dissertation Abstracts International* 37: 4992A. (University Microfilms no. 77-3557.)

Mahlberg, M. 1973. Music therapy in the treatment of an autistic child. *Journal of Music Therapy* 10:189–193.

National Society for Autistic Children. 1978. Definition of the syndrome of autism. *Journal of Autism and Childhood Schizophrenia* 8:162–169.

Nelson, D., V. Anderson, and A. Gonzales. 1984. Music activities as therapy for children with autism and other pervasive developmental disorders. *Journal of Music Therapy* 21:100–116.

O'Connell, T. 1974. The musical life of an autistic boy. *Journal of Autism and Childhood Schizophrenia* 4:223–229.

Ornitz, E. M. 1974. The modulation of sensory input and motor output in autistic children. *Journal of Autism and Childhood Schizophrenia* 4:197–216.

———. 1987. Autism. In *Encyclopedia of neuroscience,* edited by G. Adelman, 92–93G. Boston: Birkhaeuser.

Piven, J., and S. Folstein, 1994. The genetics of autism. In *The neurobiology of autism,* edited by M. L. Baumann and T. L. Kemper, 18–44. Baltimore: Johns Hopkins University Press.

Pronovost, W. 1961. The speech behavior and language comprehension of autistic children. *Journal of Chronic Diseases* 13:228–233.

Rimland, B. 1964. *Infantile autism.* New York: Appleton-Century-Crofts.

———. 1979. Language disorder and infantile autism. In *Autism, a reappraisal of concepts and treatment,* edited by M. Rutter and E. Schopler, 85–104. New York: Plenum Press.

———. 1988. Causes of infantile autism: some considerations from recent research. In *Preventive and curative intervention in mental retardation,* edited by F. J. Menolascino and J. A. Stark, 265–294. Baltimore: P. H. Brookes.

Rutter, M., and L. Bartak. 1973. Special educational treatment of autistic children: A comparative study. II. Follow-up findings and implications for services. *Journal of Child Psychology and Psychiatry* 14:241–270.

Saperston, B. 1973. The use of music in establishing communication with an autistic mentally retarded child. *Journal of Music Therapy* 10:184–188.

Schmidt, D., and J. Edwards. 1976. Reinforcement of autistic children's responses to music. *Psychological Reports* 39:571–577.

Schopler, E., and G. B. Mesibov, eds. 1984. *The effects of autism on the family.* New York: Plenum Press.

Sherwin, A. 1953. Reactions to music of autistic children. *American Journal of Psychiatry* 109:823–831.

Stevens, E., and F. Clark. 1969. Music therapy in the treatment of autistic children. *Journal of Music Therapy* 6:98–104.

Thaut, M. H. 1980. Music therapy as a treatment tool for autistic children. Unpublished master's thesis, Michigan State University, East Lansing, MI.

———. 1983. A music therapy treatment model for autistic children. *Music Therapy Perspectives* 1:7–13.

———. 1987. Visual vs. auditory (musical) stimulus preferences in autistic children: A pilot study. *Journal of Autism and Developmental Disorders* 17:425–432.

———. 1988. Measuring musical responsiveness in autistic children: A comparative analysis of improvised musical tone sequences of autistic, normal, and mentally retarded individuals. *Journal of Autism and Developmental Disorders* 18:561–571.

Trevarthen C., K. Aitken, D. Papoudi, and J. Robarts. 1998. *Children with autism.* London: Kingsley Publishers.

Warwick, A. 1995. Music therapy in the education service: research with autistic children and their mothers. In *The art and science of music therapy: A handbook,* edited by T. Wigram, B. Saperston, and R. West, 209–225. Chur, Switzerland: Harwood Academic.

Wing, L. 1976. *Early childhood autism.* New York: Pergamon Press.

———. 1979. Social, behavioral, and cognitive characteristics: An epidemiological approach. In *Autism: A reappraisal of concepts and treatment,* edited by M. Rutter and E. Schopler, 27–37. New York: Plenum Press.

9

MUSIC THERAPY IN THE TREATMENT OF SENSORY DISORDERS

Kate E. Gfeller

CHAPTER OUTLINE

Educational and Rehabilitation Practices
Music Therapy Objectives

The sense of hearing is an important source of information and pleasure. The rolling thunder or wail of a police siren signals possible danger. The lilt of a mother's lullaby comforts her infant.The voice on the six o'clock news informs us of world events. The music from the car radio offers welcome distraction from the tedium of a long drive. Our world is enriched by sound. What is sound, and how do we perceive it?

THE AUDITORY SYSTEM

Sound is a form of energy created by a host of different sources: human voices, dogs barking, car engines, musical instruments, and radios, to name just a few. Although these sound sources seem quite different, they have in common the ability to create sound energy by moving the surrounding air molecules in such a way that patterns of greater density (compression) or lesser density (rarefaction) occur. These patterns are called sound waves, and they travel through a medium such as air, water, or solids (e.g., metal) to reach your ear (see Figure 3-1).

When this repetition (or cycle) of compression and rarefaction ensues in a regular (periodic) fashion, the sound wave can be described by the number of cycles that occur per second (for example, 440 cycles per second). This rate is called the **frequency** of the sound wave. Often it is referred to using a technical label, *Hertz* (abbreviated Hz, i.e., 440 Hz). The slower the frequency of the sound wave, the lower the sound, and the faster the frequency, the higher the sound. For example, a sound wave of 880 Hz sounds higher than a sound of 440 Hz. In music, we often refer to how high or how low a note sounds with the term *pitch,* and we assign letter names of the musical scale to each pitch. For example, a sound wave of 440 Hz would be called A above middle C.

How do we perceive this sound energy? The outer portion of the ear, or *pinna,* is specially shaped to funnel sound waves into the *ear canal* and on to the portion of the hearing mechanism called the *middle ear,* which includes the *tympanic membrane* (eardrum) and ossicles (see Figure 3-2). The tympanic membrane, a flexible elastic structure, vibrates at the frequency of the sound wave. As it vibrates, it transmits that mechanical energy to three small bones, or ossicles, named the *malleus, incus,* and *stapes.* These three small bones act as levers to conduct the energy to the inner ear, or **cochlea.**

The cochlea is shaped much like a snail. If we were to peer inside this small structure, we would find a small winding canal that houses a gelatinous type of fluid and a special lining, called the *basilar membrane.* This membrane holds in place thousands of fine hair cells, known as cilia. The mechanical energy from the middle ear sets into motion the fluid in the cochlea, which then moves across the cilia. As these hair cells are stimulated, the mechanical energy is converted to electrical energy, and this electrical energy is sent via the **auditory nerve** to the brain, where the sound is processed and interpreted.

Disease or malfunction can obstruct the hearing mechanism at any point along this auditory pathway, and thus affect the quality and quantity of sound that an individual hears. Different terms are used to describe where the hearing loss originates.

TYPES OF HEARING LOSS

There are four primary types of hearing loss, each which has a different origin in the hearing mechanism. A **conductive hearing loss** is caused by disease or obstruction in the outer or middle ear, the conduction pathway through which sound reaches the inner ear. For example, scar tissue resulting from a tearing of the tympanic membrane or calcification of the ossicles reduces the flexibility and consequently the sensitivity of this part of the hearing mechanism. Therefore, more sound energy (i.e., louder sounds) is required to place the middle ear structures into motion. Conductive hearing losses often impede hearing acuity across a wide range of frequencies (i.e., low as well as high sounds). The structural damage may be slight or extensive, and in some cases, can be treated medically (i.e., reparative surgery). If the problem cannot be resolved medically, hearing aids, which amplify (make louder) the sound are often helpful.

Not all hearing losses result from problems in the middle or outer ear. A sensorineural hearing loss results from damage to, or absence of the delicate hair cells of, the inner ear. This type of loss may be due to a variety of causes **(etiology)** including infections (such as meningitis), repeated or extended exposure to extremely loud sounds, or conditions present at birth. The severity of the loss will depend on the extent of damage or malformation in the inner ear, and it is often the case that some frequencies are more easily heard than others. For example, many people with a sensorineural hearing loss will be able to hear low-pitched sounds more easily than high-pitched frequencies. In some cases, sound may be distorted.

Because of the damage to, or absence of, hair cells, there is a breakdown in the transformation of sound waves from mechanical to electrical energy. With this type of loss, provision of more sound energy through amplification (as is provided with a hearing aid) is not always helpful, because there may remain inadequate stimulation of the auditory nerve. In some cases of profound sensorineural loss, individuals may receive greater benefit from a relatively new type of assistive hearing device called a **cochlear implant.** This device essentially provides artificial electrical stimulation to the cochlear region, and subsequently the auditory nerve. However, it is important to note that a cochlear implant delivers only a portion of the sound signal, and in its present stage of technical development does not replicate normal hearing. In addition, there are very specific guidelines that physicians follow in selecting good candidates for this sort of device. Consequently, the cochlear implant is, at present time, an option for a relatively small proportion of the population with hearing losses.

A *mixed* hearing loss is the term used to describe problems that are due to structural deficiencies in both the outer or middle ear and the inner ear. If the hearing loss is due to damage or impairment to the brain or central nervous system, it is called a *central* hearing loss. In the case of a central hearing loss, although sound stimuli are transmitted to the inner ear at an adequate level of loudness, the listener, because of neurological deficits, has difficulty interpreting or understanding the sound signal. For example, the individual may acknowledge that she or he hears speech but may be unable to determine the meaning of the words. Rehabilitation of a central hearing loss is more closely related to interventions for brain injury than conductive or sensorineural losses, and therefore will not be covered in this chapter.

CLASSIFICATION OF HEARING LOSS

Hearing losses vary not only with regard to type (structural cause) but also with regard to severity. More specifically, hearing losses range from slight to profound (see Table 9-1). People with *slight* hearing losses may experience problems hearing quiet or distant speech, and may be unaware that they have a problem. They may think that others are talking too softly or mumbling. People with *profound* losses hear only very loud sounds and have considerable difficulty hearing normal conversational speech. Quiet sounds will most likely be completely undetected; loud sounds may be perceived, but will be experienced as a tactile (i.e., feeling the vibration from the sound wave) sensation rather than as a distinct sound with a specific pitch or *timbre* (tone quality). In general, the greater the severity of loss, the greater the impact the deficit has on communication. Profound or total deafness is rare. More often, people have some usable hearing, called residual hearing. Through training, people can learn to make maximum use of their **residual hearing** in order to better understand speech and environmental sounds.

ONSET OF HEARING LOSS

Another way in which hearing losses are categorized is by *time of onset,* or when the hearing loss first occurred. A *congenital* hearing loss is present at birth and may result from hereditary factors, disorders in embryological development, or toxicity or trauma during pregnancy or delivery. Hearing losses that occur after birth are known as acquired, or **adventitious** hearing losses. This type of loss may result from an infection,

TABLE 9-1 THE RELATIONSHIP BETWEEN SEVERITY OF HEARING LOSS AND COMMUNICATION DIFFICULTIES

Classification of hearing loss: effect on communication	
Slight	Frequent difficulty hearing faint speech. May demonstrate some problems in language arts subjects.
Mild	Understands conversational speech at a distance of 3 to 5 feet. May miss as much as 50 percent of conversation if not face to face. May have limited vocabulary and speech irregularities.
Moderate	Can understand loud conversation only. Will have difficulty in group discussions. Is likely to have impaired speech, limited vocabulary, and difficulty in language use and comprehension.
Severe	May hear loud voices about 1 foot from the ear. May be able to identify environmental sounds. May be able to discriminate vowels, but not consonants. Speech and language are likely to be impaired, or will deteriorate.
Profound	More aware of vibrations than tonal patterns. Relies on vision rather than hearing as the primary means of communication. Speech and language likely to be impaired or will deteriorate. Speech and language unlikely to develop spontaneously if the loss is before the development of speech (Heward and Orlansky 1988, 259–260).

Source: A. A. Darrow and K. E. Gfeller, "Music Therapy with Children Who Are Deaf and Hard of Hearing." In *Effectiveness of Music Therapy Procedures: Documentation of Research and Clinical Practice,* 2d ed., edited by C. E. Furman (Washington, DC: National Association for Music Therapy, 1996), 231.

trauma, loud noises, or drugs that are toxic to the hearing mechanism. The time of onset is particularly important with regard to speech and language development, for those losses that occur before the acquisition of language, **prelingual** losses, have a greater impact on speech and language development than do **postlingual** losses.

Postlingual losses are those that occur after the acquisition of language. In most cases, persons with postlingual losses will have developed a language base and concept of speech sounds. However, children with postlingual losses will often show a slower rate of language development than do normally hearing children, and the quality of speech can deteriorate over time because the individual has difficulty monitoring his or her own speech sounds.

THE RELATIONSHIP BETWEEN HEARING LOSS AND MODE OF COMMUNICATION

The type, severity, and onset of hearing loss all have an effect on communication. The earlier the onset and the more severe the loss, the greater the negative impact on speech and language development. The combination of type, severity, and onset of hearing loss is also likely to influence the type of communication that is most effective for the individual. For example, individuals with mild losses and greater residual hearing can generally communicate by speaking and *speech reading* (often referred to informally as lipreading) in conjunction with careful listening. This is known as an *oral communication* system. People with mild hearing losses may be virtually undistinguishable from normal-hearing people in superficial interactions, unless you happen to notice their hearing aids or very subtle differences in the sound of their speech. Some people with more severe losses (especially those with early onset) may have great difficulty forming clear, intelligible speech sounds or understanding other peoples' verbal communication. Therefore, they may prefer to communicate *manually,* or through a system of hand shapes that represent letters or words. A number of systems are used, including American Sign Language, finger spelling, and sign systems based on English syntax (see Table 9-2), (Hixon et al. 1980). Each method is based on a different philosophy of communication and uses different rules. *Total communication* refers to the simultaneous use of one or more manual communication systems and spoken language. The recipient of the message selects the most accessible aspects of the communication (Hixon et al. 1980).

OTHER TERMS AND SOCIOCULTURAL ISSUES RELATED TO HEARING LOSS

Although the types, classifications, and onset of hearing loss represent primarily the audiological status or history of the loss, other terms are used to describe hearing losses that have a basis in regulatory policy or cultural norms. For example, the term *hearing impairment* is a global term that describes all hearing losses, regardless of type, classification, or onset, and is often used in regulatory language related to the provision of special education services. It is also a term commonly used by hearing people in everyday conversations when they discuss hearing losses. However, not everyone approves of the term *hearing impaired.* Some people prefer to use the terms **deaf** or *hard*

TABLE 9-2 MODES OF COMMUNICATION USED BY PEOPLE WITH HEARING LOSSES

Modes of communication
Finger spelling—Hand shapes and positions corresponding to the letters of the alphabet that are used to spell out words.
American Sign Language (ASL)—American Sign Language is a true language in that it has its own syntactical structure, different from that of the English language. It is supplemented by finger-spelled words if no appropriate sign exists for a particular object or concept (i.e., proper names).
Sign systems based on syntax—Systems such as Signed English or Signing Exact English use many signs from ASL, but the signs are used in the syntactical structure of the English language. Additional signs are used to indicate verb tense, prefixes, suffixes, and word endings.
Total communication (TC)—This term refers to the use of combinations of sign language, sign systems, and finger spelling simultaneously with spoken language. The rationale behind TC is that the message recipient will pick out and use those aspects of the communication most accessible.

Source: Theodore J. Glattke, "Sound and Hearing." In *Introduction to Communication Disorders,* edited by T. J. Hixon, L. D. Shriberg, and J. H. Saxman (Englewood Cliffs, NJ: Prentice Hall, 1980), 102. Reprinted with permission.

of hearing to distinguish among various types of hearing losses. This is especially true for people who consider hearing loss not so much a disability, but rather a common condition within a subculture whose primary form of communication is sign language (e.g., in the United States, American Sign Language).

The word *culture* has been defined as a way of life that differentiates a specific group of people (Darrow and Gfeller, 1996). The *Deaf community,* or *Deaf culture,* refers to that subculture in the population at large that communicates through sign language and adopts social habits and values specific to this group. As is the case in any culture, there are unique rules of social interaction and manners. For example, many members of the Deaf community attend residential schools for the deaf and are members of various clubs or political organizations that support or advocate for persons who are deaf.

Members of the Deaf community often reject the term *hearing impairment,* because they believe the word *impairment* implies a broken or defective individual. Rather, they consider themselves to be culturally distinctive and differently abled only with regard to their ability to hear. Many people in the Deaf community prefer the use of terms such as *deaf* (spelled with a uppercase "D" when referring to the culture or community) to describe people with significant losses who communicate manually, and *hard of hearing* to describe people who have less severe losses, and who interact primarily with hearing individuals through oral communication.

Affiliation with the Deaf community is not simply a matter of degree of hearing loss. Members of the Deaf community can also include hearing people (e.g., children or close friends of deaf individuals) who share the values of the culture (Padden and Humphries 1988). What is more, there are individuals with significant hearing losses who do not consider themselves to be a part of the Deaf community. For example, people with serious hearing losses acquired well into adulthood may prefer to use speech reading and oral forms of communication rather than American Sign Language, because the majority of their friends and acquaintances are hearing people (Padden and Humphries 1988).

Given the considerable variation in hearing status and cultural values of those who have hearing losses, it is important to maintain a sensitivity to the issues of assigning labels. Certainly some terms are primarily audiological descriptions, and those are most useful for precise communication in medical or rehabilitative situations. Other terms, more global in nature, such as hearing impairment, deaf, or hard of hearing, have social values associated with them and, therefore, should be used with sensitivity to the specific circumstance or individual preference.

Before initiating any significant rehabilitative program with clients who have hearing losses, the music therapist should learn more about Deaf culture in order to interact appropriately and sensitively (Commission on Education of the Deaf 1988). For example, some members of the Deaf community consider music to be an art form that is "primarily for hearing people," though attitudes regarding music vary from one deaf individual to the next. The book *Deaf in America* by Carol Padden and Tom Humphries (1988) is one of many resources where issues of Deaf culture are outlined and discussed.

PROBLEMS ASSOCIATED WITH HEARING LOSS

Problems Resulting from a Hearing Loss in Early Childhood

The primary difficulty associated with hearing loss is in the area of communication, including written and spoken forms, particularly when the loss occurs early in life and is severe in nature. This is easier to understand when we consider how normally hearing children acquire language. Babies start to learn about their native language by listening to the speech of adults or children who demonstrate competent language models. In everyday life, children have many hours of exposure to *incidental language learning* (i.e., what they learn informally by engaging in or overhearing conversation). Most children by ages three or four will have acquired the basic rules of grammar for their native culture, simply by listening to language around them.

Contrast this usual scenario to that of a child with a serious hearing loss that is either undetected or little improved by assistive hearing devices. This child will either miss, or have poor examples of, language in everyday life. Consequently, there are often delays in language development, including spoken language, internal language (the mental processes associated with language), and written forms. For example, because the child cannot hear clear or complete models of adult speech, or her own speech production, she or he may have problems differentiating the range of speech sounds while listening, and will also have difficulty producing speech sounds.

Some typical problems associated with hearing loss include slower acquisition of vocabulary, slower development of proper syntax (rules of grammar), improperly formed speech sounds that make intelligibility problematic, and limited use of the voice. These difficulties in acquiring language and its spoken form (speech) have a negative impact on academic skills that are based in language; that is, any academic subject that requires reading, writing, or verbal communication. Difficulties in understanding the speech of others or in producing intelligible speech also has a negative impact on everyday communication and socialization. This may manifest itself in difficulties with following directions, poor discrimination of sounds, awkward social interactions, and social isolation (Davis and Hardick 1981).

It is important to note, however, that these difficulties are particular to acquisition of spoken language and the use of written language. Children with rich exposure to manual forms of communication in early life are likely to show similar progress in language acquisition, mastery, and social interaction in contexts where manual communication is the communicative mode of choice. For example, deaf children of deaf parents, who have regular and early exposure to a rich sign language environment, develop competency in sign language much in the same sequence and rate as normally hearing children develop speech. However, special instructional methods are typically necessary in order for these same children to acquire competence in spoken and written forms of language. It is toward that end that the music therapist may work in conjunction with other professionals (i.e., deaf education teachers, audiologists, speech–language pathologists) to maximize communication and academic development.

Problems Resulting from a Hearing Loss Acquired in Adulthood

Because those adults who acquire hearing losses in adulthood have already mastered speech and language, the types of problems experienced by these individuals are somewhat different from those found in children. Although a few speech sounds may sound less clear over time, the speech and language of most adults with acquired hearing loss can still be understood. The problems that are more prevalent for adults with acquired loss include social isolation (i.e., difficulty understanding others in conversation, hearing the words on television or radio, understanding the waiter in a restaurant, etc.) and vocational disabilities (i.e., using a phone at work; understanding the instructions of supervisors; hearing sounds important to the job, such as the sounds of an engine that warn a car mechanic there is a problem, etc.). The problems associated with a hearing loss acquired well into adulthood are ameliorated primarily through assistive hearing devices and compensatory communication strategies (i.e., hearing aids, special electronic devices for replacing doorbells, alarm clocks, etc.).

MUSIC THERAPY WITH PERSONS WHO HAVE HEARING LOSSES

It is easy to assume that music would be an inappropriate therapeutic medium for persons with hearing losses, because music is considered primarily an auditory art form. However, music can be an enjoyable art form as well as an excellent tool for therapy, as long as the auditory and communicative characteristics of the individual are accommodated (Amir and Schuchman 1985; Darrow and Gfeller 1991; Darrow and Gfeller 1996; Edmunds 1984; Fahey and Birkenshaw 1972; Ford 1985; Gfeller 1986, 1987; Hummel 1971; Riordian 1971; Vettese 1974). This section includes: (1) a description of musical perception of persons with various types of hearing losses; and (2) accommodations that can enhance music perception, including some of the primary music therapy goals and methods for persons with significant hearing losses.

Music Perception and Enjoyment by Persons with Hearing Losses

When considering the musical perception and enjoyment of persons with hearing losses, it is essential to remember that most people have some residual hearing. However, the types of musical sounds most easily heard, and the extent to which an individual actually enjoys music will depend on (1) the type and classification of the hearing loss in conjunction with the particular structural features of the music itself, (2) the type of assistive device used, and (3) personal background and preferences of the individual.

The *type or classification* of hearing loss can make a difference with regard to which musical features are most easily perceived. For example, people with sensorineural hearing losses often have better hearing acuity in lower frequencies. These individuals are more able to perceive the sounds of low-pitched musical instruments in the bass and baritone range than the relatively high frequency sounds that make up much of human speech. People who have mild to moderate hearing losses have more residual hearing through which they can perceive and enjoy music. In contrast, people with severe or profound hearing losses may perceive little more than the rhythmic beat, or the most low-frequency sounds played at a relatively loud intensity. In such instances, music that has a strong rhythmic beat may be more readily perceived and enjoyed than music that emphasizes melody and harmony (Darrow 1979, 1984, 1987; Korduba 1975).

Research studies indicate that children with hearing losses can perform at least as effectively as normal-hearing children on some types of rhythmic tasks (such as imitating a beat) if tactile (the sense of touch) or visual cues are available (Korduba 1975). For example, the child might keep a steady beat by watching a blinking light on a metronome, or by feeling the beat of a drum on the wooden frame of the instrument.

There is likely to be a greater difference, however, between children who have hearing losses and normal-hearing children for perception of melody or harmony, especially in the case of children with moderate or more severe losses. For children with enough residual hearing to perceive some frequency information, pitch discrimination improves with increased intensity (loudness). It may also be more accurate for lower pitches (i.e., the lower half of the piano keyboard, instruments like the trombone or cello). Although large pitch changes are more easily perceived than small changes (i.e., stepwise changes such as C to D), even children with severe hearing losses have been trained to recognize pitch changes as small as a minor third (i.e., C to E-flat) (Ford 1985).

Music perception and enjoyment will also be affected by the type of *assistive hearing device* used by the individual. Hearing aids function on a principle of amplifying, or making louder, sounds. However, the electrical circuitry of the hearing aids can be set to emphasize certain frequencies, often those most important in understanding speech. Consequently, musical sounds may not always sound as pleasant or natural through a hearing aid.

However, hearing aids provide a much more natural signal with regard to music than do cochlear implants, which often transmit to the individual only portions of the total sound wave. Most implant recipients to date are able to perceive basic rhythmic features of music with relative accuracy, but many implant recipients find it difficult to follow melodies. They may describe the quality of the sound as somewhat mechanical, unnatural, or noisy (Gfeller and Lansing 1991, 1992; Gfeller et al. 1997, 1998). Fortunately, the manufacturers of the cochlear implant continue to improve the technical features of the device, so future implants may provide a more satisfactory quality of sound for music listening.

The unique characteristics of the individual are also important with regard to music perception and enjoyment (Gfeller 1997b). Just as is the case for normally hearing persons, people with hearing losses vary with regard to their musical background and preferences. For example, some adults who lost their hearing well into adulthood may have had extensive musical experiences during childhood or early adulthood. This type of listening situation, in which the person can compare musical sounds they hear now to those heard prior to hearing loss, is quite different from that of persons who have a congenital or prelingual hearing loss. Those individuals cannot draw on recollection of normal listening experiences, and thus their conceptualization of music may be quite different (Gfeller 1997b).

For that segment of the population with hearing losses that does listen to and enjoy music, there are individual differences with regard to preference. For example, some people report particular enjoyment of popular music; others indicate that classical music is especially meaningful. Like normally hearing people, people using special assistive hearing devices report preference for different musical instruments or musical styles (Gfeller and Witt 1997).

Accommodations in Music Therapy for Clients with Hearing Losses: Acoustical and Language

Acoustical Accommodations The music therapist must accommodate both limited auditory acuity (how accurately one hears) and delays or deficits in communication skills when selecting musical activities or materials (Darrow and Gfeller 1991). The music therapist should take into account the auditory profile of each individual, both with regard to type and category of loss, as well as the type and benefit of any assistive hearing devices. A conversation with the client's audiologists or speech–language pathologist can be extremely helpful in determining which sounds are most easily heard by the client.

Persons with mild hearing losses may be able to enjoy most musical instruments as long as their assistive hearing device is properly adjusted. If the client has poor hearing acuity in higher frequencies (as is often the case for sensorineural losses), instruments that are in the baritone and bass range may be more readily heard than are instruments that play primarily higher frequencies. For individuals with severe or profound losses, who get little benefit from assistive hearing devices, poor auditory acuity can be accommodated by selecting rhythmic musical instruments with large vibrating surfaces, such as drums, pianos, bass tone bars, and xylophones. The rhythmic pulses of these instruments can be felt as well as heard. Instruments like the piano, or bass xylophones meet the criteria for low-frequency range and tactile access. In fact, some of these low-frequency and percussive instruments are more easily heard than human speech (which is comprised of many high frequencies). Consequently, musical instruments can be a particularly valuable therapeutic tool in therapeutic goals such as maximal use of residual hearing. Although it is true that some instruments are more readily heard by persons with severe losses, it is also important to keep in mind individual preferences (Gfeller 1997a).

Accommodations for Language Abilities or Communicative Modes The language deficiencies commonly experienced by children with serious hearing losses (Darrow and Gfeller 1996; Ford 1985) can also affect their ability to participate in music activities. In general, the music therapist needs to communicate with language that is within the present developmental level of the participant (Gfeller and Baumann 1988). For example, complex instructions and explanations may be beyond the child's language level. Words typically used to describe musical concepts may be difficult to comprehend. For example, terms such as *minor* or *harmony* are abstract descriptions of complex musical characteristics. In contrast, *fast* and *slow* are examples of more concrete terms that are easily demonstrated and more readily understood. Lyrics to songs should be examined for suitability and new vocabulary words carefully chosen and explained. Instructions should be simple and clear. In addition to considering developmental issues, the music therapist should also be sensitive to the client's system of communication. If the child uses manual communication (i.e., ASL, Signed English, etc.), the therapist should either be able to engage in two-way communication through sign, or should ensure that a qualified interpreter is available for each session.

TREATMENT GOALS FOR PERSONS WITH HEARING LOSSES

Although a severe hearing loss that is congenital or acquired in early childhood is likely to have an impact on communication skills throughout life, music therapy intervention in the areas of speech, language, or auditory perception is most likely to occur during the elementary or middle-school years. As the child with a hearing loss enters adolescence and young adulthood, the music therapist may begin to emphasize the social and emotional aspects of music, such as participation in music ensembles as a leisure-time activity and art form. The music therapist's role changes from interventionist to consultant or resource person, thus encouraging greater self-determination and responsibility on the part of the adolescent or young adult. Given these patterns of rehabilitation, and more typical job placement of music therapists, this section will focus primarily on rehabilitation goals with children who are deaf or hard of hearing.

The music therapist contributes to the rehabilitation of children with significant hearing losses in four primary ways: by (1) supplementing auditory training, (2) improving speech production, (3) reinforcing language development, and (4) providing a structured activity for social skill attainment (Darrow and Gfeller 1996). Each of these goals will be discussed in some detail.

Music Therapy for Auditory Training

Auditory training is an intervention that enables the individual to make maximum use of residual hearing, thus improving the ability to understand speech and environmental sounds. The ultimate goal of auditory training is typically to improve speech comprehension. Because music and speech share common structural characteristics (such as pitch and duration of sound), music can effectively supplement an auditory training program by motivating the use of residual hearing (Amir and Schuchman 1985; Bang 1980; Darrow and Gfeller 1996; Fisher and Parker 1994). Percussion instruments and low-pitched mallet instruments, such as xylophones or glockenspiels, can be used effectively to work on the following objectives: (1) *sound detection* (determining the absence or presence of sound), (2) *sound discrimination* (determining whether sounds are the same or different), (3) *sound identification* (recognizing the sound source), and (4) the *comprehension* (understanding) of sound (Darrow and Gfeller 1996; Erber and Hirsch 1978). The music therapist initially chooses sounds most accessible to the client and gradually increases the difficulty of the listening tasks.

> Maureen is a music therapist who works with a small group of preschool children (ages three and four) with severe hearing losses who are enrolled in a special language rehabilitation program. One of the objectives in the childrens' individualized education plans is to develop optimal use of their residual hearing. The first step toward this goal is awareness of sound versus silence. For the session, Maureen has decided to use a large tom-tom to introduce concepts of sound and silence. The head of the drum is large enough that even young children with partially developed motor skills can successfully create a sound. In addition, the beat of the drum can be felt by touching the base of the instrument. As each child takes a turn striking the surface of the drum, the other children feel the vibrations on the wooden base of the drum. Maureen and the other staff members speak and sign "I hear sound!" When the child stops playing, the adults all sign "Stop." As another way of reinforcing the concept of sound versus silence, Maureen marches to the child's rhythmic pattern and then freezes in place when the beat stops. Little Christopher loves to play this game, making people march and freeze by creating sound and silence.

Although the speech–language pathologist will want to move beyond these gross listening tasks to those involving subtle speech sounds, musical sound sources offer positive benefits in the early stages of auditory training. First, because *musical instruments are pitched in a wide range of frequencies* (from low to high) and can be played relatively loudly, they may be heard more readily than speech sounds, which have a more limited frequency (pitch) and intensity (loudness) range. These musical sounds can provide successful experiences during the early stages of sound awareness. Certain musical instruments with vibrating surfaces that are easily touched, such as the drum, piano, and xylophone, provide **tactile** as well as auditory sensations for the client experimenting with sound and silence. These tactile sensations (i.e., touching the drum while listening to the beat) can reinforce the distinction between sound and no sound (Fisher and Parker 1994).

Playing rhythm instruments allows the individual to see a cause–effect relationship between an action (striking the instrument) and the subsequent sound. For many young children, playing rhythm instruments is also a positive, motivating experience, as they actively create and listen to sounds. A high level of motivation is helpful in keeping young children with short attention spans focused and involved during therapy. The music therapist assesses progress in auditory training both through informal testing and through the use of standardized assessment procedures (Darrow and Gfeller 1996; Gfeller and Baumann 1988). Formal tests of auditory comprehension are available and are outlined by Darrow and Gfeller in the book *Effectiveness of Music Therapy Procedures: Documentation of Research and Clinical Practice* (1996, 230–266). Some of these tests require the test administrator to have specialized training in speech–language pathology or audiology.

Music Therapy for Speech Development

Children with normal hearing learn to speak by imitating the sounds of others, hearing their own speech, and making necessary adjustments. Because children with significant hearing losses hear either distorted or partial models of speech, some of their speech sounds may be formed improperly or omitted entirely (Davis and Hardick 1981). It is also common for children with severe hearing losses to have speech with improper pitch (i.e., too high) and unusual rhythm or inflection (i.e., sounding monotonous or mechanical). Individuals with profound hearing losses may use their voices very little, making only isolated sounds rather than forming clearly articulated words or phrases.

Although music therapists are not trained in the rehabilitation of articulation (the correct production of various parts of speech, such as forming a "sh" or "buh" sound), the music therapist can reinforce other aspects of speech production identified by the speech–language pathologist, which include (1) an increased use of the voice in free vocalization, and (2) an increased awareness of speech patterns and subsequent production of more natural speech rhythms, pitch, and inflections, factors that influence intelligibility (Bang 1980; Darrow 1990; Darrow and Cohen 1991; Darrow and Gfeller 1996; Darrow and Starmer 1986; Gfeller 1986).

Free vocalization and vocal imitation are encouraged through singing activities. For example,

> In Maureen's preschool group, Christopher, Robbin, and Karen are working on production of the sounds "mmmm" and "bah." In order to encourage use of these sounds, Maureen has decided to introduce the song "Old MacDonald." As the verses about the cows and sheep are introduced, Maureen models the sounds MOOO and BAAH (using methods of modeling recommended by the speech–language pathologist) and the children pretend that they are cows and sheep. Maureen works cooperatively with Natalie, the speech–language pathologist, in helping each child produce his or her best possible speech sounds. Although the initial utterances produced in rehabilitation are not always clear or correct, experimentation with the voice is an important step toward improved speech production.

Progress in speech intelligibility is difficult to assess because it is subjective in nature. For example, the first time we hear a speaker with a foreign accent, he or she may be difficult to understand. Over time, we become accustomed to the idiosyncratic speech patterns and understand more of what is said. Similarly, the therapist will find the speech of hearing-impaired persons easier to understand with greater exposure. Nevertheless, the music therapist can evaluate progress in speech intelligibility with a variety of tests, which are described by Darrow and Gfeller in the book *Effectiveness of Music Therapy Procedures: Documentation of Research and Clinical Practice* (1996, 230–266). Proper test administration, scoring, and requirements are described in the book.

Music Therapy for Language Development

A serious hearing loss not only affects the ability to hear and form intelligible speech sounds; it also has a major impact on language development. Normal-hearing children learn about vocabulary, syntax, and rules of conversation by overhearing the language of others. In contrast, hearing-impaired children have little incidental exposure to language models (Gfeller and Schum 1994). Therefore, the development of language is dependent on early and comprehensive intervention. Even with intensive training, children with serious hearing losses often lag behind their peers in language development. Common problems include reduced or improper use of vocabulary, errors in syntax, use of shorter and simpler sentences, and diminished spontaneous interactions (Davis and Hardick 1981).

Music is a nonverbal language. Why is it used toward language development goals? First, music is often paired with words in songs. Furthermore, musical activities are often facilitated with verbal instructions or directives. Activities such as writing songs or pairing sign language with music provide motivating ways to introduce or practice new vocabulary words (Darrow and Gfeller 1996; Galloway and Bean 1974; Gfeller 1987; Gfeller and Darrow 1987; Gfeller and Schum 1994). During the process of constructing a song, clients are encouraged to generate and express ideas using language skills. As group members discuss their ideas and formulate the lyrics and music, the music therapist encourages topic-related interaction among group members.

> Maureen provides music therapy for a group of lower-elementary school-aged children who have moderate to profound hearing losses. Today in music therapy the children are writing a song about favorite foods. This topic was chosen because the speech–language pathologist shared with Maureen that most of the children in the group are working on vocabulary regarding foods (i.e., spaghetti, pizza, french fries, broccoli, etc.). On a felt board, Maureen has placed pictures of the foods in the vocabulary list, and asked the children to guess which one each of their friends likes the best. Then these choices are placed in a simple song entitled "My Favorite Food," which Maureen composed for this particular activity. As each child shares his or her favorite food, Maureen models the correct sign and speech sound for each food.

Language development goals in music therapy typically focus on one of the following: (1) increased and appropriate use of vocabulary, (2) increased spontaneous or topic-related interaction, and (3) increased complexity and completeness of sentences (Darrow and Gfeller 1996; Gfeller and Baumann 1988). Interaction and sentence structure are complex and difficult to assess, requiring a language sample of the child's spoken, signed, or written communication. In order to gather a reliable sample, the therapist must be fluent in the child's mode of communication. Furthermore, interpretation of the sample requires an understanding of normal, delayed, and deviant language patterns. Therefore, unless the music therapist has had extensive training in this area, he or she should collaborate with the speech therapist to monitor progress (Gfeller and Baumann 1988).

Music Therapy for Social Skills Development

As a result of delayed language development and speech production problems, children with hearing losses miss out on many interactions with others. Furthermore, a child with limited language skills finds it difficult to understand instructions, ask questions, and express concerns or frustration. These limitations can contribute to problems in social adjustment (Meadow 1980a; Schum and Gfeller 1994).

Some children with a severe hearing loss may demonstrate immature behaviors or revert to socially unacceptable ways of expressing themselves. Because music tends to be a cooperative group event, a structured music activity offers a splendid opportunity to practice even the most basic social skills, such as taking turns, paying attention to others, following directions, sharing, working cooperatively toward a group goal, and expressing feelings appropriately (Bang 1980; Darrow and Gfeller 1996; Schum and Gfeller 1994). For some individuals, music making (i.e., playing instruments, writing songs, etc.) can be a satisfying leisure-time activity and opportunity for personal achievement.

Even clients with profound hearing losses can participate successfully in musical ensembles, song-signing, or songwriting activities if musical instruments and adaptive teaching methods have been carefully selected (Bang 1980; Darrow and Gfeller 1996; Robbins and Robbins 1980). One of the most convenient ways to measure improvement in social skills is through changes over time in the occurrence of specific problem behaviors. For example, the therapist may keep track of the number of times a client interrupts others or expresses feelings in inappropriate ways. The therapist can also use a specially designed scale, such as the Meadow/Kendall Social–Emotional Assessment Inventory for Deaf Students (Meadow 1980b), to assess social/emotional competency.

Determination of appropriate treatment goals and assessment tools should be made in conjunction with the client's speech–language pathologist or audiologist, because issues surrounding the speech, language, and auditory perception of persons with hearing losses are very complex. The music therapist must work closely with speech–language pathologists in order to develop a well-coordinated and appropriate plan of action.

SUMMARY

In summary, a hearing loss has a serious impact on a person's ability to understand speech and environmental sounds, speech production, language development, and social interaction. The extent to which speech and language development are affected depends on the type of loss, severity of loss, onset of loss, and impact of any assistive device. For those individuals who have severe and early hearing losses, intervention is required to facilitate maximal speech and language development. The structural characteristics of music and the social nature of music activities can help reduce the impact of these problems in the following ways:

1 Musical sounds encompass a wide range of frequencies, can be played at high-intensity levels, and produce tactile as well as auditory stimulation. These characteristics are useful in auditory training tasks, such as sound awareness and discrimination.

2 Like speech, music is composed of patterns that differ in pitch, duration, and intensity. Musical patterns can therefore be used to demonstrate and reinforce similar characteristics of normal speech production.

3 Music is often paired with textual information, as in song lyrics. New vocabulary and correct language usage can be reinforced through activities such as songwriting and singing.

4 Musical ensembles require social skills: following instructions, taking turns, cooperating with others, and sharing ideas. These activities provide a motivating and structured environment for learning and reinforcing appropriate social behaviors.

MUSIC THERAPY FOR PERSONS WITH VISUAL IMPAIRMENTS

The image of a blind musician playing on a street corner may come to mind when thinking of people with visual impairments and music. Many people assume that the blind are musically gifted and have extraordinary gifts of auditory perception (Pitman 1965). This myth has been reinforced by the exceptional musicality of blind people like Ray Charles and Stevie Wonder. In actuality, exceptional musical talent is as unusual among people with visual impairments as it is within the general population (Kirk and Gallagher 1979).

One of the first studies to challenge the belief that people who are blind have inherently superior auditory perception was conducted in 1918 by Seashore and Ling. They found that the auditory perception of people who are blind is more like than unlike that of sighted persons. Subsequent research suggests that, for the most part, the sighted and the blind are similar in musical aptitude and auditory perception (Drake 1939; Heim 1963; Kwalwasser 1955; Madsen and Darrow 1989; Sakurabayashi et al. 1956; Stankov and Spillsbury 1978). However, people with visual impairments, though not inherently more gifted in auditory perception, may use their intact sensory channels to fuller capacity, or may have particular subskills within the full range of auditory perception that have been highly developed (Stankov and Spillsbury 1978).

Given the fact that persons with visual impairments do not possess extraordinary musical perception, the notion of directing these persons toward careers in music as the best vocational choice is untenable. Rather, those persons with visual impairments who demonstrate talent commensurate with sighted individuals who are professional musicians are most likely to have success in musical careers.

If vocational preparation is not a prevalent music therapy goal with persons who are blind, then what therapeutic objectives are appropriate in music therapy practice with this particular disability? We can better understand rehabilitative emphases if we understand the characteristics and needs resulting from visual impairments.

Visual Impairments: Definitions and Etiology

It is a common misconception that people with visual impairments are completely without sight, or totally blind. Rather, sight impairments exist along a continuum of severity: Some are able to see some print with magnification; others can see outlines of objects or differentiate between light and shadows; a small subgroup has no useful residual vision. In general, people with visual impairments are classified into two major groups: (1) *the blind,* and (2) *the partially seeing or low-vision individuals* (Kirk and Gallagher 1979).

Blindness is defined as visual acuity from a distance of 20/200 in the better eye after correction (meaning that the person sees at a distance of 20 feet what the normal eye can distinguish at 200 feet), or a field of vision of no greater than 20 degrees (the angle of usable vision to the side of central vision). The *partially seeing* have visual acuity greater than 20/200 but not greater than 20/70 in the better eye following correction (Kirk and Gallagher 1979).

Some of the causes of blindness include infections and diseases, accidents and injuries, and prenatal influences including heredity. These can result in refractive errors (i.e., problems within the cornea or lens of the eye that cause improper focusing of the image), defective muscle control (i.e., crossed eyes or diverted gaze), disorders of receptive tissue (i.e., the optic nerve or retina that receives the image from the lens of the eye), or problems with the protective tissues (i.e., the eyelid) that cover the eyes. These conditions can be stable or progressive in nature (Codding 1982). Visual impairments may exist as the sole disabling condition or may coexist with other physical and mental impairments (Codding 1997).

Compared with other types of disabling conditions, visual impairment is a relatively low incidence impairment among children and young adults (progressive loss of visual acuity is, however, a common problem among the elderly; see Chapter 6). Furthermore, those individuals who have only a visual impairment (as opposed to multiple disabilities) make up an even smaller subgroup (Codding 1988).

Characteristics of Persons with Visual Impairments

Cognition Unless there are coexisting mental or physical disabilities, the development of children with visual impairments is more similar than dissimilar to that of normal-sighted children (Codding 1982, 1997; Kirk and Gallagher 1979). According to Kirk and Gallagher (1979), intelligence and achievement tests of children with visual impairments are only slightly below the performance of sighted children, with primary areas of delay appearing in the mastery of abstract concepts, especially those derived through spatial and other visual experiences.

Language If we exclude concepts based on visual experiences, language development of children with visual impairments is not deficient. Some usage of words such as dark, blue, yellow, or other visually based language concepts may be inappropriate. However, it is not unusual to hear a blind person use idiomatic phrases such as "Now I see what you mean," or "Look here" in proper context. Sighted persons should feel no hesitation in using these phrases around people who are blind (Kirk and Gallagher 1979).

Sensory Perception Although people have often assumed that other senses (touch, audition, smell) would be automatically strengthened if the visual sense were impaired, in fact, research does not support that opinion (Stankov and Spillsbury 1978). It may be possible, however, for persons with visual impairments to improve listening skills and use of other senses through training and practice (Kirk and Gallagher 1979).

Socioemotional Development Studies examining the impact of blindness on personality and social adjustment have been confounded by the problems of overprotectiveness or maladaptive relationships with parents and peers that may result in helplessness and dependency. Whereas some researchers have speculated that children who are blind do not initiate activities because they cannot see the consequences of their own actions (Fraiberg et al. 1968), other investigators have concluded that emotional problems of people who are blind are not necessarily a consequence of the visual impairment as much as of the attitudes of sighted persons who impose limitations (Ashcroft 1963; Cutsforth 1951).

Motor Development Research in the area of motor coordination suggests that people who are blind or partially sighted have inferior motor performance compared with that of sighted persons (Codding 1982; Kirk and Gallagher 1979). Norris, Spaulding, and Brodie (1957) found a high relationship between motor performance and blind children's opportunities for learning mobility. Kirk and Gallagher (1979) speculated that if children with visual impairments enjoy equal opportunity for physical involvement, such as climbing trees, roller skating, and other active play, they may have similar motor development to sighted peers.

As can be seen in many skill areas, the person with visual impairments has the potential for normal development. However, as a result of overprotection or lack of experiences, development may lag. Therefore, for the individual with normal intelligence, rehabilitation focuses on instructional methods and experiences that can help reduce the impact of the visual impairment on everyday learning experiences.

Educational and Rehabilitation Practices

Because those persons who have visual impairments and normal intelligence are more similar to sighted persons than not, it is not surprising that the greater majority of persons with visual impairments are educated in the public school system among sighted peers. This was not always the case. In the past, people with serious visual losses were often educated and received vocational training within schools for the blind (Kirk and Gallagher 1979). These residential facilities served essentially as homes throughout the childhood and adolescence of many people with sight impairments. Within these schools, music educators, music therapists, or musically talented staff established school orchestras, choirs, and other musical activities, with the attainment of musical skills as the primary objective (Codding 1988).

With the passage and implementation of Public Law 94-142 (Education for All Handicapped Children Act), the practice of educating the blind in remote residential schools became less prevalent (Codding 1988; Kirk and Gallagher 1979). Now those individuals who are visually impaired most often receiving residential care are those with multiple disabilities who require extraordinary physical or academic support. Visually impaired people with normal intelligence and physical functioning are typically educated in the public school system within their own communities, but receive specific types of technical support such as braille books or talking tapes in order to support educational progress.

Braille is a system of writing for the blind that uses characters made up of raised dots. Both written word and musical notation can be coded in braille, so the person who is blind can use her or his tactile sense in order to read. Some books and music are available through the music section of the National Library Service for the Blind and Physically Handicapped, Library of Congress, Washington, D.C. Other materials can be transcribed into braille through special services for the blind. However, not all people with visual impairments use braille. Some use enlarged print, magnification systems, or other special equipment for conveying print. Consequently, it is always wise to work cooperatively with the local association for the blind or local teacher of the visually impaired in order to determine what sorts of textual or musical print is most appropriate for a given individual.

Instructional methods include an emphasis on concrete learning through hearing and touch, optimizing opportunity to learn by doing, and assistance from the teacher in unifying experiences not easily perceived without the visual sense (such as understanding the totality of a farm, a grocery store, or a post office). In order to reduce the impact of visual impairment on mobility and motor development, sighted guides and programs to develop **orientation** and **mobility** are often included in the child's educational program. As these individuals approach adulthood, vocational counseling and training are an important part of the rehabilitation process.

Music Therapy Objectives

As is the case with other rehabilitative services, music therapists working with persons who are visually impaired seek to reduce the impact of the visual impairment on intellectual, social, motor, and emotional functioning. The number of music therapists serving this clientele is relatively small (Codding 1988). In the 1997 sourcebook of NAMT, some 252 music therapists indicated that they work with people who have visual impairments. However, that total includes people who have secondary disabilities such as mental retardation. The number of music therapists who work with visual impairments as a single disability is most likely much smaller in number (Codding 1997).

Unfortunately, the music therapist who works with the visually impaired has available only a small number of written resources on music perception of the blind, or therapeutic methods for this population. From 1946 to 1996, only 39 articles on music and the visually impaired were published in journals, theses, and books (Codding 1997). Relative to research on other populations, this is quite small in number. Furthermore, many of the existing articles were written well before changes in educational practices, and a number of them are case studies that pertain to very particular individual characteristics. Up-to-date resources regarding this population would be a welcome addition to the field.

However, even with the existing resources, one can find some trends. Some of the most common therapeutic objectives include: (1) to develop orientation and mobility, (2) to promote social skills and interpersonal communication, (3) to provide an outlet for appropriate emotional expression, and (4) as a form of sensory stimulation to reduce mannerisms (such as rocking or other self-stimulation) that may accompany blindness. According to Codding (1997), music is used toward those objectives in a variety of ways: (1) as a structured activity to facilitate learning of academic, motor, social, and verbal behavior; (2) as a stimulus cue or prompt for sound localization and other listening tasks; (3) as a contingency, or reward, for desired behavior; and (4) as part of musical appreciation and enjoyment (including lessons).

Orientation and Mobility **Orientation** involves the utilization of sensory processes to establish one's position in relation to objects in the environment. For example, the child needs to know her or his own body parts. Understanding the front, side, right, and left side of the body are other concepts that must be learned. The children's musical game "The Hokey Pokey" is a simple example of an activity that teaches orientation concepts. Musical sound sources can also be played throughout the movement area to facilitate localization skills. Localization involves identifying the direction from which a sound source originates in relation to one's own position (Codding 1982, 1988, 1997).

Mobility is locomotion, or movement from one's present position to a desired position in space (Codding 1982, 1997). Musical activities that include walking forward, backward, left or right, running, jumping, or galloping are all part of developing increased mobility and motor confidence. Rhythmic music can be used as a cue for tempo of movement. A variety of musical sounds, such as legato versus staccato music, can encourage different types of locomotion such as gliding or hopping.

Social Skills and Interpersonal Communication Involvement in musical organizations such as choirs, bands, or small ensembles requires cooperation with others. Social skills such as taking turns, attending, cooperation, following directions, and group problem solving are integral parts of most music groups. The music therapist structures the musical experience in order to foster social skills and cooperation. Learning social dancing to music is another way in which young persons with visual impairments can establish social skills helpful within the mainstream of life.

Emotional Expression and Development Although visual impairment per se may not have a negative impact on personality development and self-concept, the attitudes of parents, siblings, and peers toward people who are blind can have a deleterious effect on self-esteem and emotional growth. Feelings of dependence, helplessness, and lack of acceptance may exist. Activities such as writing songs or listening to relevant lyrics in a discussion group can assist in appropriate expression of feelings. Successful involvement in musical activities can promote a sense of mastery, personal accomplishment, and healthy self-concept.

Reduction of Mannerisms that May Accompany Blindness Some people who are blind may seek additional sensory stimulation in the form of rocking, rubbing eyes, or other self-stimulatory behavior. This type of behavior is most commonly seen in that segment of the population with additional disabilities such as mental retardation. In some instances, the presence of attractive musical stimuli has decreased these mannerisms and diverted attention to positive musical activities or events, such as grasping or playing an instrument (Codding 1988, 1997).

For those individuals with multiple disabilities in addition to visual impairment, therapeutic objectives may include self-help skills, achievement of preacademic knowledge, improved attention or compliance, reduction of negative behaviors, and a host of other skills (see Chapter 4 on mental retardation and Chapter 7 on orthopedic disabilities). In the case of multiple disabilities, the therapist must take into account all areas of need in addition to the impact of the visual impairment.

Therapists working with the deaf–blind face particular challenges in establishing effective interpersonal communication, because the two sensory modes traditionally used in everyday interaction are limited. The therapist may use sign language formed in the client's hand in order to communicate. For this population, the vibrations made by musical instruments such as guitars, pianos, or drums can provide a valuable source of sensory stimulation.

SUMMARY

Persons with visual impairment make up a small segment of children and young adults with disabilities. Visual impairments are generally categorized as either blind or partially sighted, and may or may not be accompanied by other physical disabilities. Visual impairments may occur in refractive, receptive, or protective tissue in the eye, or may result from lack of muscle control (directive). These conditions may be stable or progressive in nature. Those persons with normal intelligence generally have normal cognitive and language development, except in specific skills where conceptual and language development are strongly correlated with visual experiences. Contrary to common belief, people who are blind are not unusually gifted in auditory perception and musical skills, but extensive training and practice can result in optimal use of intact sensory modes. Although the people with visual impairments may demonstrate greater dependency and helplessness than sighted individuals, researchers speculate that this is due to overprotectiveness or negative attitudes on the part of parents and peers toward the disability.

One developmental area in which this population shows lower performance than sighted individuals is in motor coordination and mobility. The development of orientation and locomotor skills is often included in the educational programs of children with impaired sight. The use of special technical supports (i.e., braille, talking books, etc.) and concrete and experiential instructional methods have helped these individuals function successfully within regular educational environments.

The primary objective of music therapy is to reduce the impact of the visual impairment on social, emotional, and motor functioning. Several general objectives are commonly found in music therapy with this population: (1) development of orientation and mobility, (2) promotion of social skills and interpersonal communication, (3) appropriate emotional expression, and (4) reduction of mannerisms by using music as a form of sensory stimulation. Music is used toward those objectives in a variety of ways: (1) as a structured activity to facilitate learning of academic, motor, social, and verbal behavior; (2) as a stimulus cue or prompt for sound localization and other listening tasks; (3) as a contingency, or reward, for desired behavior; and (4) as part of musical appreciation and enjoyment (including lessons).

STUDY QUESTIONS

1 Which type of loss (conductive, sensorineural, or central hearing loss) is due to an obstruction or malformation in the outer or middle ear?
2 Briefly describe the five different levels of severity in hearing loss.
3 What is residual hearing?

4 What is another name for acquired (as opposed to congenital) hearing loss?

5 What are four basic modes of communication used by persons with hearing impairments?

6 How does the melodic and rhythmic perception of children with hearing losses compare with that of normal-hearing children?

7 What types of instruments are best for use with hearing-impaired clients?

8 What are the four primary ways in which a music therapist can contribute to the rehabilitation of hearing-impaired people? Give an example of one therapeutic goal for each intervention focus.

9 How does the musical aptitude of people with visual impairments compare with that of sighted people?

10 Describe the difference between the classifications blind and partially seeing or low vision.

11 List three causes of blindness.

12 What type of impact does a visual impairment have on cognition, language, socioemotional, and motor development?

13 List common therapeutic objectives in music therapy for people with visual impairments.

14 List common uses of music in therapeutic intervention for people with visual impairments.

REFERENCES

Amir, D., and Schuchman, G. 1985. Auditory training through music with hearing-impaired preschool children. *Volta Review* 87:333–343.

Ashcroft, S. 1963. Blind and partially seeing children. In *Exceptional children in the schools,* edited by L. M. Dunn, 413–461. New York: Holt, Rinehart and Winston.

Bang, C. 1980. A world of sound and music. *Journal of the British Association for Teachers of the Deaf* 4:1–10.

Codding, P. 1982. *Music therapy for handicapped children: Visually impaired.* Washington, DC: National Association for Music Therapy.

———. 1988. Music in the education/rehabilitation of visually disabled and multihandicapped persons: A review of literature from 1946–1987. In *Effectiveness of music therapy procedures: Documentation of research and clinical practice,* edited by C. E. Furman, 107–136. Washington, DC: National Association for Music Therapy.

———. 1997. A content analysis of music education/rehabilitation research with blind and visually impaired persons: A literature review (1946–1996). Research paper presented at the National Symposium for Research in Music Behavior, Minneapolis, MN, May 1997.

Commission on Education of the Deaf. 1988. *Toward equality: Education of the deaf.* Washington, DC.

Cutsforth, T. D. 1951. *The blind in school and society.* 2d. ed. New York: American Foundation for the Blind.

Darrow, A. A. 1979. The beat reproduction response of subjects with normal and impaired hearing: An empirical comparison. *Journal of Music Therapy* 16:6–11.

———. 1984. A comparison of the rhythmic responsiveness in normal hearing and hearing-impaired children and an investigation of the relationship of the rhythmic responsiveness to the suprasegmental aspects of speech perception. *Journal of Music Therapy* 21:48–66.

———. 1987. An investigative study: The effect of hearing impairment on musical aptitude. *Journal of Music Therapy* 24(2):88–96.

———. 1990. The effect of frequency adjustment on the vocal reproduction accuracy of hearing-impaired children. *Journal of Music Therapy* 27(1):24–33.

Darrow, A. A., and N. Cohen. 1991. The effect of programmed pitch practice and private instruction on the vocal reproduction accuracy of hearing-impaired children: Two case studies. *Music Therapy Perspectives* 9:61–65.

Darrow, A. A., and K. E. Gfeller. 1991. A study of public school music programs mainstreaming hearing-impaired students. *Journal of Music Therapy* 28(1):23–39.

———. 1996. Music therapy with children who are deaf and hard of hearing. In *Effectiveness of music therapy procedures: Documentation of research and clinical practice,* 2d ed., edited by C. E. Furman, 137–165. Washington, DC: National Association for Music Therapy.

Darrow, A. A., and G. J. Starmer. 1986. The effect of vocal training on the intonation and rate of hearing-impaired children's speech: A pilot study. *Journal of Music Therapy* 23:194–201.

Davis, J., and E. Hardick. 1981. Rehabilitative audiology for children and adults. New York: Wiley.

Drake, R. M. 1939. Factorial analysis of music tests by the Spearman tetrad difference technique. *Journal of Musicology* 1:6–10.

Edmonds, K. 1984. Is there a valid place for music in the education of deaf children? *ACEHI Journal* 10:164–169.

Erber, N. P., and I. J. Hirsch. 1978. Auditory training. In *Hearing and deafness,* edited by H. Davis and S. R. Silverman, 50–66. Chicago: Holt, Rinehart and Winston.

Fahey, J. D., and L. Birkenshaw. 1972. Bypassing the ear: The perception of music by feeling and touch. *The Music Educators Journal* 58:44–49.

Fisher, K. V., and B. J. Parker. 1994. A multisensory system for the development of sound awareness and speech production. *Journal of the Academy of Rehabilitative Audiology* 25:13–24.

Ford, T. A. 1985. The effect of musical experiences and age on the ability of deaf children to discriminate pitch of complex tones. Ph.D. diss., University of North Carolina, Chapel Hill, NC.

Fraiberg, S., M. Smith, and E. Adelson. 1968. An educational program for blind infants. *Journal of Special Education* 3:121–141.

Galloway, H. F., and M. F. Bean. 1974. The effects of action songs on the development of body-image and body-part identification in hearing-impaired preschool children. *Journal of Music Therapy* 11:125–134.

Gfeller, K. E. 1986. Music as a remedial tool for improving speech rhythm in the hearing-impaired: Clinical and research considerations. *MEH Bulletin* 2:3–19.

———. 1987. Songwriting as a tool for reading and language remediation. *Music Therapy* 6:28–38.

———. 1997a. Music therapy methods for children who are deaf or hard of hearing. Australian Music Therapy National Conference, Brisbane, Australia, August 23, 1997.

———. 1997b. Music perception and aesthetic response of cochlear implant recipients. Multidisciplinary Perspectives on Musicality: The Seashore Symposium. Iowa City, IA. October 17, 1997.

Gfeller, K. E., and A. A. Baumann. 1988. Assessment procedures for music therapy with hearing-impaired children: Language development. *Journal of Music Therapy* 25:192–205.

Gfeller, K. E., and A. A. Darrow. 1987. Music as a remedial tool in the language education of hearing-impaired children. *The Arts in Psychotherapy* 14:229–235.

Gfeller, K. E., J. F. Knutson, G. Woodworth, S. Witt, and B. Debus. 1998. Timbral recognition and apprisal by adult cochlear implant users. *Journal of the American Academy of Audiology* 9:1–19.

Gfeller, K. E., and C. R. Lansing. 1991. Melodic, rhythmic, and timbral perception of adult cochlear implant users. *Journal of Speech and Hearing Research* 34:916–920.

———. 1992. Musical perception of cochlear implant users as measured by the primary measures of music audiation: An item analysis. *Journal of Music Therapy* 29(1):18–39.

Gfeller, K. E., and R. Schum. 1994. Requisites for conversation: Engendering world knowledge. In *Let's converse: A "how-to" guide to develop and expand conversational skills of children and teenagers who are hearing impaired,* edited by N. Tye-Murray, 177–214. Washington, DC: Alexander Graham Bell Association.

Gfeller, K. E., and S. Witt. 1997. A qualitative assessment of music listening experiences by adult cochlear implant recipients. National Association for Music Therapy National Conference Research Session, November 21, Los Angeles, CA.

Gfeller, K. E., G. Woodworth, D. A. Robin, S. Witt, and J. F. Knutson. 1997. Perceptions of rhythmic and sequential pitch patterns by normally hearing adults and adult cochlear implant users. *Ear and Hearing* 18:252–260.

Heim, K. E. 1963. Musical aptitude of seven high school students in residential schools for the blind as measured by the Wing Standardized Test of Musical Intelligence. Master's thesis, University of Kansas, Lawrence.

Heward, W. L., and Orlansky, M. D. 1988. *Exceptional Children.* Columbus, OH: Merrill Publishing Co.

Hixon, T. J., L. D. Shriberg, and J. H. Saxman, eds. 1980. *Introduction to communication disorders.* Englewood Cliffs, NJ: Prentice Hall.

Hudgins, C. V. 1949. A method of appraising the speech of the deaf. *Volta Review* 51:597–601, 638.

Hummel, C. J. 1971. The value of music in teaching deaf students. *Volta Review* 73:224–228.

Kirk, S., and J. Gallagher. 1979. *Educating exceptional children.* 3d ed. Boston: Houghton Mifflin.

Korduba, O. M. 1975. Duplicated rhythmic patterns between deaf and normal-hearing children. *Journal of Music Therapy* 12:136–146.

Kwalwasser, J. 1955. Exploring the musical mind. New York: Colman Ross.

Ling, D., and M. Milne. 1981. The development of speech in hearing-impaired children. In *Amplification in education,* edited by F. Bess, B. A. Freeman, S. Sinclair, and J. S. Sinclair, 10–27. Washington, DC: Alexander Graham Bell Association.

Meadow, K. 1980a. *Deafness and child development.* Los Angeles: University of California Press.

———. 1980b. *Meadow/Kendall social-emotional assessment inventory for deaf students.* Washington, DC: Gallaudet College.

Music Therapy Sourcebook 1997. 1997. National Association for Music Therapy: Colesville, MD.

Norris, M., P. Spaulding, and J. Brodie. 1957. *Blindness in children.* Chicago: University of Chicago Press.

Padden, C., and T. Humphries. 1988. *Deaf in America.* Cambridge, MA: Harvard University Press.

Pitman, D. J. 1965. The musical ability of blind children. *American Foundation for Blind Research Bulletin* 11:63–79.

Riordian, J. T. 1971. *They can sing too: Rhythm for the deaf.* Springfield, VA: Jenrich Associates.

Robbins, C., and C. Robbins. 1980. *Music with the hearing-impaired: A resource manual and curriculum guide.* St. Louis, MO: Magnamusic-Baton.

Sakurabayashi, H. Y., Y. Satyo, and E. Uehara. 1956. Auditory discrimination of the blind. *Japanese Journal of Psychology of the Blind* 1:3–10.

Schum, R., and K. Gfeller. 1994. Engendering social skills. In *Let's converse: A "how-to" guide to develop and expand conversational skills of children and teenagers who are hearing impaired,* edited by N. Tye-Murray, 147–176. Washington, DC: Alexander Graham Bell Association.

Seashore, C. E., and T. Ling. 1918. The comparative sensitiveness of blind and seeing persons. *Psychological Monographs* 25:148–158.

Stankov, L., and G. Spillsbury. 1978. The measurement of auditory abilities of sighted, partially sighted, and blind children. *Applied Psychological Measurement* 2:491–503.

Vettese, J. 1974. Instrumental lessons for deaf children. *Volta Review* 76:19–22.

10

MUSIC THERAPY IN THE TREATMENT OF MEDICAL CONDITIONS

Kate E. Gfeller

CHAPTER OUTLINE

The use of music in the treatment of medical conditions is centuries old. In ancient times, priests and witch doctors used chants and rhythms to ward off the evil spirits assumed to cause illness and affliction. Music was believed to possess supernatural powers and could either heal directly or through appealing to beneficent gods (Gfeller 1990).

In modern times, music is still used in medical treatment, but the rationale has changed. Contemporary applications of music for the treatment of chronic and acute medical conditions are based on scientific principles substantiated through research. As a member of the medical team, the music therapist works with the patient to alleviate the negative impact of disease, trauma, or a debilitating condition.

Music therapists serve a variety of patient groups in a variety of medical settings (Standley 1986). In a general hospital, the therapist may work with patients undergoing surgical procedures or chemotherapy, women in labor and delivery, burn victims, and persons with acute or chronic illness. In an outpatient facility, a music therapist may assist clients suffering from chronic pain or undergoing tedious or uncomfortable rehabilitation. Hospice programs, which provide support and comfort for terminally ill patients, may offer music therapy services. Although patient needs vary, they can be grouped into two broad areas: (1) *physical needs* and (2) *psychosocial needs.*

PHYSICAL NEEDS

The physical needs of medical patients differ depending on their conditions. However, there are two common foci of music therapy services: (1) *pain reduction and tolerance for treatment procedures* and (2) *improved muscular functioning.*

Pain Reduction and Tolerance for Treatment Procedures

Pain is a complex phenomenon (Sarafino 1997). It can be acute (i.e., of short duration) or chronic. It can have sudden or gradual onset. It may be sensed in a location far removed from the location of injury, and it can vary in quality (stabbing, dull, throbbing, searing, etc.). It may stem from tissue damage and insult to nerve endings but cannot simply be explained in physical terms. Emotional and cognitive factors contribute to the severity of perceived pain (Anderson and Masur 1983; Gracely et al. 1978; Jacox 1977; Sarafino 1997). Anxiety, tension, fear, and perceived loss of control can accompany and exacerbate feelings of distress and pain. Anxiety and tension contribute to the perception of pain in several ways. These negative emotions can lead to increased muscle tension, which, in turn, can create greater pressure on already sensitive nerve endings (Jacox 1977). Tension can also interfere with normally relaxed breathing patterns and cause deoxygenation, or oxygen deficits, in muscle tissue (Clark et al. 1981). This, too, can increase discomfort. Moreover, anxiety or fear can heighten a person's attention to the pain, thus increasing its perceived severity.

Many aspects of pain perception can be explained by a principle known as the Gate Control Theory of Pain (Melzack and Wall 1965, 1982; Sarafino 1997). According to this theory, actual physical insult occurs in nerve endings throughout the body, but awareness and interpretation of the stimulation takes place in the central nervous system (CNS). A neural "gate" can be opened or closed to varying degree, thus modulating the incoming pain signals before they reach the brain (Sarafino 1997). When a pain signal enters the spinal cord and the gate is open, transmission cells send the pain impulses freely. But if the gate is closed, the strength of the pain signal to the brain will be modulated. The extent to which the gate is open or closed depends on (1) the amount of noxious stimulation (the more pain, the more active the pain fibers), (2) the amount of sensation in other peripheral fibers (competing stimuli such as massage or rubbing), and (3) the messages that descend from the brain (e.g., the effects of some brain processes such as anxiety or excitement can open or close the gate for all or some types of inputs).

This theory, developed in the 1960s, has been upheld by numerous research studies over the past few decades, and continues to be one of the most influential and important theories of pain perception. In particular, it has been able to demonstrate the tremendous importance of psychosocial variables, and it accommodates biological aspects of pain as well (Sarafino 1997).

How might this theory be illustrated in everyday life? Even while pain stimuli is occurring, the central nervous system is taking in other stimuli as well: the sound of people talking, the smells in the room, a program on television, and car horns honking in the street. Because the CNS can process only limited amounts of information at any given time, these sensations compete with the pain stimulus for attention. As a result of the limited capacity of conscious awareness, our perception of pain is reduced to the extent that we direct attention to other internal or external stimuli (i.e., conversation, music, etc.) (Farthing et al. 1984). In other words, if conscious awareness (attention) can be focused on a strong, positive stimulus rather than the pain, the perception of pain can thus be attenuated (Anderson and Masur 1983; Farthing et al. 1984; Jacox 1977; Melzack and Wall 1982).

> Nine-year old Carlos is home from school today because he has strep throat. He hates being sick! He hates the fiery feeling in his throat, and it hurts whenever he swallows. His forehead is pounding, and all his joints and muscles feel just rotten. How can he possibly endure this for another minute? After school, his friend George stops by to visit, and tells him all about the big event at school today. Evidently, some of the frogs got out of the classroom terrarium and started jumping all around the room. The girls were screaming and the teacher was racing around in her high heels and nice dress, trying to catch the frogs. It was complete chaos!
>
> Carlos's mother has just stopped by his room to see how he is feeling and is surprised to see her suffering son with a smile on his face. His pain, for now, seems bearable. The stronger and entertaining stimulus of George's story of the frogs at school (which acts as a form of distraction) has won the battle for attention from Carlos's central nervous system.

A number of methods of pain management based on the Gate Control Theory of Pain have been developed, including distraction. There are many examples of positive stimuli that can act as distractors. Researchers have used stimuli such as video games, tapes of music or comedy routines, movies, and stories (Anderson and Masur 1983). In everyday life, nurses and other caregivers have found conversation, mental tasks (i.e., solving a puzzle), and forms of entertainment (TV, music) to be of assistance (Jacox 1977; Sarafino 1997). In the clinical setting, some forms of stimuli are more easily provided than others. Music is one stimulus that can be administered with little expense or inconvenience.

Music Therapy Interventions for Pain Control

In today's world of sophisticated medications and treatments, why would the use of music as an aid to pain control be of value? First, because perception of pain is influenced by mental as well as physical factors, it is important to address both areas (Colwell 1997; Gfeller et al. 1990; Godley 1987; Jacox 1977; Sarafino 1997; Standley 1986).

Second, some medical conditions cannot be remedied through surgical methods, and analgesics may not provide adequate relief over extended periods of time. For example, someone with cancer may suffer great pain and receive only partial relief from medication (Sarafino 1997). Furthermore, some patients object to the confusion or other negative side effects that accompany strong narcotics.

Maintaining mental clarity is of particular concern for patients in hospice care. Hospice, or palliative, care consists of the reduction or abatement of pain and other troubling symptoms experienced by terminally ill patients (Munro 1984). Hospice care personnel typically serve individuals with terminal illnesses who no longer wish to have extraordinary measures taken to prolong life; rather, these terminally ill persons wish to spend their remaining days in an environment as close to normal as possible, which provides physical and emotional support. In preparation for death, many individuals feel the need to secure the financial welfare of their families and come to terms with feelings about their own mortality. In order to attend to these issues, mental clarity is important. Therefore, the use of heavy medication may be undesirable.

In some instances, it is important to reduce the amount of anesthesia administered during surgery, especially if the standard dose might suppress respiratory functioning or cause mental sluggishness. For example, it is important to avoid the latter problem in outpatient surgeries. Childbirth is another area for which an adjustment is indicated, because anesthesia might place the baby at risk.

Techniques that make use of the power of the human mind to reduce the perception of pain are called *cognitive pain control strategies* (Sarafino 1997). Cognitive pain control methods are not intended to eliminate traditional pharmacological painkillers. However, there are circumstances in which medication is contraindicated or a reduced dosage is desirable (Scartelli 1989). In these instances, cognitive means for reducing pain should be considered.

There are several ways that music can be used in conjunction with cognitive pain control strategies to reduce the perception of pain: (1) *as a stimulus for active focus or distraction,* (2) *to facilitate a relaxation response,* (3) *as a masking agent,* (4) *as an information agent,* and (5) *as a positive environmental stimulus.*

Music as a Stimulus for Active Focus or Distraction One method of reducing pain perception is to use a preferred selection of music as a positive and competing stimulus to reduce attention to the negative aspects of pain or an uncomfortable medical procedure (such as outpatient surgery, cardiac testing, or dental procedures). This approach is based on the Gate Control Theory of Pain. According to Clark and colleagues (1981), the music is an active focal point, and the patient is coached and encouraged to focus on and follow the music, thereby taking a more active role in his or her pain management. When used as a distractor or focal point, the selected music must hold the interest and attention of the patient. It should either be chosen directly by the patient or at least be a style he or she enjoys (Clark et al. 1981; Gfeller et al. 1990; Godley 1987; Standley 1986).

Jeannie is a music therapist at Mercy Hospital. One of the services she provides is helping expectant mothers prepare for childbirth. She joins the Lamaze teacher at a number of Lamaze classes, and explains to the mothers-to-be how they can use music to help manage their pain during labor and delivery. Jeannie explains that music can act as a distractor or focal point to help reduce the intensity of the pain. Because each of the expectant mothers in the class has different musical tastes, Jeannie knows that one kind of music will not work for everyone. If the music is being used as a focal point or for distraction, it needs to hold the attention of the individual. That might mean upbeat music rather than slow or relaxing music.

Jeannie meets with the mothers, has them fill out inventories that describe what kinds of music they enjoy, including particular favorites, and then works with each mother to select music for an individualized tape for the delivery room. After each of the expectant mothers has her childbirth tape ready, Jeannie works with the group to practice how distraction or focus can be used as a pain management strategy in preparation for the big event.

The use of music to reduce the pain or discomfort in surgery or a treatment procedure has been documented in a number of medical settings, including dental treatment (Gardener and Licklider 1959; Gfeller et al. 1990; Monsey 1960; Standley 1986), labor and delivery (Burt and Korn 1964; Clark 1986; Clark et al. 1981; Hanser et al. 1983; Standley 1986), chronic pain programs (Colwell 1997; Godley 1987), pediatric units, to reduce distress response to injections and other procedures (Malone, 1996), and surgical units (Locsin 1981; Standley 1986; Walters 1996). Although this strategy can be effective, research has shown that no single pain control technique works for every person in every circumstance (Anderson and Masur 1983; Jacox 1977). For example, distraction can be especially useful as a technique for people who like to ignore or avoid the procedure as it occurs. However, other people, referred to in pain research as "monitors," tend to feel less anxious if they can receive continual information about what is happening and why (Sarafino 1997). For that kind of individual, distraction may be less effective. Another limitation of active focusing is that it requires sustained concentration. If the patient experiences intense and prolonged pain, fatigue eventually sets in and reduces the effectiveness. Other strategies must then be engaged (Jacox 1977). Therefore, therapists assisting in pain management should be skilled in a variety of pain control methods (Sarafino 1997).

Music as a Cue for Relaxation Response Muscular relaxation is another approach that can reduce pain (Clark et al. 1981; Colwell 1997; Godley 1987; Jacox 1977; Standley 1986). Relaxation is a response that is considered incompatible with tension (Jacox 1977; Scartelli 1989). As relaxation occurs, the patient experiences reduced muscle tension, along with deeper and more even respiration. This reduces muscular pressure on nerve endings and reinstates a steady supply of oxygen to muscle tissue. In addition, relaxation can reduce anxiety and fear, psychological correlates that can make the pain or treatment seem more intolerable (Godley 1987; Jacox 1977; Robb et al. 1995; Standley 1986).

Music can be used in conjunction with relaxation techniques (Bonny 1989; Clark et al. 1981; Colwell 1997; Godley 1987; Jacobsen 1934; Robb et al. 1995; Scartelli 1989). The music therapist assesses the patient's musical preference, and together they select music that is pleasurable and promotes relaxation. For example, a slow, steady beat can prompt even, deep respiration. Music that evokes vivid images can guide thoughts to pleasant scenes such as serene meadows or a bank of fluffy white clouds.

One limitation to relaxation strategies is that the techniques must be learned and practiced over a period of time in order to be effective (Clark et al. 1981; Godley 1987; Jacox 1977; Scartelli 1989). Therefore, they are used infrequently in cases of acute pain or singular treatment procedures (such as a tooth extraction). If, however, lingering pain or repeated treatments are anticipated, or if adequate preparation time is available (as in childbirth), the patient can learn to relax using music in conjunction with other methods, such as progressive relaxation or guided imagery. The role of the music therapist, then, includes not only selecting and providing music, but also training and coaching the client on relaxation techniques (Clark et al. 1981; Godley 1987; Standley 1986).

Music as a cue for relaxation can be beneficial in a variety of treatment settings, including chronic pain control (Colwell 1997; Godley 1987), rehabilitation programs for physically disabled clients with muscle tension (Scartelli 1982, 1984), labor and delivery (Clark 1986; Clark et al. 1981; Hanser et al. 1983), and medical–surgical units, including pediatric surgical units (Robb et al. 1995; Siegel 1983).

Let's go back to Jeannie's program for expectant mothers. In addition to introducing music as a distractor or focal point, Jeannie explains that music can be an effective tool in conjunction with relaxation techniques. If music is used for this purpose, Jeannie will work with the patient to identify music that will be relaxing to the patient, can help induce steady and deep breathing, and may be useful in eliciting beautiful and relaxing images. Because no single pain management technique works for all people in all situations, Jeannie's two-pronged approach—giving the mothers music for distraction or focus, and other music to promote relaxation—gives the expectant mothers a menu of pain control strategies they can chose from as needed during delivery.

Music as a Masking Agent A number of factors contribute to fear and anxiety during medical treatment. Some are external elements, such as the sounds produced by equipment or cries of pain from other patients. For example, some people find the sound of the dental drill anxiety producing (Rankin and Harris 1984). As the drill whirs and whines, the patient's tension mounts. In hospital settings, the clanging of equipment or the cries of other patients can be unnerving (Clark et al. 1981). Music played through headphones can mask some of these unpleasant sounds and therefore avert some of the anxiety caused by outside agents (Gfeller et al. 1990; Standley 1986).

Music as an Information Agent One of the cognitive interventions believed to reduce negative psychological correlates of pain is the provision of information regarding the experience of pain during medical procedures (Anderson and Masur 1983; Jacox 1977; Sarafino 1997). For example, it is common for nurses or doctors to explain or interpret physical sensations (i.e., "You will feel a short sting, followed by some pressure") when they administer injections as a way of reducing the anxiety about the procedure. Preparing an individual for a medical procedure such as surgery can assist in alleviation of fear and can facilitate postprocedural recovery (Sarafino 1997).

Music as a carrier of information has proven beneficial toward this end (Chetta 1981). For example, preoperative teaching sessions for hospitalized children can include songs imparting information about surgery and the various people (doctors, nurses) who will be encountered.

One of Jeannie's responsibilities at the hospital is to help children in pediatrics prepare for surgery or other uncomfortable procedures. In the music therapy cart that she wheels to pediatrics, she has not only some musical instruments, but also puppets that are dressed liked doctors, nurses, and other kinds of medical personnel. Kyle, a four-year-old who is scheduled for surgery the next day, is on Jeannie's list to receive music therapy today. She goes to his room and puts on a puppet show with the medical puppets, in which she introduces the primary personnel that Kyle will meet, and the sorts of basic procedures they will do as they prepare Kyle for surgery. Jeannie sings the song, "Who Are the People in the Hospital?" as she introduces each puppet, and each special puppet is introduced with a particular song that Jeannie has written. Although this looks like play time, specialists in pediatric care have found that such play can make a significant difference in helping children adjust to the hospital and procedures.

Music as a Positive Environmental Stimulus Medical treatment often takes place is a sterile environment unfamiliar to the patient. The room may be filled with unpleasant smells (such as the odor of disinfectant), large ominous-looking equipment, and bustling medical personnel who do not always have the time to establish a rapport with, and address the psychological concerns of, each patient. Especially for young children, an environment so radically different from home and school can create fears and anxiety (Barrickman 1989; Marley 1984; Rudenberg 1985; Sarafino 1997; Schwankovsky and Guthrie 1985). Furthermore, the patients are frequently the passive recipients of treatment intervention, with little control over their schedules or even their own bodies. This lack of control is another source of stress and can exacerbate perception of pain (Gfeller et al. 1990; Langer 1983; Lefcourt 1982; Meinhart and McCaffery 1983; Sarafino 1997).

Even though perceived loss of control may be unavoidable in some medical circumstances (e.g., if an arm must be strapped to an IV, or if a patient is too ill to control his or her own activities), patients can reestablish some control and introduce familiarity into the environment with access to preferred music (Barrickman 1989; Gfeller et al. 1990). In addition, music as an aesthetic medium provides positive sensory stimulation in an otherwise sterile, isolated, or seemingly hostile environment. For example, Christenberry (1979) reported that burn patients, as a result of isolation policies aimed at infection control, often lack appropriate sensory stimulation. As a result, patients may turn to inappropriate internal self-stimulation (i.e., hallucinations) or become less tolerant of the medical procedures. Music provides a positive form of sensory stimulation in this sterile, isolated environment.

The positive influence of music in a medical environment can be demonstrated not only through psychological measures of perceived well-being, but also through physiological changes. For example, Chapman (1975) and Caine (1991) found that premature infants exposed to lullabies and other appropriate musical stimuli showed greater weight gain and were discharged from the hospital sooner than infants without this positive stimulation. Cassidy and Standley (1995) found that the introduction of lullabies to low-birth-weight infants in a neonatal intensive care unit results in positive effects on oxygen saturation levels, heart rate, and respiratory rate. Several studies comparing medical treatment with and without music have demonstrated reduction in blood pressure or heart rate in the music condition (Bonny 1983; Locsin 1981; Oyama et al. 1983). Studies by Locsin (1981) and Burt and Korn (1964) found that musical stimuli in conjunction with medical procedures led to reduced doses of pain medication.

The Future of Pain Control: Biochemical Aspects As we have seen, pain perception is complex. Researchers are actively searching to learn how pain functions and how it can be reduced. Recent studies have shown that the human body responds to pain or stress by producing various chemicals. Some of these substances are a by-product of pain or stress. Others like endogenous opioids (such as endorphins) are chemicals the body produces that actually help reduce discomfort (Sarafino 1997; Scartelli 1989). These chemicals seem to function in a similar way to reduce pain as do drugs such as morphine. Preliminary research (Goldstein 1980; Rider et al. 1985; Tanioka et al. 1985) suggests that musical stimuli may influence biochemical production and subsequently reduce discomfort. Although further research is needed to fully understand this avenue of inquiry, it is already apparent that this area of research holds important implications for future treatment interventions.

Improved Muscle Functioning

In some instances, treatment of a medical condition includes a period of physical therapy and rehabilitation. For example, after a stroke some people must "relearn" how to walk or use their limbs. This requires many hours of tedious, tiring exercise. Music can provide an ideal background for rehabilitation. First, enjoyable or inspirational music can reduce the patient's awareness of the negative aspects of therapy, such as its discomfort and monotony. Second, a strong, rhythmic beat provides a steady auditory cue to help with motor planning. In other words, the patient can use the musical beat as a signal to move one or more limbs (Lucia 1987; Rudenberg and Royka 1989; Standley 1986; Staum 1983; Thaut 1985).

Adequate muscle functioning not only involves mobility of the arms and legs, but also includes internal organs, such as the lungs. Proper expansion of the lungs is important because it helps reduce congestion and improve respiratory function. Playing wind instruments or singing can help promote the lung activity of bedridden patients. Such activities can also help maintain the level of respiratory function in patients with chronic conditions, such as asthma (Behrens 1982; Bolger 1984; Rudenberg and Royka 1989; Schwankovsky and Guthrie 1985; Standley 1986).

PSYCHOSOCIAL NEEDS

Acute and chronic medical conditions have an impact not only on a person's physical well-being, but also on emotional and social functioning (Christenberry 1979; Colwell 1997; Godley 1987; Munro 1984; Rudenberg and Royka 1989; Sarafino 1997; Schwankovsky and Guthrie 1985; Standley 1986). According to Schwankovsky and Guthrie (1985), a person with an acute or chronic medical condition characteristically has a number of psychosocial needs:

1 To adapt to the illness and its limitations
2 To help the family adjust to the illness
3 To adjust to the hospital environment
4 To learn and use appropriate coping mechanisms
5 To reduce fear and anxiety about the illness and prescribed treatment
6 To maintain an environment as close to normal as possible, or normalization
7 To continue cognitive and social development
8 To prevent or overcome developmental delays resulting from the illness or the treatment
9 To engage in physical activity
10 To face issues related to one's own mortality

Some of these concerns are direct by-products of the illness itself. For example, a patient with a respiratory illness may have difficulty adjusting to loss of vitality. Other needs result from the subsequent loss of independence, normal routine, and quality of life that accompany hospitalization or convalescence. For example, a patient hospitalized for eye surgery may be unable to read, drive, or work. These limitations could lead to increased dependence on others for financial support, transportation, and activities of daily living.

The music therapist can help the patient adjust to these limitations through (1) *provision of normalizing activities that promote social, motor, and cognitive development,* and (2) *provision of emotional support through music activities that explore or encourage appropriate expression of feelings related to the illness.*

Normalization

Normalization is the process of integrating objects, events, and interactions that resemble everyday life (are normal) into the medical environment. Patients, both young and old, can benefit from normalization of the hospital environment. However, given the developmental differences between children and adults, the types of intervention will differ. First, let us consider normalization in the pediatric (children's medicine) setting.

Normalization in Pediatrics In a normal environment, a child's typical day includes school, playtime and other social activities, and household responsibilities. Children interact with their parents, teachers, siblings, and peers. In contrast, a hospitalized child spends many hours in an unfamiliar bed in an unfamiliar room with unfamiliar adults who administer injections, intravenous (IV) lines, and X rays. The youngster has limited exposure to family members and other children. The typical routines of going to school, participating in Scouts, and feeding the dog are disrupted. These changes can create anxiety and frustration, which may be expressed through tantrums, withdrawal, or other inappropriate coping mechanisms (Barrickman 1989; Schwankovsky and Guthrie 1985). If prolonged hospitalization is required, the child misses school as well. Consequently, development of social and academic skills may be arrested or delayed. Hospitalization is not a typical childhood experience, but musical activity is. Music can be a valuable tool for normalization of the medical environment, by providing opportunities for play and physical activity, social interaction with peers, and cognitive growth. Each of these areas is briefly discussed in the following section.

Play and Physical Activities Play is a natural means for young children to explore the environment, express thoughts and feelings, and learn new skills (Froelich 1984; Schwankovsky and Guthrie 1985). Learning musical games, playing with musical toys (windup animals, mobiles, and rhythm band instruments), singing, and moving to music are all common childhood activities (Barrickman 1989). Even toddlers can enjoy these experiences because music involves sensory and motor experiences within the developmental capability of the young child (Barrickman 1989; McDonald and Simons 1989). Familiar childhood songs, such as "Old MacDonald," the "Itsy-Bitsy Spider," and "London Bridges," seem like old friends in a strange or seemingly hostile environment. According to Marley (1984), musical games and activities reduce stress-related behaviors in infants and toddlers.

Unfortunately, illness or medical treatments can impede normal childhood motor activity. Children with chronic respiratory or heart conditions may lack the physical strength and vitality to run and play. Children recovering from surgery or orthopedic interventions may have diminished mobility because of IV tubes, traction, or casts. These limitations may prohibit participation in jump rope, baseball, or other games that require full mobility and endurance. But physical activity need not end altogether. The music therapist can involve the child in music and movement activities to the extent physically possible. For example, a patient with one arm immobilized because of a cast or an IV can vigorously play a rhythm instrument with the other arm. Children confined to bed or wheelchairs can participate in action songs or finger plays (children's songs that use finger motions to help illustrate the story in the song, such as "Where Is Thumbkin?" or "Two Little Blackbirds") that encourage upper body or facial movement (Barrickman 1989).

Structured Social Interaction In nursery schools all over the world, children hold hands, sing, and move as a group during music activities. Even independent two-year-olds can be drawn into a group activity featuring a favorite musical game (McDonald and Simons 1989). Music, traditionally a medium for social involvement, can be introduced into the medical milieu to increase social interaction (Gfeller 1990). Group singing, rhythm band activities, action songs, and finger plays provide opportunities to cooperate, become aware of others, and share ideas. Even shy children can participate nonverbally by playing rhythm instruments, clapping, or performing actions to songs (Barrickman 1989).

Preacademic Activities Because a serious illness interferes with school attendance, academic development can suffer. Educational services, such as homebound or hospital-based teachers, can help the child maintain academic progress. The music therapist can help by introducing or reinforcing academic and preacademic concepts (colors, numbers, shapes, and other knowledge learned prior to kindergarten) through music activities that are fun and age appropriate. Many childhood songs ("Mary Has a Red Dress," "The Wheels on the Bus," "Old MacDonald," etc.) teach information about colors, shapes, community helpers, animals, and other concepts learned in preschool and elementary classrooms (Barrickman 1989; Schwankovsky and Guthrie 1985).

Normalization and Adults The cries and screams of a young child that can accompany medical treatment are clear indicators that the child is afraid. But we should not assume from the relatively quiet demeanor of an adult receiving medical treatment that all is well. Adults, too, have negative reactions to a sterile hospital room and a disruption in lifestyle (Sarafino 1997).

Normalization of the hospital environment for adult patients occurs by providing social opportunities and meaningful leisure activities adapted to fit the individual's level of functioning. For example, group singing or improvisation on musical instruments encourages socialization among patients or between a patient and his or her family (Munro 1984; Standley 1986). The tedium of long-term hospitalization or restricted movement can be ameliorated through involvement in musical leisure activities. Small, portable instruments, such as synthesizers, autoharps, or kalimbas, can be learned in a short period of time, even by patients with minimal musical training (Munro 1984).

Emotional Support

Chronic and acute illnesses have adverse effects on emotional, as well as physical, well-being. Fear or anxiety concerning the illness or treatment, separation from loved ones, adaptation to the illness, and awareness of one's own mortality are all important concerns during medical treatment. One dramatic example is the emotional concerns of patients with AIDS, a failure of the immune system that presently has no cure. Because of the typically fatal outcome of this condition, people who contract AIDS may be ostracized or the focus of negative comments. Feelings of isolation, guilt, or helplessness may be as devastating as the physical effects of the condition (Maranto 1988).

As was discussed in Chapter 3, music has long been regarded as a powerful form of communication through which we express our deepest emotions. Music with special spiritual or sentimental meaning can provide comfort and support. The music therapist facilitates activities such as writing songs, listening to music, relaxing to music, and drawing to music that encourage emotional expression and well-being (Colwell 1997).

In a hospice setting, music therapy can be an important tool for exploring and expressing feelings about impending death (Gilbert 1977; Munro 1984; O'Callaghan 1997; West 1994). Some individuals, for example, have found music an effective way to share feelings with family and friends. For example, Munro (1984) tells of a terminally ill patient who, with the assistance of a music therapist, created a musical collage on tape as a parting gift for loved ones.

Expression of feelings has particular importance in the pediatric ward because young children often find it difficult to articulate their emotions in an unfamiliar setting. Research by Froelich (1984) indicated that hospitalized children involved in music therapy were more willing to verbalize feelings than were a similar group of children who had experienced more traditional forms of intervention. In short, the music therapist can offer important support in reducing the psychological and emotional impact of medical conditions. Although the music therapist's greatest reward is a smile of relief or giggle of happiness, it is nevertheless important for the therapist to determine treatment effectiveness through objective as well as subjective assessment.

ASSESSMENT PROCEDURES

The needs and physical characteristics of medical patients vary greatly. Therefore, the music therapist is challenged to select realistic, appropriate tools for assessing the patient's condition. In so doing, we must not underestimate the importance of sensitive, subjective evaluation by the therapist. Subtle changes in behavior or seemingly incidental remarks by the patient can provide important clues about physical and emotional status. Careful documentation of progress is best achieved with a variety of objective assessment tools applicable to short- or long-term treatment.

Self-Report Measures

One valuable source of information is the patient, who can provide input on physical distress, anxiety, tension, and satisfaction with treatment through interviews or written forms (Sarafino 1997). Extent of physical discomfort can be reported on descriptive or numerical scales, in which the patient indicates the intensity of pain on a horizontal or vertical line (see Figure 10-1). Other types of standardized scales, such as the McGill-Melzack Pain Questionnaire or the Stewart Pain–Color Scale provide qualitative information about pain (Stewart 1977). Similar inventories can measure anxiety or emotional well-being. For example, the State-Trait Anxiety Inventory assesses the patient's level of anxiety (Spielberger et al. 1970). Because children differ from adults with regard to cognitive abilities and language, special measures specifically designed for children should be used for young patients (Sarafino 1997).

Observation of Behavioral Responses

Observational ratings can also document patient status (Sarafino 1997). For example, muscle relaxation inventories have been used in music therapy programs during childbirth by Codding (1982) and Winokur (1984). Such inventories require that the observer indicate the level of relaxation for specific body areas, such as the forehead, jaw, neck and shoulders, and arms. Observational data on intensity, frequency, and duration of such behaviors as crying, facial distortions, restlessness, or treatment resistance can signify the patient's level of comfort or anxiety (Standley 1986). Children may demonstrate different types of behavior in response to pain than do adults, so the age of the patient should be taken into account when selecting behaviors for observation (Sarafino

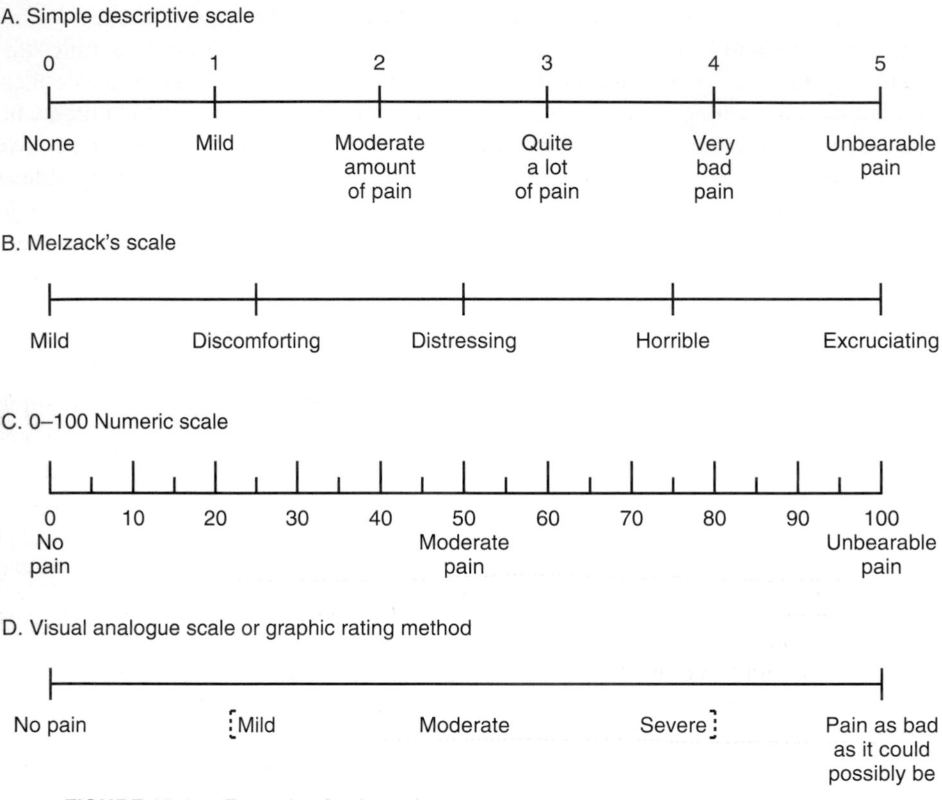

FIGURE 10-1 Example of pain scales.

1997). Because pain is a subjective phenomenon, it may be advisable to gather both self-report and observational data to get a reliable measure of patient status.

Clinical Measures

Physiological and clinical measures can also provide insight into patient progress. Blood pressure, pulse, and exhalation ability are indicators of patient status. The amount of medication needed for pain control or the length of hospitalization are sometimes appropriate measures of patient satisfaction and treatment effectiveness (Sarafino 1997; Standley 1986).

A number of measures can be used in a medical setting to determine physical or psychosocial conditions. Selection of a specific assessment tool should reflect its potential as a meaningful indicator of the patient's condition and its ease of use in the clinical milieu. Assessment should neither interfere with treatment nor inflict further distress on an already vulnerable client.

In conclusion, the music therapist working in a medical setting will find patients of all ages, and with a wide variety of conditions. The sorts of problems they encounter will depend on the nature of the condition or illness, the patients' ages, the types of procedures required, and a host of personal circumstances. All these factors need to be considered in determining the patients' needs, the appropriate sorts of interventions, what kinds of music will be acceptable, and the measures that will provide reliable information about progress. Further, the music therapist must be flexible and cooperative in working with the entire medical team, because most patients receive a variety of tests and treatments.

SUMMARY

Music therapists serve individuals who suffer from chronic or acute medical illnesses in a variety of settings, including hospitals, clinics, and hospice programs. Although the specific symptoms and problems of clients vary, music therapists generally use music to reduce the impact of physical or psychosocial problems related to the patient's illness. Music therapy may be used for the following objectives:

1 *To reduce perception of pain:* Music is used as a cognitive pain control strategy in the following ways: (a) as an active focal point or distractor to reduce awareness of pain, (b) as a cue for relaxation response, (c) as a masking agent for anxiety-producing sounds in the environment, (d) as an information agent, and (e) as a positive stimulus in the environment.

2 *To improve muscular functioning:* Music provides motivation and structure for physical activity required in rehabilitation, including mobility and respiratory functioning.

3 *To normalize the medical environment:* Musical activities provide opportunities for play and physical activity, social interaction, leisure, and academic development. Normalization can reduce the impact of hospitalization on the development of young children and enhance the emotional well-being of adults.

4 *To provide emotional support:* Music, a form of communication associated with emotions, can provide an outlet for emotional expression and be a source of comfort.

STUDY QUESTIONS

1 What is the basic principle behind the Gate Control Theory of Pain?

2 Why is music used to help relieve pain, despite the sophistication of today's medications and painkillers?

3 List and describe five ways in which music is used to reduce the perception of pain.

4 Give several examples of how music might be used toward improved muscle functioning.

5 What are some of the psychosocial needs of persons with acute or chronic medical conditions?

6 What does the term *normalization* mean?

7 Describe ways in which music is used as play and as a physical outlet for children with chronic or acute illness.

8 Describe ways in which music is used to foster social interaction among clients with chronic or acute illness.

9 Describe ways in which music is used to support the preacademic progress of children with acute or chronic illness.

10 Describe ways in which music is used to provide emotional support.

11 Describe several types of assessment methods that a music therapist might use to measure progress of patients with chronic or acute medical conditions.

REFERENCES

Anderson, K. O., and F. T. Masur. 1983. Psychological preparation for invasive medical and dental procedures. *Journal of Behavioral Medicine* 6:1–41.

Barrickman, J. 1989. A developmental music therapy approach for preschool hospitalized children. *Music Therapy Perspectives* 7:10–16.

Behrens, G. A. 1982. The use of music activities to improve the capacity inhalation and exhalation capabilities of handicapped children's respiration. Master's thesis, Kent State University, Kent, OH.

Bolger, E. P. 1984. The therapeutic value of singing. *New England Journal of Medicine* 311:1704.

Bonny, H. L. 1983. Music listening for intensive coronary care units: A pilot project. *Music Therapy* 3:4–16.

———. 1989. Sound as symbol: Guided imagery and music in clinical practice. *Music Therapy Perspectives* 6:7–10.

Burt, R. K., and G. W. Korn. 1964. Audioanalgesia in obstetrics: White noise analgesia during labor. *American Journal of Obstetrics and Gynecology* 88:361–366.

Caine, J. 1991. The effects of music on the selected stress behaviors, weight, caloric and formula intake, and length of hospital stay of premature and low-birth-weight neonates in a newborn intensive care unit. *Journal of Music Therapy* 33:180–192.

Cassidy, J. W., and J. M. Standley. 1995. The effect of music listening on physiological responses of premature infants in the NICU. *Journal of Music Therapy* 32:208–227.

Chapman, J. S. 1975. The relation between auditory stimulation of short gestation infants and their gross motor limb activity. Ph.D. diss., New York University.

Chetta, H. 1981. The effect of music and desensitization on preoperative anxiety in children. *Journal of Music Therapy* 23:74–87.

Christenberry, E. 1979. The use of music therapy with burn patients. *Journal of Music Therapy* 16:138–148.

Clark, M. E. 1986, Music-therapy-assisted childbirth: A practical guide. *Music Therapy Perspectives* 3:34–41.

Clark, M. E., R. R. McCorkle, and S. B. Williams. 1981. Music-therapy-assisted labor and delivery. *Journal of Music Therapy* 18:88–109.

Codding, P. A. 1982. An exploration of the uses of music in the birthing process. Master's thesis, Florida State University, Tallahassee, FL.

Colwell, C. 1997. Music as a distraction and relaxation to reduce chronic pain and narcotic ingestion: A case study. *Music Therapy Perspectives* 15(1):24–31.

Farthing, G. W., M. Venturino, and S. W. Brown. 1984. Suggestions and distraction in the control of pain: Test of two hypotheses. *Journal of Abnormal Psychology* 93:266–276.

Froelich, M. A. 1984. A comparison of the effect of music therapy and medical play therapy on the verbalization of pediatric patients. *Journal of Music Therapy* 21:2–15.

Gardener, E., and J. C. Licklider. 1959. Auditory analgesia in dental operation. *Journal of the American Dental Association* 59:1144–1150.

Gfeller, K. E. 1990. Cultural context as it relates to music therapy. In *Music therapy in the treatment of adult mental disorders,* edited by R. Unkefer, 63–69. New York: Schirmer.

Gfeller, K. E., H. Logan, and J. Walker. 1990. The effect of auditory distraction and suggestion on tolerance for dental restoration in adolescents and young adults. *Journal of Music Therapy* 27:13–23.

Gilbert, J. P. 1977. Music therapy perspectives on death and dying. *Journal of Music Therapy* 14:165–171.

Godley, C. A. 1987. The use of music therapy in pain clinics. *Music Therapy Perspectives* 4:24–28.

Goldstein, A. 1980. Thrills in response to music and other stimuli. *Physiological Psychology* 8:126–129.

Gracely, R. H., P. McGrath, and R. Dubner. 1978. Validity and sensitivity of ratio scales of sensory and affective verbal pain descriptors: Manipulation of affect by diazepam. *Pain* 5:768–769.

Hanser, S. B., S. C. Larson, and A. S. O'Connell. 1983. The effect of music on relaxation of expectant mothers during labor. *Journal of Music Therapy* 20:50–58.

Jacobson, E. 1934. *You must relax.* New York: McGraw-Hill.

Jacox, A. D., ed. 1977. Pain: A source book for nurses and other health professionals. Boston: Little, Brown.

Langer, E. 1983. *The psychology of control.* London: Lawrence Erlbaum.

Lefcourt, H. 1982. *Locus of control.* London: Lawrence Erlbaum.

Locsin, R. 1981. The effect of music on the pain of selected post-operative patients. *Journal of Advanced Nursing* 6:19–25.

Lucia, C. M. 1987. Toward developing a model of music therapy intervention in the rehabilitation of head and trauma patients. *Music Therapy Perspectives* 4:34–39.

Malone, A. 1996. The effects of live music on the distress of pediatric patients receiving intravenous starts, venipunctures, injections, and heel sticks. *Journal of Music Therapy* 33:19–33.

Maranto, C. 1988. AIDS: Information and issues for music therapists. *Music Therapy Perspectives* 5:78–81.

Marley, L. S. 1984. The use of music with hospitalized infants and toddlers: A descriptive study. *Journal of Music Therapy* 21:126–132.

McDonald, D. T., and G. M. Simons. 1989. *Musical growth and development: Birth through six.* New York: Schirmer Books.

Meinhart, N. T., and M. McCaffery. 1983. *Pain: A nursing approach to assessment and analysis.* Norwalk, CT: Appleton-Century-Crofts.

Melzack, R., and P. D. Wall. 1965. Pain mechanisms: A new theory. *Science* 150:971–979.

———. 1982. *The challenge of pain.* New York: Basic Books.

Monsey, H. L. 1960. Preliminary report of the clinical efficacy of audioanalgesia. *Journal of the California State Dental Association* 36:432–437.

Munro, S. 1984. Music therapy in palliative/hospice care. St. Louis, MO: Magnamusic-Baton.

O'Callaghan, C. 1997. Therapeutic opportunities associated with the music when using song writing in palliative care. *Music Therapy Perspectives* 15:32–38.

Oyama, T., K. Hatano, Y. Sato, M. Kudo, R. Spintge, and R. Droh. 1983. Endocrine effect of axiolytic music in dental patients. In *Angst, schmerz musik in der anasthesie,* edited by R. Droh and R. Spintge, 143–146. Basel, Switzerland: Editiones Roche.

Rankin, J. A., and M. R. Harris. 1984. Dental anxiety: The patient's point of view. *Journal of the American Dental Association* 109:43–47.

Rider, M., J. Floyd, and J. Kirkpatrick. 1985. The effects of music, imagery, and relaxation on adrenal corticosteroids and the re-entrainment of circadian rhythms. *Journal of Music Therapy* 22:46–58.

Robb, S. L., R. J. Nichols, R. L. Rutan, B. L. Bishop, and J. C. Parker. 1995. The effects of music-assisted relaxation on preoperative anxiety. *Journal of Music Therapy* 32:2–21.

Rudenberg, M. T. 1985. Music therapy for orthopedically handicapped children. In *Music therapy for handicapped children,* vol. 3, edited by W. Lathom and C. Eagle, 37–116. Lawrence, KS: Meseraull Printing.

Rudenberg, M. T., and A. M. Royka. 1989. Promoting psychosocial adjustment in pediatric burn patients through music therapy and child life therapy. *Music Therapy Perspectives* 7:40–43.

Sarafino, E. P. 1997. *Health psychology: Biopsychosocial interactions.* 3d ed. New York: Wiley.

Scartelli, J. P. 1982. The effect of sedative music on electromyographic-biofeedback-assisted relaxation training of spastic cerebral-palsied adults. *Journal of Music Therapy* 19:210–218.

———. 1984. The effect of EMG biofeedback and sedative music, EMG biofeedback only, and sedative music only on frontalis muscle relaxation ability. *Journal of Music Therapy* 21:67–78.

———. 1989. *Music and self-management methods.* St. Louis, MO: Magnamusic-Baton.

Schwankovsky, L. M., and P. T. Guthrie. 1985. Music therapy for other health-impaired children. In *Music therapy for handicapped children,* edited by W. Lathom and C. Eagle, 119–167. Lawrence, KS: Meseraull Printing.

Siegel, S. L. 1983. The use of music as a treatment in pain perception with post-surgical patients in a pediatric hospital. Master's thesis, University of Miami, Coral Gables, FL.

Spielberger, D. D., R. L. Gorsuch, and R. Luschene. 1970. *State-trait anxiety inventory.* Palo Alto, CA: Consulting Psychologist Press.

Standley, J. M. 1986. Music research in medical/dental treatment: Meta-analysis and clinical applications. *Journal of Music Therapy* 21:184–193.

Staum, M. L. 1983. Music and rhythmic stimuli in the rehabilitation of gait disorders. *Journal of Music Therapy* 20:69–87.

Stewart, M. L. 1977. Measurement of clinical pain. In *Pain: A source book for nurses and other health professionals,* edited by A. K. Jacox, 107–137. Boston: Little, Brown.

Tanioka, F., T. Takzawa, S. Kamata, M. Kudo, A. Matsuki, and T. Oyama. 1985. Hormonal effect of anxiolytic music in patients during surgical operation under epidural anesthesia. In *Angst, schmerz, musik in der anasthesie,* edited by R. Froh and R. Spintge, 285–290. Basel, Switzerland: Editiones Roche.

Thaut, M. 1985. The use of auditory rhythm and rhythmic speech to aide temporal muscular control in children with gross motor dysfunction. *Journal of Music Therapy* 22:108–128.

Walters, C. 1996. The psychological and physiological effects of vibrotactile stimulation, via a somatron, on patients awaiting scheduled gynecological surgery. *Journal of Music Therapy* 33:261–267.

West, T. M. 1994. Psychological issues in hospice music therapy. *Music Therapy Perspectives* 12:117–124.

Winokur, M. A. 1984. The use of music as an audio-analgesia during childbirth. Master's thesis, Florida State University, Tallahassee, FL.

11

MUSIC THERAPY IN NEUROLOGICAL REHABILITATION

Michael H. Thaut

CHAPTER OUTLINE

STROKE

Prevalence

Stroke constitutes one of the most common and disabling neurological diseases in adult life. It is estimated that 450,000 to 500,000 people are affected by some form of stroke each year, and the estimated financial cost for the health care system exceeds $7 billion per year. The majority of stroke victims survive over an appreciable time (fatality rate in acute stroke stage is only 15 percent). However, 50 percent of all survivors will suffer permanent neurological disability resulting in a complete or partial loss of some physical or cognitive function (Wade et al. 1985).

Definition

The technical term for stroke is cerebralvascular accident (CVA). A stroke occurs when blood supply to a part of the brain is suddenly interrupted. The cells in the affected part of the brain do not receive the necessary supply of oxygen to function and consequently die or become damaged (Wade et al. 1985).

Etiology and Diagnosis

Several causes of stroke have been identified at various frequencies among stroke victims. The different causes are usually categorized into two main groups: **ischemia** and **intracranial hemorrhage.**

Ischemic strokes are caused by blockage of an artery (blood vessel) that supplies blood to the brain. For example, arteriosclerosis (a disease causing thickening and hardening of the walls of the arteries that supply the brain with blood) or fatty deposits on the inner walls of the arteries may obstruct blood flow to the brain. If the obstruction is only temporary, an incomplete stroke or **transient ischemic attack** (TIA) may occur, which can last from a few seconds to several minutes. A TIA must be considered a signal for an impending complete stroke in the future. Other ischemic strokes may be caused by a blood clot, also called **thrombus,** which may develop on the arteriosclerotic deposits within an artery, closing off an artery and resulting in a condition called *cerebral (brain) thrombosis.* A third type of arterial blockage, embolism, is caused by a moving blood clot, called an **embolus,** which has broken away from a thrombus, usually in the heart, and lodges in an artery, cutting off blood supply to the brain.

The most common causes of a stroke that is due to intracranial hemorrhage are hypertension (high blood pressure) and **cerebral aneurysm.** Strokes caused by hypertensive hemorrhage are usually the result of sudden increases in blood pressure that lead to the rupture of arteries and bleeding inside the brain. Cerebral aneurysm refers to a condition where the wall of an artery bulges because of a weakness in the tissue of the artery, then breaks, leading to interruption of blood flow and bleeding inside the brain. Less frequent than ischemia or hemorrhage are brain tumors, which may cause a stroke by pressing on a blood vessel and shutting off blood supply to the brain, or by pressing on the brain tissue itself and causing damage (Brookshire 1978; Johns 1978; Pedretti 1985).

Some of the factors that predispose an individual to a CVA besides arteriosclerosis and hypertension are obesity, diabetes, smoking, or congenital vascular weakness. Unfortunately, at this time there is no proven medical treatment for stroke. The death of brain tissue because of lack of blood supply occurs very rapidly, which makes it impossible to administer treatment quickly enough to alter the situation (Wade et al. 1985). In some cases, surgery has been found to be helpful if bleeding in the brain occurs because of hemorrhage. If the stroke is progressing over several hours or days, some physicians favor the use of medication that prevents blood clotting (Wade et al. 1985). According to Swenson (1984), the severity of a stroke is dependent on five factors: (1) the cause of the stroke, (2) the location of the stroke, (3) the quantity of brain tissue involved (sometimes a large quantity of actual tissue damage results in a relatively minimal dysfunction or vice versa), (4) the health status of the patient before the stroke, and (5) the number and types of complications occurring after the initial CVA. The actual neurological effects are dependent on the site of the lesion in the brain.

Recovery of physical and cognitive functions after brain damage is a very important but complicated matter. Following the injury to the brain, the victim may loose consciousness and may remain unconscious for a substantial length of time. Once consciousness is regained, a phase of confusion, disorientation, and memory loss usually follows. In this phase, more or less specific symptoms become apparent, too, such as impairment of movement (paralysis), speech, or vision. After this acute phase, a period of recovery begins that can last from several weeks to several months. During this time, lost physical, intellectual, or sensory functions may spontaneously return in the patient. Most of the spontaneous recovery occurs within three to six months after the injury to the brain.

The degree of deficit and recovery are influenced in all types of brain injury by the extent and placement of the lesion and by the rapidity with which the lesion is produced. Generally, the smaller the lesion, the smaller will be the resulting deficit. However, the location in the brain and the distribution of the lesion between the brain hemispheres will also affect the recovery outcome. It is also generally accepted that lesions that develop slowly frequently result in smaller disruptions of functions than does sudden damage (Cohen 1993).

There is much conjecture about why a patient can regain, seemingly without medical intervention, lost functions that were controlled by damaged areas in the brain. The more reasonable explanations are based on the general concept that intact brain tissue surrounding the damaged area takes over for the destroyed tissue. More recent neuroscience research on brain plasticity has begun to show that networks of brain areas responsible for specific functions can change and become reorganized because of spontaneous mechanisms or external influences such as training and learning experiences.

The exact understanding of these neurophysiological processes, however, is still subject to much research and remains a challenge for our understanding of brain mechanisms.

Recent advances in pharmacological treatments may also help reduce the effects of lesions on functional impairments in patients by, for example, limiting the amount of cell death after the brain accident in areas immediately surrounding the damaged brain tissue.

Assessment

Assessment of stroke patients involves the identification and description of lost functions and the severity of any loss. Four major areas are commonly assessed: cognitive function, communication, physical function, and socioemotional function.

Cognitive Function The term *cognitive function* is usually used to describe a wide variety of mental and intellectual abilities including memory, attention, perception, reasoning, and general state of consciousness. In the initial stages of a stroke, almost 50 percent of all patients suffer from some alteration of the level of consciousness (Wade et al. 1985). Some patients may be unconscious for a prolonged period of time (comatose); others may just suffer from confusion, disorientation, or may appear apathetic and lethargic for a few hours or days.

To test for impairments in intellectual and reasoning abilities, IQ tests are often administered. These tests can be used by the neuropsychologist to help determine the level of functioning in areas such as the comprehension of written and spoken information, retention of general knowledge and math, reasoning and understanding abstract information (How are an axe and a saw alike?), attention span, memory, and visual perception. Almost any injury to the brain produces memory problems (Hayden and Hart 1986). Memory skills that are often affected in stroke patients are retention of information, ability to learn new material, and the ability to remember and generalize knowledge from one setting to another.

Neglecting one side of the body is a problem that highlights some of the perceptual problems stroke patients experience. Our central nervous system is cross-wired, that is, one side of the body is controlled by the opposite side (hemisphere) of the brain. Therefore, for example, damage to the visual control centers on the left side of the brain will lead to restricted or completely lost visual perception in the right visual field. It is important to note that the patient is not visually impaired in the right eye; rather, the brain centers that receive visual information from the eye are destroyed. Sometimes visual, auditory, and tactile sensory signals from an entire side are disregarded. A patient may ignore you when you speak if you are standing on the affected side of the body. When patients get dressed they may forget to put the shoe on the foot of the affected side of the body. Eating only the food on one-half of a plate, or reading only one-half of a page vertically are other examples of this perceptual neglect.

Communication Most stroke victims will suffer from some form of communication disorder. Problems with communication abilities can range from understanding spoken language, producing speech, reading and writing, to using any symbol system for communication such as gestures, sign language, or selecting pictures from visual communication charts. Especially susceptible to severe communication problems are stroke victims with damage to the left side of the brain; it is estimated that in 90 percent of all right-handed and 75 percent of all left-handed people the major language centers are located in the left brain hemisphere (Springer and Deutsch 1985).

Three distinct kinds of communication disorders may be encountered as a result of stroke. The first, **aphasia,** is defined as an impairment of the ability to use language as a result of brain damage (Wade et al. 1985). More specifically, aphasia refers to the inability to understand and interpret language symbols and formulate language in symbols. For example, an aphasic patient may be unable to understand spoken language (receptive aphasia), or may be unable to formulate his or her thoughts in spoken words (expressive aphasia). If receptive and expressive problems coexist in a patient, the disorder is referred to as *global aphasia.*

The second communication disorder, *dysarthria,* is a speech disorder that results from damage to the neuromuscular systems that control the mechanism of speech production. These include the structures required for breathing, swallowing, vocalizing, and movements of the jaw, lips, tongue, and palate, which are necessary for articulation and resonance in speech production. Dysarthric speech is slow and slurred. The patient speaks in a monotonous, nasal voice. Often the flow and phrasing of speech is disrupted because the patient has difficulties coordinating breathing and speaking.

The last disorder we shall discuss, **apraxia** of speech, is a disorder of planning and positioning, in proper sequence, the speech muscles involved in articulation of words. Thus, the sound sequence of spoken language is severely disturbed. In other words, the patient is trying to say one sequence of sounds, and another comes out. Apraxia of speech affects voluntary speech activity. Involuntary activities, such as automatic, reflexlike speech, are not affected. For example, the speech therapist may, without any success, ask the patient to say "good morning" during the therapy session. A little while later, the patient may say "good morning" fluently in response to somebody greeting him or her in passing in a hospital hallway.

Physical Function One of the most common physically disabling conditions, as a result of stroke, is paralysis: the loss of voluntary control over movement of the limbs (Wade et al. 1985). Most frequently seen in stroke patients are paralysis conditions of the right or left side of the body, which are called right- or left-sided hemiplegia, respectively. Because the central nervous system is cross-wired to a large extent, that is, nerves originating on one side of the brain cross over to the other side of the body on the cranial and spinal level, damage to the motor areas of the left brain hemisphere will result in right-sided hemiplegia and vice versa.

The physical disability of stroke victims can be described by four categories: strength and endurance, flexibility, muscle tone, and coordination.

Muscular strength and endurance is initially greatly diminished and will prohibit or limit purposeful movement. As part of the overall physical recovery, strength usually returns to the unaffected side. However, the affected side of the body will almost always remain weaker.

Flexibility refers to the range of motion of muscles around a joint. Flexibility of the elbow, wrist, shoulder, knee, ankles, and so on, may be affected by a stroke. Limited range of motion can be a result of poor muscle strength or disturbed muscle tone. Normal muscle tone involves a background level of muscular contraction that allows us to move our bodies against the forces of gravity. Motor recovery in hemiplegia usually progresses through different stages of muscle tone impairment. In the period immediately following the brain injury, muscle tone is usually very flaccid, that is, weak, so no limb movement or very limited movement can be initiated. In the next stage, the beginning of muscle tone recovery, a state of spasticity develops in which the muscles are stiff and contracted, making movements awkward, uncoordinated, and limited in range.

Synergistic mass movements dominate discrete limb movements in this stage; for example, when trying to reach forward with the hemiplegic arm the patient will move the whole arm, trunk, and shoulder forward in one pushing motion to compensate for the flexor spasticity that limits the normal ability to extend elbow, wrist, and fingers. In the final stages of motor recovery normal muscle tone reappears and smooth motor coordination becomes possible again. The stages of recovery of muscle tone are well described by Brunnstrom (1970).

The term motor coordination is used to describe the well-timed and well-planned execution of complex movements in time and space, and with proper muscle force. Well-coordinated movement usually involves movement patterns that consist of various combinations of sequential, alternating, simultaneous, unilateral (one-sided), or bilateral (two-sided) limb motions.

Socioemotional Function Stroke patients not only experience severe cognitive and physical problems, but also are confronted with many serious social and emotional consequences of their medical condition. The experience of a sudden and very severe loss of physical and intellectual abilities can be emotionally devastating and may lead to depression, feelings of hopelessness, and anxiety states. These emotional reactions can be compounded by confusion, restlessness, or irritability of the patient as a result of memory failure, or inaccurate and distorted sensory input because of impaired hearing or vision, for example. Immediately after the CVA many patients go through a stage of emotional lability where they suffer from mood swings, extreme emotional reactions, and so forth. This loss of emotional control is often embarrassing and frustrating to the patient as well as the caregivers.

Social concerns of a stroke patient center around an often dramatic change in living conditions. The patient may not regain the ability to live independently and may require hospitalization and extended care in a nursing home. Even if the patient can return to his or her normal living environment, activities of daily living may pose a major problem. The spouse or children may have to take over many functions, and adaptions of the physical environment may have to be made, such as making the house wheelchair accessible. Another source of frustration and experience of loss may occur in the area of leisure activities. The patient may no longer be able to pursue previous activities that have given him or her a sense of fulfillment and were an important part of his or her social life with friends and family.

TRAUMATIC BRAIN INJURY

Prevalence

Traumatic brain injury is the major cause of death and disability in the United States for persons under the age of 35, killing more people than all other diseases combined. Approximately 700,000 Americans suffer a head injury each year. Of those injured, 10 percent to 15 percent will never return to their preaccident lifestyles.

Definition

Head injuries caused by an accident occur without warning. The sudden and often severely disabling life changes cause many problems, not only for the injured victim but also for family and professional caregivers. A traumatic head injury results in many and complex physical, linguistic, cognitive, social, emotional, and behavioral changes in an individual. When the brain is injured without penetration of the skull, it is called a *closed-head injury.* An injury of this type usually causes widespread and diffuse damage to the brain. Brain damage because of stroke or penetrating head injuries is usually more localized and causes more specific behavioral deficits.

Etiology and Diagnosis

Closed-head injuries can be the result of three external forces acting simultaneously or successively on the brain during an accident situation: (1) compression of brain tissue, (2) tearing of brain tissue, and (3) shearing, as areas of the brain slide over other areas. For example, such damage can occur when the head in motion is suddenly stopped, such as when it hits the windshield in a car accident. The head will continue forward and smash into the windshield, thereby causing the brain to impact the front of the skull. After collision, the head will rebound, and the brain will hit the back of the skull. This injury is termed *coup-contrecoup injury* (National Head Injury Foundation 1984). During the back-and-forth head motion of this type of injury the brain moves over the rough bones at the base of the skull. This motion causes damage to the brain stem, which usually results in a coma state (a prolonged state of unconsciousness where there is no meaningful response to outside stimuli).

Further complications during closed-head injury can occur because of swelling of the brain or bleeding in or around the brain. If not medically corrected these conditions can cause further brain damage or lead to the death of the accident victim. Twenty years ago, 90 percent of all patients with severe head injuries died. Because of advances in emergency care, such as surgical treatments, medical technology to preserve vital functions, and speedier rescue procedures, today at least 50 percent of all brain injury victims survive. However, the quality of life for the accident victim is very often seriously diminished.

One of the major factors affecting a person's chances for recovery is the time spent in coma. The longer the person is comatose the more likely the existence of severe and widespread brain damage.

Assessment

One of the most reliable and most frequently used measurement tools to assess comatose states is the Glasgow Coma Scale (GCS) (O'Shanick 1986). The GCS measures three clinical features: eye movement, motor response to pain stimuli or command, and verbal response. A numerical rating scale gives an assessment of the severity of the coma state (mild = 13 or more, moderate = 9 to 12, severe = 8 and below).

Glasgow Coma Scale

Eye opening:

1 None (not due to facial edema)
2 To pain (stimulation to chest/limb)
3 To speech (nonspecific response)
4 Spontaneous

Motor response to pain stimulus or command:

1 No response (flaccid)
2 Extension (decerebrate)
3 Abnormal flexion (decorticate)
4 Withdrawal (normal flexor response)
5 Localizes pain (purposeful movement)
6 Obeys command

Verbal response:

1 None
2 Incomprehensible (moans)
3 Inappropriate (loose associations)
4 Confused (delirious)
5 Fully oriented

The Rancho Los Amigos Hospital located in Downey, California, has developed an assessment tool to describe and categorize the behavior of patients as they emerge from coma. Their Levels of Cognitive Functioning Scale is organized into eight stages:

1 *No response:* Unresponsive to any stimulus.

2 *Generalized response:* Limited, inconsistent, nonpurposeful responses, often to pain only.

3 *Localized response:* Purposeful responses; may follow simple commands; may focus on presented object.

4 *Confused, agitated:* Heightened state of activity; confusion, disorientation, aggressive behavior; unable to self-care; unaware of present events; agitation appears related to internal confusion.

5 *Confused, inappropriate, nonagitated:* Appears alert; responds to commands; distractible; does not concentrate on task; agitated responses to external stimuli; verbally inappropriate; does not learn new information.

6 *Confused, appropriate:* Good directed behavior; needs cuing; can relearn previously known activities of daily living; serious memory problems; some awareness of self and others.

7 *Automatic, appropriate:* Robotlike appropriate behavior; minimal confusion; poor insight into own condition; initiates tasks but needs structure; poor judgment, problem-solving, and planning skills.

8 *Purposeful, appropriate:* Alert and oriented; recalls past events; learns new activities and can continue without supervision; independent living skills at home; capable of driving; weaknesses in stress tolerance, judgment, abstract reasoning will persist; may function socially and professionally at reduced levels in society (Hagen et al. 1979). The behavioral deficits of head-injured patients are usually evaluated in four areas during the rehabilitation process: (1) cognitive problems, (2) sensorimotor problems, (3) medical problems, (4) socioemotional problems.

Cognitive Problems According to Pedretti (1985) the cognitive problems a head-injured patient experiences involve problems with memory, expressive and receptive language abilities, attention and concentration, and the use of cognitive strategies to solve problems. An individual may have difficulties in learning and retaining new information, maintaining attention and focus on a given task, and may be easily frustrated. The ability to comprehend spoken or written language or follow complex, sequential directions may also be impaired. Left hemispheric brain injuries frequently affect verbal memory skills, whereas right hemispheric damage frequently affects spatial/perceptual skills. Often, head-injured patients have great difficulties in analyzing and integrating information to solve problems (Ashley and Krych 1995).

Sensorimotor Problems Closed-head-injured patients usually show a wide variety of physical and sensory deficits. Damage to the auditory or visual nerve is frequent and results in impaired perceptual skills in hearing and vision. Motor impairment may affect all four limbs in regard to coordination, balance, range of motion, endurance, muscle tone, and body awareness. Because of the more widespread and diffuse localization of closed-head injury, affected individuals show motor problems more frequently on both sides of the body compared to stroke patients where hemi- (one-sided) paresis is the common clinical picture. Also, because of damage to the lower levels of the brain, primitive reflexes, such as seen in normal infants, may reappear, and protective reflexes, for example, maintaining balance, may be disturbed, thus limiting voluntary and skilled motor performance.

Medical Problems Head-injured patients may develop associated medical conditions that further complicate the rehabilitation process. Frequently seen in affected individuals are heart conditions, seizures, hypertension, diabetes, or lung diseases. Also, some individuals may develop substance abuse problems (Lynch and Maus 1981).

Socioemotional Problems The sudden and severe alteration of lifestyle may increase the risk of serious emotional and social problems for the head-injured individual. Depression, anxiety, low self-esteem, sexual dysfunction, or aggressive behaviors will interrupt the social and emotional relationships the patient has with his or her family and friends. Furthermore, the patient and his or her caregivers will have to deal with impaired self-care skills with regard to independent living, personal hygiene, dressing, feeding, employment, and use of transportation. Many closed-head-injured patients exhibit a personality change. Lezak (1976) lists some of these behavior features of personality change:

1 Lack of initiative

2 Rigidity, as manifested in the inability to adapt behavior to changing demands of social or professional situations in daily life

3 Impulsiveness and overactivity, as manifested in the inability to stop ongoing behavior

4 Poor self-awareness, inappropriate social behavior, lack of anxiety over situations

5 Lack of foresight and social judgment

Frequently seen are combativeness and emotional lability. These changes in personality are considered a result of damage to the frontal lobe, an area of the neocortical part of the human brain responsible for high-level intellectual, sensory, and motor functions.

REHABILITATION TECHNIQUES IN NEUROLOGICAL REHABILITATION

Principles of Neurological Rehabilitation

As we discussed earlier, most individuals who suffer from stroke and traumatic brain injury will show some degree of spontaneous recovery of lost function during the first weeks or months after the accident. Recovery is fastest in the early weeks, and most measurable recovery is complete within three to six months. However, it is now accepted that long-term training can still significantly improve a patient's functional abilities (Bach-y-Rita 1992). Many branches of medicine have developed treatments to accelerate or improve the natural recovery process. Although it is often difficult to discern and evaluate separately the distinct contributions of treatment and the spontaneous recovery process to the improvement of the patient, it is widely accepted that therapy can help make the recovery process more efficient.

Wade and associates (1985) discuss five general ways in which therapy can help the rehabilitation process. First, therapy should help prevent complications, such as illness, muscle weakness, or contractures, which can obstruct the natural recovery process. Second, the therapist may teach adaptive strategies so that the patient can learn to use the unaffected part of the body in place of the affected one. Third, therapy is directed at retraining the affected parts of the nervous system through specific exercise techniques, for example, in the areas of motor performance and speech. Fourth, therapy should ensure the availability and proper use of correct physical aids (sticks, wheelchairs, lifts, ramps) in the patient's daily environment. Fifth, many rehabilitation specialists claim that some long-term disabilities seen in brain-injured individuals are not due to the original loss but rather to learned nonuse that results when the patient does not use the affected limb even though movement is possible (Taub 1980).

It is important to recognize that several distinct treatment approaches have been developed over the last 40 years in neurological rehabilitation. They are based on different models of understanding how the brain works regarding the control of movement, speech, and cognitive functions, for example. A detailed discussion would exceed the scope of this text, but some brief examples of three major models in motor control will be useful to introduce some key concepts (Shumway-Cook and Woollacott 1995).

The oldest model in therapy is based on the reflex model. The reflex model originated in the earlier part of the twentieth century from the work of neurophysiologists who studied the nerve pathways of motor reflexes in order to understand the basic mechanisms of the motor system. The reflex model emphasizes the importance of stimulating normal reflex patterns from the outside, for example, through sensory stimulation, to facilitate normal motor behavior because reflexes are considered the basis for all movement.

The hierarchical model of motor control emerged in the 1930s and has dominated the understanding of movement control for many decades. This model states that control of movement is organized hierarchically from the lowest levels in the spinal cord to the intermediate levels to the highest levels in the neocortex. Internal motor programs drive movement patterns. These programs are built by contributions from different brain and spinal cord systems, ranging from *most automatic control* on lower brain centers to *most volitional* in higher brain regions. The hierarchical model suggests that damage interrupts the control hierarchy at some level and that therapy should, for example, emphasize the inhibition of lower-level reflex patterns so that higher brain areas can regain control. This model also implies that normal motor function will only reappear in a steplike fashion after damage, from lower, mostly reflexive, to higher, more volitional, levels. Approaches in physical therapy based on this model are, for example, the Bobath or NDT (neurodevelopmental treatment) methods.

The most recent model assumes a systems approach to motor control, where movement arises out of the interaction between different systems in the central nervous system and the environment without a necessary distinction between higher or lower levels. Control is not based on reflex stimulation or hierarchically organized muscle activation patterns; rather it relies on strategies generated to achieve movement goals. The most persuasive evidence in recent research supports the systems approach because (1) the development of motor skills in children (e.g., kicking, reaching, walking) does not necessarily show a developmental sequence from reflexive to internally commanded movement, and (2) in complex movements, the distinctions between automatic and volitional commands are becoming increasingly blurred. When planning and executing a movement it may be more useful to speak about both aware and unaware adjustments in posture, direction of reaching, speed of walking, or strength of muscle activation, for example. However, both adjustment processes are equally complex.

The systems model leads to two principles for the development of treatment techniques. First, therapy should emphasize functional, task- and goal-oriented activities and exercises. Second, the therapist should use effective learning and training strategies by emphasizing the training of functional movements in a highly repetitive, patterned, and rhythmic manner.

Again, as discussed in the assessment section of this chapter, efforts in neurological rehabilitation generally can be grouped into four deficit areas: cognitive deficits, communication deficits, physical deficits, and socioemotional deficits. In the following section we will give a brief overview of the major focus of therapy in each deficit area.

Cognitive Deficits

In cognitive rehabilitation two major efforts stand out in the clinical setting: memory and attention/perception training. In memory training, therapy methods can be divided into compensatory external aids (diaries, wristwatch alarms, computers, etc.) that assist the patient in memory deficits, and compensatory internal aids that provide the patient with strategies to remember information, recall performance, and so on. Examples of internal aids are visual imagery, rhymes, or songs that structure the sequence of information and facilitate memorization and simple repetition, group related information (chunking), or relate new information to previously learned and well-consolidated material.

Attention/perception training focuses on the accurate use of the senses in perception as well as the ability to attend to important events and stimuli in an appropriate manner. Of concern in this area are problems such as visual inattention and visual or other sensory neglect syndromes of one side of the body. Individuals may read only one-half of a newspaper page or eat only the food on one-half of a plate. Cognitive training that makes patients aware of their deficits, as well as methods such as picture completion and object assembly have proved useful. Auditory, visual, and tactile training and body awareness training are also important components of a perceptual retraining program. Attention training may also focus on using proper attention span and adapting appropriate attention strategies, for example, to maintain attention or to select, shift, and divide attentional focus between important events.

Communication Deficits

Because aphasia is the most common disorder of communication in brain-injured persons it has received the most attention in developing therapy techniques. Depending on the site of the brain lesion, expressive or receptive channels of verbal communication may be damaged. Aphasia is usually divided into the expressive or the receptive type according to the site of the lesion. Many techniques have been developed to treat aphasia. Some of the more general techniques to improve overall communicative ability are promoting aphasics communicative effectiveness (PACE), Amerind (gesture system), Bliss (visual symbol system), and visual communication charts. The above-mentioned techniques are predominantly nonverbal and emphasize getting a message across rather than training spoken language.

More direct techniques foster the use of spoken language. For example, deblocking tries to unlock communicative channels by presenting the information in an undamaged mode before using it in the damaged mode. A patient who has difficulty understanding what he or she reads may be presented with the written material in spoken form before seeing it written down. A second technique emphasizing the recovery of spoken language is melodic intonation therapy (MIT), which will be discussed in detail in the section on music therapy methods. A third technique is the stimulation approach, which attempts to trigger reflexlike speech by encouraging patients to complete automatic phrases, for example, good ________________ (morning), or previously learned songs or rhymes.

Treatments for **dyspraxia** (disturbance in the sequence of spoken language) and **dysarthria** (slow, slurred speech) are not as well understood as those for aphasia. In dyspraxia, two different approaches exist. One emphasizes the use of automatic or reflexlike speech, MIT, or the stimulation approach. The other approach encourages direct work on articulation and sequencing of sounds.

Therapy for dysarthria focuses on breath control, rate of speech, and intonation exercises that improve vocal power, melodic and rhythmic inflection, and clarity of articulation. Severely dysarthric patients will need help eating because swallowing and tongue movement may be impaired.

Physical Deficits

Recovery of physical abilities is a primary concern of therapists who work with brain-injured patients. It is a general observation that some degree of muscle function is recovered during the first weeks after the accident. Most consideration in therapy is given to the recovery of walking ability and the independent use of arms and hands. Many specific techniques for treating movement disability and muscle dysfunction have been developed by physical and occupational therapists. These techniques, such as the Bobath approach, Rood method, and Brunnstrom approach, rely on different physical exercise programs to normalize muscle tone and posture, work through abnormal movement reflexes, regain range of motion and muscle strength, and develop movement coordination. A more recent approach in therapy has been the introduction of biofeedback methods (Basmajian 1984). By using visual or auditory feedback to indicate unconscious muscle activity, patients can be helped to regain control over weak muscles. In general, current theory favors active and repetitive training exercises of functional movements. A systems approach in motor control has changed some of the more traditional views on how to rehabilitate motor functions.

Experimental studies have shown that therapy administered during the early stages of recovery can significantly improve and sustain gains in physical functioning. However, it is difficult to demonstrate the superiority of one method over another. One very important factor frequently mentioned by professionals is patient motivation, which seems to have considerable influence on the success of therapy. However, little research data are available in this area (Wade et al. 1985).

Socioemotional Deficits

Life after severe brain injury often requires extensive adaptations to new roles by the patients and their caregivers. Four stages in adapting to the brain injury have been identified by Holbrook (1982). The first stage, crisis, is characterized by shock, confusion, and a high level of anxiety. In the second stage, treatment, patient and family usually develop high expectations of recovery coupled with the denial that the disability is permanent. In this stage, which usually takes place during hospitalization, patients and family may be highly motivated and enthusiastic about treatment progress. However, therapy staff should try to develop realistic expectations without dampening hope or enthusiasm. The third stage, realization of disability, usually coincides with discharge from the hospital or active treatment. During this period there is often grief and bereavement over the disability, which may lead to feelings of despair and frustration. The experience of an altered and diminished quality of life very frequently leads to depression. Supportive counseling by professionals usually helps assist the patient and the family through this stage. In the fourth stage, adjustment, the patient ideally has adopted and adjusted to a new lifestyle where he or she finds ways to contribute meaningfully to the family life and to participate in occupational and leisure activities. Depending on the severity of the injury, however, many patients never reach this stage, or may take years to do so.

MUSIC THERAPY FOR PATIENTS WITH STROKE AND TRAUMATIC BRAIN INJURY

Our previous discussion makes it clear that stroke and traumatic brain injury affect many different aspects of an individual's lifestyle, behavior, and level of functioning. A brain-injured individual has emotional, physical, social, and cognitive problems that need to be addressed in the rehabilitation process. Therefore, brain injury rehabilitation is carried out by an interdisciplinary treatment team that usually consists of physicians, psychologists, social workers, and rehabilitation specialists in physical therapy, speech therapy, occupational therapy, and related disciplines. A rehabilitation music therapist will often be a member of such a team, and will frequently be asked to collaborate with other therapy disciplines in a client's treatment. Music therapy offers a specialized set of techniques and activities that addresses the rehabilitation needs of the patient in the areas of cognitive, communication, physical, and socioemotional deficits. Additionally, musical exercises offer a wide range of structural options to integrate patients into a group therapy setting where music applications can be scaled to each patient's level of functioning and yet contribute to a meaningful musical group experience. The music therapist thus can become a very effective transdisciplinary and patient-oriented therapy facilitator in an inpatient or outpatient rehabilitation setting.

Music Therapy with Cognitive Deficits

Music therapy techniques in this area of treatment can be grouped into the following categories: sensory stimulation, reality orientation, attention training, memory training, perceptual training, executive strategies training. Music materials are frequently used to activate a maximum of sensory channels when trying to trigger responses from comatose patients in a sensory stimulation program. Often, songs or instrumental pieces with which the patient was familiar before the accident are used to evoke reactions.

In the early stages of recovery, brain injury patients are often confused and agitated. Music, especially familiar and patient-preferred pieces, can be used to relax the patient and provide nonthreatening, pleasant, and familiar sensory stimulation to decrease anxiety and help orient the patient to his or her environment.

Many studies have shown that background music or the use of music to present nonmusical information can improve attention span, reduce distractibility, and ascertain task focus (Jellison 1988).

The perception of the rhythmic, melodic, harmonic, and dynamic patterns in music is very effective in consciously and subliminally focusing and organizing the flow of our attention. Even untrained musical listeners are immediately attracted to and pay attention to music they like, as well as recognize and remember significant parts of the music, for example, melodic or rhythmic phrases, almost instantaneously. These attributes of music can be used with brain-injured patients to retrain general attentional abilities. For example, during a musical task the rhythmic, dynamic, melodic, and harmonic structures of the music can be used to train a patient's ability to recognize and discriminate temporal, spatial, or visual cues. An attentional task in music may require the patient to recognize rhythmic or melodic patterns, or to remember spatial patterns of tone sequences on a keyboard or percussion set. These training experiences may be a first important step in regaining attentional abilities, which may then be extended to nonmusical events. Music can also be used to help control the attention of patients by focusing them on important nonmusical functional information presented in song form. In neglect training, musical tasks and cues can be used effectively to train awareness of the neglected body side by playing instruments bilaterally or practice visual scanning by turning to sounds from different directions during a music and movement exercise. Thus music can be used nonspecifically as background stimulus to improve motivation and attention during the process of relearning activities of daily living. However, elements and perceptual features in musical patterns can also be used in a very specific and functional manner to train attentional control.

Music is also very useful for memory retraining programs. The efficiency of music as a mnemonic (memory) device has been well documented in research (Gfeller 1983; Wallace 1994; Claussen and Thaut 1997). Rhythm and melody provide excellent structures to organize, sequence, and remember verbal information. Rhythm and melody can become strongly associated with a verbal text, for example, in a song, and recalling a short melodic excerpt can trigger recall of long lines of words and sentences. Rhyme is another structure often used in music that helps memory recall. Melodic and rhythmic phrasing in a song or chant also helps "chunk" verbal information. Rhythmic, melodic, and harmonic elements are used in music to create larger patterns that are easily recognizable. In fact, phrase pattern organization is probably one of the most important organizational elements when creating or remembering music (Deutsch 1983). Chunking refers to the organization of single small pieces of information into larger units that are remembered as a whole. To better understand this important concept of efficient memory storage, think of how we recall telephone numbers. We tend to recall them as one chunk rather than seven separate numbers. A simple illustration of the phrasing process in music to create more manageable memory chunks is the ABC song. Musical phrasing creates 4 easily remembered bits of information out of 26 letters. Remembering 26 separate bits of information ordered in a rather arbitrary fashion is a considerable challenge for our memory storage capacity. Therefore, songs, chants, rhymes, and so forth, are used very efficiently by the music therapist to train memory function. For example, instructional songs or chants may help the patient remember important information. Rehearsing familiar or new songs and chants may help the patient train memory function.

If auditory perception is impaired by brain damage, the music therapist may assist in auditory training using musical materials (Thompson et al. 1990). Auditory sensory acuity, that is, the discrimination of pitch, loudness, timbre, and time in single tones or sound patterns, may be trained within musical tasks to improve memory and discrimination in general auditory perception that is important for the perception of speech or environmental sounds. It is no surprise, therefore, that the rhythm section of the Seashore Test of Musical Aptitude is still used as a part of the Halstad-Reitan test, a widely used neuropsychological assessment tool with brain-injured patients.

Music Therapy with Communication Deficits

Music therapists assist with musical materials and methods in two treatment approaches to aphasia rehabilitation. One form of treatment is melodic intonation therapy (MIT) (Sparks et al. 1974). MIT utilizes the client's unimpaired ability to sing, which is frequently seen in aphasics, to facilitate spontaneous and voluntary speech. Simple phrases and sentences, which should pertain to the patient's activities of daily living, are sung and chanted to melodies that resemble natural speech intonation patterns. Therapy starts with the patient and therapist singing in unison, and progresses to a level at which the patient is able to sing answers to simple questions. Subsequently, the patient moves from singing to chanting where the melodic and rhythmic inflection is closer to normal speech prosody. In a final step, the patient's intonations are moved back into normal speech inflection. MIT is most successful with aphasic patients who have good auditory comprehension but impaired verbal expression (expressive aphasia). The neurological theory explaining the effectiveness of MIT was based on the assumption that singing by activating the right undamaged brain hemisphere bypasses the damaged motor speech function of the left brain hemisphere (Kandel and Schwarz 1985). However, some recent brain imaging studies have found that after the completion of MIT training the normal speech areas in the left hemisphere had been reactivated (Belin et al. 1996).

The other form of aphasia treatment where musical materials can play a beneficial role is the *stimulation* approach as developed by Basso and colleagues (1979). This approach is based on the observation that aphasics, although unable to give an intentional and voluntary language response, can sometimes produce it automatically in response to a facilitating stimulus. To understand this rationale we have to realize that in daily life we use many speech phrases almost automatically in conversation with others. For example, we respond verbally to phrases like Hi, How are you? and Good morning with little thinking because in daily use these phrases have become overlearned. In certain frustrating situations an angry word or exclamation such as "damn" may slip across our tongues without our conscious awareness. Musical materials, such as song texts, can also become overlearned and thus easy to recall. If somebody intones "Silent Night" or "God Bless America" we may automatically join in and continue with the appropriate words. The stimulation approach uses musical materials among other materials to trigger automatic speech, for example, by singing with the patient and using song lyrics completion ("Silent night, holy ____________"; "God bless ____________"), or rhythmic chanting in question and answer format to evoke overlearned verbal responses. The stimulation approach tries to trigger a response first in a more automatic way, and later in a more voluntary, intentional way by gradually removing the facilitating stimuli.

Because the rehabilitation of dyspraxia is less understood than that of aphasia, music therapy methods are less clear-cut than in aphasia. Some clinicians find it useful to adapt MIT and stimulation approach techniques with dyspraxic patients. Another treatment approach uses techniques to practice positions of the oral apparatus and muscles (lips, jaw, tongue, etc.) with and without sound before proceeding to speech–sound production. The music therapist can support this approach by using wind instruments and vocal exercises with the desired vowel and consonant combinations to practice and reinforce oral motor movements and positions and sound production.

With dysarthric patients the music therapist can support rehabilitation efforts by applying relaxation exercises, especially in the upper trunk, neck, shoulder, and head regions. An important contribution to dysarthria rehabilitation can be made in music therapy with rhythmic cuing to control the rate of speech. Many dysarthric patients benefit in intelligibility from slowing their speech rates. This may seem counterintuitive because dysarthric speech is already very slow. However, articulatory clarity, prosodic patterns, and muscular and breath control do benefit from decelerated rhythmic cuing (Pilon et al. 1998). Furthermore, dysarthric patients will benefit from breathing exercises to develop good breath support and regular synchronization of breathing and speech phrases. Vocal exercises used by singers to attain good phonation and resonance in voice control are helpful in dysarthria, too. Finally, singing or chanting exercises that work on proper speed, articulation, and refined melodic and rhythmic speech inflection will improve the dysarthric patient's speech intelligibility (Lucia 1987).

In summary, applications to speech and language rehabilitation in music therapy comprise the following techniques: (1) melodic intonation therapy, (2) nonpropositional speech stimulation, (3) rhythmic speech cuing, (4) vocal intonation therapy, (5) therapeutic singing, and (6) oral motor exercises.

Music Therapy with Physical Deficits

Music therapists integrate movement and music when working in physical rehabilitation to provide motivation, purpose and structure, and physiological facilitation to the therapeutic exercises and activities of the patient (Thaut 1988).

Two basic concepts help clients meet their goals: movement to music and movement through music. In methods using movement to music, music is used as a movement accompaniment to provide a timekeeper, or pacemaker, and muscular entrainment signal. One very important aspect of well-coordinated movement is proper timing. The muscles of our body have to move at the right time in relationship to one another. Even simple motions, which we take for granted, such as bringing a coffee cup from the saucer to the mouth and tilting it properly so the coffee can be drunk, require an enormous amount of complex muscular control. Any physical rehabilitation program is therefore most concerned with restoring the capacity for functional movement. Music therapists can support these efforts very efficiently using music and movement techniques. Using music as a facilitating stimulus in physical exercise is based on three physiological mechanisms:

1 *Patterned sensory stimulation:* Music is organized in rhythmic patterns. Rhythmic accents and phrases are predictable timing cues because they occur regularly in the same sequence and in predictable proportional time relationships. Thus learning to follow a rhythm not only helps synchronize the timing of a movement to a beat, but also helps plan, program, and execute, in a well-organized fashion, longer sequences of complex movement patterns, for example, reaching for, grasping, and lifting a cup.

2 *Rhythmic entrainment:* Music is perceived via the auditory sense. Hearing, moreover, is the sense in which the comprehension of timing develops earliest and most efficiently (Gallahue 1982). For example, when we try to tap our hands along with rhythmic patterns of sounds or flashing lights, our rhythmic accuracy will always be better when following sounds. The motor system is very sensitive to the input of time information from the auditory system. Timing signals in the auditory system can entrain movement responses very quickly and accurately, even at levels below the perceptual threshold (Thaut et al. 1998). Rhythmic entrainment occurs when the frequency and pattern sequence of movements become locked to the frequency and pattern of an auditory rhythmic stimulus, such as in metronome pulses or the metric and rhythmic patterns in music. Recent research has shown that, when one moves in synchrony with a rhythmic beat, the primary synchronization strategy of the brain is not to synchronize the motor response to the beat event but to scale the duration of the movement to the duration of the beat interval (Thaut et al. 1998). This means, for therapeutic applications of rhythmic entrainment, that auditory rhythm enhances time stability and movement planning and execution during the whole duration of the movement and not just at the endpoints of the movement. For example, when moving the arm in synchrony with a beat from one point on a table surface to another, the brain synchronizes the movement by scaling the duration of the arm movement between reaching the points to the time interval between the beats. Therefore, rhythmic cuing of movement is not just a pacemaker cuing the coincidence of a movement event (e.g., tapping the table surface with the finger) to a beat, but a cue to give time stability to the whole movement trajectory (e.g., the travel path of the arm through space). This finding is extremely important in order to understand why auditory rhythm improves the temporal, spatial, and force aspects of the total movement pattern in therapy and not just the timing of movement endpoints in coincidence with a beat.

3 *Audiospinal facilitation:* Sound activates the motor system in our central nervous system. In order to perceive a sound, first the the nerve cells (neurons) in the auditory system have to become activated. However, through the reticular formation, a structure in the brain stem, the excitation patterns in the auditory nerve are passed on to the neurons of the motor system in the spinal cord which are set into a state of raised excitability and readiness for action. The most dramatic effect of sound triggering the motor system is the startle reflex. However, the auditory priming effect of the motor system to facilitate functional movement works most effectively when sound is below the intensity level of the startle reflex, and when sound is organized in rhythmic patterns (Rossignol and Melvill-Jones 1976). The muscles will become activated in synchrony with the rhythm which helps the muscles anticipate and time the movement properly.

The concept of movement through music refers to playing musical instruments to exercise physical functions, such as fingers, hands, arms, shoulders, legs, and oral motor muscles. By selecting the appropriate musical instrument, specific physical movements that are damaged in a patient (such as the ability to move fingers independently) can be exercised. Because the patient produces musical patterns during the exercise, the above-mentioned three mechanisms of movement to music are also true in this application. However, there are three additional therapeutic mechanisms in the use of musical instruments:

1 *Auditory feedback and purposeful movement:* When patients perform therapeutic movements using musical instruments they receive immediate feedback if the movement has been performed properly because they will have produced a musical tone or beat alone or appropriately placed within a whole sound pattern. This feedback process gives the patient immediate and rewarding knowledge of the results of his or her efforts, thus reinforcing goal-oriented movement performance.

2 *Affective/motivational arousal:* Most patients, if appropriate instruments are selected within a well-crafted therapeutic music experience (TME), will enjoy playing musical instruments. Thus, musical instruments can be an important tool to stimulate and maintain a patient's motivation for a physical rehabilitation program.

3 *Motor memory:* The rhythmic and melodic patterns that a patient produces while exercising with a musical instrument will also help him or her remember the muscular movements that produced these patterns. So, again, we discover music as a mnemonic device, however, in this context facilitating motor memory. An example is the pianist who can play, sequentially and simultaneously, many notes in a few seconds without having to remember every single note (the attempt of which would actually prevent his or her performance). What the admiring layperson may refer to as "the fingers remember the music" alludes to the process where the melodic and rhythmic patterns actually have helped the commitment of finger and hand motions to a specific type of memory in our nervous system, the motor memory or ability to remember movement sequences. On a more elementary level, the same mnemonic process can help a patient perform and remember more efficiently longer and more difficult sequences of movement, for example, combining different finger movements, or using hands and arms in a coordinated way.

In clinical practice music therapists use the above-discussed therapeutic mechanisms as rationales to develop scientifically valid and effective treatment techniques. Music therapists may provide rhythmic stimuli to improve walking patterns of patients or to accompany physical therapy exercises (e.g., rotating shoulders, moving arms, and hands, etc.) with appropriate music. More specifically, music therapists can retrain functional movements using musical instruments. For example, keyboard exercises can benefit finger dexterity. Playing percussion instruments can train eye–hand coordination; help coordination of hands and arms on both sides of the body; improve range of motion of the elbow, shoulder, or wrist; or increase muscular strength. It is important to analyze the physical strengths and weaknesses of the patient and then match them with an instrument that requires positioning and motions appropriate to his or her physical ability. All these applications can be systematically organized in three categories of treatment methods:

1 *Rhythmic auditory stimulation (RAS):* RAS is a specific technique to facilitate rehabilitation of movements that are intrinsically biologically rhythmical. One of the most important of these rhythmical movements is gait. Therefore, the most prominent application of RAS is to gait disorders, for example, in stroke patients (Thaut et al.

1993; Thaut et al. 1997; Prassas et al. 1997) and traumatically brain-injured patients (Hurt et al. 1998).

2 *Patterned sensory enhancement (PSE):* PSE uses rhythmic, melodic, harmonic, and dynamic aspects of music to provide temporal, spatial, and force cues for movements that reflect functional exercises and activities of daily living. PSE is broader in application than RAS because (a) it is applied to movements that are not rhythmic by nature (e.g., most arm and hand movements, functional movement sequences such as during dressing or sit-to-stand transfers) and (b) it provides more than just temporal cues. PSE uses musical patterns to assemble single, discrete motions (e.g., arm and hand movements during reaching and grasping) into functional movement patterns and sequences and cue them temporally, spatially, and dynamically during training exercises (Thaut et al. 1990).

3 *Therapeutic instrumental music playing (TIMP):* TIMP uses the playing of musical instruments to exercise and simulate functional movement patterns. Appropriate selection of musical instruments and performance patterns can train gross and fine motor movements in a therapeutically meaningful way by emphasizing, for example, range of motion, endurance, strength, functional hand movements and finger dexterity, limb coordination, and so on (Elliot 1982; Clark and Chadwick 1980).

Music Therapy with Socioemotional Deficits

As we have discussed earlier, the social and emotional consequences of brain injury are very serious and require attention in the rehabilitation process. Music therapists can help meet the social and emotional needs of brain-injured patients in three ways.

One way is to reduce anxiety and alter depressed feelings in the patient who has experienced traumatic changes in quality of life. Pleasant and rewarding music experiences can be helpful in promoting relaxation, alleviating anxiety, and providing uplifting mood experiences.

Second, music experiences can be used to help the patient cope with the new lifestyle to which he or she must become accustomed. Rather than succumb to functional deficits, the patient should compensate for them by finding meaningful new ways to do things. The patient can only accomplish this if stages of denial or hopelessness are overcome. The patient, in other words, must come to terms with a new lifestyle by accepting the disability and developing new ways of adapting. This process of acceptance can be helped by talking to counselors or other supportive persons about feelings and thoughts of grief, pain, and despair. The music therapist, by using music experiences in the process of therapy, can effectively serve as a facilitator and catalyst in encouraging the patient to experience and express some of these feelings and thoughts, and to induce hope and motivation.

Finally, music experiences can be used to fulfill the patient's needs for social interaction and support. It is important for the patient to become a member of support groups that assist in recovery efforts. Also, family support groups, composed of the patient and family members, have proven helpful as well. The music therapist can help clients experience social interaction through musical group activities that are enjoyable and emotionally uplifting.

PARKINSON'S AND HUNTINGTON'S DISEASES

We will discuss Parkinson's and Huntington's diseases together in this section of the chapter because they are both disorders of the basal ganglia, a subcortical brain structure essential for normal cognitive and motor function. In addition to a common location, both diseases are manifested by severe disturbances of movement. However, the malfunctioning neurological systems in the basal ganglia, the cause and progression of the disease, and the nature of the disease symptoms have certain features in common and are quite different in others.

Prevalence

Parkinson's disease (PD) is a neurological disease whose prevalence increases with older age. Reported figures indicate 1 per 1,000 under the age of 60, 5 per 1,000 at the age of 70, and 20 per 1,000 over the age of 85 (Caird 1991). The median age for onset reported in most epidemiological studies is in the late 60s. However, the disease can already appear in persons below the age of 50. The prevalence of PD is equally distributed across the world, and gender incidence is virtually equal between men and women. The prevalence pattern of PD thus gives very few clues about possible causes of PD.

Huntington's disease (HD), on the other hand, is an inherited neurodegenerative disease that is fairly rare compared to other neurological diseases. However, compared to other genetically transmitted neurological diseases it is relatively common (1 in 10,000) (Harper 1991). The onset of HD is usually between the ages of 40 and 50. However, any onset age is possible, yet very early or late onset ages are comparatively rare (10 percent before age 20; 15 percent after age 60).

Definition

In Parkinson's disease it is important to differentiate between the idiopathic form and other forms, usually called Parkinsonism or Parkinsonian symptoms. All Parkinsonian disease states are characterized by four features: (1) tremor in certain body parts; (2) muscular rigidity; (3) slowness and poverty of movement (bradykinesia or hypokinesia); (4) postural instability (Caird 1991). Parkinson's disease that occurs by itself, that is, is not associated with the simultaneous occurrence of other diseases or degenerative brain states, is called idiopathic and is by far the most common form of Parkinson's disease. Other forms of Parkinsonism can be induced by drugs, postencephalitis, head injuries (e.g., in boxers), Alzheimer's disease, or various forms of brain atrophy, that is, deterioration or degeneration of areas in the brain.

Huntington's disease is an inherited neurodegenerative disease transmitted by a dominant genetic defect. The deficient gene can be transmitted by the mother or the father to the child. Thus, almost all patients with HD have a long family history of the disease.

Etiology and Diagnosis

Both PD and HD are diseases of the basal ganglia, a brain structure centrally located below higher cortical areas and above the brain stem. The basal ganglia has close connections to the neocortex from where it both receives and sends sensory and motor information. The basal ganglia play a critical role in processing sensory information and in the control of movement, especially in initiating, maintaining, and sequencing movement patterns. In idiopathic PD, dopamine, which is an important neurotransmitter for normal basal ganglia function, is depleted. The basal ganglia receive the neurotransmitter from dopamine-producing cells in an area of the brain stem called *substantia nigra.* In idiopathic PD, more and more substantia nigra cells die and thus the basal ganglia receive less and less dopamine necessary for normal functioning. The cause of the cell death in the substantia nigra is unknown. Eighty percent of the normal dopamine level has to be lost before Parkinsonian symptoms develop. However, the dopamine concentration in the brain and the number of cells in the substantia nigra decrease as part of the normal aging process anyway. Therefore, it may be difficult to decide in very old age if Parkinsonian symptoms are due to the advanced age of the person or the onset of idiopathic PD.

HD is an inherited disease which is almost completely dominant in genetic transmission. In 1993, a research group located the HD gene on chromosome 4. Genetic testing can identify with very strong reliability if a person has inherited the Huntington gene. The causes for the genetic defect are not well understood at this time. Unlike in PD, dopamine deficiency is not the cause of the disease process in HD. Rather, there is a strong assumption that faulty metabolic processes in the brain chemistry (glucose) of the basal ganglia structure itself may play a significant role. The errant chemical process leads ultimately to cell death in the basal ganglia.

Assessment

In PD, frequently one of the first symptoms is a tremor in one hand which may spread to the other hand and other parts of the body. The tremor frequency in PD is characteristically around 5 per second (5 Hertz). Limbs are usually rigid and show resistance to movement when pushed from the outside. Poverty of movement is one of the most debilitating problems in PD. Patients have great difficulty initiating or stopping movement. Walking and arm movements are very slow. Alternating limb movements are especially affected. The slowness of movement, called *bradykinesia,* may increase to a state of complete lack of movement, called *freezing* or *akinesia.* Sequencing different movements together, for example, changing directions while walking, can trigger freezing episodes. Postural instability is evident in stooped posture, stiff movement of the joints (for example, the knee or hip), and poor righting reflexes. All these factors put the PD patient at a high risk of falling, especially during walking. Speech may also be affected in PD patients. A frequent symptom is slurring and poor articulation characteristic of dysarthria (see under stroke treatment). In the later stages of PD, cognitive impairments and dementia can develop in addition to the original movement disorder. One of the most frequently used assessment tools in PD is the Hoehn and Yahr scale (Hoehn and Yahr 1967).

In HD, one of the most visible disease symptoms is the onset of chorea, that is, involuntary jerking movements involving the whole body. Choreitic movements can interfere severely with normal activities of daily living. However, although most noticeable to the observer, they are not the most detrimental aspect of the disease. Higher-functioning patients may have very strong chorea, whereas more severely affected patients in the later stages of the disease may actually show fewer chorea symptoms. HD affects the overall ability to control voluntary movement, which will become progressively worse during the disease. Swallowing and speech are frequently affected, too. Furthermore, the disease will affect the psychological and cognitive abilities of the patient. Depression, cognitive deterioration all the way to dementia, perceptual deficits, poor attention and memory, decreasing motivation, and emotional instability are all part of the typical disease progression.

Treatment

A difference in rehabilitation strategies exists between plateau diseases such as stroke or Traumatic Brain Injury (TBI) in which the disease does not continually progress after the initial damage, and neurological disorders such PD and HD, which show a progressive worsening of the patient's status. Whereas in nondegenerative disease relearning, retraining, and compensatory strategies are important, maintaining and facilitating functions as long as possible is the primary strategy with degenerative diseases. In PD and HD, functional exercise and sensorimotor and cognitive facilitation of existing functions are a strong component of recommended treatment. The most common and very beneficial basis of treatment in PD is pharmacological, using drugs (L-Dopa) to replace the lost dopamine in the basal ganglia. However, the beneficial effect of drugs tends to diminish over the course of the disease. New advances in treatment research are studying surgical interventions in the basal ganglia, dopamine-producing cell implants in the brain stem, and facilitation of movement through sensory stimulation, that is, most commonly in the auditory or visual modality. Surgery in areas of the basal ganglia seems to be most promising in reducing tremors. Auditory and visual stimuli seem to be effective in substituting for or enhancing missing or faulty internal neural signals of the basal ganglia necessary for movement that are not generated because of a lack of dopamine.

No single treatment that makes a substantial difference in the course of HD has been found so far. Medication can alleviate some of the symptoms of restlessness, chorea, movement slowing, anxiety, depression, fear, or cognitive deterioration. However, the severity of the disease symptoms, unlike in PD, can only be moderately alleviated. Therapeutic exercise in the areas of physical, cognitive, and speech function, as well as relaxation training, psychological counseling, and nutritional regimens are considered useful components in a therapy program for patients with HD.

MUSIC THERAPY FOR PATIENTS WITH PARKINSON'S OR HUNTINGTON'S DISEASE

Music therapists have a very effective tool in music to facilitate movement in PD. Several studies have demonstrated that PD patients can synchronize their gait movements to rhythmic stimuli and, through entrainment, can improve their walking patterns through better posture, more appropriate step rates (step cadence) and stride length, and more efficient and symmetrical muscle activation patterns in their legs (Richards et al.

1992; Thaut et al. 1996; McIntosh et al. 1997; Miller et al. 1996). In case of walking patterns that are unsafe because of very fast yet short and shuffling strides, rhythmic cuing can be used to entrain slower, safer gait patterns.

Furthermore, rhythmic facilitation can cue effectively advanced gait exercises, such as turning, walking on inclines, stopping and starting, stair stepping, and so forth. Functional arm and hand movements can also be cued effectively with auditory rhythm. Arm and hand tremors sometimes can be reduced during musical tasks; however, music performance may not always have a lasting effect on tremor reduction. Rhythmic cuing of dysarthric speech patterns in patients with PD has shown good success in controlling speech rate and enhancing intelligibility. Research has shown that patients with HD can benefit from auditory rhythm in improving slowness of movement, especially in walking (Thaut et al. 1996). Thus, music therapy can play a beneficial role in maintaining functional movement abilities as long as possible. However, the selection of appropriate musical materials is crucial for therapeutic success. Research has shown that patients with HD respond better to metronome rhythm than musical–rhythmic cues when trying to synchronize their movement, especially in more severe stages of the disease. This is probably caused by the cognitive decline and disturbances in sensory perception that commonly occur in HD, especially in the more advanced stages of the disease.

SUMMARY

This chapter has provided an overview of diseases frequently encountered in neurological rehabilitation, rationales and techniques for rehabilitation, and the specific role of neurological music therapy in the treatment process. Strokes (cerebrovascular accidents) are caused by an interruption of the blood supply to the brain either by blockage (ischemia) or rupture (intracranial hemorrhage) of blood vessels. The damage to the brain that results is dependent on the location of the stroke and can result in cognitive, communication, physical, and socioemotional dysfunction. Spontaneous recovery of some or all abilities will occur in most cases during the first three months after the stroke. During this time, rehabilitation efforts are the most effective.

Traumatic head injuries are the leading cause of death and disability for Americans under the age of 35. Head injuries that are due to external trauma cause diffuse brain damage and often damage the brain stem, which can lead to a state of prolonged unconsciousness (coma). Once the client begins to awaken from the coma, a long and complicated recovery process begins, often lasting six months or more. Problems associated with head injury include deficits in cognitive, communicative, sensorimotor, and socioemotional abilities.

Parkinsons' disease and Huntington's disease are disorders of movement caused by basal ganglia dysfunctions. In both diseases, cognitive and perceptual deficits will appear in the later, more advanced stages of the disease process. Patients with Parkinson's disease suffer from tremors, especially in the upper limbs, and slowing or akinesia of movement. Gait is especially affected by the poverty of movement which increases with disease duration. Pharmacological treatment (L-Dopa) is very effective, but the benefits diminish with prolonged use of medication. New treatment approaches include surgical interventions and sensory-based training and facilitation techniques.

Huntington's disease is a genetically dominant disorder that is characterized by choreitic movements and a severe deterioration of functional movement and cognitive abilities.

Music therapy is a unique treatment modality that uses specialized neurological and psychological techniques including sensory stimulation, memory retraining, melodic intonation therapy (MIT), rhythmic auditory stimulation (RAS), patterned sensory enhancement (PSE), and functional motor exercises through therapeutic instrumental music playing (TIMP) to facilitate the recovery or retraining of lost functions or maintenance of deteriorating functions.

STUDY QUESTIONS

1. The two most common causes of cerebralvascular accidents are __________ and __________.
2. What are the four areas of lost function most commonly assessed in stroke patients? Give an example of a lost function for each area.
3. How does the type of brain damage differ between closed-head injury and stroke?
4. Name and describe the two commonly used measurement instruments that assess comatose and postcomatose states in brain-injured patients.
5. What are the five ways in which therapy can help in rehabilitating brain-injured patients?
6. What are the methods a music therapist can use when rehabilitating cognitive deficits of brain-injured patients?
7. What methods in music therapy remediate communication deficits of stroke patients?
8. Describe three methods, musical materials, and rationales for music therapy in physical rehabilitation.
9. How can the music therapist meet the social and emotional needs of the brain-injured patient through music-based methods?
10. What are some of the techniques the music therapist can apply to therapy for patients with Parkinson's and Huntington's diseases?

REFERENCES

Ashley, M. J., and D. K. Krych. 1995. *Traumatic brain injury rehabilitation.* New York: Appleton-Century-Crofts.

Bach-y-Rita, P. 1992. Recovery from brain damage. *Journal of Neurologic Rehabilitation* 6: 191–200.

Basmajian, J. V., ed. 1984. *Therapeutic exercise.* Baltimore: Williams and Wilkins.

Basso, A., E. Capatini, and L. A. Vignolo. 1979. Influence of rehabilitation on language skills in aphasic patients. *Archives of Neurology* 36:190–196.

Belin P., P. Van Eeckhout, M., Zilbovicius, P. Remy, C. Francois, S. Guillaume, F. Chain, G. Rancurel, and Y. Sampson. 1996. Recovery from nonfluent aphasia after melodic intonation therapy. *Neurology* 47:1504–1511.

Brookshire, R. H. 1978. *An introduction to aphasia.* Minneapolis: BRK.

Brunnstrom, S. 1970. *Movement therapy in hemiplegia.* New York: Harper & Row.

Caird, F. I. 1991. *Rehabilitation in Parkinson's disease.* New York: Chapman and Hall.

Clark, C., and D. Chadwick. 1980. *Clinically adapted instruments for the multiply handicapped.* St. Louis, MO: Magnamusic-Baton.

Claussen, D., and M. H. Thaut. 1997. Music as a mnemonic device for children with learning disabilities. *Canadian Journal of Music Therapy* 5: 55–66.

Deutsch, D. 1983. Organizational processes in music. In *Music, mind, and brain,* edited by M. Clynes, 119–136. New York: Plenum.

Elliot, B. 1982. *Guide to the selection of musical instruments with respect to physical ability and disability.* St. Louis, MO: Magnamusic-Baton.

Gallahue, D. 1982. *Understanding motor development in children.* New York: Wiley.

Gfeller, K. E. 1983. Musical mnemonics as an aid to retention with normal and learning disabled students. *Journal of Music Therapy* 20:179–189.

Hagen, C., D. Malkmus, and P. Durham. 1979. Levels of cognitive functioning. In *Rehabilitation of the head-injured adult: Comprehensive physical management,* edited by Professional Staff Association of Rancho Los Amigos Hospital, 46–68. Downey, CA: Rancho Los Amigos Hospital.

Harper, P. S., ed. 1991. *Huntington's disease.* London: Saunders.

Hayden, M., and T. Hart. 1986. Rehabilitation of cognitive and behavioral dysfunction in head injury. *Advanced Psychosomatic Medicine* 16:194–229.

Hoehn, M. M., and M. D. Yahr. 1967. Parkinsonism: Onset, progression, and mortality. *Neurology* 17:427–442.

Holbrook, M. 1982. Stroke: Social and emotional outcome. *Journal of the Royal Collage of Physics* 16:100–104.

Hurt, C. P., R. R. Rice, G. C. McIntosh, and M. H. Thaut. 1998. Rhythmic auditory stimulation in gait training for patients with traumatic brain injury. *Journal of Music Therapy,* in press.

Jellison, J. A. 1988. A content analysis of music research with handicapped children (1975–1986): Applications in special education. In *Effectiveness of music therapy procedures: Documentation of research and clinical practice,* edited by C. E. Furman, 85–97. Washington, DC: National Association for Music Therapy.

Johns, D. F. 1978. Clinical management of neurogenic communicative disorders. Boston: Little, Brown.

Kandel, E., and J. Schwarz. 1985. Principles of neural science. New York: Elsevier.

Lezak, M. D. 1976. *Neuropsychological assessment.* New York: Oxford University Press.

Lucia, C. M. 1987. Toward developing a model of music therapy intervention in the rehabilitation of head trauma patients. *Music Therapy Perspectives* 4:34–39.

Lynch, W. J., and N. K. Maus. 1981. Brain injury rehabilitation: Standard problem list. *Archives of Physical Medicine and Rehabilitation* 62:223–227.

McIntosh, G. C., S. H. Brown, R. R. Rice, and M. H. Thaut. 1997. Rhythmic auditory-motor facilitation of gait patterns in patients with Parkinson's disease. *Journal of Neurology, Neurosurgery, and Psychiatry* 62: 22–26.

Miller, R. A., M. H. Thaut, G. C. McIntosh, and R. R. Rice. 1996. Components of EMG symmetry and variability in parkinsonian and healthy elderly gait. *Electroencephalography and Clinical Neurophysiology* 101: 1–7.

National Head Injury Foundation. 1984. *Coma: Its treatment and consequences.* Framingham, MA: National Head Injury Foundation.

O'Shanick, G. J. 1986. Neuropsychiatric complications in head injury. *Advanced Psychosomatic Medicine* 16:173–193.

Pedretti, L. W. 1985. Occupational therapy practice skills for physical dysfunction. St. Louis, MO: C. V. Mosby.

Pilon, M. A., K. W. McIntosh, and M. H. Thaut. 1998. Speech rate control in dysarthria rehabilitation. *Brain Injury,* in press.

Prassas, S. G., M. H. Thaut, G. C. McIntosh, and R. R. Rice. 1997. Effect of auditory rhythmic cuing on gait kinematic parameters of stroke patients. *Gait and Posture* 6:218–223.

Richards, C. L., F. Malouin, P. J. Bedard, and M. Cioni. 1992. Changes induced by L-Dopa and sensory cues on the gait of parkinsonian patients. In *Posture and gait: Control mechanisms,* vol 2, edited by M. Woollacott and F. Horak, 126–129. Eugene: University of Oregon Books.

Rossignol, S., and G. Melvill-Jones. 1976. Audio-spinal influences in man studied by the H-reflex and its possible role in rhythmic movement synchronized to sound. *Electroencephalography and Clinical Neurophysiology* 41:83–92.

Shumway-Cook, A., and M. H. Woollacott. 1995. *Motor control: Theory and practical applications.* Baltimore: Williams and Wilkins.

Sparks, R., N. Helm, and A. Martin. 1974. Aphasia rehabilitation resulting from melodic intonation therapy. *Cortex* 10:303–316.

Springer, S. P., and G. Deutsch. 1985. *Left brain, right brain.* New York: Freeman.

Swenson, J. R. 1984. Therapeutic exercise in hemiplegia. In *Therapeutic exercise,* edited by J. V. Basmajian. Baltimore: Williams and Wilkins.

Taub, E. 1980. Somatosensory differentiation research with monkeys: Implications for rehabilitation medicine. In *Behavioral psychology in rehabilitation medicine,* edited by L. P. Ince, 371–401. Baltimore: Williams and Wilkins.

Thaut, M. H. 1988. Rhythmic intervention techniques in music therapy with gross motor dysfunction. *Arts in Psychotherapy* 15:127–137.

Thaut, M. H., H. W. Lange, R. Miltner, C. P. Hurt, and V. Hoemberg. 1998. Velocity modulation and rhythmic synchronization in gait of Huntington's disease patients. *Movement Disorders,* in press.

Thaut, M. H., G. C. McIntosh, R. R. Rice, R. A. Miller, J. Rathbun, and J. M. Brault. 1996. Rhythmic auditory stimulation in gait training for Parkinson's disease patients. *Movement Disorders* 11:193–200.

Thaut, M. H., G. C. McIntosh, R. R. Rice, and S. G. Prassas. 1993. Effect of rhythmic auditory cuing on EMG and temporal stride parameters in hemiparetic gait of stroke patients. *Journal of Neurologic Rehabilitation* 7:9–16.

Thaut, M. H., R. A. Miller, and L. M. Schauer. 1998. Multiple synchronization strategies in rhythmic sensorimotor tasks: Phase versus period corrections. *Biological Cybernetics,* in press.

Thaut, M. H., R. R. Rice, and G. C. McIntosh. 1997. Rhythmic facilitation of gait training in hemiparetic stroke rehabilitation. *Journal of Neurological Sciences* 151:207–212.

Thompson A. B., J. C. Arnold, and S. E. Murray. 1990. Music therapy assessment of the cerebrovascular accident patient. *Music Therapy Perspectives* 8:23–30.

Wade, D. T., R. Langton-Hewer, C. E. Skilbeck, and R. M. David. 1985. Stroke: A critical approach to diagnosis, treatment, and management. Chicago: Yearbook Medical Publications.

Wallace, W. T. 1994. Memory for music: Effect of melody on recall of text. *Journal of Experimental Psychology* 20:1471–1485.

12

GROUP MUSIC PSYCHOTHERAPY IN CORRECTIONAL PSYCHIATRY

Michael H. Thaut

CHAPTER OUTLINE

Penal institutions in the United States are in pressing need of psychiatric services. Many studies have documented the growing number of prisoners with severe mental problems. For example, a study of the Alabama prison system reported 10 percent of all inmates as psychotic, and 60 percent as having severe psychiatric disturbances (Leuchter 1981). One of the contributing factors may be that the deinstitutionalization of many psychiatric patients over the last 20 years, and the lack of community-based outpatient psychiatric programs, have victimized many patients by driving them into criminal activity because of lack of adequate health and welfare services.

Psychiatric services are one of the least available health services for prisoners (Valdiserri 1984). Two reasons may account for this. First, correctional psychiatry often stands in conflict with penal philosophies, which do not support the concept of rehabilitation and treatment in prisons. Second, the prison environment presents a very stressful and uninviting professional environment that may deter qualified professionals from working there.

Correctional psychiatry should be distinguished from the more popular field of forensic psychiatry. Whereas a correctional mental health professional works in prisons with prisoners who have been found guilty and sentenced by the courts but have a psychiatric diagnosis, forensic psychiatry involves psychiatric evaluations of prisoners and treatment of patients with criminal records who have been found not guilty by reason of insanity. Forensic psychiatry usually works outside prisons in special wards of regular state hospitals. In this chapter, we will discuss the role of psychiatric services in corrections, professional considerations for the music therapist, three styles of group music psychotherapy, and a specific model for therapeutic music improvisation called the *musical semantics* model. The reader should keep in mind that the information provided here specifically for corrections, can be applied to the forensic setting when adapted to the differences in institutional rules, goals, therapeutic milieu, and background of the patients. Furthermore, much of the information on group music psychotherapy and the model of therapeutic improvisation are relevant for music therapists in general who work in psychiatric settings.

MUSIC THERAPY IN CORRECTIONAL PSYCHIATRY: RATIONALES AND GOALS

Music therapy can be a very successful psychosocial treatment modality in the prison system (Thaut 1987). Involvement in music therapy may provide an incarcerated psychiatric patient with strong emotional and motivational ties to reality, for two reasons. One, the musical experience may become a surrogate for healthy *real-life* experiences, which do not exist in the individual's incarcerated environment. Two, the musically induced mood and emotional response of the patient can facilitate a learning process in thinking, feeling, and behavior that is therapeutically meaningful.

Music therapy interventions provide the imprisoned psychiatric patient with an adaptive and enjoyable medium to express and release personal thoughts and feelings in a constructive, structured manner. Through musical experiences, the individual may learn to properly formulate and organize personal feelings and thoughts. The prisoner may also learn discipline, impulse control, and social skills in individual and group settings (Thaut 1987). Music-based therapy experiences may be used to motivate the severely disturbed patient to reenter reality through a nonthreatening medium. Reducing anxiety, stress, hostility, and combativeness, and using music for positive mood induction are also essential goals for the correctional music therapist.

Research in correctional settings has shown that music experiences can be used as a therapeutic tool to alter mood, anxiety, and thoughts about self in psychiatric prisoner–patients (Thaut 1989a, 1989b).

Some of the major goal areas in correctional music therapy are:

1 Increase self-esteem, learn respect for others.
2 Provide a means of self-expression for feelings, thoughts, and memories.

3. Provide theme-centered structures for social interaction in group therapy and improve group cohesiveness and awareness of others.
4. Reduce aggressive and hostile behavior.
5. Facilitate psychosocial development and adjustment.
6. Provide a nonthreatening and motivating reality focus.
7. Induce mood change.
8. Promote social interaction and interpersonal support.
9. Promote emotional learning in the following steps:
   a. Experience emotions.
   b. Identify emotions.
   c. Express emotions appropriately.
   d. Perceive emotions of others.
   e. Modulate own emotional experiences through feedback from others.

In summary, in music, as an affective and pervasive sensory stimulus, real-life experiences and feelings can be recreated. Reality contact can be made attractive and rewarding. Healthy and appropriate structures of social feedback and interaction can be built. Tension, stress, and anxiety can be channeled and diffused constructively. All of this is possible through music in an environment that has very little tangible and physical means to produce these experiences, which are indispensable for a therapeutic milieu.

PROFESSIONAL CONSIDERATIONS FOR THE CORRECTIONAL MUSIC THERAPIST

The correctional music therapist needs to understand the prison-specific rules of conduct and social dynamics of a penal institution. Prisons are societies within our society, with their own rules, values, and behavior codes. The music therapist, in order to be efficient, must have knowledge about typical prisoner behaviors, power structures among inmates, manipulative behavior, prison jargon, and the development of different prisoner personalities formed during incarceration. Otherwise, the therapist will fail in his or her attempt to develop a therapeutic relationship with the prisoner–patient, or worse, may become a victim of the prisoner's manipulations.

Every institutional regulation in a prison is made to support and strengthen institutional security, which is the main rule and overrules every other concern and program. The music therapist is responsible for security in his or her working area. Competence and responsibility in handling security issues will enhance the respect for the therapist by the inmates and security staff. Good communication and cooperation with the security staff is necessary to build a successful music therapy program.

There are several other prison-specific professional concerns with which the music therapist must deal. For one, the hierarchical and security-dominated organization of a penal psychiatric unit seems, at first, largely contradictory to a desirable therapeutic milieu. The music therapist needs to accept the reality of a prison setting and develop adapted techniques within the institutional framework. Less equipment may be available than in other clinical settings. Hours of programming may be restricted. At times, the music therapist may feel more like a guard than a therapist. Emotional sharing and openness have to be handled cautiously and may not always be therapeutic goals among prisoners themselves and between the therapist and the prisoners.

Imprisonment may exacerbate psychiatric symptoms in a patient, which may lead the therapist to believe that efforts to create a therapeutic environment are in vain. On the other hand, malingering and other forms of manipulation to exploit their illnesses to their benefit are also frequently seen in prisoner–patients.

The music therapist should be familiar with the criminal record of the patient. However, the therapist must learn to separate treatment issues from criminal issues. The music therapist will very likely experience ambivalent feelings toward the prisoner, such as anger or cynical and punitive attitudes and overwhelming empathy, at some time during his or her employment. Both attitudes will make the therapist less efficient.

Three steps will help the music therapist maintain an efficient professional attitude. First, the therapist needs to constantly realize that even small therapeutic contributions can make dramatic differences in a prisoner–patient's therapeutic progress. Second, the music therapist needs to establish him- or herself firmly as an integral part of the treatment team and develop supportive interpersonal relationships with other staff members. Third, therapeutic interventions should be brief, time-limited, focused on the here and now, and guided by realistic and attainable treatment goals and objectives.

Therapy should be presented as an opportunity for the prisoner to work on specific therapeutic goals. However, the responsibility for appropriate improvement in therapy has to remain with the prisoner–patient. In building relationships with prisoner–patients, the therapist should develop a firm and friendly rapport. It is advantageous to spell out to the patient the terms of the relationship; that is, the specific limitations the therapist wishes to set or the environment dictates, as well as the interpersonal rapport that can be achieved.

THREE TYPES OF GROUP MUSIC PSYCHOTHERAPY

Three different types of group music psychotherapy have been found to be highly successful in working with psychiatric prisoner–patients: supportive group music therapy using guided music listening and counseling techniques, therapeutic music improvisation, and music and relaxation (Thaut 1987).

Guided Music Listening and Counseling

In this technique the patients describe their current moods, feelings, and concerns in the initial part of the session. In a second step the patient is asked to formulate a personal agenda, which should spell out a behavioral goal or an area of concern the patient wishes to work on during the session. The third phase of the session involves listening to recordings of music pieces that each patient selects. The music should relate to the personal agenda of the patient, for example, by matching the current mood, by altering the mood in desired directions, by expressing important personal feelings and thoughts, by facilitating positive associations or recall of important memories, or by providing a source of motivation for the patient to make therapeutic progress.

Following each musical excerpt, the patients are encouraged to discuss the feelings and thoughts provoked by the music. These may include joy, nostalgia, loneliness, struggle, depression, love, thoughts about the past and loved ones, or concerns about the future. In the next phase, personal interpretations of the musical experience as they relate to the meaning of the experience in terms of each patient's personal agenda are encouraged and guided by the therapist. Following these interpretations, therapeutic goals are formulated for each patient for the following days or weeks.

Therapeutic Music Improvisation

Instrumental group improvisation sessions permit communication between patients through a variety of chosen or assigned pitched and nonpitched percussion instruments. The patients learn to express and communicate appropriately feelings such as anger, joy, celebration, relief, grief, and so on, on their instruments. The therapist sets up simple jazz-type improvisational structures in which the patients learn to alternate between playing as a group and individual free playing. Often, patients who cannot communicate verbally in an appropriate manner interact and express themselves in an organized and coherent manner on musical instruments. After the instrumental improvisations, the ensuing group discussion focuses on the musical experience as a behavioral learning experience to practice social interaction, to experience and communicate emotions, to experience success, to release tension and reduce anxiety, and to experience reality in a nonthreatening and rewarding manner.

Music and Relaxation

In music and relaxation sessions the initial phase is spent with the patients to identify feelings of anxiety, stress, tension, and the sources of these experiences in the prisoners' lives. This phase is followed by teaching and applying stress management techniques. A technique that can be taught quickly and gives the patient a successful relaxation experience is progressive muscle relaxation (Jacobson 1974). Progressive muscle relaxation requires no imagery, will power, or suggestion, and is therefore especially suited for severely mentally ill patients. While going through the relaxation exercises the patients listen to soft background music, which they can choose according to their preferences, to enhance the state of psychological and physiological relaxation (Unkefer 1990). After the exercise portion the patients are given the opportunity to discuss their experiences during the session as well as ways to apply music and relaxation outside music therapy.

A MUSICAL SEMANTICS MODEL OF THERAPEUTIC MUSIC IMPROVISATION

One of the most effective ways to facilitate group psychotherapy experiences in music therapy is through therapeutic music improvisation. In this modality patients actively engage in music performance on instruments using musical elements and forms that can be quickly mastered by musically nontrained individuals. The basic goal in all forms of therapeutic improvisation is the use of active music making to experience and communicate nonmusical thoughts and feelings that are related to important therapeutic issues.

Although therapeutic music improvisation is widely used clinically and often described in the literature in great technical detail, several key issues in the therapeutic understanding of this technique are unresolved. This may be one of the reasons the technique has not been widely accepted by the general psychotherapy community as a viable form of intervention. One of the major unresolved issues refers to the question of *meaning* in music when the music therapist asks the patient to play music, or when the music therapist tries to respond to or interpret the patient's musical utterance.

The model described here has been found to be very useful for applying therapeutic music improvisation to psychotherapy in many settings. The model is based on the recognition that music does not directly communicate referential information like verbal language. The meaning or "semantics" of language is based on the fact that in speech we use sound patterns as words that stand for concepts known to us by definition or experience. The word *ball* refers to, for example, a round object, an object for certain games, or a colloquial expression for an experience (having a ball). It is generally agreed in the study of music theory and aesthetics (Raffman 1992) that sound patterns in music do not have these meanings. Therefore, inherent conceptual problems arise immediately when the therapist asks the patient to improvise music for nonmusical goals, for example, by expressing a feeling word or an emotional experience, or when the patient's musical expressions are interpreted in nonmusical terms. Such a way of looking at a patient's musical performance cannot result in satisfactory results because it assumes that there is a way for literal and referential translations of musical patterns into nonmusical "language." Therefore, a frequent observation in therapeutic improvisation is that literal translations or interpretations are neither musically satisfactory nor therapeutically meaningful. The music suffers when the patient tries to create direct analogies between musical events and feelings and thoughts. The therapeutic understanding suffers, because the therapeutic meaning of a patient's musical response has to be interpreted by creating analogies between musical events and nonmusical events.

The musical semantics model holds that these analogies are musically restraining as well as arbitrary in therapeutic interpretation because they are based on an impossibility, that is, asking music to express referential meaning similar to language. Even the emphasis on expressing feeling states through music does not solve that dilemma because it is still assumed that music can directly communicate stereotyped emotional responses such as joy, jealousy, love, fear, anger, and so forth.

Therapeutic music improvisation based on the musical semantics model evolves within a hierarchy of three levels. The musical semantics model states that the meaning and validity of musical expressions, even in a therapeutic setting, is initially determined entirely within the music itself. Therefore, on the first level, a patient's musical playing always represents, no matter if on very simple or rather sophisticated performance levels, primarily his or her musical thoughts and not his or her nonmusical thoughts. Therefore, as a first step, the therapist tries to encourage good musical expression in the patient's or the patient group's improvisation. The patient is asked to improvise music in a rhetorical style reminiscent in principle concept of Baroque schools of improvisation (Schulenburg 1995), that is, to communicate musical thoughts through musical improvisation, for example, by improvising on a brief melody, a change in timbre, a rhythmic pattern. The meaning of this improvisation is found in the particular expression of a musical feeling or thought and should not be interpreted immediately as a referential expression of a nonmusical thought or emotion. The therapeutic value of the musical response develops in the expression of musical coherence, for example, through a simple musical phrase expressing tension and stability, a beginning and an ending, a variation on a previous motive, a surprise turn in a melody, a sensitive and controlled change in tempo or dynamic level, and so on.

On the first level, the therapist encourages and evaluates musical expression in improvisation by the criterion of musical coherence as one aspect of the general state of cognitive or emotional coherence of the patient. Remember that musical coherence is not defined by the sophistication of the music. Very simple musical responses can be coherent or incoherent. The therapist tries to help the patient achieve satisfactory musical expressions, that is, musical coherence, not as a literal translation of a nonmusical thought or feeling experience but as a means to help the patient achieve cognitive and emotional coherence in one area of his or her general behavior and mental status. Thus musical improvisation can be used as a diagnostic tool in the therapy process, or as a training tool for improvement in cognitive and affective coherence prototypical for nonmusical cognitive or affective behavior (Perilli 1996).

The counseling process which embeds any therapeutic music experience will provide the appropriate direction and understanding of this therapeutic process for the patient. The patient understands that musical improvisation is not an end in itself. Yet the patient interprets and analyzes his or her musical expressions initially in terms of creating music. This analysis leads naturally to an analysis of general issues of behavioral coherence, for example, by discussing with the patient how he or she was able to create, communicate, and adapt coherent thoughts in music and how that process relates to general issues of behavioral coherence. Thus, the musical improvisation is structured musically yet is also a functional therapeutic experience. However, this counseling process is only meaningful if the process of creating musical coherence was fully explored and experienced by the patient. Therefore, the emphasis in the improvisation must be placed on the coherence of the musical process in order to create therapeutic relevance that is congruent with the capacity of musical communication.

On the second level, appropriate *coherent* musical expressions are considered in order to reflect appropriately ordered sensory behavior that can be molded into appropriate social interactions and group experiences. Musical forms can express and simulate an infinite variety of interactive relationships, for example, playing solos, playing as a group, creating musical dialogs, alternating individual vs. group playing, and so forth. Thus, the structure of the therapeutic improvisation facilitates appropriate interactive behavior based on the appropriateness of the musical behavior. The appropriate expression of musical thoughts and feelings becomes the avenue that allows one to enter the reality of an appropriate social experience.

It is important to recognize that on both levels of therapeutic music improvisation patients will report emotional experiences that already go beyond the musical emotion. Two frequent types of responses comment on the musical experience as (1) a change agent, offering a different perspective on a person's thinking and feeling about self; and (2) an intensification, accessing, or release of existing emotions (Thaut 1989a). Those emotional or cognitive responses are therapeutically very useful because they reflect an introspective thinking and feeling process of the patient. It is important to realize, however, that these responses are not reflecting a literal translation of music in which a musical response directly expresses a nonmusical thought or emotion. Actually, asking patients to use music as a referential expression of thoughts and feelings may stifle their emotional development of the music because they can never experience the full communicative quality of the music, which can only unfold within its own "semantic" value, that is, the communication of musical patterns. Rather, the coherence of the musical experience creates a cognitive and affective state in which more general inner reflections about self are possible (Sloboda 1992).

It has been an interesting clinical observation that prisoner–patients, when given a choice list of "feeling" words (happy, sad, angry, etc.) and one nonfeeling word (memory) to improvise on, very consistently chose the nonfeeling word "memory." However, the musical improvisations were richer in musical content than when they were asked "to play a feeling word," possibly because the nonfeeling word gave them fewer constraints than the feeling word when they tried to literally and awkwardly translate to a musical instrument what it sounds like to feel angry. This fact comes as no surprise when using the musical semantics model for musical expression because according to this model music cannot communicate such concepts directly.

The first two levels of therapeutic music improvisation are prerequisites for the introduction of the third level in which a patient can make referential or inferential transformations from a musical statement to a nonmusical statement. On this level, patients may be able to improvise musical patterns that they experience as representative of a nonmusical thought or feeling, thus using music effectively to communicate "language" in analogy. However, this process is a translation of music into a nonmusical, more linguistic understanding of a musical event that is only meaningful if the musical expression is fully appreciated in musical terms first. Two examples illustrate this point. The first example illustrates by analogy: A meaningful translation of a text from one language to another can be accomplished only if the original text is intelligible and meaningful. The second example refers to musical experiences: A patient may repeat a certain rhythmic phrase over and over during an improvisation. Without an understanding of musical semantics, the therapist may be tempted to interpret this as maladaptive, for example, a translation of compulsive behavior into music. However, a musical analysis may yield this as the emergence of musical coherence reflective of a general improvement in mental functioning because the patient tries to create musically meaningful patterns. In another scenario, a therapist may ask a patient to express a feeling word in music and then use this experience to generate insight into emotional experiences. However, the musical task, because of its literal translating character, could restrain the patient's musical expression in such a way that the ensuing discussion would lack depth because the foundational musical experience lacked cognitive and affective musical significance for the patient. Therefore, the basis of transformatory adaptations of music, which can be very effective in the therapeutic process, is the therapeutic emphasis on musical coherence as a tool for behavior learning and change in the patient.

In summary, the musical semantics model emphasizes a hierarchy of three steps in the therapeutic process related to music improvisation:

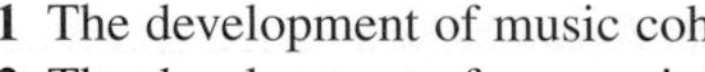

1 The development of music coherence.
2 The development of appropriate behavior.
3 The development of transformations of music to "language" expressions.

CLINICAL CONSIDERATIONS

Clinical reality in a psychiatric prison hospital is characterized by several factors that need to be taken into account in the clinical practice of correctional music therapy. First, many prisoners function on low intellectual levels, especially as far as verbal skills are concerned. Second, prisoners crave immediate tangible rewards and gratification in an environment where only the basic necessities of daily life are provided and where emotional and physical survival is a daily challenge. Third, a therapeutic program cannot contradict basic prison structures regarding security and codes of behavior conduct. If it does, it will become a source of behavior confusion for the inmates, and it will put at risk the physical safety of the inmates as well as the staff. Fourth, normal emphasis in group and individual therapy on self-disclosure, empathy, and sharing can only find limited application in a prison setting.

Power hierarchies among inmates, exploitation of weaker inmates, and use of private information for extortion, control, and manipulation of others require a selective and prudent use of self-disclosure, empathy, and sharing in therapy. However, a therapeutic program that, within these limitations, can offer therapeutic support and meaningful choices and thus return self-respect, identity, and responsibility to its patients, will be greeted with enthusiasm and support by the patients and the staff.

The personal agenda technique (Yalom 1983), discussed in the previous sections of this chapter in conjunction with guided music listening, is a safe and efficient approach to therapy in the prison setting. Its here-and-now focus and emphasis on individual goal setting is very adaptable to the specific requirements of a correctional music therapy group. It also requires cooperative behavior within a group and offers opportunities to become socially involved without forcing everybody's involvement in an individual's therapeutic issues. However, in order to have his or her own personal agenda met, a patient has to tolerate and respect everyone else's agenda in the session.

In selecting the music for therapy, three factors need to be considered. First, the therapist has to allow for individual choices as much as possible to maintain a patient's interest and motivation. When using the personal agenda technique, individual music selections should match individual agendas. Second, a survey of theories of music perception regarding emotion and meaning in music (Thaut 1990) suggests that meaningful responses to music, whether in listening or performing, can occur only within a person's preference for and familiarity with a musical style. It is therefore imperative for the music therapist to offer therapeutic music experiences in musical styles that are familiar to and preferred by the patients. Third, in order to facilitate a patient's response to the therapeutic music experience, the therapist needs to explain to the patient the ways in which music can evoke emotional and motivational responses, stimulate thoughts and memories, give feelings of energy and activation, or provide the activity structure for performance-based therapeutic experiences.

Verbal responses of prisoner–patients are varied and range from monosyllabic and noncommittal utterances to brief answers and interpretations in response to events in the group, to responses that show insight into the patient's own behavior and express the desire to change. Some patients may be so acutely confused that meaningful verbal participation is not possible. However, musical experiences can be perceived on very different levels of emotional or intellectual functioning and evoke meaningful responses on different levels of behavioral functioning. Thus music therapy offers graded opportunities for the mentally ill prisoner to reenter reality and engage in a rewarding behavioral learning process at his or her level of functioning. The uniqueness of music therapy as a performance-based therapy with strong affective–motivational qualities makes it an effective treatment modality in correctional psychiatry.

SUMMARY

As we have learned, correctional music therapy is a rewarding but difficult field. Psychiatric services in the penal system are much needed and not always sufficiently available. The penal environment poses unique challenges to psychiatric treatment. Clinical practice has to adapt to many limitations and restrictions that are inherent in the structure of a prison system.

We have outlined how music therapy can meet the challenge of the penal environment and provide meaningful therapeutic interventions for the incarcerated mentally ill. We have also discussed the special personal and professional challenges the correctional music therapist faces. Therapeutic music experiences can provide strong emotional ties to reality for the incarcerated mentally ill.

Three types of therapy groups have been found to be highly successful at providing meaningful therapeutic music experiences for penal patients: supportive group therapy incorporating counseling techniques and guided music listening, therapeutic music improvisation, and music and relaxation. A new model for therapeutic music improvisation was introduced that emphasizes the inherent attributes of music in providing therapeutic change.

In conclusion, we have addressed some clinical considerations that are specific to correctional music therapy. A thorough understanding of the prison environment is necessary as well as adaptive approaches to conducting therapy. However, music therapy is a modality that can exert a far-reaching influence on the psychiatric prisoner–patient's behavior.

STUDY QUESTIONS

1. What are the three steps of the musical semantics model in therapeutic music improvisation?
2. Three types of group music psychotherapy discussed in this chapter are ____________, ____________, and ____________.
3. What steps can the correctional music therapist take to maintain an effective professional attitude?
4. What are some of the major goal areas in correctional music therapy interventions?

5 What is the personal agenda technique?
6 Discuss some of the clinical considerations for the correctional music therapist in regard to prisoner behavior and music choices.

REFERENCES

Jacobson, E. 1974. *Progressive muscle relaxation.* Chicago: University of Chicago Press, Midway Reprint.

Leuchter, A. F. 1981. The responsibilities of the state for the prevention and treatment of mental illness among prisoners. *Journal of Forensic Science* 26:134–141.

Perilli, G. G. 1996. Music therapy in a psychiatric rehabilitation program: From deficit to psychosocial integration. In *Music therapy within multidisciplinary teams,* edited by I. N. Pedersen and L. O. Bonde, 59–74. Aalborg, Denmark: Aalborg University Press.

Raffman, D. 1992. Proposal for a musical semantics. In *Cognitive bases of musical communication,* edited by M. Riess Jones and S. Holleran, 23–32. Washington, DC: American Psychological Association.

Schulenburg, D. 1995. Composition and improvisation in the school of J. S. Bach. In *Bach perspectives,* edited by R. Stinson, 1–42. Lincoln, NB: University of Nebraska Press.

Sloboda, J. A. 1992. Empirical studies of emotional response to music. In *Cognitive bases of musical communication,* edited by M. Riess Jones and S. Holleran, 33–50. Washington, DC: American Psychological Association.

Thaut, M. H. 1987. A new challenge for music therapy: The correctional setting. *Music Therapy Perspectives* 4:44–50.

———. 1989a. The influence of music therapy interventions on self-rated changes in relaxation, affect, and thought in psychiatric prisoner–patients. *Journal of Music Therapy* 26:155–166.

———. 1989b. Music therapy, affect modification, and therapeutic change. *Music Therapy Perspectives* 7:55–62.

———. 1990. Neuropsychological processes in music perception and their relevance in music therapy. In *Music therapy in the treatment of adults with mental disorders,* edited by R. F. Unkefer, 3–32. New York: Schirmer.

Unkefer, R. F., ed. 1990. *Music therapy in the treatment of adults with mental disorders.* New York: Schirmer.

Valdiserri, E. V. 1984. Psychiatry behind bars. *Bulletin of the American Academy of Psychiatry Law* 12:93–99.

Yalom, I. 1983. *Inpatient group psychotherapy.* New York: Basic Books.

13

MUSIC THERAPY IN THE SCHOOLS

Kate E. Gfeller

CHAPTER OUTLINE

Sara Wilson is the music teacher at Whitmore Elementary School. However, she not only teaches general music to all the students in kindergarten through sixth grade, but also provides music therapy services. The principal at the school is quite pleased to have a music teacher who has her certification in music therapy, because a number of students enrolled at Whitmore have disabilities that require special educational accommodations.

In any given school day, Sara will serve students in a variety of settings. For example, some of the students with disabilities participate in regular music classes along with nondisabled peers. Sometimes she needs to design modifications in her lesson plans in order for those students to participate successfully. She also teaches several special music classes and music therapy sessions for disabled students whose instructional needs are significantly different from those of their peers. Today, Sara will also serve as a music therapy consultant to Mr. Jansen, the band director. He has a new student in his band, Stewart, who is mildly retarded. Mr. Jansen has asked Sara to help him figure out some instructional approaches that will help Stewart keep up with the others. As a consultant, Sara does not provide direct instruction to Stewart but, rather, assists Mr. Jansen in designing and facilitating a suitable accommodation.

If a music teacher from the first half of the twentieth century were to visit Sara Wilson's school, the teacher would be amazed to see students with disabilities learning and playing with nondisabled students, for the notion of including these special children in the regular classroom is a relatively recent phenomenon. How were children with disabilities educated in the past, and how did current practices come about?

EDUCATING CHILDREN WITH DISABILITIES: A HISTORICAL PERSPECTIVE

As we look back in history, we discover that the provision of education for children who have chronic disabilities is a relatively recent practice. The first educational program for persons with disabilities was established in the United States in 1817. During the nineteenth century, a number of asylums or *residential institutions* were established for children who were deaf, blind, and mentally and physically disabled (Adamek 1996). These institutions were often located in remote sites far away from the general public. Historical records dating back to the early 1800s indicate that music programs, including classes, lessons, and ensembles, were considered an important aspect of the education of disabled children, especially those children who were deaf, blind, or mentally disabled (Heller 1987; Sheerenberger 1953; Solomon 1980).

Some of these early music training programs were established with therapeutic goals in mind (Heller 1987; Sheerenberger 1953; Solomon 1980). For example, singing was promoted as a way to improve breathing and articulation. Musical activities were also considered a valuable form of auditory training for students who were deaf. The development of musical knowledge and skills was considered an important curricular emphasis, and participation in music activities was seen as a worthy form of social activity. Because many of these institutions were residential, some students became "lifelong" members of the institution's bands or orchestras. Had Sara Wilson been a music teacher at a state school for the blind, for example, a day's work might have included teaching a music appreciation class, giving private music lessons using braille music, rehearsing the elementary school-age children in the beginning orchestra, and taking the advanced orchestra of adolescents and adults to play a concert for the local music study club.

By the first half of the twentieth century, there was still no consistent federal policy regarding the education of students with chronic conditions. Some children who were cared for at home received no formal instruction at all. Some, especially those with more severe disabilities, continued to be educated in residential institutions. By 1910, *special education classes* within public schools were gaining in popularity. Many educators thought that small and separate classes for students with disabilities were the best possible educational placements for these students. Many people assumed that students would benefit from small teacher-to-student ratios, and that the curriculum would be specially tailored to the unique characteristics of each child. Unfortunately, by 1940, it had become clear to many parents and educators that special education classes were far from ideal. Too often, these special classes became dumping grounds for a hodgepodge of students with a wide range of capabilities and needs. The teachers were often poorly trained and the instruction was little more than custodial in nature (Adamek 1996).

Eventually, public pressure motivated the state and federal governments to improve and expand public school services for children with disabilities. By the 1970s, large numbers of children were moved out of institutions and back into their home communities, where the local school systems were expected to provide a more "normal" yet suitable education. This movement to normalize the education of students with disabilities received an enormous boost when it became federal law. This law, Public Law (PL) 94-142, the Education for All Handicapped Children Act of 1975, stipulated that no child could be denied free and appropriate education, and that the education must take place in the least restrictive environment. The term, *least restrictive environment (LRE),* means that instruction should be provided in an instructional setting as close as possible to normal and also with the sort of educational support necessary to help the student learn.

Since the passage of PL 94-142, a number of amendments to the law have been passed to update or refine the delivery of educational services to children with disabilities. In 1990, for example, Public Law 101-476, the Individuals with Disabilities Act (IDEA), was passed by Congress. This law retained many of the basic principles of PL 94-142, but the term *handicapped* (as was used in PL 94-142) was replaced with the term *disability* and more specific and extensive services were included in this more recent legislation. IDEA was reauthorized (PL 105-17) in 1997, and subtle but important modifications were made to federal guidelines regarding the education of students with disabilities. Over time, state and federal legislators will continue to modify these regulations in response to public pressure or new information about best instructional practices.

As a result of these laws, the manner in which children with disabilities are educated has changed dramatically. In the past, many children with chronic conditions lived their childhoods, or even their lifetimes, in remote institutions. Nowadays, although a child with a particularly severe condition may need temporary hospitalization or residential care, the majority of students with disabilities will receive instruction in their local community schools. Within the halls of the local schools, one can find children with a wide range of disabilities—mental and physical disabilities, emotional disorders, and chronic medical conditions—learning and playing alongside their nondisabled peers.

LEAST RESTRICTIVE ENVIRONMENT: A CONTINUUM OF SERVICES

Although laws such as the Individuals with Disabilities Act (PL101-476) protect the rights of children with disabilities to a free and appropriate public education, the laws do not specify exactly what sort of instruction each child should have. Rather, the regulations require that each student's educational program include two components: (1) Each child should be educated in a setting that is as close to normal as is possible, and thus includes the student to the extent possible in instruction with nondisabled peers. (2) The instructional setting must provide an appropriate instruction given the child's individual needs. In some cases, the instructional needs are not adequately provided in a regular classroom.

Because school-age children have many different kinds of disabilities, which also range in severity, there is no single program for all disabled students. Rather, there exists a continuum of instructional services, from closest to normal (i.e., the regular classroom) to most restrictive (such as a residential educational or medical facility). The least restrictive environment should be selected for each student, based on that individual's unique strengths and instructional needs. In addition to selecting the placement, there are additional decisions to be made regarding various supporting therapies. For example, a student with serious physical disabilities may require the services of a physical or occupational therapist as well as academic instruction. A student with a hearing loss may require the services of a speech–language pathologist or audiologist.

Let us consider examples of students that represent various points along that instructional continuum.

> Tony, a student with a congenital foot abnormality, may function without any special support except in physical education, where he may need to have a few modifications in his footwear or type of participation. Tony attends the regular music classes, and the only time his disability seems to be an issue is during activities that require quick movement to music. Tony represents one extreme on the continuum of instructional service. For Tony, the least restrictive environment (remember, that means close to normal placement that provides suitable instructional support) is the regular classroom, and his instructional needs can be met with very few and minimal adaptations.
>
> At the other end of the continuum, we find Tara, a teenager who has profound retardation and severe physical disabilities because of cerebral palsy. Although she is 14 years of age, her mental age is approximately equivalent to that of a 3-month-old infant. Tara has considerable spasticity and is capable of limited purposeful movement. She requires a feeding tube for nutrition because she cannot chew or swallow her own food. Given the severity of Tara's disabilities, her physical and instructional needs are quite unlike those of the typical 14-year-old's. Therefore, the least restrictive environment for Tara will be quite different from Tony's. Tara is taken in a special bus each morning to a rehabilitation facility where her teachers and therapists work on goals such as grasping, lifting her head, range of motion, and other very basic motor skills needed for optimizing her independence. Three times a week, John, the facility's music therapist works with Tara on range of motion, head control, and grasping skills.

There are also children whose point on this continuum of instructional services may fluctuate considerably over time. For example,

> Brad is a fifth grader whose behavioral disorder is characterized by impulsiveness and disruptive actions. Much of the time, he can control his behavior fairly well as long as his instructional environment is highly structured and his teacher facilitates the behavioral program designed by the school psychologist, Mr. Dennis. Brad meets weekly with Mr. Dennis, and this seems to help keep Brad on an even keel. At this time, the least restrictive environment for Brad is the regular classroom (including regular music classes), with social and behavioral support provided by the school psychologist. This has not always been the case, however.
>
> Last year, when Brad was in the fourth grade, his father abandoned the family and Brad's behavior problems started to escalate. He became so disruptive that he was placed in a psychiatric facility for a few weeks where he would receive more intensive counseling and behavioral management. While in the hospital, Brad not only received daily therapy sessions, but also attended academic classes in the hospital's school. Twice weekly he participated in music therapy sessions designed to help him with identification and appropriate expression of feelings. At that time, the least restrictive environment for Brad was a short-term hospital setting with inhospital education and more intensive therapeutic services.
>
> Once Brad's behaviors started to stabilize, he was discharged and he returned to school. The least restrictive environment, immediately following hospitalization, was a special education classroom for students with behavioral problems, along with special support services such as weekly music therapy and two sessions weekly with the school psychologist. By the end of spring, Brad seemed to be coping much better. Eventually, his teacher recommended his return to the regular classroom, where he has been throughout the fifth grade. Within less than 12 months, the least restrictive environment, that is, the point along the continuum of educational services most appropriate for Brad, has changed three times.

Brad's situation illustrates the point that students' educational needs can change, and that a particular special program may not be suitable for even one student over time. Therefore, in order to determine the most appropriate educational programming for each student, a group of specialists (usually the teacher, school psychologist, and therapists), along with the student's parents or guardian, will meet annually to write up an **individualized education plan (IEP),** a basic plan that states (1) what instructional and support services should be provided and (2) where the instruction will take place. For example, will the student be in a regular classroom, a special education classroom, or a special school? Will the student receive physical therapy or music therapy? The placement should always be the one that, given the child's current needs, is most like a regular classroom, and that results in maximum time with nondisabled peers, but that also provides adequate instructional support.

Given the variety of disabilities students may have, and the continuum of educational and rehabilitative services provided, the role of a music therapist in the educational system can vary considerably. Although there can be considerable variation in the way different school systems organize instruction and supporting therapies, there are several common types of services that a music therapist is likely to provide within the educational system.

DIRECT SERVICES PROVIDED BY MUSIC THERAPISTS IN EDUCATIONAL SETTINGS

Teaching the Inclusive Music Education Class

Sara Wilson's first period this morning is with the third grade music class. The third grade students have just started a special unit on playing the recorder and, in this lesson, the students are learning correct fingerings for the various notes. Sara needs to modify the instructional materials for this unit for Jonas, who has a visual impairment. He needs a special braille version of the fingering charts and music. Jonas's special education teacher and the State Commission for the Blind have assisted Sara with the preparation of special braille music books. In addition, these specialists recommended to Sara instructional approaches for students who can't rely on vision. For example, when Jonas first moved to Whitmore Elementary, Sara started to realize how many times she used instructions that required vision: "Watch me, class." "Look over here." "Which of the instruments is black?" With some adjustments in Sara's teaching methods and materials, Jonas participates in music class as readily as do his classmates.

During third period, Sara teaches music to the fifth grade class. Brad, a student with a behavioral disability attends this class. Sara helps Brad participate effectively in the regular music class primarily by helping him maintain appropriate behavior. Sara displays in a prominent place a list of rules indicating how to behave in her class. Even more important, she (like all of Brad's teachers) also follows the behavioral program designed by Brad's psychologist. That helps Brad by establishing consistent expectations for his behavior throughout the school. Unless Brad is having a particularly "bad" day, he is usually a productive member of music class.

Both Jonas and Brad are **mainstreamed** into the regular music classes. The term *mainstreaming* is sometimes used in a variety of ways but, in general, it means that students with disabilities are included in classes with nondisabled students. Another word, *inclusion,* is sometimes used to describe the concept of education in the regular classroom. When Jonas and Brad attend regular music classes, they are expected to learn the same skills and information that other children learn in music education. Sometimes the IEP may also indicate a secondary goal of *social integration* when students are placed in regular music education. However, it is important to realize that friendships and cooperation do not necessarily occur just by placing a student with disabilities in a class with nondisabled students. Rather, successful integration both academically and socially requires that the music teacher take into account any unique instructional needs of the individual student.

Academic success can be facilitated in a variety of ways. In some cases, the music teacher/therapist may use a *remediation* approach in order to ensure successful participation. That is, a student may need a little extra time, tutoring, or special instructional approach in order to learn all of the same skills and knowledge introduced in the music class. For example, the music teacher may assign a capable and friendly student in the class to tutor Brad on the song lyrics to be learned for the spring musicale.

In other cases, a *compensatory approach* might be more appropriate. That means that the instructor determines that the student will be unlikely to achieve all of the same instructional goals as the nondisabled students in the class. The teacher helps the students *compensate* for their limitations by assigning them alternative learning tasks that are within their ability level. For example,

> Kim, a student with a physical disability is unlikely to develop the motor precision necessary to play a complex samba rhythm that the class is learning. Therefore, Sara has Kim play a different rhythm that doesn't require such a high level of precision.

Social integration also requires direct instructional attention. According to research studies (Darrow and Schunk 1996; Humpal 1991; Jellison et al. 1984), students with disabilities are more likely to fit into the social fabric of the classroom if the music teacher designs instructional tasks that require and reward cooperation of small groups of students. For example,

> Sara might have her fifth grade class of 25 students break into five small groups to make up short plays illustrating the life of Mozart. She tells her class that the group that cooperates the most will get to perform their play for Mr. Rolland, the PE teacher. Brad, who sometimes finds it rather intimidating to suggest ideas in front of the entire class, may find it a little easier to interact with and get to know a small group of only four other students.

The type of instructional *accommodation* (i.e., adjustment or modification) necessary in the regular music class will depend on the type and severity of disability of the student. For example, students with visual impairments will need instructional modifications that reduce dependence on visual information. Students with mental disabilities will require instructional techniques helpful for students who learn slowly. A student with physical disabilities is more likely to require special help with playing instruments or movement. Behavioral management techniques are often the primary accommodation for students who have emotional or behavioral problems. This means that the music teacher or therapist who is serving a student with a disability in the regular music classroom needs to (1) identify the impact that the disability has on learning various musical tasks, (2) determine what special instructional methods or materials will be most helpful in overcoming the disability, and (3) facilitate positive interaction between disabled and nondisabled students.

Teaching the Self-Contained Music Class

Sometimes, the impact of a disability is so great that a student may have difficulty participating effectively in a regular music class. In such cases, the least restrictive environment for music instruction might be a *self-contained* music class. That means the student will attend a music class, often slightly smaller in size, that is designed especially to meet the instructional needs of students with particular disabilities.

> The deaf education teacher has told Sara Wilson that the students in her deaf education class seem to have difficulty participating in the regular music class. Therefore,

Sara has worked with the school principal to find a time for a special music class just for the deaf and hard-of-hearing students. In this class, the students will spend less time on singing and melody recognition than is the case in the regular music class. Instead, Sara will emphasize rhythmic activities that the students can learn through visual imitation and vibrotactile feedback. Sara will also introduce some special remediation on melodic tasks to help the students participate more effectively in the regular music class.

The self-contained class has several instructional advantages: (1) It is often smaller than the regular music class, so the music teacher can give special attention to individual needs. (2) The teaching methods can be designed expressly for unique learning needs related to the individual student. However, there is considerable debate about the relative merits of mainstreaming versus placement in a special class. Some research suggest that self-contained classes do not necessarily improve the academic, emotional, or social functioning of students any more than does a well-facilitated placement in the regular classroom. Those studies suggest that the positive role models and peer pressures from nondisabled students can motivate students with disabilities to interact and study more normally. Other studies, however, suggest that some types of disabilities may be better served in a self-contained classroom (Darrow and Schunk 1996).

Music Therapy as a Related Service

In addition to teaching the general music classes and the self-contained special music classes, Sara Wilson also spends several class periods each week providing direct music therapy services to students whose individual education plans call specifically for music therapy as a related service. John is one of the students that she sees in music therapy. John looks pretty much like other students his age, and he has normal intelligence. However, no matter how hard he tries, he is failing in math. He has recently been diagnosed as having a specific learning disability in mathematics. Because of his considerable interest in music, his IEP committee thought that music therapy might be a good related service to support the goals in special education.

Because there are many different types of learning disabilities, Sara will need to individualize John's music therapy intervention specifically for his disability. There is no standard method or approach deemed effective for all types of learning disabilities. However, Sara has identified four basic categories of music therapy goals that she is likely to use in working with students like John. Music therapy can be used (1) as a tool for teaching or rehearsing specific academic information, (2) as a reinforcer for desired academic behaviors, (3) as a means of promoting socioemotional development, and (4) as support for adaptive music education (Gfeller 1984).

Support for Academic Tasks One way in which music therapy can support academic concepts is through music activities that reflect skills emphasized in the classroom (Gfeller 1984). Musical activities can easily be designed to demonstrate basic cognitive constructs such as object classification (the labeling of objects by color or shape), seriation (the relationship of objects by size, quantity, or quality), spatial relationships (such as in/out, to/from), and temporal relations (the chronological ordering of events, such as first, next, last). For example, if the student has been learning the labels for basic shapes or sizes, musical instruments of varied size and shapes, such as drums, triangles, or woodblocks, can provide novel representations of those concepts. Fast and slow music can be used to illustrate the concept of tempo.

Manner of presentation is as important as content. Good educational practices are especially important when working with marginal learners, and traditional educational methods may not be effective. The therapist should be familiar with methods and materials designed for the special learner and consult with the special education team when determining teaching strategies.

Music is also used as a *carrier of information.* Academic information can be incorporated into catchy, attractive tunes or rhythmic verses to aid recall. You may remember singing songs about the alphabet, animals, colors, and community helpers.

The successful use of music as a memory aid, or **mnemonic** device, has been useful with students who have poor memory, such as those with mental retardation or specific learning disabilities. For example, Shehan (1981) found that the pairing of verbal information with short melodic phrases and visual aids improved recall. Similarly, Gfeller (1982) found that short, simple melodies can help children recall information, such as multiplication tables. Using musical jingles as a novel form of rehearsal can increase motivation and attending, both important prerequisites for memory (Gfeller 1982). Pairing new information with familiar information, such as a well-known melody, can also facilitate recall. For example, many children have learned the alphabet to the familiar song, "Twinkle, Twinkle, Little Star."

Whether music is used to represent academic concepts or as a mnemonic strategy, this intervention should be selected and designed in close cooperation with the special education staff. Regular and open communication between the music therapist and the students' various teachers (most particularly the primary classroom teacher) is one of the key elements to successful music therapy interventions.

Music as Reinforcement As a number of research studies have demonstrated (Eagle 1982), music is a valued, enjoyable stimulus and social event for many people. As such, the opportunity to listen to music or participate in musical activities can be used as a *reinforcer* (reward) in behavior modification programs. Music can be an effective reward for reinforcing proper behavior, but more important, it can also be effective in improving the quality of the students' academic work (Dorow 1976; Eisenstein 1974; Madsen 1979; Madsen et al. 1976). That is, studies show that the quality of academic work will not improve simply by rewarding the student for sitting quietly in his or her seat (in-seat behavior). Rather, reinforcement of accurate responses results in an overall increase in accuracy with or without reinforcement of in-seat behavior. Therefore, if music is used to improve academic behavior, it is important that the reward is linked with the desired academic outcome, not just with good behavior (Treiber and Lahey 1983).

As in all contingent uses of music, the musical experience used as a reward must be truly enjoyable for the student. The music therapist can determine individual preferences through prior assessment. Furthermore, the student must understand what specific behavior is expected in order to earn the music reward. How might a music therapist use music as a reinforcement?

John's special ed teacher, Mr. Jamison, has noticed that John not only has difficulty with mathematical computation, but also, as a result of his frustration, tends to rush through problems. Mr. Jamison would like to encourage John to work more carefully by finding a realistic way to reward careful and accurate work. Because John has been successful in music class and seems to like music, Mr. Jamison decides to talk the situation over with Sara Wilson. Mrs. Wilson says that she can set up a reinforcement program for John that will encourage careful work in mathematics.

First, Sara Wilson meets with John and explains that Mr. Jamison is concerned about his rushing through math exercises. "John, Mr. Jamison tells me that you do much better in your math when you work carefully, but sometimes you hurry. Mr. Jamison was wondering if you and I could work together to improve your math. I think we can find a way."

Next, Mrs. Wilson explains to John that he can earn special music time by doing careful and accurate work in math. Sara discusses with John his favorite musical activities, and John tells Mrs. Wilson that he really likes to play the electronic keyboard in the music therapy room, but he doesn't know how to use all the special buttons. Mrs. Wilson tells John, "For every math problem you do correctly in a week, you will earn three minutes of time playing the keyboard. I will be available to help you learn the special buttons, if you wish."

Sara Wilson and Mr. Jamison work out a time at the end of each week when John can "cash in" his correct math problems and go to the music therapy room to play the electronic keyboard. This example of music as reinforcement has several key ingredients: First, John was rewarded for correct work, not just for finishing the problems. Second, Sara determined, by talking with John, what type of music activity would be enjoyable and thus rewarding. Third, Sara has clearly defined what John must do in order to earn his reward.

Socioemotional Development A structured musical activity can create a motivating environment in which appropriate social behaviors are modeled by the therapist and practiced by the student. Social skills targeted in special education can be integrated into the rules of participation in musical ensembles or creative activities. Furthermore, through activities such as lyric analysis, songwriting, and music listening, emotions can be evoked and expressed in appropriate ways. These types of activities also provide excellent opportunities to work on problem-solving and group cooperation skills (Gfeller 1984).

The special education teacher, Mr. Jamison, has expressed some concern in the faculty lounge that several of the learning-disabled students, including John, not only have academic difficulties, but also have immature social skills: They tend to interrupt others, curse when they feel upset, do not take care of their schoolbooks and equipment, and seem inconsiderate of others. Mrs. Wilson tells Mr. Jamison that she would be willing to set up a music therapy group for five of the students in which social skills and appropriate interaction would be practiced. Mrs. Wilson and Mr. Jamison confer and set up specific behavioral objectives that will be emphasized in the music therapy group.

John, Jason, Brian, Carrie, and Damien all attend music therapy group two times weekly for 30 minutes. The group participates in a number of different music activities, including putting together a rock band and writing songs. This group is different from a regular music group, in that Mrs. Wilson not only teaches musical skills to the students, but also emphasizes appropriate behavior during the group process. For example, each student must earn the opportunity to lead the rock group by using appropriate language and by not interrupting others. Each student is expected to take proper care of the guitars, synthesizer, and percussion equipment. In addition to rewarding appropriate behavior, Mrs. Wilson focuses on appropriate expression of feelings by having the group write song lyrics about a variety of emotions, such as frustration, worthlessness, loneliness, and confidence. Throughout the group, Mrs. Wilson models desired social behaviors by taking good care of the equipment herself, using appropriate language, not interrupting others while they are expressing an idea, and treating each person with respect.

These examples represent just a few of the numerous therapeutic goals and interventions that a music therapist might facilitate in an educational setting. The specific therapeutic goals and interventions selected will depend on the particular type and severity of disability, and the individual differences and interests of each student.

THE MUSIC THERAPIST AS A CONSULTANT

It's 3:00 P.M., and the halls are empty. Although the students have gone home for the day, Sara Wilson's work is not yet over. In addition to working on her lesson plans for next week, she has also promised to meet with Mr. Jansen, the school's band director. Mr. Jansen mentioned in the faculty lounge last week that Stewart wants to join the band. Sara knows Stewart pretty well. He is mildly retarded, and used to be in Sara Wilson's music therapy group for at-risk preschoolers. Stewart has progressed nicely as a result of early intervention and good consistent education, but he is still slower in learning than his peers, and he can be easily distracted. Mr. Jansen worries that this may hamper Stewart's participation in band.

Mr. Jansen had Sara attend the two o'clock band rehearsal, where she observed Stewart's participation in the percussion section. Sure enough, he sometimes got off the beat, and he had difficulty keeping his eyes on the conductor. In her meeting with Mr. Jansen, Sara suggested a number of instructional strategies, including peer tutoring by the more advanced drum students, and slightly easier drum parts, to help Stewart be a more productive part of the band.

Music therapists, because of their professional training, have special knowledge in adaptive music techniques and behavioral management. They can provide useful recommendations to the regular classroom teacher who is seeking alternative instructional or therapeutic interventions. The music therapist is needed to offer practical ideas about accommodating a student in band, choir, or other music experience, because music educators have often received only limited preprofessional preparation in the accommodation of special learners.

VARIATIONS IN JOB REQUIREMENTS FOR MUSIC THERAPISTS IN SCHOOLS

> Last month, Sara Wilson attended a conference for music educators from across the United States, and was particularly pleased to swap professional tips with Dana Rodriguez, a music therapist who, like her, works in a school system. Sara was surprised, however, when Dana described her job requirements and responsibilities, for there are some interesting differences. For example, Dana is certified only as a music therapist. She does not have dual certification in music education and music therapy as does Sara. In the state where Sara lives, a music therapist must also have a teacher's certificate in order to work in the schools. The state regulation where Dana works does not require dual certification. Unlike Sara, Dana does not teach regular music classes. Rather, Dana's direct services include only self-contained music classes and music therapy sessions. Dana also spends many hours each week as a consultant to the music teachers in the entire school system. Consequently, her case load requires her to travel to five different schools throughout the district.

Sara Wilson's various responsibilities illustrate common types of services that a music therapist might provide in a school system. However, as Dana's job description indicates, not all music therapists are required to fulfill all those services. The range of responsibilities will vary from school to school. Sometimes these differences are a result of state-by-state variations in educational rules and policies (e.g., whether or not a music therapist must also have a teacher's certificate to work in the schools).

No matter which services the school music therapist provides, it is important for a music therapist in the schools to have a broad knowledge of disabling conditions and the sort of impact that such conditions can have on learning. For example, a music therapist in a large school system may work with children who have any of the following conditions: mental retardation, physical disabilities, emotional impairments, blindness, deafness, autism. Prior chapters in this book have introduced the unique problems and special therapeutic needs that children with different conditions will have. The music therapist needs to understand the various disabilities, and must plan therapeutic and educational interventions accordingly.

The music therapist must also be ready to modify the delivery of services as a child's instructional and therapeutic needs change over time. For example, sometimes children with disabilities or medical conditions require intensive treatment in medical facilities. As their conditions stabilize or improve, these children often return to classes and playgrounds at their local schools. The music therapist plays an important role in helping meet the unique health and instructional needs of children while still providing an instructional environment that is as much like normal education as is possible.

SUMMARY

Some music therapists are employed in school settings. This is because children with disabilities, whenever possible, are expected to attend classes in their local schools alongside their nondisabled peers. Because educational settings serve students having a wide range of disabilities, the music therapist in the public schools may serve a number of functions: instruction of students with disabilities alongside nondisabled students in regular music classes; instruction of self-contained music classes for students whose instructional needs are not well served in the regular class; provision of music therapy services for children whose IEPs indicate music therapy intervention; and consultation with other teachers regarding adaptation of music instruction or use of music to reinforce other classroom concepts.

Each student has unique problems and needs, thus music therapy interventions must be individualized. However, there are four basic therapeutic categories that are commonly emphasized in the educational setting:

1 *Music activities can support academic tasks.* Music can be used to reflect academic skills emphasized in the classroom, as a carrier of information, or as a mnemonic device to aid memory.

2 *Music can be used as a reinforcer.* Appropriate behavior and completion of academic tasks can be rewarded through events such as listening to music or participating in music activities.

3 *Music activities can provide socioemotional support.* Structured music activities provide opportunities to practice appropriate social behaviors and express feelings.

4 *Music therapy can support music education.* Because learning-disabled students may experience difficulties in music education, the music therapist may provide consultation in adaptive methods to ensure that the learning-disabled student participates successfully in the mainstream music environment.

STUDY QUESTIONS

1 Give several examples of how music therapy can be used to support academic concepts.
2 Think of one way in which music might be used as a reinforcement for a student with learning difficulties.
3 How might music therapy be used to support social and emotional growth?
4 What is Public Law 94-142, and what did it require?
5 What is a self-contained music class?
6 What does the term *least restrictive environment* mean?

REFERENCES

Adamek, M. S. 1996. In the beginning: A review of early special education services and legislative regulatory activity affecting the teaching and placement of special learners. In *Models of music therapy interventions in school settings: From institution to inclusion,* edited by B. L. Wilson, 3–12, Silver Spring, MD: National Association for Music Therapy.

Darrow, A. A., and Schunk, H. 1996. Music therapy for learners who are deaf/hard-of-hearing. In *Models of music therapy interventions in school settings: From institution to inclusion,* edited by B. L. Wilson, 184–199, Silver Spring, MD: National Association for Music Therapy.

Dorow, L. G. 1976. Televised music lessons as educational reinforcement for correct mathematical responses with the educable mentally retarded. *Journal of Music Therapy* 13:77–86.

Eagle, C. 1982. *Music therapy for handicapped children:* Washington, DC: National Association for Music Therapy.

Eisenstein, S. R. 1974. Effects of contingent guitar lessons on reading behavior. *Journal of Music Therapy* 11:138–146.

Gfeller, K. E. 1982. The use of melodic-rhythmic mnemonics with learning-disabled and normal students as an aid to retention. Ph.D. diss., Michigan State University, East Lansing.

———. 1984. Prominent theories in learning disabilities and implications for music therapy methodology. *Music Therapy Perspectives* 2:9–13.

Heller, G. N. 1987. Ideas, initiatives, and implementations: Music therapy in America, 1789–1848. *Journal of Music Therapy* 24:35–46.

Humpal, M. 1991. The effects of an integrated early childhood music program on social interaction among children with handicaps and their typical peers. *Journal of Music Therapy* 28:161–177.

Jellison, J. A., B. H. Brooks, and A. M. Huck. 1984. Structuring small groups and music reinforcement to facilitate positive interactions and acceptance of severely handicapped students in regular music classrooms. *Journal of Research in Music Education* 32:243–264.

Madsen, C. K. 1979. The effect of music subject matter as reinforcement for correct mathematics. *Council for Research in Music Education Bulletin* 59:54–58.

Madsen, C. K., L. G. Dorow, R. S. Moore, and J. U. Wemble. 1976. Effect of music via television as reinforcement for correct mathematics. *Journal of Research in Music Education* 24:51–59.

Sheerenberger, R. 1953. Description of a music program at a residential school of the mentally handicapped. *American Journal of Mental Deficiency* 57:573–579.

Shehan, P. K. 1981. A comparison of medication strategies in paired-associate learning for children with learning disabilities. *Journal of Music Therapy* 18:120–127.

Solomon, A. L. 1980. Music in special education before 1930: Hearing and speech development. *Journal of Research in Music Education* 28:236–242.

Treiber, F. A., and B. B. Lahey. 1983. Toward a behavioral model of academic remediation with learning-disabled children. *Journal of Learning Disabilities* 16:111–115.

PART THREE

PROFESSIONAL ISSUES IN MUSIC THERAPY

14

THE MUSIC THERAPY TREATMENT PROCESS

William B. Davis
Kate E. Gfeller

CHAPTER OUTLINE

REFERRAL
ASSESSMENT
  What Is an Assessment?
  Why Is Assessment Important?
  Assessment Tools
TREATMENT PLAN
  Therapeutic Goals and Objectives
  Data Collection Systems
DOCUMENTATION
  Methods of Documentation
EVALUATION AND TERMINATION OF TREATMENT
PROFESSIONAL ETHICS
  Confidentiality

According to Cohen and Gericke (1972), "the cornerstone upon which to develop a responsible and meaningful treatment–rehabilitation program is the accumulation and synthesis of accurate, significant patient data" (161). After this information has been collected and analyzed, it is used to formulate treatment goals, objectives, and strategies. Assessment of client needs also assists the therapist in evaluating and documenting clinical change that occurs during treatment (Cohen and Gericke 1972; Hanser 1987; Isenberg-Grezeda 1988; Punwar 1988). This chapter will discuss areas of professional accountability, including assessment of client needs, development of the treatment plan, evaluation of clinical change, documentation of progress, and professional ethics.

Mary is a 58-year-old woman with a diagnosis of depression. One contributing factor is the recent death of her husband. Her personal physician has referred her to the Cherryvale Mental Health Center for outpatient therapy, which will include music therapy. We will follow Mary through her course of therapy, including referral, assessment, treatment, documentation, and issues related to professional ethics.

REFERRAL

Requests for music therapy services for a client may come from various sources, including physicians, psychologists, occupational therapists, physical therapists, speech and language pathologists, teachers, parents, social workers, and occasionally, clients themselves. In a hospital setting, referral for music therapy services is generally initiated by a physician. In a public school setting, the referral may be generated by parents, the school psychologist, or the interdisciplinary team. A request for music therapy in a nursing home may come from a staff member, physician, family member, or the activity director. The staff of Cherryvale Mental Health Center has learned that, at one time, Mary played piano for Sunday services at her church and sang in the community chorale. Although she has not participated in these activities for 20 years, she has expressed an interest in redeveloping her music skills. Mary's psychiatrist believes that development of leisure skills is a crucial part of her treatment plan. Noting her background in music, he has ordered a music therapy assessment to determine if music could be a meaningful leisure activity for her.

ASSESSMENT

An assessment is completed prior to the start of treatment. It provides an overall view of the client's history and present condition, which in turn is used to develop treatment strategies and estimate the duration of treatment. One type of assessment is based on a prescriptive framework, in which the therapist designs a treatment plan based on the client's weaknesses and limitations, with little or no input from the client. In recent years, this framework has generally been replaced with a **felt needs** approach, which incorporates client interests, values, and attitudes into the treatment plan (Hasselkus 1986; Lewis 1989).

What Is an Assessment?

An assessment is an analysis of a person's abilities, needs, and problems, and it is completed prior to treatment (Cohen and Gericke 1972; Punwar 1988). The results of the assessment guide the nature and scope of services recommended for the client. Assessment information can be acquired by interviewing the client and/or family members, observing the client in cognitive, physical, or other tasks, viewing the client's interactions with others, or reviewing the client's records. Ideally, assessment data are gathered in multiple ways.

Frequently, client needs are assessed by members of an interdisciplinary team. This group of health professionals works together to coordinate treatment. The team may consist of a physician, psychologist, occupational therapist, speech and language pathologist, physical therapist, social worker, and others. Each team member completes part of the assessment in his or her area of expertise. For example, the physician evaluates the client's medical history and current health status. The occupational therapist may compile information on the person's social, leisure, and vocational skills. The psychologist tests cognitive ability and personality; the physical therapist learns about the client's gross motor function; and the social worker assesses family and other relationships. The music therapist evaluates musical interests, abilities, and skills. In addition, he or she may evaluate strengths and weaknesses in nonmusic domains that are amenable to assessment by musical stimuli. These areas include, but are not limited to, auditory perception, memory, auditory discrimination, gross and fine motor coordination, and social and emotional behaviors (Hanser 1987). The treatment team's assessment provides information in the following areas:

Medical Past medical history and current health status are representative of this category.

Cognitive Areas assessed include comprehension, concentration, attention span, memory, and problem-solving skills.

Social This includes self-expression, self-control, and quality and quantity of interpersonal interaction.

Physical Range of motion, gross and fine motor coordination, strength, and endurance are representative of this category

Vocational/Educational This category includes adequacy of work skills and preparation for the workplace.

Emotional This area includes appropriateness of affect and emotional responses to various situations.

Communication This includes expressive and receptive language skills.

Family Family relationships and needs are noted in this section.

Leisure Skills This category includes awareness of recreational needs and interests, participation in meaningful leisure activities, and knowledge of community resources.

Why Is Assessment Important?

There are several reasons why music therapists need to know how to administer assessments. One of the most important reasons is that the information learned from an assessment helps determine the nature and scope of treatment. The data help the music therapist decide if the client is suited for music therapy and, if so, what treatment goals and techniques are appropriate.

A second reason for assessing client needs is to provide a reference against which progress during treatment can be measured. In other words, we can't tell how far we have gone if we don't know where we started. If progress is not satisfactory, the therapist can modify the treatment plan. At the end of treatment, a final evaluation helps determine the level of improvement over the initial evaluation.

Third, the continued growth and development of the music therapy profession is dependent upon the ability to accurately assess, monitor, and evaluate treatment (Isenberg-Grezeda 1988). According to Cohen, Averbach, and Katz (1978), no profession, whether it is music therapy or another discipline, can legitimately attain true professional stature without a viable assessment system, not merely the completion of an assessment form. Such an assessment system must underscore the uniqueness of music therapy and contribute to the fulfillment of an individualized client treatment, training, and habilitation plan (92).

Mary's interdisciplinary treatment team completed a comprehensive assessment during her early visits to the mental health center. The results are summarized below.

Medical: Mary is slightly overweight and has elevated blood pressure controlled with medication. She has no other significant medical problems. Vision and hearing are normal.

Cognitive: Mary's intelligence falls within the normal range, but she has difficulty concentrating. She has a short attention span, poor memory, and poor problem-solving skills. These deficits in cognitive performance are attributed to her depression.

Social: Since the death of her husband, she has withdrawn from social activities. She reports feeling lonely but avoids social interaction.

Physical: Mary appears to have normal gross and fine motor control, strength, and coordination for a woman of 58. She complains of a lack of energy and is easily fatigued, which is a symptom of depression.

Vocational/Educational: Mary has not held a job for about 15 years, but she has worked as a teacher's aide, a secretary, and a salesperson. She attended college for two years and majored in music education.

Emotional: Because of her depression, Mary demonstrates little affect. She reports feeling hopeless about the future and has contemplated suicide. She has not emotionally worked through the loss of her husband.

Communication: Mary speaks only in response to direct questions and with only one or two words. Eye contact is minimal.

Family: Mary has two adult children who live out-of-state and have not visited Mary since their father's funeral. Mary reports feeling alienated from her children. There are no other relatives nearby.

Leisure skills: Mary spent the past several years caring for her husband after his stroke. She indicated that she had little time for recreational activities except for occasional trips to the bowling alley with a friend. During the assessment by the occupational therapist, Mary mentioned that many years ago she had played piano for church, wedding, and funeral services and had sung in the community chorale. She acknowledged an interest in redeveloping her skills in music.

The assessment confirms the diagnosis of depression. The team believes that Mary's depression will respond to treatment with antidepressant medication and supportive group therapy, but there is concern that her lack of involvement in the community after discharge may lead to a relapse. The treatment team wonders if music might provide an avenue for Mary to become more involved with others. Does she have the interest and skills in music to pursue it as a leisure activity? To answer this question, the team has referred Mary to the music therapist, Hal, who will perform an in-depth assessment of her music skills.

Assessment Tools

The tools used in assessment vary according to the type of disability and the focus of the person doing the assessment. For example, a mentally retarded child has different characteristics and needs than does an elderly person in a nursing home. In addition, because different professionals are concerned with different aspects of a person's functioning, they will seek different kinds of information. A psychologist uses different assessment tools than an occupational therapist, who uses different assessment tools than a physical therapist, and so forth.

Reliability and validity are two constructs that are important in evaluating the usefulness of an assessment tool. Reliability refers to the consistency with which a test measures a behavior or behaviors. To be reliable, a test must measure a behavior in the same way each time. Validity, on the other hand, has to do with how well a test really measures what it is supposed to. For example, a blood cholesterol test is considered valid if it measures your level of cholesterol (rather than your hemoglobin or white cell count) and reliable if it produces consistent results each time.

Assessment information gained by psychologists, physical therapists, physicians, occupational therapists, and other professionals contains nonmusical information about physical, social, cognitive, and medical functioning that can be helpful to the music therapist. In addition, music therapists have developed some assessment tools that evaluate musical and nonmusical functions in a variety of populations.

Assessments have been constructed for use with persons who are mentally retarded (Boxhill 1985; Cohen et al. 1978; Cohen and Gericke 1972; Wasserman et al. 1973), persons with psychiatric disorders (Braswell et al. 1983, 1986), institutionalized elderly persons (York 1994), and people with hearing impairment (Gfeller and Baumann 1988). In addition, tests have been used to assess cognitive development in adults and children (Rider 1981), in children who are emotionally disturbed using improvised music (Crocker 1955), and in children who are autistic (Nordoff and Robbins 1977). Assessment scales have also been developed for general clinical populations (Bitcon 1976; Bruscia 1987). The drawback for many of these tests is that reliability and validity have not been established, so caution must be used when interpreting the results.

Time constraints often mandate how thoroughly a client can be assessed. Clinical therapists perform assessments along with their other duties, so an exhaustive assessment is frequently unrealistic. Fortunately, there are types of assessments that can be administered expeditiously: (1) selective assessment, (2) checklist assessment, (3) patient-specific assessment, and (4) running assessment.

Selective Assessment By reading reports submitted by the psychologist, physician, occupational therapist, physical therapist, and other members of the treatment team, the music therapist can gain valuable information from which to develop treatment goals and interventions. Hal could develop Mary's treatment plan from information contained in the assessments that have already been performed. The drawback to this approach is that he may miss vital information.

Checklist Assessment Many assessments gather information through a written narrative, which is comprehensive but time consuming. A checklist of behaviors is much quicker to administer but not as thorough. Hal may wish to assess Mary's musical abilities and interests with a checklist.

Patient-Specific Assessment In this method, the therapist supplements information already gathered by other team members with a few well-chosen questions that provide enough additional information from which to devise an appropriate treatment plan (Cohen and Gericke 1972). After reading the various assessment reports submitted by others, Hal could ask Mary a few questions that will guide his development of the treatment plan.

Running Assessment Frequently, assessment occurs during actual music therapy sessions, using therapeutic music experiences that are structured to reveal client strengths and needs. Over time, a treatment plan can be formulated based on the information that has been gathered. The advantage of this method is that it can be used for a new member in an ongoing music therapy group. The disadvantage is that it may take longer to collect the data necessary to develop an effective treatment plan. A running assessment probably would not be used in Mary's case, because she has been referred for a short-term process with a specific focus.

Within a few weeks, Mary's depression is less severe because of medication and supportive therapy, and her eating and sleeping patterns have nearly returned to normal. She is more communicative and better able to concentrate and solve problems. Hal, the music therapist at Cherryvale, will now play an important role in helping Mary integrate into the community through the development of music as a leisure activity. In order to help Mary, Hal needs to determine the following:

Her motivation to redevelop her music skills

Her level of piano and vocal skills

Her knowledge of community resources (music stores, music teachers, and performing groups)

Her work habits (punctuality, reliability, problem solving, and time management)

Using selective assessment, Hal has determined the following:

Mary remembers her previous involvement in music activities fondly and is eager to redevelop her skills. She has a realistic view about her present skill level but feels confident that, through hard work, she can once again become proficient at voice and piano.

Not surprisingly, Mary's music skills have deteriorated over the years. She will need extensive practice before being able to play piano at the level necessary to perform in public. Her vocal skills have also declined but will require less work than piano to become functional.

Although Mary has lived in the community for many years, she shows little knowledge about the availability of community resources to help her in her quest to improve her music skills.

Hal noted that Mary has not been punctual for many of her therapy appointments at Cherryvale. She will need to improve her punctuality and reliability before she can successfully participate in community activities.

TREATMENT PLAN

Once assessment data has been gathered and analyzed, the next step is to establish a music therapy treatment plan. Mary needs to work on improving her music skills, gaining knowledge about community music resources, improving her work habits, and continuing to work on grief issues related to her husband's death. Hal will design a treatment plan to start at Mary's current level of functioning and progress step-by-step until she reaches a predetermined point of desired behavior.

Therapeutic Goals and Objectives

The essence of a treatment plan lies in therapeutic goals and objectives, which are based on established treatment priorities. A goal may be defined as a broad statement of the desired outcome of treatment. Thus, in consultation with Mary, Hal has developed the following treatment goals:

1 To improve vocal skills
2 To improve piano skills
3 To improve punctuality
4 To utilize community music resources
5 To resolve grief issues

Whereas goals are broad statements of desired changes in client behavior, objectives are more specific and short term. A goal is broken down into a series of short-term objectives. Each objective describes an immediate goal, which may be viewed as a small step in the process of attaining a final goal. Listed below are examples of an objective for each of Mary's goals in music therapy:

Goal 1: To improve vocal skills
Objective: Mary will PRACTICE HER VOCAL SKILLS daily for at least one-half hour "three times during the next week."
Goal 2: To improve piano skills
Objective: Mary will PRACTICE HER PIANO SKILLS daily for at least one-half hour "three times during the next week."
Goal 3: To improve punctuality
Objective: Mary will BE ON TIME for three music therapy sessions "next week."
Goal 4: To utilize community music resources
Objective: "By the next music therapy session," Mary will VISIT one LOCAL MUSIC STORE AND PURCHASE one PIECE OF SHEET MUSIC.

Goal 5: To resolve grief issues
Objective: "During the next music therapy session, Mary will CONTRIBUTE at least four COMMENTS with appropriate affect related to her grief issues

Notice that each objective consists of several distinct parts. The behavior to be observed is in caps. The criterion, which is underlined, is described quantitatively, using a number or percent. The termination date, in quotes, gives a target date of achievement. In addition, an objective sometimes contains a qualifier, which stipulates certain conditions under which the objective will be valid. As you can see, objectives clearly indicate what the client is working toward. As such, they can be difficult to construct but provide the best indicator of client progress.

Once Hal has developed Mary's treatment goals and objectives, he can design interventions to help her get there. She will meet with Hal three times weekly for one hour for approximately three months. During the sessions, they will work on piano and vocal skills as well as discuss work habits and community resources. Hal will keep track of Mary's progress through data collection procedures described below. When Mary meets an objective, a new one will be developed that will systematically bring her closer to her goal.

Data Collection Systems

Monitoring progress throughout a client's therapeutic process is one of the most important aspects of a therapist's job (Ottenbacher 1986). It allows the therapist to make adjustments in the treatment plan if progress is not occurring, and ultimately measures the success or failure of a treatment program.

As we have learned, objectives are carefully written to reflect precisely what the client needs to do to meet the treatment goal. Because the behavior can be observed by the therapist, it can also be accurately recorded and matched against a baseline, or level at which the behavior was occurring before treatment was begun. A baseline measure is important to obtain, because it indicates the severity of the problem and serves as a reference point for later evaluation of the effectiveness of the treatment program (Hall 1974).

There are many different strategies for collecting client data, but two of the easiest and most popular methods are frequency and duration recording (Hall 1974; Ottenbacher 1986; Sulzer-Azaroff and Mayer 1977).

Frequency Recording In this very practical observation technique, the therapist simply counts the number of discrete (separate) occurrences of the behavior under observation. In other words, how often does a particular behavior occur? In some instances, the treatment objective may call for a reduction in behavior. For example, a patient may be very restless and unable to participate in group therapy. In order to determine if restlessness has subsided, the therapist may count the number of times the patient leaves his or her seat during a music therapy session. Or perhaps we wish to see some type of purposeful and healthy behavior increase. Therefore, the music therapist may count the number of guitar chords learned in a given period of time. Any behavior that can be counted may be measured using frequency recording. Other examples include number of verbalizations, number of times late for a class or session, and number of musical instruments identified.

The advantages of frequency recording are that it can be used without disrupting ongoing tasks, and the data are easy to record and graph. The therapist simply tallies the behavior on a piece of paper or with a digital counter. The data can then be transferred to a graph (discussed below), which provides a visual representation of the client's progress.

Duration Recording Sometimes it is important to measure how long a particular behavior lasts, or its duration. Duration can be measured either in the total amount of time (seconds, minutes, hours) or in the percentage of time that a behavior occurs during a given period. For example, the therapist working with a hyperactive child who spends a great deal of time out of her or his seat might want to record elapsed time of out-of-seat behavior during the session. A period of 10 minutes out-of-seat during a 20-minute session could either be recorded as 10 minutes or as 50 percent. A stopwatch can be used for precise time measurement, or a standard clock or watch can be used if less precise measurement is adequate. Other behaviors that can be measured using duration recording include time engaged in a task or minutes late for a session.

Hal uses both frequency and duration recording to obtain data about Mary's progress. A frequency count is used to measure all five objectives in her treatment plan. Hal keeps track of the number of times Mary practices piano and voice each week, the number of times Mary is on time for her sessions, the number of contacts she makes with community music resources, and the number of comments she makes that are related to her grief issues. Hal also uses duration recording to monitor the length of time Mary practices piano and voice each week and the extent of her lateness to music therapy sessions. These data are graphed and used to evaluate Mary's progress.

DOCUMENTATION

Organizations must maintain accurate and complete records on the diagnosis, treatment, and care of all clients. This information provides a chronological account of the client's treatment and is considered a legal document (Miller 1986). It also contains information used to monitor quality (effectiveness of treatment), cost effectiveness, and efficiency. In the future, music therapy progress reports may be used to justify charges to insurance companies, Medicare, and Medicaid (Lewis 1989; Punwar 1988). On a more immediate scale, the record establishes an important communications link among all caregivers involved with the client.

The submission of regular and accurate written reports is a fundamental responsibility of all music therapists. These reports should contain assessment data, goals and objectives, treatment plans, progress notes, and a final report. The information must be written in a clear, concise manner using nonjudgmental, objective terminology. After each session, Hal writes a summary of his work with Mary in her permanent medical record.

Methods of Documentation

Reporting requirements and formats vary greatly among organizations. One method of documentation frequently used in hospitals is called APIE (Luksch 1997). Each APIE note consists of four sections:

A = Assessment In this section the therapist states ongoing needs as identified in the initial assessment as well as specific client functioning during and after each session.

P = Plan The therapist lists all goals worked on during each session and notes the music therapy interventions used.

I = Intervention In this section, the therapist describes in subjective and objective terms what has been observed and how the therapist intervened with the client. Also included is the length of the session, number of clients in the group, quality of session, and notable affective expression.

E = Evaluation In this final stage, the therapist will state if goals and objectives were met for the session, evaluate overall progress of the client, and evaluate the effectiveness of the experience in relation to stated goals and objectives.

The following example of a progress note is from one of Hal's sessions with Mary. It follows the APIE format:

A(ssessment): Mary is a 58-year-old outpatient who has been diagnosed with depression related to her husband's death. Client needs to increase verbal expressions of feelings about her husband's death to staff and peers. In addition, Mary experiences problems with punctuality at music therapy sessions and at community music activities. Client also needs to improve knowledge about available community music resources and activities. Practice time on voice and piano needs to be increased.

At today's session, Mary's posture was slumped, she avoided eye contact with therapist, and did not initiate verbal interaction with therapist or peers until the final therapeutic music activity. The client reported that she felt better after music therapy. Mary was five minutes late to group.

P(lan): Mary continues music therapy sessions once per week on an outpatient basis. At the beginning of today's session, Mary was asked about the number of times and duration she practiced piano and voice during the past week, her punctuality at choir rehearsals, and the number of contacts she made during the last week with community music resources. During today's music therapy session, song writing and instrumental improvisation were used to elicit comments concerning grief issues surrounding her husband's death.

I(ntervention): To help Mary feel more comfortable in verbalizing her feelings about her husband's death to peers and staff, the therapeutic song writing and instrumental improvisation were used. Mary declined to participate in the song-writing experience when the therapist asked her to contribute a sentence to the song being written by group members to reflect feelings about their depression. This experience appeared to be threatening to Mary. During the instrumental improvisation, Mary selected the xylophone which she played for the duration of the experience (15 minutes). During this time, her posture improved and she frequently smiled and made eye contact with the therapist and group members. At the end of the instrumental improvisation, Mary contributed two comments related to her mood, indicating that she felt much better than when she first arrived for music therapy. There were eight clients present for today's 45-minute session.

E(valuation): Mary indicated that she practiced her voice and piano four times last week, 30 minutes per time. Objective was met. Mary reported that she was on time for both choir rehearsals, but was late by five minutes to today's music therapy session. Although she has improved her punctuality, she continues to be late for her weekly music therapy sessions. Objective not met. Mary continues to do well exploring community music resources. Last week she purchased sheet music from a local music store for both her voice and piano lessons. Objective met. During the instrumental improvisation, Mary contributed two verbal comments related to her feelings of depression. Although Mary is becoming more comfortable expressing her feelings, she did not meet the criterion of four verbal comments related to her grief issues. Objective not met.

Another way to document client progress is with a graph. The visual representation of data conveys an immediate sense of how a client is progressing (or not progressing). Figure 14-1 is a graph of data from Mary's music therapy program, showing the number of minutes late to her sessions over the past two months. As you can see, she has been inconsistent with punctuality. A graph could be constructed to document Mary's progress for each of her goals.

EVALUATION AND TERMINATION OF TREATMENT

When a client has met his or her treatment goals, or when the treatment team decides that the client has derived the greatest possible benefit from therapy, treatment is discontinued. At that time, the music therapist writes an evaluation of the entire music therapy process, including the initial goals that were set and progress that was made. The therapist may include recommendations for further treatment or other services.

Mary has been involved in outpatient music therapy for three months. She has met most of her goals and is doing well. In Hal's summary, he recommends that she continue music therapy sessions once a week and use her redeveloped piano and vocal skills as a leisure activity, with an emphasis on those pursuits that allow her to be with other people.

PROFESSIONAL ETHICS

Most professional organizations, including Cherryvale Hospital, are concerned not only with the knowledge of practitioners, as demonstrated through successful completion of

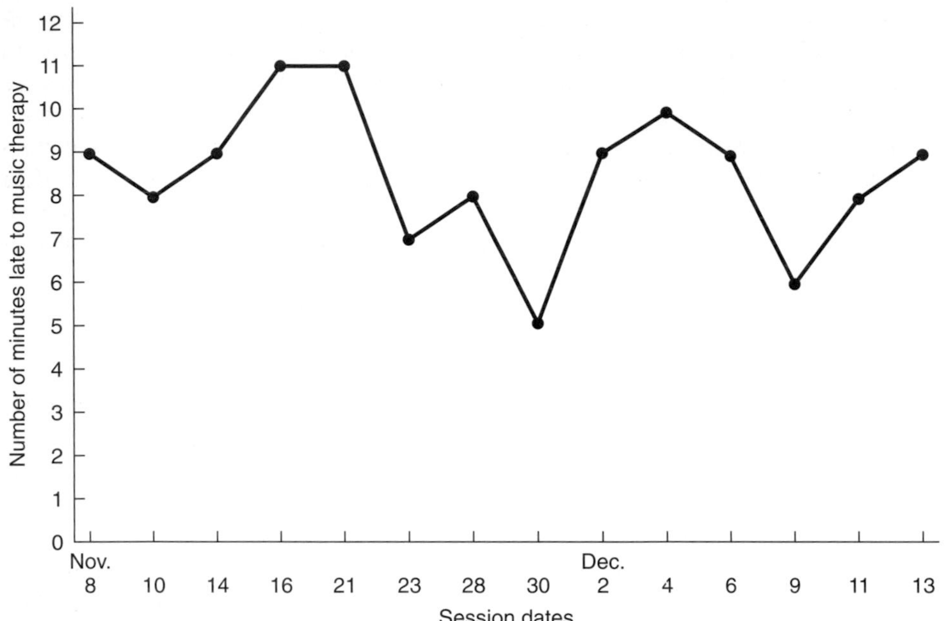

FIGURE 14-1 This graph depicts the number of minutes that Mary was late to her music therapy sessions over a five-week period.

required educational preparation and examinations, but also with their ethical behavior. The term *ethics* refers to the standards of conduct that guide professional practice. Ethical standards are sometimes related to legal statutes (i.e., through state or federal laws), but may sometimes be self-imposed by a professional organization. Organizations such as the American Psychological Association, the National Association of Social Workers, the American Psychiatric Association, and the American Music Therapy Association, to name just a few, have formulated codes of ethics that outline appropriate behavior of the therapist in relation to the client and society in general (Corey et al. 1993). Although the specific behaviors outlined within each code of ethics differ from organization to organization, there are several key issues that are considered of particular importance by most health care professions, including music therapy. These include professional competence and appropriate therapist–client relationships.

Professional competence is a complex issue, but several concerns are commonly found within the ethical codes of health care professions. One is an adequate preparation for the specific profession in question. In order to practice their profession, music therapists, like Hal, must have completed a music therapy program accredited by AMTA, have successfully completed an internship, and use methods that conform with standards of practice endorsed by their professional organization. The therapist should also be aware of personal and professional limitations that might interfere with appropriate provision of care. For example, the music therapist is not qualified to administer or prescribe medication. If the music therapist suspects that the client's problem requires medication, that client should be referred to a physician for evaluation.

The overriding concern in the therapist–client relationship should be the welfare of the client. This means that the client has the right to the most efficacious treatment in an environment that fosters safety, respect, and self-determination. Therapy should be terminated or referrals made when the client no longer benefits from therapy. In addition to providing good care, it is important that the therapist refrain from dual relationships with the client. This means that the therapist should avoid situations that interfere with professional judgment or objectivity (i.e., a romantic relationship or personal friendship) (NAMT 1987). Related to the issue of therapist-client relationship is that of confidentiality.

Confidentiality

Confidentiality, which means that the therapist will not share or discuss matters (outside the group of professionals directly providing care) that arise in therapy, is not only found in most codes of ethics, but is also addressed in many state laws and institutional policies (Corey et al. 1993). Principles of confidentiality seek to protect the client's right to privacy within the boundaries of the law. They are applicable to all treatment settings, including public organizations, private organizations, and private practice.

Most health professions have addressed the issue of confidentiality in their professional standards of ethics. The *Code of Ethics* adopted by the National Association for Music Therapy (1987) includes a section on confidentiality. An important component is the expectation that the therapist keep all client information confidential, whether that information is contained in a written record, a pictorial account, a tape recording, or an informal conversation. However, the release of confidential information to other health professionals involved with the client is acceptable, as is its release in other limited circumstances. For example, the words or actions of a client may be revealed (1) when an individual poses imminent danger to her- or himself or to others (i.e., if a client has informed a therapist that she or he intends to kill a former boyfriend or girlfriend, the therapist is legally obligated to inform the threatened individual and the proper authorities so protective action can be taken); (2) in the case of abuse of minors; (3) and when the information has become an issue in a court action (Corey 1996).

Confidentiality is a very important part of music therapy practice. Students need to understand and practice the principles of confidentiality prior to their first visit to a clinical site.

These are only a few of the many complex concerns that are addressed in ethical standards for music therapists and other health care professionals. Not all ethical considerations are subject to formal legal action, but the individual who breeches ethical conduct may be subject to censure or sanctions by the professional organization. Over and above possible enforcement, each professional has an obligation to conform to these guidelines in order to protect the rights and dignity of each client as well as to uphold the standards of the profession.

SUMMARY

In this chapter, we have learned about the music therapy process, including referral, assessment, treatment, and documentation. Before treatment begins, an assessment is completed, generally by an interdisciplinary team made up of professionals from different specialties. This information helps determine the proper approach to treatment.

Treatment begins with the development of goals and objectives. Goals are broad statements of intent, whereas objectives precisely describe what the client will accomplish. During the course of treatment, client progress is monitored by gathering objective and subjective data. This information helps determine accountability, treatment effectiveness, and efficiency of the therapy. It allows the therapist to make changes in a program that is not working.

Progress is recorded in the client's record, generally after each session. There are a variety of formats for writing progress notes, which may include a graph of relevant data. Written reports, as well as other information pertaining to the client's treatment, are governed by principles of confidentiality.

The final step in the therapy process is the evaluation and termination of treatment. At that point, the therapist prepares a discharge summary of the treatment process and may make recommendations for follow-up.

STUDY QUESTIONS

1. What is an assessment?
2. Why does an assessment need to be completed before treatment?
3. What is an interdisciplinary team, and who are some of the professionals that comprise this group?
4. Define reliability and validity.
5. What is a patient-specific assessment?
6. Describe the elements of a treatment plan.
7. Define goals and objectives, and discuss how they relate to the treatment plan.
8. What is the purpose of data collection?
9. Discuss the importance of documenting client progress.
10. What are APIE notes?
11. When does a therapist terminate treatment?
12. When is it appropriate for a therapist to share confidential client information with persons not involved with the patient's treatment?

REFERENCES

Bitcon, C. 1976. *Alike and different: The clinical and educational use of Orff-Schulwerk.* Santa Ana, CA: Rosha Press.

Boxhill, E. H. 1985. *Music therapy for the developmentally disabled.* Rockville, MD: Aspen Systems.

Braswell, C., D. M. Brooks, A. Decuir, T. Humphrey, K. W. Jacobs, and K. Sutton. 1983. Development and implementation of a music/activity therapy intake assessment for psychiatric patients. Part 1: Initial standardization procedures on data from university students. *Journal of Music Therapy* 20:88–100.

———. 1986. Development and implementation of a music/activity therapy intake assessment for psychiatric patients. Part 2: Standardization procedures on data from psychiatric patients. *Journal of Music Therapy* 23:126–141.

Bruscia, K. 1987. *Improvisational models of music therapy.* Springfield, IL: Charles C Thomas.

Cohen, G., J. Averbach, and E. Katz. 1978. Music therapy assessment of the developmentally disabled client. *Journal of Music Therapy* 15:88–99.

Cohen, G., and O. L. Gericke. 1972. Music therapy assessment: Prime requisite for determining patient objectives. *Journal of Music Therapy* 9:161–189.

Corey, G. 1996. *Theory and practice of counselling and psychotherapy.* 5th ed. Pacific Grove, CA: Cole.

Corey, G., M. Corey, and P. Callanan. 1993. *Issues and ethics in the helping professions.* 4th ed. Monterey, CA: Brooks/Cole.

Crocker, D. B. 1955. Music as a projective technique. *Music Therapy* 5:86–97.

Gfeller, K., and A. A. Baumann. 1988. Assessment procedures for music therapy with hearing-impaired children: Language development. *Journal of Music Therapy* 25:192–205.

Hall, R. V. 1974. *Managing behavior: 1.* Lawrence, KS: H & H Enterprises.

Hanser, S. B. 1987. *Music therapist's handbook.* St. Louis, MO: Warren H. Green.

Hasselkus, B. R. 1986. Assessment. In *The role of occupational therapy with the elderly,* edited by L. J. Davis and M. K. Kirkland, 123–127. Rockville, MD: American Occupational Therapy Association.

Isenberg-Grezeda, C. 1988. Music therapy assessment: A reflection of professional identity. *Journal of Music Therapy* 25:156–169.

Lewis, S. C. 1989. *Elder care in occupational therapy.* Thorofare, NJ: Slack.

Luksch, B. C. 1997. Colorado State University music therapy handbook. Unpublished manuscript.

Miller, R. D. 1986. *Problems in hospital law.* 5th ed. Rockville, MD: Aspen.

National Association for Music Therapy (NAMT). 1987. *Code of ethics.* Washington, DC: National Association for Music Therapy.

———. Notes: *1987. Code of Ethics,* July/August, September/October 1990. Washington, DC: National Association for Music Therapy.

Nordoff, P., and C. Robbins. 1977. *Creative music therapy.* New York: John Day.

Ottenbacher, K. J. 1986. *Evaluating clinical change.* Baltimore, MD: Williams and Wilkins.

Punwar, A. J. 1988. *Occupational therapy: Principles and practice.* Baltimore: Williams and Wilkins.

Rider, M. 1981. The assessment of cognitive functioning level through musical perception. *Journal of Music Therapy* 18:110–119.

Sulzer-Azaroff, B., and G. R. Mayer. 1977. *Applying behavior analysis procedures with children and youth.* New York: Holt, Rinehart and Winston.

Wasserman, N., R. Plutchik, R. Deutsch, and Y. Takemoto. 1973. A music therapy evaluation scale and its clinical applications to mentally retarded adult patients. *Journal of Music Therapy* 10:64–77.

York, E. 1994. The development of a quantitative music skills test for patients with Alzheimer's disease. *Journal of Music Therapy* 31:280–296.

15

THE ROLE OF RESEARCH IN MUSIC THERAPY

Kate E. Gfeller
William B. Davis

CHAPTER OUTLINE

The word *research* may bring to mind mysterious scientists in remote, sterile laboratories filled with test tubes and cages of white rats. As the white-coated researchers peer through microscopes, they mumble polysyllabic formulas for obscure chemical reactions. This image shrouds research in a "white coat" of isolation and obscurity. Actually, research is related to basic events of everyday life. Why do leaves turn different colors in the fall? What causes heart attacks? How do birds find their winter homes during migration? Why does the music in a horror movie make us feel anxious?

The effect of music on mood and behavior has long been a subject of curiosity. In ancient times, people believed that music was a magical force that could affect thinking and feeling. Modern scientists still believe that music influences human behavior; however, we no longer credit its effects to supernatural powers. Rather, through scientific inquiries, we have identified many characteristics of music that influence social, physiological, and psychological response.

Intellectual curiosity alone has motivated extensive inquiry into musical response. However, music therapists conduct research for pragmatic reasons as well. As health care providers, music therapists serve individuals with specific physical or psychological needs. It is the ethical responsibility of the therapist to provide the most effective and efficient care possible. To do so, the therapist compares possible interventions and evaluates each one for its relative merit. Objective scientific inquiry plays an important role in this process. This chapter will introduce you to some of the important concepts and types of music therapy research.

THE VALUE OF RESEARCH

Music therapists have formally acknowledged the value of research for many years. In 1964, the National Association for Music Therapy (NAMT) established the *Journal of Music Therapy,* a publication dedicated to the dissemination of current research and clinical practice (Solomon 1984). In 1969, the *Constitutional Bylaws* of NAMT were expanded, to state that the basic purpose of NAMT was the advancement of training and research in the music therapy profession (NAMT 1969). Over the past three decades, research studies have been regularly presented at professional meetings of the National Association for Music Therapy and the American Association for Music Therapy (as mentioned earlier, these organizations merged in 1998 to form the American Music Therapy Association). Additional research-oriented journals (*Music Therapy Perspectives* and *Music Therapy,* the official journal of the American Association for Music Therapy) were established. According to Duerksen (1968), the "advancement of knowledge and practice in music therapy depends on the quality of the research performed and used by its practitioners." That statement is as true today as it was in 1968.

DEFINITION OF RESEARCH

Research may be defined as "the goal-directed process of looking for a specific answer to a specific question in an organized, objective, reliable way" (Payton 1988). Research produces new knowledge and involves the collection, analysis, and interpretation of data. When done properly, research helps explain and predict behavior. The ultimate benefit is to assist the music therapist in selecting the most useful treatment for his or her clients.

How do we learn? According to Payton (1988), there are four ways to accrue knowledge:

1 *Intuition:* The intuition method is best described as "I know it because I know it" and guides much of our daily behavior. Intuition helps us make clinical judgments about a client's treatment. However, it is not the appropriate basis for scientific study.

2 *Authority:* The authority method of learning might best be described as "this is true because an expert said it was so." Experts in a particular field are a valuable source of information but, remember, at one time we believed that mental illness was caused by demons or unhappy gods. Of course, over time this notion was proved false, but for many centuries people believed it because someone in a position of authority said it was so.

3 *A priori:* The a priori method of learning uses reason and logic to draw conclusions about an event. Reason, of course, is important in interpreting events, but it does not include the important element of systematic observation.

4 *Scientific method:* The scientific method of learning combines intuition, authority, and reason and adds systematic observation. Intuition helps guide the formulation of research questions, authority helps us learn what has already been discovered, and reason helps us interpret data and explore how the results can be applied to our clients.

The combination of these three methods of knowing plus systematic observation are the key elements in the scientific method.

HOW RESEARCH CAN INFLUENCE MUSIC THERAPY PRACTICE

There are three ways in which research can influence music therapy practice. First, because music is the therapeutic medium through which music therapists work, the clinician needs to understand normal reactions to musical stimuli. The music therapist's use of music should take into account the many cultural, physiological, and psychological aspects of musical response. An understanding of normal musical response assists the therapist in selecting appropriate music for a given situation.

Second, music therapists need to evaluate the effectiveness of specific interventions with different types of disorders. Just as doctors prescribe medicine based on knowledge about how certain diseases react to different chemicals, the music therapist should select an intervention based on how people with a particular disorder respond to specific applications of music and music activity.

Finally, research findings help refine theories about music therapy practice. According to Webster's *Dictionary,* a theory is "a systematic statement of principles that guides and acts as a rationale for any given discipline." These principles are the basis for practical actions (Feder and Feder 1981). The theories of any discipline are subject to scrutiny and change as new evidence gained from research challenges previously held beliefs (Rainbow and Froehlich 1987). For example, during the time of the Revolutionary War, doctors theorized that disease was caused by ill humors (phlegmatic liquids in the body) or excessive vascular pressure. If the humors could be balanced and vascular pressure reduced, the patient would be cured. In keeping with this theory, physicians applied leeches to their patients in order to remove impurities and to reduce blood pressure. As a result of the efforts of medical researchers who challenged this theory, physicians began to understand the role of infections and viruses in causing disease. As theories about illness changed, so did treatments. Consequently, more effective pharmacological interventions were put into place.

Similarly, music therapists base their clinical practices on theories, or beliefs, about how music influences behavior. Over the years, research findings have differentially supported, refuted, and refined various commonly held views about music therapy practice. For example, one theory states that music is a unique stimulus that is intrinsically (for its own sake) enjoyable, which can therefore serve as an effective reinforcement or reward to modify behavior. This theory likely arose from clinical observations of many therapists who noted that clients often became more alert or cooperative when allowed to hear or play music. A number of research studies have since supported the theory that music can be an effective reinforcement. For example, in a study of children with behavioral disorders, Hanser (1974) noted that children who showed a high incidence of disruptive behavior in a classroom interrupted the class less frequently when rewarded with the opportunity to listen to favorite musical selections.

More recent studies, however, have suggested that a refinement of this theory is in order. In a study of music therapy for persons with multiple disabilities, Wolfe (1980) investigated the use of music as a reward to encourage control of neck muscles. The subjects, because of their physical disability (cerebral palsy), had difficulty holding their heads erect. This inability to maintain head control interfered with eye contact, attending skills, and interpersonal interaction. The researcher sought to determine whether music would serve as an incentive to control neck muscles. Each subject was allowed to listen to music as long as the head was held erect. If the chin dropped, the music was stopped.

As predicted, some individuals did indeed strive to maintain head and neck control; we would surmise that this effort was made in order to hear the music. Others, however, made little or no effort to hold their heads erect and therefore were not allowed to listen to the music. These individuals did not respond in the predicted manner. Why?

Wolfe's conclusions hold important implications for practicing music therapists. The author determined that music may have been rewarding only to a portion of the participants in the study. He noted that several of the subjects who failed to establish erect head posture lived in a care facility that was often noisy and filled with cries or unpleasant sounds. Wolfe hypothesized that some individuals may have found silence a novel relief that was even more rewarding than music. It is also possible that the particular musical selection was not enjoyable to individual subjects.

Research findings such as these help us refine our theories about music as a reinforcement. Wolfe's objective inquiry pointed out that music may not be intrinsically rewarding in every instance. Music may be more or less effective as a reinforcement in different situations and under different conditions. These differences should be considered when implementing music therapy interventions.

Testing and refining theory and practice is an ongoing process. According to Rainbow and Froehlich (1987), the task of research is to test proposed theories that may assist humans in understanding themselves and their environments. Frequently, we learn that doctors have tested and found a new and more effective medicine for the treatment of a physical or mental condition. In a similar fashion, music therapists continue to challenge their methods of practice, refining and improving interventions.

In summary, demonstrating the effectiveness of music therapy techniques is essential. It is accomplished by carefully accumulating data that support or disprove a theory. As therapists, we must be able to show that our interventions for specific populations and specific clinical environments produce beneficial results. Lacking such documentation, the music therapy profession risks skepticism from our clients and other health care professionals (Ottenbacher 1986).

Research is the most important tool that we have to validate the music therapy profession and, fortunately, there are many types of research available.

Let us consider a hypothetical clinical situation in which research influences music therapy practice.

Janine is a music therapist working in a rehabilitation center. At a team meeting, the physical therapist has expressed concern about a group of elderly patients who have gait irregularity (uneven walking patterns) as a result of strokes. The physical therapist believes that rehabilitation can improve gait irregularities. Unfortunately, the group as a whole has poor tolerance for physical discomfort and lacks motivation to maintain regular exercise. Janine knows that some of these patients will endure a long, difficult walk down the corridor in order to attend music therapy sessions in the day room. Janine wonders whether music might be incorporated into rehabilitation plans to improve motivation. As she ponders this problem, a number of questions come to mind. Has music ever proven effective for rehabilitation of gait disorders? If so, what kind of music would be best? Are there particular techniques that can improve therapy efficiency or effectiveness?

Janine could answer some of these questions through a long process of trial and error. However, she can make more intelligent choices if she considers the research findings reported by others who have asked similar questions. Where can she find this information?

A common practice among researchers is to report the results of their experiments in professional publications, such as the *Journal of Music Therapy.* Janine could visit the library to determine if there are published studies related to her area of interest. A second approach is to attend professional meetings, such as The American Music Therapy Association's annual national conference, where research papers that detail the latest findings are presented. Janine may find one or more presentations that will be helpful in designing her treatment plan. Through these methods of distributing research results, music therapists can benefit from the work of others.

TYPES OF RESEARCH

There are six basic types of research beneficial to the music therapist. **Descriptive** and **qualitative research** are two types that describe "what is" under current circumstances. **Experimental** and **single systems research** both investigate "what will be" if particular factors or conditions are in effect. **Philosophical research** expresses a researcher's opinion about "what ought to be" (Gilbert 1979; Phillips 1989; Rainbow and Froehlich 1987; Wheeler 1995). **Historical research** reflects "what was," helping us understand the past as it relates to the present. Let us consider the problem of Janine, our music therapist, and see how these various types of research might assist her in her practice.

Descriptive Research

Because Janine believes that music might provide motivation for sustaining an exercise program, it is important that she know what types of music the patients enjoy. She can learn about musical preferences of the elderly in descriptive research, which describes what exists at present. Research Example 1, a descriptive research project by Alicia Clair Gibbons, provides such information and may help Janine select music that will be enjoyable and interesting to the rehabilitation group.

RESEARCH EXAMPLE 1 : Descriptive Research

Title of Article →

Popular Music Preferences of Elderly People

Author and Affiliation →

Alicia Clair Gibbons
University of Kansas

Abstract →

A basic premise in music therapy practice is that most adults prefer music of their young adult years to music of other life periods, and that preferred music is more likely to promote participation in music therapy activities than nonpreferred music. It is also quite commonly assumed that elderly adults tend to prefer sedative to stimulative musical experiences. In order to test these assumptions about elderly persons' musical preferences, a study was conducted (N = 60) to determine: (1) whether or not elderly people tend to prefer music that was popular in their young adult years to music that was popular later in their lives; and (2) whether or not elderly people prefer stimulative to sedative music. Results of the study indicated that elderly persons strongly prefer popular music of their young adult years to popular music of life periods after young adulthood (p < .001). Results also indicated that there were no statistically significant differences in preferences for sedative or stimulative music. However, the raw data showed that elderly persons tend to prefer stimulative to sedative music in all age categories.

The study supports the music therapy premise that adults prefer music of their young adult years, but refutes the notion that elderly persons tend to prefer sedative to stimulative music. If music preference is a factor in successful music experiences for elderly adults, then popular music of young adult years may more likely promote successful experience than popular music of later life periods.

Introduction and Related Literature →

Gerontology, or the study of aging, has gained great attention since 1900, especially in the last 20 years (Birren and Clayton 1975). However, even with the growing interest and study of aging, a clear definition of who is old has not been determined. In American society one is considered old when he or she reaches the point of reduced productivity. That age is most often defined at 65 years, the age for employment retirement.

The literature indicates that in American society a person's worth is measured by what he or she can produce or will produce. Retirement not only means that one is quitting production, but is incapable of it (Twente 1970). Retirement often brings about a crisis in the meaningful use of time when a person must shift out of the customary work role, such as gainful employment, child rearing, or homemaking, into

---

Publication Information →

Journal of Music Therapy, XIV(4), 1977, 180–189

Alicia Clair Gibbons, RMT, is a doctoral aspirant and instructor in music therapy, Department of Music Education and Music Therapy, University of Kansas, Lawrence, Kansas.

Introduction and Related Literature →

a substitute role (Havighurst 1970). The older person is left with no definite purpose in life and opportunities for self-esteem are minimal.

Older persons seem to derive satisfaction from associating with one another when given the opportunity to do so (Jeffers and Nichols 1970; Palmore and Luikart 1974). Programs for the elderly should provide these opportunities. It would seem that such programs should serve to acknowledge and develop physical and social strengths and that program focus should be on positive qualities, not disabilities and failures. Music and musical activities may serve to stimulate successful activity which would contribute to self-esteem, aesthetic expression, and gratification. Most important, music may provide for a structured use of time (Sears, note 1).

Music is an integral part of most people's lives since it has many cultural and societal uses. Culture and society define music and determine how it is used. It is a basic premise in the field of music therapy that music of cultures other than one's own has little or no meaning (Gaston 1968) and that one will not respond to or participate in it. A part of that premise is that most adults prefer music of their young adult years to music of other life periods (Gaston 1966), and that preferred music is more likely to promote participation in music therapy activities than nonpreferred music. It is also quite commonly assumed that elderly adults tend to prefer sedative to stimulative musical experiences (Cotter 1965). On the basis of such assumptions music therapists and others design music activities for the elderly which include popular music of the young adult years. Those activities may emphasize music of a sedative nature. If the assumptions are incorrect, music activities may not be programmed to best facilitate the elderly person's involvement or successful experience with music.

While no recent study has been made of the effect music has upon the elderly person, earlier studies of the effect of recorded music upon geriatric, institutionalized patients indicated an increase in appropriate behavior and personal appearance, less aggression, less physical and verbal reaction to hallucinations, reduced incidences of incontinency, and a lowering of undesirable patient noise (Cotter 1960; Griffin 1959; Kurz 1960). Music may also increase environmental awareness in withdrawn, hospitalized geriatric patients (Leiderman 1967; Bright 1972).

The purpose of this study was to determine if elderly people have a preference for popular music of their young adult years compared to popular music from periods after young adulthood, or if the elderly person has no particular popular music preference. In addition, the study attempted to determine if elderly people prefer stimulative or sedative music. Young adult years were arbitrarily defined as that age between 20 and 30 years of age. Legal adult age and clarity of research design were considered in the definition of young adult years.

Method

Subjects

Methodology →

Sixty verbal, ambulatory, and nonambulatory persons between the ages of 65 and 95 years were asked to volunteer as subjects. Persons were randomly selected from various residential situations throughout the Lawrence–Kansas City, Kansas, area.

Each subject was presented with a verbal explanation of the study. To ensure that the explanation was understood, each person was asked to reiterate verbally the

Methodology →

general content stated in the explanation. After the prospective subjects verified their understanding, they were asked to volunteer to participate in the study. The study was conducted immediately after the subjects volunteered.

Setting

The study was conducted in an available meeting room at six sites to which elderly persons had access. Materials and equipment used in the study included a Wollensak Solid State Monophonic Tape Recorder, three experimental tapes, response sheets, pencils, and a piano.

Procedure

Music selections, representative of popular music in each 10-year period from 1900 through 1976, were tape-recorded. The piano medium was used to eliminate instrumental, orchestral, and vocal variables among the selections. The selections were randomly chosen from popular music charts and publications in each period in consultation with musicians familiar with music from the period. In order that the musical examples would be as representative as possible for each period, each sample consisted of an equal number of stimulative and sedative pieces. Judgments of stimulative and sedative music from each period were confirmed by a panel of music experts.

A pianist familiar with a wide range of popular music and musical styles tape-recorded the music. The most familiar section of each selection was played. The selections from various periods were randomized on the experimental tape with sedative selections alternated with stimulative selections. Each selection was of approximately 20 seconds in duration with a 20-second response interval before the next selection was played. Each experimental tape was of approximately 14 minutes in duration.

The first selection on all three experimental tapes was a familiar, patriotic song. The subjects were asked to verbally indicate whether or not they could hear the music. The first selection served to allow the experimenter to adjust the loudness to a comfortable, audible level and to familiarize the subjects with the testing procedure. After the first selection the tape was stopped and subjects were permitted to ask questions concerning the task. When all questions were answered, the experimental task began and was not interrupted until its completion. Most subjects participated in groups of approximately five persons, and participated in the experimental task only once.

During the 20-second response interval that followed each selection, each subject judged whether he or she liked or disliked the selection on a continuum from zero (dislike greatly) to 10 (like greatly). An equal-appearing interval scale (Edwards 1957) was used for recording responses. No subject indicated the need for additional response time.

Since the age range of subjects was broad, it was necessary to focus on three different periods of time which were defined as the young adult years. For those individuals from age 65 to age 75, the young adult years covered the period from 1920 to 1940. For individuals from age 76 to 85, the young adult years were from 1910 to 1930. Finally, for individuals from age 86 to age 95, the young adult years were from 1900 to 1920. A certain amount of overlap was thought necessary to compensate for

Methodology

individuals who fell between the end ages of each group. In addition, there was the unknown factor of diffusion time for popular music.

Since three different young adult periods were defined, it was necessary to construct three separate instruments or experimental tapes to measure popular music preference. In addition to the first selection which was consistent on all tapes, each tape presented eight popular songs from the young adult years group. Each group covered two decades, and two stimulative and two sedative songs were selected from popular music in each decade. Each tape also consisted of eight other songs, four stimulative and four sedative, randomly chosen from music popular in the years following 1950. The eight songs selected from the later life periods, after 1950, were consistent for all three experimental tapes. Each of the three tapes consisted of 16 popular music selections in addition to the trial selection. Table 1 gives the song selections in the sequence presented for each period.

TABLE 1 SONG SEQUENCE FOR EXPERIMENTAL TAPES BY LIFE PERIOD WITH TYPE DESIGNATION

Table

	SONG TITLES		
Type	65–75 years	76–85 years	86–95 years
1. Sed	Sentimental Journey	*I'm Sorry	Moonlight Bay
2. Stim	*You're 16, You're Beautiful & You're Mine	If You Knew Susie	Over There
3. Sed	*Roses Are Red	Moonlight & Roses	*I'm Sorry
4. Stim	Deep in the Heart of Texas	*The Lion Sleeps Tonight	My Little Margie
5. Sed	I Only Have Eyes for You	*Roses Are Red	*Roses Are Red
6. Stim	*Raindrops Keep Falling on My Head	Baby Face	*Sixteen Tons
7. Sed	*Mandy	Always	Always
8. Stim	Marzidoats	*Raindrops Keep Falling on My Head	*The Lion Sleeps Tonight
9. Sed	Over the Rainbow	*The Way We Were	*Mandy
10. Stim	*The Lion Sleeps Tonight	I've Got Rhythm	Darktown Strutters Ball
11. Sed	*I'm Sorry	Girl of My Dreams	Let Me Call You Sweetheart
12. Stim	I've Got Rhythm	*You're 16, You're Beautiful & You're Mine	*You're 16, You're Beautiful & You're Mine
13. Sed	I'm in the Mood for Love	*Mandy	*The Way We Were
14. Stim	*Sixteen Tons	My Little Margie	*Raindrops Keep Falling on My Head
15. Sed	*The Way We Were	I'm in the Mood for Love	I'm Always Chasing Rainbows
16. Stim	You Are My Sunshine	*Sixteen Tons	Alexander's Ragtime Band

*Songs that were popular after 1950.

Analysis of Data

Data were analyzed for 38 of the 60 subjects tested. Data for 22 subjects could not be used due to mismarked score sheets, failure to complete the task, or failure to discriminate among the selections. Eighteen individuals ranged in age from 65 to 75 years, 16 persons ranged in age from 76 to 85 years, and four individuals fell in the 86 to 95 age range.

Results

Results →

The results of the analyses show that the interaction term (AB) is not significant (see Table 2). There was no significant interaction among the variables. Therefore, the experimental results may be directly interpreted.

Table 2 shows that variable A, the effect of the music period, is significant ($p < .001$). The hypothesis which states there is no difference among the means for preferences may thus be rejected.

There is significant difference between preference for music of the young adult years and music of later life periods. Musical preference indicates that elderly people prefer music of their young adult years to music of later life periods (see Figure 1).

Table 2 indicates that no significant differences existed in preferences for stimulative or sedative music. Figure 2, however, suggests that the elderly population may prefer stimulative to sedative music in the life periods defined in this study.

Results of the study indicate that elderly persons strongly prefer popular music of their young adult years to popular music of later life periods. There also seems to be a tendency for elderly persons to prefer stimulative to sedative music that was popular in all life periods. The study supports the music therapy premise that elderly adults prefer music of their young adult years, but refutes the notion that elderly persons tend to prefer sedative to stimulative music. Therefore, if music preference is a factor in successful musical experiences for elderly adults, then popular music of young adult years may more likely promote successful experience than popular music of later life years.

Discussion or Summary →

Discussion or Summary

In music therapy practice with the elderly, ages may vary from 65 to 95 years and more. If people in that broad age range are grouped together, preferred music may be

TABLE 2 SUMMARY OF FACTORIAL ANALYSIS OF VARIANCE

Source of variation	SS	df	MS	F
A (period of music)	50.658	1	50.65	11.53**
B (type of music)	15.635	1	15.63	3.56*
AB (interaction)	2.301	1	2.30	1.00
Within cells	650.366	148	4.39	
Total	728.959	151		

*$p < .100$.
**$p < .001$.

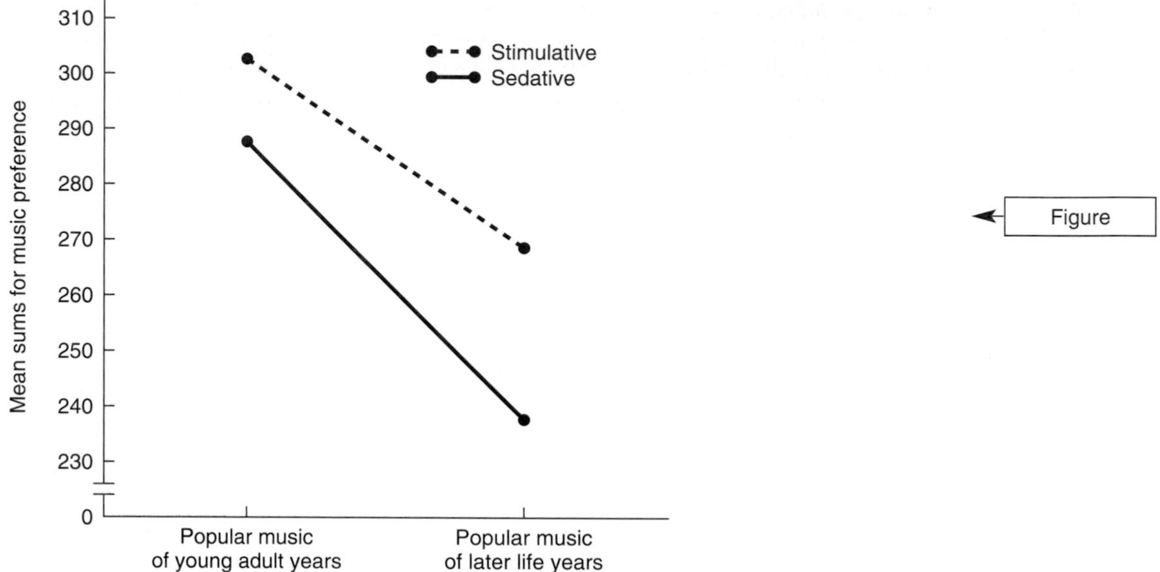

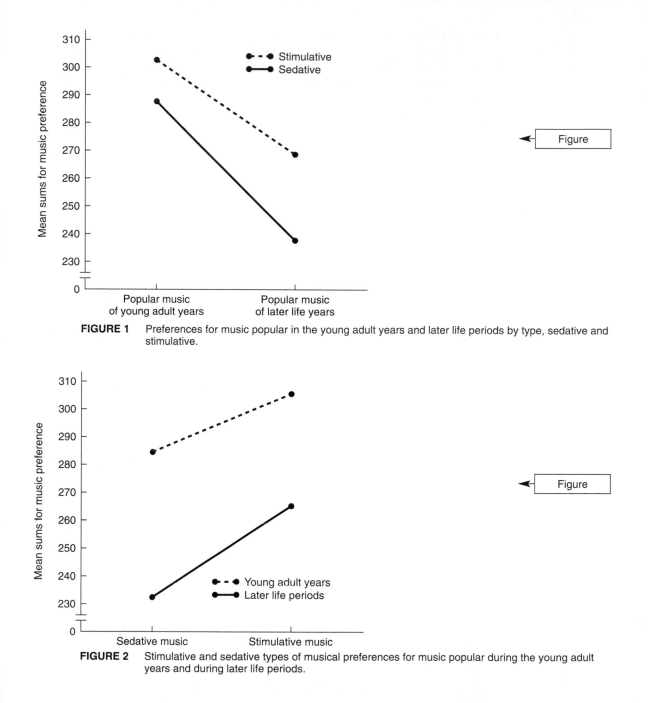

FIGURE 1 Preferences for music popular in the young adult years and later life periods by type, sedative and stimulative.

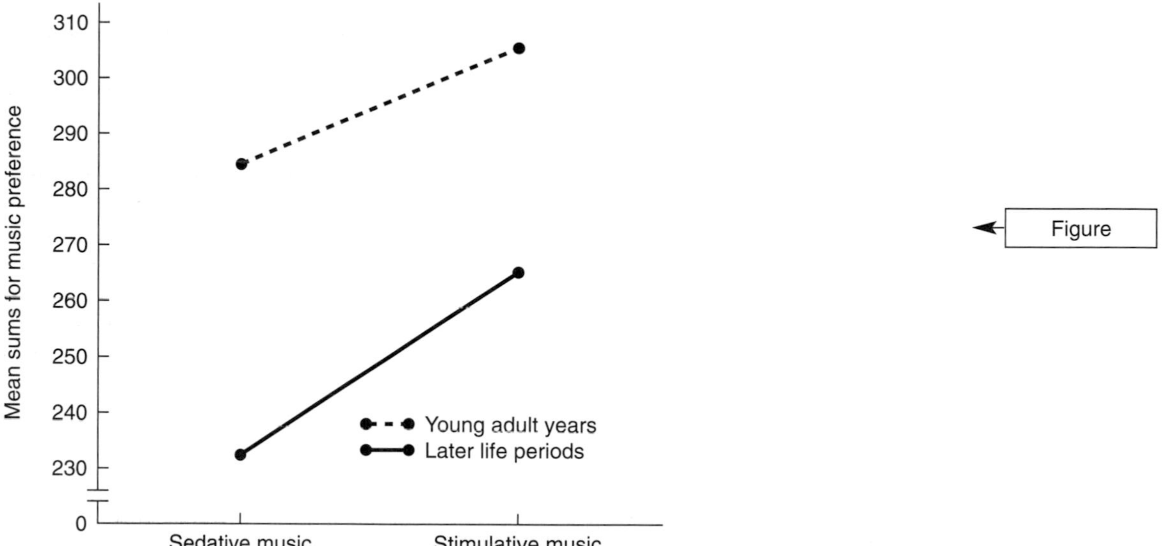

FIGURE 2 Stimulative and sedative types of musical preferences for music popular during the young adult years and during later life periods.

widely varied since there are great differences in young adult periods among group members. The music therapist may erroneously assume that any old, popular music will best facilitate commitment to, and success in, music activities. This study indicates that music of each person's young adult years is preferred to other popular

Discussion or Summary

music. If preference influences participation, it would seem well for the clinician to consider popular music in young adult periods for individual members of the group. In addition, the clinician should not assume that only sedative music facilitates commitment to the music therapy experience since some elderly people may tend to prefer stimulative to sedative music.

Reference Note

References

1 W. W. Sears. Music is time-ordered behavior. Informal discussion. University of Kansas, June 29, 1976.

References

Birren, J. E., and V. Clayton. 1975. History of gerontology. In *Aging,* edited by D. Woodruff and J. Birren. New York: Van Nostrand.

Bright, R. 1972. *Music in geriatric care.* New York: St. Martin's Press.

Cotter, V. W. 1960. Effects of the use of music on the behavior of geriatric patients. Unpublished master's thesis, University of Kansas, Lawrence, KS.

———. 1965. Music therapy for geriatric patients with behavioral disorders. In *An analysis, evaluation and selection of clinical uses of music in therapy,* edited by E. T. Gaston, 76–92. Cooperative Research Project F-044, HEW, University of Kansas, Lawrence, KS.

Edwards, A. 1957. *Techniques of attitude scale construction.* Englewood Cliffs, NJ: Prentice Hall.

Gaston, E. T. 1966. Sound and symbol. *Journal of Music Therapy* 3:90–92.

———. 1968. Man and music. In *Music in therapy,* edited by E. T. Gaston. New York: Macmillan.

Griffin, J. E. 1959. The effects of a planned music program on habits of incontinency and interest in music activities of geriatric patients. Unpublished master's thesis, University of Kansas, Lawrence, KS.

Havighurst, R. J. 1970. Leisure and aging. In *The daily needs and interests of older people,* edited by A. Hoffman. Springfield, IL: Charles C Thomas.

Jeffers, F. C., and C. R. Nichols. 1970. The relationship of activities and attitudes to physical well-being in older people. In *Normal aging,* edited by E. Palmore. Durham, NC: Duke University Press.

Kurz, C. E. 1960. The effects of a planned music program on the day hall sound level and personal appearance of geriatric patients. Unpublished master's thesis, University of Kansas, Lawrence, KS.

Leiderman, P. C. 1967. Music and rhythm group therapy for geriatric patients. *Journal of Music Therapy* 4:126–127.

Palmore, E., and C. Luikart. 1974. Health and social factors related to life satisfaction. In *Normal aging II,* edited by E. Palmore. Durham, NC: Duke University Press.

Twente, E. E. 1970. *Never too old.* San Francisco: Jossey-Bass.

In order to glean useful information from the study, one needs to understand the various sections of a research article and what information each part provides. Example 1 shows the major components of descriptive research articles.

Publication Information Information about the journal includes the name *(Journal of Music Therapy),* volume and issue number (vol. 14, the fourth issue), year of publication (1977), and page numbers of the article (180–189). This publication information helps the reader to locate a particular article in the library.

Title of Article The title of a research article is often lengthy and may seem cumbersome. However, the author attempts to include in the title as much information as possible about what is being studied and with whom. The title of Example 1, "Popular Music Preferences of Elderly People," tells us that the article reports on the types of music that older people enjoy.

Author and Affiliation The name of the author(s) and the institution where the research was carried out are located at the beginning of the article. Alicia Clair Gibbons completed this research while affiliated with the University of Kansas. If a therapist or another researcher needs to find out more about this research, he or she can contact the author at her place of employment.

Abstract The abstract provides a brief summary of the information found in the article. It usually includes the purpose of the study, who participated in the study (referred to as "subjects"), behaviors or events that were observed and analyzed, and what was learned. The abstract is a valuable tool for the clinician or researcher because it helps determine whether or not the research paper contains relevant information without taking the time to read the entire article. From reading this abstract, Janine surmises that the article is closely related to one of her questions, so she chooses to read the entire paper for a more detailed account.

Introduction and Related Literature The beginning of the article provides background information for the research study. The introduction describes the problem being studied, what previous researchers have learned about the problem, and what questions remain unanswered. The author generally identifies which aspect of the problem he or she plans to examine. In Example 1, Gibbons briefly summarizes previous studies about the musical interests of the elderly population. She also explains what she plans to study, based on unanswered questions from previous research.

Method The method section describes how the author(s) conducted the study, including a description of people who participated in the study (subjects), where the study took place, special equipment or tests that were used, and the procedures used to collect information. The author should give enough detail so that another researcher could replicate (repeat) the study. Gibbons studied 60 elderly subjects selected from a variety of settings around the Kansas City area. Using music from various time periods, she attempted to determine if elderly people have a preference for popular music of their young adult years versus popular music from other periods in their lives versus no particular preference. She also wondered if elderly people showed a preference for stimulative (lively) music versus sedative (quiet, slow) music.

Results The results section describes what the author(s) discovered. In both descriptive and experimental research, there is usually a statistical analysis of the quantitative data (numbers of objects, length of event, percentage of accuracy, etc.) collected by the researcher. The author generally describes the results in a narrative form, but the outcome may also be summarized in a table or figure. The Gibbons study concludes that elderly people prefer stimulating music of their young adult years.

Tables An efficient way to present data is in tables. In this example, the author indicates which particular statistical test was used and summarizes the outcome. The small asterisk in Table 1 indicates that both the time in which the music was popular and the type of music had an important impact (described as statistically significant, or beyond a chance occurrence) on the listener's preference.

Figures Figures provide a helpful visual representation of the results. For example, in Figure 1 in Research Example 1 the drop indicates that popular music of young adult years was preferred over popular music from later years.

Discussion or Summary Some articles have a separate discussion section, but in this particular article, it appears as the final paragraph in the results section. In the discussion, the author interprets the findings of the study. In other words, what does it mean? Are there any implications for clinical practice? Are there special precautions the reader should take when interpreting the outcome? This section may also suggest areas that merit future study. In Gibbons' summary, she recommends that therapists working with elderly clients consider using music from the clients' young adult years. She also suggests that music choices not be limited to sedative selections because the subjects in this study tended to prefer more stimulating music.

References The reference section includes a list of all previous research studies to which the author referred when writing the current article. Each citation is comprised of the title of the article, the name of the author, and descriptive information about the publication in which it appeared.

One of the interesting findings of this article was that elderly subjects preferred stimulative music, in contrast to a common belief that older people prefer sedative music. Frequently, such common beliefs are based on the therapist's own perspective and may not always be accurate. One of the values of research is to help us understand clinical situations from a broader and more objective perspective.

Experimental Research

Experimental research has a format similar to that of descriptive studies. Although these two types of research share many common features, there are important differences in the kind of information we can learn. Descriptive research describes "what exists," whereas experimental research suggests "what might be."

We often associate experimental research with laboratories and scientists wearing white coats. However, it encompasses a much broader range of inquiry. In an experimental study, the researcher uses a controlled environment to determine whether or not a particular variable (characteristics or event, such as a particular type of medicine, method of teaching, or brand of toothpaste) has an important effect on the outcome. For example, a dentist may have some of her patients use brand X toothpaste; others are given brand Z. At the end of a year, the dentist may find that the patients using brand X have fewer cavities than those using brand Z.

Can the dentist assume that brand X is more effective? Only if she has eliminated all other possible explanations for the difference between the two groups. Perhaps significantly more of the patients using brand X live in a neighborhood with fluoridated water. Or perhaps the brand X patients were more conscientious about brushing their teeth. In order to feel confident that the difference in number of cavities was because brand X worked more effectively, the researcher must have controlled for other factors (or variables) that could have influenced the outcome.

Just as a dentist might compare two toothpaste brands in order to help a patient reduce the number of cavities they produce, a music therapist might compare different treatment interventions to determine if one is more effective than the other. In Research Example 2, an experimental study, the author has examined the effects of a particular music therapy intervention.

RESEARCH EXAMPLE 2 : Experimental Research

Music and Rhythmic Stimuli in the Rehabilitation of Gait Disorders

Myra J. Staum
University of the Pacific

This exploratory study investigated the application of rhythmic auditory stimuli as a superimposed structure in facilitating proprioceptive control of rhythmic gait. Twenty-five subjects of varying ages and gait disorders listened to individually determined music and rhythmic percussive sounds and attempted to match their footsteps to the stimuli. As rhythmic control increased, stimulus conditions were gradually faded for internalization and independence of the motor pattern. Results indicated that all subjects evidenced gains in rhythmic, even walking, and/or consistency in walking speed. Dependent measures included cumulative timed deviations between footfalls in hundredths of a second and cadence inconsistencies counted in consecutive 10-second intervals. Improvement was also determined by college observers who watched and rated randomly arranged videotape segments of baseline and treatment conditions. Overall, and on specific components of gait, observers differentiated significantly between baseline and treatment conditions. Treatment with music/pulse and fading of music/pulse yielded significant nondifferentiation in ratings, indicating the observable strength and effectiveness of the fading procedures. Proprioceptive control of rhythmic walking was best facilitated in hemiparetic stroke patients, spastic disorders, and painful arthritic or scoliotic conditions.

Neuromuscular and skeletal disorders, affecting 20,000,000 people in the United States, rank first among disorders which seriously alter the quality of people's lives in their long-term debilitating effects (Kelsey et al. 1978). Many of these disabilities are both painful and limiting in normal daily functioning and are costly and require long-term, sometime arduous rehabilitation. In particular, disorders impeding mobility may prohibit independence in working, socializing, and completing the daily routine of living. While compensatory systems for independent mobility are continuously being developed, the psychological effects and integrity of individuals dependent on others may far outweigh the many advances in rehabilitative technology.

While traditional methods for rehabilitating ambulatory disorders are effective, many individuals, particularly elderly ones, may require prolonged assistance or a motivating structure to pursue self-initiated practice. Geriatric and stroke patients may

---

Journal of Music Therapy, XX (2), 1983, 69–87

Myra Jo Staum, Ph.D., RMT, is an assistant professor at the University of the Pacific, Stockton, California. This paper is a report of her dissertation research completed at The Florida State University.

have limited concentration and frequent emotional lability, and may require a more specialized, nontraditional method of treatment. Similarly, young children with limited tolerance for repeated practice may be responsive only to those structures which are readily enjoyable. For those individuals whose neuromuscular connections are severely disturbed, acquiring control over the muscles and limbs may be a monumental task.

Research in the area of motor learning and rehabilitation has addressed the facilitation of a variety of movement tasks in normal and abnormal populations for which external auditory cues have been particularly influential (Carsloo and Edfeldt 1963). In reading, listening, and motor learning tasks with normal individuals, the implementation, withdrawal, or interruption of sound has been used contingently in the presence of specified criteria for motor behavior (Adams et al. 1972; Madsen and Wolfe 1979; Reynolds and Adams 1953). In training muscle responses, the facilitory effect of contingent auditory feedback has been observed in controlling jaw movement and thumb-twitching (Hefferline and Keenan 1963; Hefferline and Perera 1963), in decreasing the rate of multiple tics (Barrett 1962), and in modifying poor posture (Azrin et al. 1968; O'Brien and Azrin 1970). In some instances, the intensity of auditory cues faded over time still maintained a substantial level of response (Hefferline and Perera 1963).

Contingent tonal stimulation has also been applied to special and institutionalized populations. With cerebral palsied and quadriplegic individuals, continual tone reinforcement improved performance on a rotor pursuit target (Sachs and Mayhall 1972). Contingent music listening and instrument playing improved the motor skills of severely retarded children (Holloway 1980) but did not increase motor behavior with severely and profoundly retarded adults (Metzler 1974). Distorted and interrupted music successfully reduced the rocking behavior of a blind retarded child (Greene et al. 1970) yet did not substantially decrease self-stimulation in retarded children (Greenwald 1978). The use of contingent music was effective with a majority of cerebral palsied clients in acquiring proper head posturing control (Wolfe 1980).

The inherent effect of music/rhythmic stimulation on the motor system has been observed in the movement of newborns (Owens 1979), gum chewing (Wagner, note 1), pursuit rotor tasks (Mikol and Denny 1955), typing (Jensen 1931), swimming (Dillon 1952), cardiovascular endurance (Anshel and Marisi 1978), and physical education performance (Beisman 1967). Results, while variable, demonstrate a stronger positive effect on movement in the presence of music/rhythmic stimulation.

Auditory stimulation for gait training has been limited primarily to the contingent use of tones, buzzes, and single sounds. Under conditions of auditory horn feedback, no feedback, and faded feedback, foot dragging of an athetoid cerebral palsied individual decreased from 71 percent to 2 percent under feedback conditions (Spearking and Poppen 1974). With chronic footdrop in hemiparetic patients, audio and visual feedback facilitated improvement and retention of dorsiflexion twice as much as traditional therapeutic exercise (Basmajian et al. 1975). Electromyographic visual and tone feedback was also successful in helping a hemiplegic patient gain function of both upper and lower right limbs (Nafpliotis 1976). In addition, audiofeedback improved hemiparetic patients with dorsiflexion of the ankle, facilitated monitoring of very weak muscles, a spastic gastrocnemius muscle, a quadriceps muscle, and aided monitoring of weak hamstrings in other abnormal spastic conditions (Basmajian 1979). For children exhibiting toe walking, a footswitch worn on the bottom of the shoe with a portable buzzing sound device attached to the waist aided appropriate heel contact during extended practice (Conrad and Black 1980).

Amputees used auditory tones to signal appropriate force levels, where gradual amplification occurred as weight bearing increased on the affected leg. Variable magnitude of tone feedback also indicated varying force levels (Warren and Lehmann 1975).

In hemiparetic stroke patients, a feedback cane was used to facilitate weight transfer from the cane to the weakened leg. When the weight placed on the cane handle met or exceeded a preset threshold, a tone sounded as thresholds were gradually set to more sensitive levels. Results with this device indicated that only a few weeks of practice produced sufficient proprioceptive control to eliminate need for the feedback cane (Baker et al. 1979).

Research examining gait training with music stimuli is minimal. Aside from auditory feedback, only the direct application of vibration to spastic and flaccid muscles has been investigated (Basmajian 1979).

The present study examined the use of rhythmic auditory stimuli to increase independent, even control of ambulation in individuals with uneven or arrhythmic gait patterns. As the reintegration of normal ambulatory patterns requires control and modification of external sensations by proprioceptive impulses and by muscle tone, the use of augmented auditory cues might facilitate this control.

Method

Subjects

Nine children (ages 5–19 years) and 16 adults (ages 52–87) were selected for the study; all evidenced observable gait arrhythmias or inconsistent walking speeds (cadence abnormalities). Gait disabilities included those associated with spastic, athetoid, and ataxic cerebral palsy, spastic hemiplegia due to brain trauma, hemiplegia due to cerebrovascular accident (CVA), scoliosis, poliomyelitis, parkinsonism, and osteoarthritis (see Table 1). The children were selected from special education programs in two public school systems; the older patients were from two different nursing homes, an extended care facility of a medical hospital, and a senior citizens' housing project.

Selection and Recording of Musical Excerpts

Several marches were analyzed by the experimenter for a clear and strong beat pattern with which the subjects could match their footsteps. The following five marches were chosen as maintaining the most consistent tempo: "Stars and Stripes Forever," "Colonel Bogey," "Grand March" from Verdi's *Aida,* "76 Trombones" from *The Music Man,* and "Semper Fidelis." All selections were recorded at eight different metronomic

TABLE 1

Subject	Age	Sex	Disability	Subject	Age	Sex	Disability	Subject	Age	Sex	Disability
A	11	M	Cerebral palsy ataxic	J	68	F	CVA R. hemiplegia (also arthritis of knee)	S	66	M	CVA R. hemiplegia (also mild expressive aphasia)
B	5	F	Cerebral palsy athetoid	K	76	M	CVA partial R. hemiplegia (also global aphasia)	T	72	F	Poliomyelitis; neuromuscular scoliosis (also arthritis of knees; pain in L. knee and hip)
C	7	M	Spina bifida (also scoliosis)	L	72	F	Osteoarthritis of knees & hip (also edema of ankles)	U	11	F	Spastic R. hemiplegia (brain trauma)
D	5	F	Cerebral palsy spastic	M	64	F	CVA R. hemiplegia (also severe confusion)	V	11	M	Spastic R. hemiplegia (also blind; retardation)
E	80	F	Parkinson's disease (also severe confusion and depression)	N	86	F	CVA R. hemiplegia	W	19	M	Cerebral palsy spastic L. hemiplegia (also slight retardation)
F	87	F	CVA L. hemiplegia	O	81	F	CVA R. hemiplegia (also global aphasia)	X	11	M	Mild L. hemiplegia (also retardation)
G	52	M	CVA R. hemiplegia (also expressive aphasia)	P	74	F	CVA spastic R. hemiplegia (also severe depression)	Y	9	M	Mild spastic L. hemiplegia (also retardation)
H	83	F	CVA L. hemiplegia	Q	68	F	CVA R. hemiplegia (also arthritis of ankle)				
I	75	F	CVA L. hemiplegia (also cardiovascular disease)	R	66	M	CVA L. hemiplegia				

speeds from a variable speed record player (Audiotronics 450-VT). Recording occurred for 2 minutes with a pause of 5 seconds between selections.

On eight separate cassette tapes, rhythmic pulses were taped by tapping two tone blocks to the same eight tempi as the music selections. These "pulses" were taped for two minutes with one tempo per cassette tape. Thus, treatment materials consisted of eight tapes, each containing two minutes of five musical selections, and another eight tapes with two minutes of rhythmic pulses. Both groups of tapes were recorded at increasing metronomic speeds to accommodate the range of slow to fast walkers (3 steps/minute–119 steps/minute). For purposes of this study, all marches were expressed in groups of four beats. Subjects were directed to step either on the first beat, on the first and third beats, or on all four beats depending on individual ability. Very slow walkers were allowed to step once every eight beats.

Setting and Apparatus

Settings varied among subjects to include areas convenient to the specific environment. As some of the disabilities were prevalent only in the balance associated with turning corners, a straight pathway and a circular turning area were provided in all settings and remained consistent throughout each individual's treatment.

A small cassette tape recorder (Realistic Minisette 9-14-812) was hung from the shoulder of the experimenter with two lightweight headphones (Panasonic EAH 740 and Calrad 15-129) connected to its input. Headphones were worn by both the subject and experimenter so that decibel level, beat matching, and cessation of trials could be monitored. In addition, the experimenter wore a watch with a sweep second hand and walked to the side and slightly behind the subject during each trial. An additional experimenter was present for videotaping and assisting with wheelchairs between trials. A videotape machine (Sony Betamax SLQ-340) was used twice a week for obtaining progressive data.

Design and Procedure

A baseline (B_1), treatment with pulse and music stimuli (X_1), and fading of stimuli (X_2) comprised the format of the changing criterion design implemented in this study. For three consecutive days prior to baseline videotaping, the experimenter walked individually with patients for approximately five minutes to habituate them to the routine, provide exercise for those whose recent ambulation was minimal, determine individual beat-matching abilities, and ascertain the motor functioning level in other body parts. On the fourth day, subjects walked for one minute with the experimenter, rested for one minute, then walked six more times interspersed with sitting and resting. Videotapes of these six trials focused only below the knee for analysis of cadence (number of steps per minute), timed deviations between left/right footfall, inconsistencies in speed (cadence inconsistencies), and abnormal gait characteristics. The analysis of cadence yielded information relevant to the specific tempo selection to be used during treatment.

On each treatment day, subjects were exposed alternately to three music selections and three rhythmic pulse conditions. During treatment, subjects were directed to listen to the auditory selection through headphones, tap a hand or predetermined functioning body part along with the selection for one minute, and vocalize any verbal sound to the beat of the music. After one minute of tapping, subjects stood and were requested to "walk with the music/pulse" in the same rhythmic manner in which they had been gesturing. After a minute of walking, subjects were seated, the experimenter changed tapes, and the process was repeated with the next selection of alternating music or pulse selections.

When the experimenter determined an adequate change or control in walking, music and pulse sounds were gradually faded by an increasing number of seconds. During walking, the experimenter gradually decreased the volume of the tape recorder until it was off for the predetermined period of time, with a gradual increase in volume until the end of the one-minute trial. When walking was not adequate, fading was reversed by one consecutive second per trial until the subject regained sufficient control. On consecutive trials, music and pulse were faded by a progressive number of seconds until, by the end of the three-week treatment period, auditory cues were completely eliminated for all subjects.

Measurement and Evaluation

The six baseline periods were averaged to obtain a single baseline performance score. Biweekly samples were isolated during treatment conditions in the second and third weeks for evaluation.

For purposes of this study, arrhythmia was defined as the inconsistent timed deviations between footfalls (swing phase) within one minute. Based on normative pilot data, deviations exceeding 2.00 seconds were considered arrhythmic. To measure this deviation, two microswitches (Unimax) were connected independently to two 1/100-second interval timers (Lafayette Co. 54014 and Standard Electric Co. S-1); the microswitches were pressed to activate the timers and released to stop them. The right switch was activated when the subject's right heel contacted the floor, and released when the foot was released, thus providing measurement concerning the left swing phase. Similarly, the left switch monitored the right swing phase. At the end of one minute, cumulative seconds in swing phase were notated for both feet. The differences between the two sets of figures for each trial constituted "cumulative deviations between footfalls" or "arrhythmia." Based on normative data, gait evenness would be expected to improve as deviations approximated zero. Interobserver reliability of videotape analyses with the switch/timer device was obtained on eight different occasions for eight different one-minute samples, resulting in .996 observer agreement.

Number of steps per minute or "cadence" was first evaluated for baseline purposes by counting the number of steps patients took per minute and by averaging the results of six minutes of walking to obtain the individual's average rate of speed. This information was used only in selecting the appropriate tape and beat pattern for treatment.

To measure tempo inconsistencies, however, cadence was evaluated by counting steps taken every 10 seconds during one-minute periods from videotaped segments. Each 10-second interval was then compared to each previous 10-second interval, and the total number of discrepancies or "changes" was determined. Again, based on normative pilot data, inconsistencies would not be expected to exceed 1.31 steps/minute in a normal consistent speed of walking. Inconsistency for this study was defined as a discrepancy total greater than three steps per minute. Counters (Wolfe

1980) connected to the microswitch/timer apparatus also individually totaled right and left leg cadences, thus providing a continuous monitor of the total number of steps per minute for subjects who needed to increase or decrease their overall walking speed.

Two subjective evaluations were made by college music students. In the first, student observers watched three 45-second segments of subjects before treatment (B_1), during treatment with music/pulse (X_1), and at the end of fading when walking occurred without auditory cues (X/xb/2). The ordering of segments was randomized for all 25 clinical subjects, and the volume control of the television monitor was turned off to provide only visual assessment. Observers were requested to look at the segments as many times as they wished and to order them overall as "worst," "next best," and "best" walking. In the second task, different observers saw the same order of tapes with an additional first segment repeated again as a fourth segment. The task required observers to indicate an increase or decrease in improvement by comparing consecutive tape segments of 15 different components of normal and abnormal gait on a scale ranging from –3 to + 3 (Figure 1).

Results and Discussion

Analysis of walking yielded improvement with treatment in all subjects where arrhythmia was prevalent (Table 2). The most impressive gain was a 66-year-old male stroke patient (subject R) who decreased from a deviation of 29.56 seconds between feet in baseline to .61 seconds by the end of treatment. Ten subjects (45 percent) achieved a normal rhythmic evenness, with an additional nine subjects (41 percent) approaching differences of only two to three seconds. An 87-year-old female stroke patient (subject F) who did not achieve a normal rhythmic pattern decreased from a deviation of 26.20 seconds to 7.83, and a seven-year-old male spina bifida child (subject C) from 17.10 to 8.23; both represented extraordinary improvement. Only one subject's gain was minimal with an increase from 14.87 to 20.54 seconds before settling to 12.67 seconds. Three subjects were already within the normal range of rhythmic evenness; therefore, assessments for them were not reported.

Arrhythmic walking demonstrated only a slight increase at the end of fading for 32 percent of subjects, while an additional 52 percent demonstrated continuous improvement over time. The increase in arrhythmia may be attributed to premature fading for specific individuals who perhaps could have benefited from a more prolonged training period.

Consistency in speed, although variable, improved for 68 percent of the subjects. Eight percent were extremely variable with no particular trend; 12 percent did not improve; and 4 percent, while demonstrating improvement, did not deviate initially from the norm. Twelve percent were already considerably consistent in relation to normative data; therefore, no further measurements were obtained for them (Table 3).

In observer ratings of overall gait, significant visual discrimination was made in the actual order of tapes, i.e., B_1 was perceived as "the worst," X_1 as "next best," and X_2 as "best" (Table 4). In ratings of specific gait components, observers differentiated among baseline and both treatment tapes in the category of rhythmic, even steps, with observations significantly accurate in the direction of actual treatment for all six comparison orders ($p < .001$ and $p < .02$, Table 5).

Observer #____ Subject #____ Comparing Tape ____ with ____

1.	____ Unbalanced	−3 −2 −1 0 1 2 3	____ Balanced
2.	Walks on part of foot: ____ heel ___ toe ____ side ___ flat footed	−3 −2 −1 0 1 2 3	____ Walks on whole foot: heel then toe
3.	____ Stops or pauses	−3 −2 −1 0 1 2 3	____ Walks without stopping or pausing
4.	____ Steps sideways ____ Steps backward ____ Steps twice on same foot	−3 −2 −1 0 1 2 3	____ Walks in continuous right–left progression
5.	____ Arrhythmic or uneven steps	−3 −2 −1 0 1 2 3	____ Rhythmic, even steps
6.	____ Rigid, stiff or choppy steps	−3 −2 −1 0 1 2 3	____ Even, smooth steps
7.	____ Width between feet: ____ too wide ____ too narrow ____ crosses over midline of body	−3 −2 −1 0 1 2 3	____ Width between feet about normal
8.	___Inconsistent width between feet	−3 −2 −1 0 1 2 3	____ Consistent width between feet
9.	One or more feet turned: ____ outward ____ inward	−3 −2 −1 0 1 2 3	____ Feet straight ahead
10.	____ Distance of feet off floor: ____ too high ____ too low or shuffling	−3 −2 −1 0 1 2 3	____ Distance of feet off floor about normal
11.	____ Feet inconsistent distance off floor	−3 −2 −1 0 1 2 3	____ Feet consistent distance off floor
12.	____ Speed of walking: ____ too slow ____ too fast	−3 −2 −1 0 1 2 3	____ Speed of walking about normal
13.	____ Inconsistent speed of walking	−3 −2 −1 0 1 2 3	____ Consistent speed of walking
14.	____ Stride length too long ____ Stride length too short	−3 −2 −1 0 1 2 3	____ Stride length about normal
15.	___Inconsistent stride length	−3 −2 −1 0 1 2 3	____ Consistent stride length

FIGURE 1 List of specific gait components for observation by raters.

For tempo inconsistencies, the categories of consistency and slow/fast speeds were collapsed and again yielded significant differentiation in treatment order ($p < .001$) for all comparisons; the only exception was X_1 (treatment with music/pulse) compared with X_2 (fading), where observations were perceived significantly as similar ($p < .001$). Two other related components were analyzed including rigid, stiff, choppy steps which resulted in significant differentiation in the correct order for all tape comparisons except for the comparison of X_2 with X_1.

Results of the study demonstrated improvement in objective measures of rhythmic and

TABLE 2 CUMULATIVE DEVIATIONS BETWEEN FOOTFALLS IN 1-MINUTE SAMPLES: ARRHYTHMIA

		Week 2		Week 3	
Subject	Baseline	Tuesday	Thursday	Tuesday	Thursday
A	2.02	2.20	2.64	.97	1.49
B	1.19	Within normal range			
C	17.10	16.44	5.31	6.72	8.23
D	15.15	6.06	7.19	8.06	3.26
E	19.96	1.41	5.98	2.85	3.17
F	26.20	8.13	7.15	9.13	7.83
G	.39	6.11	2.09	1.00	.83 (foot-foot)
	9.38	6.24	1.70	.80	3.25 (foot-cane)
H	7.5	5.19	4.04	3.10	.01
I	12.03	4.41	7.21	6.75	2.21
J	9.07	4.47	1.99	1.90	.28
K	10.97	1.30	.41	.42	1.59
L	23.41	4.35	5.60	.29	.20
M	6.99	1.56	1.31	1.76	1.82
N	9.75	.82	1.45	.12	.13
O	14.87	8.34	20.54	13.32	12.67
P	.78	Within normal range			
Q	.56	Within normal range			
R	29.56	3.12	4.37	3.06	.61
S	9.60	.98	.44	.52	.17
T	17.16	6.97	3.69	2.60	3.87
U	8.59	1.35	3.16	4.74	2.55
V	14.66	5.04	5.07	4.64	3.24
W	10.31	3.21	3.20	2.88	3.44
X	8.38	5.16	7.21	2.31	3.34
Y	6.49	1.10	3.16	3.01	1.88

consistent walking as well as strong visual recognition of treatment effects by naive observers. Strength of the procedures was evidenced by the continued decrease in step deviations even when auditory cues were minimized, and by observers' nondifferentiation between treatment with music/pulse and subsequent gradual fading. The fact that 88 percent of the subjects maintained rhythmic, even control throughout fading procedures is consistent with literature concerning maintenance of muscular response with the gradual removal of conditioned auditory stimuli (Hefferline and Perera 1963).

In addition to rhythmic and even walking, other related gait anomalies improved. These included some decreased midline crossing in spastic and ataxic disorders and an extinction of ipsilateral stepping in stroke patients, results which were corroborated by naive observers.

Subject variability functioned both to enhance and deter individual gait training. Particularly affecting treatment were cardiac problems resulting in hyperventilation, and fear of falling which increased tension in the lower extremities. Comprehension of the task was sometimes decreased with receptive aphasic subjects, retarded

TABLE 3 TOTAL NUMBER OF CHANGES IN 1-MINUTE SAMPLES: CADENCE INCONSISTENCIES

		Week 2		Week 3	
Subject	Baseline	Tuesday	Thursday	Tuesday	Thursday
A	19	9	9	6	1
B	5	5	2	2	5
C	14	3	4	6	2
D	11	2	4	3	2
E	5	6	7	5	4
F	5.6	1	3	4	1
G	2	------------------------- Consistent tempo ------------------------			
H	12	5	5	5	2
I	6	9	4	3	1
J	12.6	6	3	21	10
K	17.5	8	10	8	7
L	4.5	0	1	1	1
M	10	2	4	4	3
N	2	------------------------- Consistent tempo ------------------------			
O	2	------------------------- Consistent tempo ------------------------			
P	4	3	1	0	0
Q	25	65	64	60	60*
R	6.5	6	2	6	3
S	8	0	7	4	1
T	12	1	8	2	0
U	14	2	2	4	2
V	9	12	6	12	6
W	4	4	8	7	4
X	13	7	3	1	6
Y	12	3	8	8	5

*Subject Q was consistent but needed to increase the number of steps taken per minute.

TABLE 4 OBSERVER RATINGS OF OVERALL GAIT ($n = 375$)

Category	B_1	X_1	X_2	X^2	$p <$
Worst	254	52	69	200.85	.001
Next Best	51	184	140	73.46	.001
Best	71	137	167	38.60	.001
	B_1	X_1	χ^2		$p <$
	254	184	11.18		.001
	B_1	X_2	χ^2		$p <$
	254	167	17.97		.001
	B_1	X_2	χ^2		$p <$
	184	167	.823		.50

TABLE 5 OBSERVER RATINGS OF SPECIFIC GAIT COMPONENTS

Comparison of tape segments	*n*	Worse	Same	Better	χ^1	*p* <
			Rhythmic, even steps			
B_1–X_1*	121	23	13	85	75.44	.001
X_1–B_1	129	89	23	17	74.23	.001
X_1–X_2	114	32	29	53	9	.02
X_2–X_1	129	64	37	28	16.33	.001
B_1–X_2	139	11	40	88	65.28	.001
X_2–B_1	120	89	17	14	90.15	.001
			Cadence/tempo inconsistencies			
B_1–X_1	233	23	62	148	105.34	.001
X_1–B_1	254	142	85	27	78.11	.001
X_1–X_2	236	50	88	98	16.31	.001
X_2–X_1	245	87	106	52	18.38	.001
B_1–X_2	242	25	67	150	100.33	.001
X_2–B_1	234	160	50	24	133.64	.001
			Rigid/stiff/choppy steps			
B_1–X_1	120	19	26	75	46.55	.001
X_1–B_1	129	82	29	18	54.46	.001
X_1–X_2	121	32	40	49	3.59	.20
X_2–X_1	130	60	42	28	11.88	.01
B_1–X_2	130	14	24	92	67.81	.001
X_2–B_1	120	82	24	14	67.40	.001
			Stops/pauses			
B_1–X_1	120	22	21	77	51.35	.001
X_1–B_1	130	86	34	10	69.66	.001
X_1–X_2	120	26	44	50	7.80	.05
X_2–X_1	129	52	55	22	15.48	.001
B_1–X_2	129	7	28	94	95.86	.001
X_2–B_1	121	93	16	12	103.36	.001

*To be read as "X_1 compared to B_1:" B_1 tape shown first followed by X_1 tape.

youngsters, mentally confused subjects, and inattentive patients. Fatigue in all subjects was evidenced by less precision and attentiveness by younger children and a diminished ability to move in older patients.

Because of widespread nerve and muscle damage, patients with a flaccid type of paralysis were even less responsive. Motivation to walk, however, was the greatest variable in gait improvement; this resulted in diligent work during gait training and active practice of rhythmic walking outside of training by covert repetition of the rhythmic pattern or by walking to a self-initiated beat.

While music and pulse trials did not yield differing results, most subjects indicated their enjoyment of the music. A few others expressed greater ease in synchronizing their footsteps to the clarity of the pulse.

Summary and Recommendations

This study investigated the use of rhythmic auditory stimuli to rehabilitate gait disorders. Externally superimposed auditory cues (rhythmic music and percussion pulses) were used to facilitate proprioceptive control of even and coordinated walking. Treatment effects for 25 individuals with varying gait disorders were evaluated by examining (1) cumulative deviations between footfalls in hundredths of a second (arrhythmia), (2) total changes in number of steps per minute in consecutive 10-second intervals (cadence inconsistencies), (3) overall subjective ratings of videotaped segments, and (4) subjective ratings of specific gait components. Results indicated that all subjects improved in rhythmic and/or consistent walking. Furthermore, observer ratings of randomized videotaped samples yielded significant discrimination in observation of baseline and treatment conditions on overall and specific gait components. Observer nondiscrimination between treatment with pulse/music and fading treatment substantiates the generalization of gait improvement following withdrawal of auditory stimuli.

A controlled laboratory setting might be preferable for gait research; however, a natural setting was felt to be equally important as one's functioning is frequently based on the perception of normality by others in daily tasks. While the clinical nature of this study prohibited control of all factors, videotaping from the waist down with some emphasis on consistent clothes and footwear as well as a straight directional walking path would perhaps enhance the consistency of evaluation. The two subjective measures substantiated results achieved by objective measures of arrhythmia and cadence inconsistencies; however, further validation of the subjective measures should be obtained for any future replication.

For ataxic and athetoid cerebral palsy subjects, where length of time in swing phase varies sporadically from one foot to another, documentation between every consecutive left-right or right-left step might yield a more accurate account of arrhythmia. In these patients, the alternating arrhythmia balanced out the timers over a minute, resulting in deviations which appeared small or nonexistent. Measurement and improvement of hemiparesis, however, was most apparent through time deviational measures because the longer swing phase always accumulated more time than the shorter one.

The functional value of long-term training should, as in all clinical procedures, be of paramount concern to the therapist treating gait disorders. For patients requiring personal assistance in walking, initial balance training followed by specifically selected assisting devices and longer practice periods might be a more desirable prerequisite. For younger and less severely disabled individuals this method may facilitate slower, more consistent, or even gait, thus increasing stability of movement and consequently providing greater control of locomotion.

With the increasing occurrence of cerebrovascular accidents resulting in hemiparesis, this form of gait training may very well provide an effective and enjoyable technique for the ensuing prolonged rehabilitation. The long-term effectiveness of auditory stimuli in facilitating proprioceptive control of rhythmic gait lies in the patient's desire and motivation to practice the necessary skills. As a means of gait rehabilitation, superimposed music and auditory stimuli can produce substantive modifications which may generalize to the individual's enhanced appearance, increased stability, and independent mobility. However, continued research in this exploratory area is warranted to differentiate the potential uses of this therapeutic tool.

Reference Note

1 D. K. Wagner. An Electromyographic Investigation of the Frequency and Amplitude of Adult and Adolescent Gum Chewing Behavior During Three Music Conditions. Unpublished manuscript, 1981.

References

Adams, J. A., P. H. Marshall, and E. T. Goetz. 1972. Response feedback and short-term motor retention. *Journal of Experimental Psychology* 92:92–95.

Anshel, M. H., and D. Q. Marisi. 1978. Effect of music and rhythm on physical performance. *Research Quarterly* 49:109–113.

Azrin, N., H. Rubin, F. O'Brien, T. Ayllon, and D. Roll. 1968. Behavioral engineering: Postural control by a portable operant apparatus. *Journal of Applied Behavior Analysis* 1:99–108.

Baker, M. P., J. E. Hudson, and S. L. Wolf. 1979. A "feedback" cane to improve the hemiplegic patient's gait. *Physical Therapy* 59:170–171.

Barrett, B. H. 1962. Reduction in rate of multiple tics by free operant conditioning methods. *Journal of Nervous and Mental Disease* 135:187–195.

Basmajian, J. V., ed. 1979. *Biofeedback—principles and practice for clinicians.* Baltimore: Williams and Wilkins.

Basmajian, J. V., C. G. Kukulka, M. G. Narayan, and K. Takebe. 1975. Biofeedback treatment of foot-drop after stroke compared with standard rehabilitation technique: Effects on voluntary control and strength. *Archives of Physical Medicine and Rehabilitation* 56:231–236.

Beisman, G. L. 1967. Effect of rhythmic accompaniment upon learning of fundamental motor skills. *Research Quarterly* 38:172–176.

Carsloo, S., and A. W. Edfeldt. 1963. Attempts at muscle control with visual and auditory impulses as auxiliary stimuli. *Scandinavian Journal of Psychology* 4:231–235.

Conrad, L., and E. E. Black. 1980. Augmented auditory feedback in the treatment of equinus gait in children. *Developmental Medicine and Child Neurology* 22:713–718.

Dillon, E. K. 1952. A study of the use of music as an aid in teaching swimming. *Research Quarterly* 23:1–8.

Greene, R. J., D. L. Hoats, and A. J. Hornick. 1970. Music distortion: A new technique for behavior modification. *The Psychological Record* 20:107–109.

Greenwald, M. A. 1978. The effectiveness of distorted music versus interrupted music to decrease self-stimulatory behaviors in profoundly retarded adolescents. *Journal of Music Therapy* 15:58–66.

Hefferline, R. F., and B. Keenan. 1963. Amplitude-induction gradient of a small-scale (covert) operant. *Journal of Experimental Analysis of Behavior* 6:307–315.

Hefferline, R. F., and T. B. Perera. 1963. Proprioceptive discrimination of a covert operant without its observation by the subject. *Science* 139:834–835.

Holloway, M. S. 1980. A comparison of passive and active music reinforcement to increase preacademic and motor skills in severely retarded children and adolescents. *Journal of Music Therapy* 17:58–69.

Jensen, M. B. 1931. The influence of jazz and dirge music upon speed and accuracy of typing. *Journal of Educational Psychology* 22:458–462.

Kelsey, J. L., H. Pastides, and G. E. Bisbee, Jr. 1978. *Musculo-skeletal disorders: Their frequency of occurrence and their impact on the population of the United States.* New York: Prodist.

Madsen, C. K., and D. E. Wolfe. 1979. The effect of interrupted music and incompatible responses on bodily movement and music attentiveness. *Journal of Music Therapy* 16:17–30.

Metzler, R. K. 1974. The use of music as a reinforcer to increase imitative behavior in severely and profoundly retarded female residents. *Journal of Music Therapy* 16:97–110.

Mikol, B., and M. R. Denny. 1955. The effect of music and rhythm on rotary pursuit performance. *Perceptual and Motor Skills* 5:3–6.

Nafpliotis, H. 1976. Electromyographic feedback to improve ankle dorsiflexion, wrist extension, and hand grasp. *Physical Therapy* 56:821–825.

O'Brien, F., and N. Azrin. 1970. Behavioral engineering: Control and posture by information feedback. *Journal of Applied Behavior Analysis* 3:235–240.

Owens, L. D. 1979. The effects of music on the weight loss, crying, and physical movement of newborns. *Journal of Music Therapy* 16:83–90.

Reynolds, B., and J. A. Adams. 1953. Motor performance as a function of click reinforcement. *Journal of Experimental Psychology* 45:315–320.

Sachs, D. A., and B. Mayhall. 1972. The effects of reinforcement contingencies upon pursuit rotor performance by a cerebral-palsied adult. *The Journal of Nervous and Mental Disease* 155:36–41.

Spearking, D. L., and R. Poppen. 1974. The use of feedback in the reduction of foot dragging in a cerebral palsied client. *Journal of Nervous and Mental Disease* 159:148–151.

Warren, C. G., and J. F. Lehmann. 1975. Training procedures and biofeedback methods to achieve controlled partial weight bearing: An assessment. *Archives of Physical Medicine and Rehabilitation* 56:449–455.

Wolfe, D. E. 1980. The effect of automated interrupted music on head posturing of cerebral palsied individuals. *Journal of Music Therapy* 17:184–206.

Articles on experimental research follow a format that is very similar to that of descriptive research articles. However, in experimental research, the investigator introduces something new and studies its effects rather than look at something that already exists. In Example 2, Staum studies the effects of rhythmic music during gait rehabilitation.

In the introduction to the problem, the author points out that rehabilitation of gait disorders can be a tedious and uncomfortable process. She cites several studies suggesting that rhythmic stimulation with tones or buzzes can be a valuable cue in the motor planning of people with physical disabilities, but reports that only limited research exists using music as a source of rhythmic information. Because other studies suggest that music can be an enjoyable and rewarding stimulus, Staum hypothesizes that music might serve as a motivator as well as an auditory cue.

In the method section, Staum describes the people who participated in the study, the type of music used, the place where the study took place, and how gait regularity was measured. She also discusses how the effectiveness of treatment intervention was measured. In this study, the researcher compared the gait of each person before the treatment started (called baseline in this particular study, but also known as pretest) with his or her gait after treatment.

The results section of an experimental research article includes an assessment of whether the experimental treatment was effective in changing the outcome. In Staum's article, we learn that the treatment yielded improvement in all subjects with uneven walking patterns. The author then discusses the types of conditions that benefited the most from the treatment.

Based on the results, summary, and recommendations of this article, Janine could predict with some confidence that music might be a positive addition to gait-training exercises for elderly stroke victims.

The previous two articles illustrate descriptive and experimental research, both of which often use quantitative information presented in statistical tables and graphs. Both of these types of research report information about a large number of people. In contrast, single systems research, which shares some similarities with experimental and descriptive research, is typically conducted with individuals or small numbers of participants in their normal environment.

Single Systems Research

There are two primary reasons for using single systems approaches. The first is to monitor changes in an individual's behavior or performance during the course of therapy. The other reason is to study the effects of a particular intervention on a client's behavior to determine if there is a cause and effect relationship (Hanser 1995; Ottenbacher 1986). For example, does music improvisation change the level of a client's interaction with others, or does listening to music reduce pain during a medical procedure?

In single systems research (SSR), the examiner systematically applies and withdraws a music therapy intervention (also referred to as the *treatment variable*) over a series of time periods, called *phases*. There are three distinct phases of SSR, which can be applied in multiple configurations:

1 *Baseline:* This is a time period in which the treatment variable is not applied (we will call it A). This is the level of behavior the person demonstrates under everyday conditions.

2 *Intervention:* This refers to a time period in which the treatment variable is introduced (B). In other words, how the person under study will respond to the music therapy treatment.

3 *Reversal:* Sometimes used in SSR, reversal is a return to baseline following an intervention phase (A). This reversal helps confirm that a change in behavior was due to the treatment and not from other influences.

The most common research design for SSR studies is the ABA, or reversal design, with many variations possible.

Measurements of the *dependent variable* (the behavior specifically under study) occur regularly and frequently throughout the various phases of SSR. For example, the researcher may want to find out how much pain a patient reports under different treatment conditions. In this case, pain is the dependent variable.

Analysis of the data is accomplished through various quantitative (statistical) methods as well as through qualitative analysis (i.e., "eyeballing" the data). The researcher looks for patterns of change associated with the introduction and withdrawal of the treatment variable, that is, the type of intervention tested in the study.

Let's look at an example of SSR in music therapy practice.

> A therapist wants to determine if a new music therapy technique is effective in increasing a client's use of her right arm following a stroke (cerebrovascular accident, or CVA). Using an ABA(B) study design, the therapist finds during the baseline phase that the client uses her right arm 15 percent of the times requested (the dependent variable) during five separate 15-minute sessions. Next, the therapist introduces an intervention consisting of a rhythm-based music experience (the treatment variable). During the next five sessions, the client's use of her right arm has risen to 75 percent. To determine if the change is due to the music therapy intervention, the therapist initiates the reversal phase by withdrawing the rhythm-based music experience. During subsequent sessions, the client's use of her right arm decreases to 18 percent, close to the baseline level. The therapist then reintroduces the music therapy intervention, and use of the client's right arm increases rapidly once again to a level of 78 percent. The therapist concludes that the new music therapy technique was responsible for the increased use of the client's right arm. Figure 15-1 depicts the data collected during the ABA(B) study.

Because one of the intentions of SSR is to establish cause and effect, the approach exhibits similarities to experimental research. A comparison of the two approaches may be helpful.

Both experimental research and SSR rely on measurements of one or more dependent variables that remain constant throughout the investigation. However, in experimental research, there are limited measurements of the dependent variable, generally once before the treatment variable is introduced and once after completion of the study. With SSR, the dependent variable is measured with much greater repetition and frequency. Perhaps the most important difference between experimental research and SSR lies in the numbers of subjects involved. Experimental research relies on groups of subjects, divided into experimental and control groups, to establish a cause and effect relationship between the treatment and dependent variables. In SSR, the individual serves as his or her own control by moving through phases that alternate between intervention and nonintervention conditions. Because of this unique difference between the two approaches, SSR is generally easier to integrate into the clinical music therapy than experimental research.

Other important types of inquiry, such as qualitative, philosophical, and historical research, rely on more qualitative forms of information.

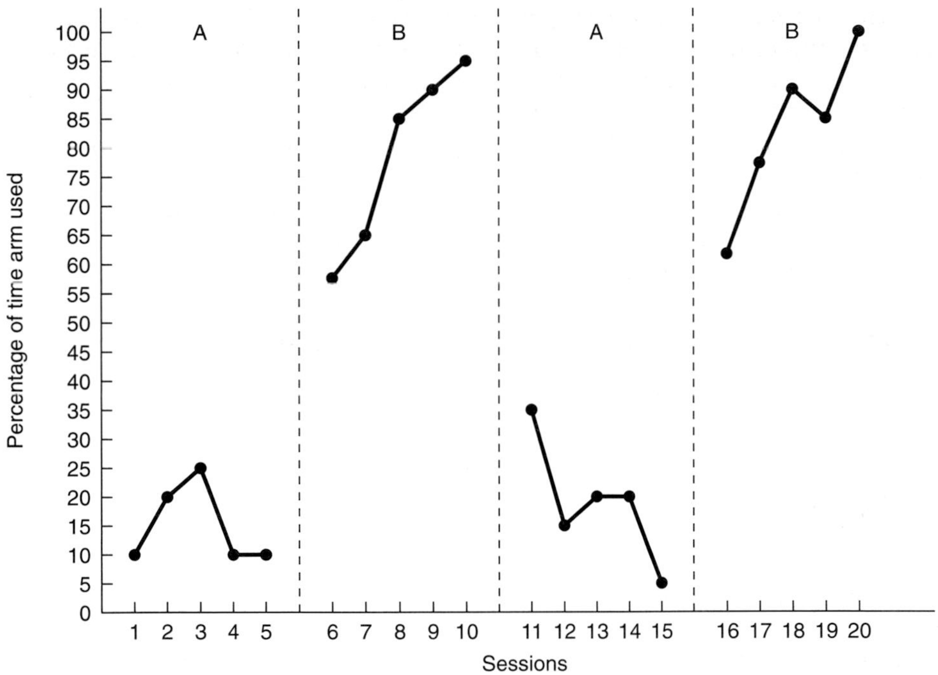

FIGURE 15-1 ABA(B) study.

Qualitative Research

Qualitative research is rapidly emerging as an accepted mode of inquiry for music therapists and others engaged in social sciences research. In contrast to experimental research, qualitative research is descriptive and focuses on people's perceptions and feelings. Using inductive reasoning (arriving at a general conclusion based on specific data or information), the music therapist draws conclusions about the effectiveness of an intervention's process and outcome. Because qualitative research occurs in the client's social environment, it frequently can be integrated into the therapeutic process more easily than other types of investigation (e.g., experimental research). It is especially helpful for music therapists who work with clients over an extended period of time (Aigen 1995; Ottenbacher 1986).

Qualitative research methods include three major types of data collection:

1 Direct observation of the persons being studied.
2 Examination of written records.
3 In-depth interviews.

These same basic procedures can be used in experimental and descriptive research as well. However, in qualitative research, the researcher will collect somewhat different kinds of information, and in somewhat different ways.

Data generated through an interview results in valuable information about a subject's feelings, experiences, opinions, interests, attitudes, values, and knowledge. The direct observation method of data collection yields important understanding about a client's behaviors and interactions with others. For example, in observing a subject, an experimental researcher may tally the number of times a particular behavior occurs, thus quantifying that event. In contrast, a qualitative researcher will likely write up a very detailed description of the individual or group's response, thus emphasizing differences or subtleties among the responses observed. Information that might be considered subjective is acceptable in qualitative research.

By reviewing written records, such as questionnaires, diaries, and journals, the therapist gains helpful insight into the client's feelings, beliefs, and motivations (Berg 1998; Denzin et al. 1994; Patton 1991).

Unlike experimental and certain other types of scientific study, qualitative research data are not measured in terms of quantity or frequency (i.e., the number of times a participant plays a drum or makes a verbal statement). Instead, researchers analyze the data for patterns and themes that help them understand the meaning that an individual derives from her or his experiences. In so doing, the therapist is better able to identify a client's unique responses to an intervention and individualize the therapeutic music program more effectively (Aigen 1995). It is important, however, to note that qualitative research does not lend itself to cause and effect conclusions because the sorts of controls and research methods needed to draw such cause and effect relationships are not a strength of this type of research, and a therapist should take care in applying the findings of the study to larger populations (Ottenbacher 1986).

> Our music therapist, Janine, decides to use one of the methods of qualitative research—in-depth interviews—with her clients who are undergoing gait rehabilitation. She expects to gain a better understanding of her clients' feelings and attitudes toward rehabilitation, preferred music styles, and perceived treatment benefits. By collecting important information about her clients' unique perspectives, she believes the treatment approach will be more meaningful and effective.

In summary, qualitative research pursues answers to questions by investigating people within their social settings. Qualitative researchers seek information about how people live and interact in their environments in order to better understand how they derive meaning from their experiences. As with other types of research, effectiveness requires specific training and expertise in the unique methodologies of qualitative research. For more information about qualitative research, an excellent resource is *Qualitative Research Methods for the Social Sciences* by Berg (1998).

Philosophical Research

Philosophical research also differs from experimental or descriptive research in many respects. One obvious difference is the organizational structure of the article. Philosophical research is similar in format to historical research, but there are major differences in the kinds of information presented. Historical research describes what has occurred in the past, whereas philosophical research proposes what ought to be. According to several sources (Codding 1988; Gilbert 1979; Jellison 1973), philosophical inquiries are much less common in music therapy publications than descriptive, experimental, and historical research. Furthermore, the number of philosophical studies over the past 10 to 15 years has declined. Philosophical research was in greater evidence during the early years of professional organization.

Whereas experimental researchers seek to answer questions by measuring particular events in a controlled environment, philosophical research attempts to determine truths or principles based on reflective or critical thinking. Phelps, Ferrara, and Goolsby (1993) emphasized that these reflective procedures are disciplined and orderly. Knowledge and truth are derived through logic and reasoning rather than through analysis of data.

Philosophical research serves several purposes (Phelps et al. 1993). One objective is to evaluate current practices in music therapy and determine, through logic and critical thinking, which methods should be retained, abandoned, or modified. A second purpose is to define or clarify principles or concepts related to professional concerns. For example, a philosophical essay may lend validity to a music therapy program for a particular population. A third reason for philosophical research is the application of existing theories to music therapy practice. As an illustration, an investigator may compare various theories of musical response as they relate to music therapy practice.

Research Example 3 is a philosophical essay written by Leonard Meyer (1955), a well-known music psychologist and philosopher, who theorized about meaning and emotion in music. The purpose of this article is to relate theories of musical response to uses of music in therapy. The author refutes theories that view musical response as absolute and isolated.

Meyer points out that musical meaning is related to the cultural orientation, associations, and habits of the listener. This view implies that the music therapist must take into account the cultural orientations of the client when selecting music for therapeutic intervention.

RESEARCH EXAMPLE 3 : Philosophical Research

Learning, Belief, and Music Therapy

Leonard B. Meyer, Ph.D.
Department of Music
University of Chicago

The psychology of music has, until recently, been plagued by three interrelated errors: hedonism, atomism, and absolutism.

Hedonism is the confusion of aesthetic experience with the agreeable and the sensuously pleasing. As Langer notes, earlier psychologists based their experiments . . . on the assumption that music was a form of pleasurable sensation. . . . This gave rise to an aesthetic based on liking and disliking, a hunt for a sensationist definition of beauty. . . . But beyond a description of tested pleasure–displeasure reactions to simple sounds or elementary sound complexes . . . this approach has not taken us (Langer, note 1).

The attempt to explain and understand music as a succession of separable, discrete sounds, and sound complexes is what was referred to as the error of atomism. But even the meager achievement which Langer allows to studies of this kind must be still further depreciated. The tested pleasure–displeasure reactions were not what most of these psychologists tacitly assumed them to be: they were not universals, but products of learning and experience.

This draws attention to the third error mentioned—the error of absolutism: the belief that the responses obtained by experiment or otherwise were universal, natural, and absolute. This absolutist approach was also related to the time-honored search for a physical, quasi-acoustical, explanation of musical enjoyment—the attempt, that is, to account for musical communication in terms of vibrations, ratios of intervals, and the like.

Even those not haunted by the ghost of Pythagoras have often unwittingly fallen into the error of absolutism. For instance, much of the research into the problem of the "emotional response" to music (which usually involves studies of what is actually a mood response) tacitly assumes that the findings made are good for all times and all places. Thus the "sad" effect of the minor mode, to cite but one example, was not as a peculiarity of European art music of the past 250 years, but as a kind of necessary universal. For to most of these ethnocentric scholars there was no music save Western music.

Today we are, I think, able to take a more enlightened view of these matters. The easy access which almost all individuals have to great music makes it quite apparent that a Beethoven symphony is not a kind of musical banana split, a matter of purely sensuous pleasure. The work of the Gestalt psychologists has shown beyond doubt that

L. B. Meyer. 1955. Learning, belief, and music therapy. Fifth Book of Proceedings of the National Association for Music Therapy, 27–35. Lawrence, KS: National Association for Music Therapy, Inc.

understanding is not a matter of perceiving single stimuli or simple sound combinations in isolation, but rather a matter of grouping stimuli into patterns and relating patterns to one another. And finally, the studies of comparative musicologists, bringing to our attention the music of other cultures, have made us increasingly aware of the fact that the particular organization developed in Western music is not absolute, natural, or God-given.

Studies in the psychology and aesthetics of music, as well as those in the realm of music theory, have for the most part abandoned the view that the universe of discourse which musical communication presupposes and upon which musical experience depends is universal or absolute. The perception of and response to tonal patterns as well as the awareness of and response to the connotations and associations to which music gives rise are no longer viewed as naive, reflex reactions. It is now generally recognized that musical experiences are dependent upon learned habit responses and that the musical styles of different cultures and various epochs are, in the last analysis, artificial constructs developed by musicians within a particular culture and at a specific time.

Musical styles are social facts, not physical ones. They are to be found not in the over-tone series or in the reactions of naive, unpracticed individuals, but in the habit responses of those who have learned through practice and experience to understand and feel the relationships established in a particular style. The case is well stated by Aiken: We speak of "traditions," styles of art, "meanings," and so on as if these things had a kind of independent reality of their own which is eternally attached to works of art. But traditions and meanings are kept alive only through the dispositions and habits which form the subjective contexts of countless individuals. . . . There can be no aesthetic response whatever apart from the responses of individual men which give it meaning (Aiken, note 2).

These dispositions and habits are learned by constant practice in performing and listening—practice which should, and usually does, begin in early childhood when habit responses are most easily formed. Conceptual understanding does not provide the automatic, instinctive responses which will enable the listener to comprehend the swift, changeable course of the musical stream. Nor is such objective knowledge necessary. Applying to music what Russell said of language: "understanding music is not a matter of dictionary definitions—it is not a matter of knowing this or that rule of musical grammar or musical form—rather it is a matter of habits correctly acquired in one's self and properly presumed in others" (Russell, note 3).

It is not enough, for example, for the listener to know in a conceptual sense that in the Western music of the past 300 years a combination of tones, the dominant seventh chord, creates an expectation that another combination of tones, the tonic, will be forthcoming. The expectation must have the status of an instinctive ideomotor set—a felt urgency—before it can be truly comprehended or strongly felt. The story of the young composer who left his bed, ran to the piano, and resolved such a dominant seventh chord to its tonic is a good instance of this power of felt urgency—of ingrained habit.

As Russell observes, not only must habits be correctly acquired in the listener, but they must also be properly presumed in others. That is, our trained habits of discrimination and response must be relevant to the particular musical style in question if they are to be of any use. For the habits acquired are not universal, but are developed and learned in connection with a specific musical style, though it is, of course, possible for one listener to have acquired habits appropriate to several styles, just as one person may learn to understand several languages.

Music, then, is not a "universal language." The tongues of music are many. They vary from culture to culture, from epoch to epoch within the same culture, and even within a single epoch and culture. A westerner must learn to understand Japanese music just as he must learn to understand the spoken language of Japan. A person familiar only with the tradition of recent European music must practice playing and listening to the music of the Middle Ages just as he must practice reading and speaking the language of Chaucer. Even within one and the same culture and era it is the exception rather than the rule when a musical style is understood by all members of the culture. Witness, for instance, the difficulties which the devotees of "serious" music have in responding to the subtleties and nuances of jazz—and vice versa.

The fact that musical experience depends upon learned habit responses and dispositions has obvious implications for the music therapist. It means that if music is to have a specific effect—acting as something more than a kind of general socializing agent—then it must be carefully selected, keeping in mind the learned habits, associations, and orientations of the particular patient or group of patients being treated. Indeed, music whose style is unfamiliar and which is, therefore, at best only partially intelligible may well arouse undesirable apprehensions, tensions, and anxieties.

Reference Notes

1 Susanne K. Langer. Philosophy in a New Key (New York: Mentor, 1951), 171.

2 Henry D. Aiken. "The Concept of Relevance in Aesthetics." *Journal of Aesthetics* 48 (1947) VI: 159.

3 Bertrand Russell. *Selected Papers* (New York: Modern Library, 1957), 42.

This research has important implications for Janine's clients. The rehabilitation center where Janine works as a practicing music therapist serves large numbers of clients from an old ethnic neighborhood. Many elderly people in her city are of German heritage. Given Meyer's commentary about the importance of cultural orientation, Janine may want to consider inclusion of some German folk music in the gait rehabilitation program.

Historical Research

Whereas descriptive and experimental researchers seek to discover what is and what will be, historical researchers attempt to learn, in a precise and systematic manner, what has happened in the past. Of interest to music therapists are the people, places, events, and past practices that have helped shape the profession.

According to Phelps, Ferrara, and Goolsby (1993), there are a number of reasons for pursuing historical research. First, the past may be helpful in understanding present conditions that influence music therapy practice. For example, Solomon (1980) presented evidence to support the hypothesis that special-education classrooms in the nineteenth and early twentieth centuries used music as an important tool to diagnose and treat speech and hearing defects. Solomon concluded that the use of music in special-education classrooms is not a new idea, but one with a lengthy history that can be traced to the early nineteenth century. Today, music is used to help diagnose and treat hearing-impaired children, a precedent set 100 years ago.

A second reason for undertaking historical research is to identify the institutions, hospitals, and schools where music therapy has been practiced. We know, for example, that music therapy was used on Blackwell's Island in New York City during the latter part of the nineteenth century. However, we lack specific information about the daily routine of the hospital and the music therapy techniques used with the many hundreds of mentally ill clients. A more complete account of music therapy practiced on Blackwell's Island would help us better understand the techniques and status of the profession during the last few decades of the nineteenth century.

Third, biographical data concerning early, prominent music therapists is important but also scarce. Eva Vescelius, Harriet Ayer Seymour, and Willem Van de Wall were important music therapists who lived during the early and middle part of the twentieth century, yet we know very little about their lives or music therapy activities. Without a record of the contributions of music therapy pioneers, we are missing worthwhile information that could provide encouragement for today's music therapists (Solomon and Heller 1982).

Research Example 4 is a historical study written by Dale Taylor (1981). The article describes how music therapy was used to treat physical and mental disorders during the first half of the twentieth century in general medical settings. Taylor indicates that music therapy played an important role in physical and psychological rehabilitation in clinics, hospitals, and other medical settings such as dental offices. This article is important because it compiles information from a variety of sources and demonstrates an ongoing interest in music therapy practice and research by medical and music specialists during the first decades of the twentieth century.

RESEARCH EXAMPLE 4 : Historical Research

Music in General Hospital Treatment from 1900 to 1950

Dale B. Taylor
The University of Kansas

Beginning at the turn of the century, this report examines the effect of the recently invented phonograph on practical and experimental efforts to reconcile the century-old separation of medicine and music. Progressing chronologically, events are examined which affected the use of music in physical medicine during the first half of the twentieth century. Topics include the first college course work in hospital music, important theories regarding the neurological basis of musical effects, early research investigating the influence of music on physiological behavior, the inclusion of permanent musical hardware in hospital construction, social and physical rehabilitation in orthopedic medicine, psychological applications in pediatrics and psychosomatic medicine, and the use of music to combat pain in surgical, dental, obstetrical, and gynecological procedures.

As the music therapy profession grows in both amount and range of service, new and existing areas of clinical application are being explored and expanded. Some areas which may seem new within the music therapy profession may actually be receiving renewed interest after a period of inactivity. A review of the historical development of a specific area of application may assist music therapists in discovering what has been formerly proven or disproven and in making informed decisions concerning present and future actions.

In a recent review of the relationship between music and medicine, Kuemmel (1978) emphasized that music and medicine were integral in the training and practice of physicians from A.D. 800 to 1800. During the late eighteenth and nineteenth centuries the two fields diverged, although an affinity still existed between them (Boxberger 1963). With Edison's invention of the phonograph in 1877 and the introduction in 1896 of commercially feasible disk records, renewed interest was directed toward use of music in hospital treatment. Music was used as a diversion during the day and as a sleeping aid at night. Its early use was also reported in operating rooms to mitigate fears of operations and to provide assistance during administration of local anesthesia (Boxberger 1963).

The phonograph also expedited the scientific investigation of musical effects by physicians interested in the medical applications of music. In 1899, Dr. James Corning of New York City experimented by covering the face with a hood to exclude

Journal of Music Therapy, XVIII (2), 1981, 62–73 © 1981 by the National Association for Music Therapy, Inc.

Dale B. Taylor, RMT, is director of music therapy at the University of Wisconsin, Eau Clair, Wisconsin, and a doctoral candidate at the University of Kansas.

unintended sounds, using tubes to connect the ears with an Edison phonograph. His conclusion was that consciousness was not essential, and that large areas of the cerebrum were beneficially affected (Gatewood 1921). In 1903, Tarchanoff conducted similar experiments using an apparatus known as an ergograph; he also concluded that consciousness was not necessary and that the physiological effects of music were of primary importance. Around the turn of the century, the physiological effects of music were investigated through laboratory experiments with both animals and humans. These experiments demonstrated changes in cardiac output, respiratory rate and volume, pulse rate, blood pressure, and body secretions related to various types of music (Light et al. 1954).

The first official acknowledgement by the American Medical Association of possible therapeutic applications of music in general hospital treatment came in 1914 through publication in their journal of a letter written by Dr. Evan O'Neill Kane. He reported using a phonograph in his operating room for "calming and distracting patients from the horror of the situation" (Kane 1914, 1829) before general anesthesia and during local anesthesia. The advantage of the phonograph was that it continued producing sounds despite the surgeon, anesthetist, or assistants. Too often, assistants instructed to talk to the patient only compounded the problem by asking if he or she was in pain; on other occasions, brief exchanges about the weather were followed by silence. With the phonograph, some patients reportedly conversed animatedly about the musical selections with the anesthetist throughout the operation.

In a comprehensive essay written in 1917, Eva Vescelius, founder of the National Therapeutic Society of New York City, predicted, "When the therapeutic value of music is understood and appreciated, it will be considered as necessary in the treatment of disease as air, water and food" (1918, 376). She expressed hope for a time when the equipment of a hospital, asylum, or prison would include a department for music under the direction of a competent musical supervisor, and when appropriations for music would be considered as necessary as for any other civic department.

One year later, Columbia University announced the inauguration of a new course called "Musicotherapy" taught by Margaret Anderton, a British musician who had worked extensively with Canadian soldiers wounded in World War I. Her technique in orthopedic and paralysis cases was to have the men produce the music themselves. She theorized that the major healing potential of music was in the timbre of an instrument, especially in wind instruments made of wood. The research background for her work came from tests performed on healthy men which had determined that certain pitches or harmonic combinations had specific physiological effects. For example, one hospital was investigating the effect on the throat of playing a given chord in a certain key, with the ultimate goal of treating paralysis of the jaw ("Columbia University to heal wounded by music" 1919).

The most extensive account of music in general hospitals appearing during the first half of this century concerned its use in conjunction with anesthesia and analgesia. The cornerstone of this movement was the published text of an address delivered by Esther L. Gatewood, Ph.D., in 1920. Recognizing the importance of employing musical selections preferred by the patient, she advocated a physiological explanation for changes in the type of selection most enjoyed at different times. She also emphasized the importance of music "in keeping with the mood and attitude to be desired not by the patient but by the physician in charge" (1921, 48). In calling for a gradual mood change in the music, she described what has since become widely referred to as the "iso principle" of mood change. Gatewood offered as a scientific basis for music's beneficial effects the "neurological fact" that two separate sensory stimuli entering the nervous system simultaneously tend to neutralize each other with only the stronger, more persistent one entering into consciousness. Therefore, if the attention of an individual is sufficiently centered on one stimulus such as music, this stimulus may effectively exclude all others. Within her presentation, Dr. Gatewood issued a call for experimental research on musical influence:

The problem still remains to determine more specifically the basic principles governing the particular type of rhythm, melody, and harmony, and its organic reaction. Such definite information is essential to the intelligent use of music in practical situations of which the administration of anesthesia is one (48).

One of those to answer this call was Ida L. Hyde of the State University of Kansas, who studied the pulse rate and pressure, systolic and diastolic pressures, relative velocity of blood flow, and electrocardiogram of 15 subjects. Of particular interest in applying results of her study to physical medicine was the following general conclusion:

The indications are that those selections of music rendered either vocally or instrumentally that exert a favorable reflex action on the cardiovascular system, have also a favorable influence upon the muscle tone, working power, digestion, secretions and other functions of the body (Hyde 1924, 223).

The next major impetus in general hospital music came through formation by Isa Maud Ilsen of the National Association for Music in Hospitals. Ilsen (1926) claimed to have 20 years of experience investigating and applying music as a remedial agent to relieve suffering from disease and surgical operations. Her basic theory was that hospital music must "arouse the vital functions of the body [which] are all rhythmic when in a state of perfect health; to this state the rhythm of the music should accord" (15).

Although Ilsen identified rhythm as the basic therapeutic element in music, the existing public bias against jazz was reflected in her characterization of "mere jazz" as having rhythmic effects "out of harmony" with the need for soothing agents in the sick room. She also considered doleful music inappropriate for a patient depressed with physical suffering and separation from family and friends. She predicted that soon a department of music founded on thorough hospital training, medical ethics, and scientific and therapeutic management would be a branch of hospital service.

After three decades of efforts to convince medical experts of the importance of music, the first permanent commitment to hospital music was made in 1929 with the construction of Duke University Hospital. All bed patients could receive radio reception through earphones, sponge rubber cushioned reception units, or wall-mounted speakers on children's and infants' floors. Similar speakers were installed in ward utility and preparation rooms for music during monotonous tasks, and both tap-ins and speakers were present in all recovery rooms (Pickrell et al. 1950).

With increased music therapy research and application, improved technology, and publications describing music in hospitals, interest spread from the operating room to other treatment areas. Specialists in obstetrics and gynecology were informed of progress in the therapeutic uses of music by McGlinn (1930), who reviewed the negative side effects of gaseous anesthetic agents (i.e., nausea, vomiting, and pulmonary irritation), the problems associated with remedies such as preanesthesia doses of morphine and scopolamine, and the advantages and disadvantages of spinal anesthesia. Music was then indicated as the best means of overcoming fear and objections to chemical agents. Music did not interfere with operating room technique and could be changed for each patient to provide optimum diversion. McGlinn also reported that many hospitals were using the radio to accompany local anesthesia in children's tonsillectomies.

Although most of McGlinn's supporting information described music applications in a wide variety of surgical procedures, he suggested that obstetricians and gynecologists specifically should employ music. Music reportedly provided a diversion and a better atmosphere for surgical patients, relaxed tension of the operator and attending personnel, and entertained the operating room suite force during preparation and cleanup procedures. The author concluded that "there is no question that the patients are better for the lack of psychic shock and lessened preanesthetic drugging" (682).

Until this time, music used during operations had been played not only for the patient but through speakers which could be heard by everyone in the room. In 1932, A. F. Erdmann presented his "silent gramophone" for calming patients. Instead of a complete phonograph, it included only a turntable on ac current with an electrical pickup, a separate volume control device, telephone earpieces to place on the head or under a pillow, and a separate receiver for the anesthetist. This apparatus effectively delivered selected music at a specific time to a limited number of persons (Erdmann 1934).

Several New York newspapers and periodicals publicized the Erdmann procedure immediately following his December 1932 presentation to the New York Society of Anesthesiologists. These included the *Brooklyn Daily Eagle,* the *Scientific American, Medical Economics, Science Service,* and the *New York Times.* The latter newspaper continued its coverage of music and medicine with a report of a practical demonstration for the International New Thought Alliance. The presentation was made by Ada Cox Fisher with pianist Harriet Ayer Seymour and baritone Everett A. Engstrom. Their contention was that music "plus constructive thought has the power . . . to cure pain and disease" ("200 Test Music Cure" 1933).

Although Esther Gatewood provided the neurological foundation 15 years earlier, only in 1935 was the use of music to combat specific stimuli associated with pain detailed. A dentist named E. S. Best divided sounds into two classes, tunes and noises. According to Best, noises of dental machinery aggravated pain through bone conduction, which notified the patient that the dreaded moment had arrived. Using the neurological principle explained earlier by Gatewood, Best pointed out that the central nervous system focused on one stimulus when multiple stimuli entered. Best and his associates then designed a "radio chair," based on their discoveries that bone-conducted sound tended to supersede air-transmitted vibrations and that patients tended to concentrate on music. After experimenting with various areas of the skull, they concluded that amplifiers applied to the "mastoid portion of the temporal bones offered by far the best conduction" (Best 1935, 265). Through this procedure, they purported to introduce tunes directly into the auditory centers of the brain by bone conduction, thereby rendering less audible the unpleasant noises associated with the grinding of teeth.

Pediatric and orthopedic wards began to receive attention in 1938 when the *New York Times* carried a story describing the work of Harriet Ayer Seymour, Chairman of the Hospital Music Committee, State Charities Aid Association, and Isabel Parkman of Bellevue Hospital. They suggested symphonic music for respiration and heartbeat, "out-of-door" music for the tubercular, and marches for "cripples." Case descriptions included a girl born without limbs who had become first trombone player in her school orchestra, using an instrument adapted with leader cuffs, rings, hooks, and zipper. Also described were physically handicapped children with arms and legs immobilized who delighted in playing rhythm instruments (" 'Healing' by music" 1938).

Esther Goetz Gilliland, recognized leader in early attempts to organize the music therapy profession, published numerous articles in medically and educationally related periodicals. In a 1944 article, she asserted that experiments had proven "irrefutably" the power of music to elicit such physiological changes as increased body metabolism, increased or decreased muscular energy, accelerated respiration with decreased regularity, changes in cardiovascular response, lowered thresholds for sensory stimuli, and increased internal glandular secretions. Although most of her work was devoted to neuropsychiatric applications, such statements by an author of her stature advanced the use of music in physical medicine.

In 1944, a major project was initiated by Kenneth Pickrell and associates using music in all phases of the surgical procedure and in other hospital departments. Their goal was to eliminate fear, establish confidence, and allay apprehension by producing a congenial atmosphere. They believed that "the introduction of music in the patient's room, the anesthesia room, the operating room, and the recovery room simplifies the task of the surgeon, the house officers, the nurses, and perhaps of even greater importance, the patient" (Pickrell et al. 1950, 144).

As the project progressed, Pickrell and his associates found music useful in avoiding previously unidentified auditory sources of patient anxiety. After admission, music helped sooth and comfort the patient who was often left alone. Music was used during the operation for patients under local, spinal, or regional anesthesia. Music played directly to patients through earphones helped distract them from attending to the noise of surgical instruments and conversations concerning details of the operation and their pathology. During the postoperative phase, the surgical staff used music to distract the patient from pain and discomfort and to avoid apathy, imagined exaggeration of symptoms, and "cerebral inactivity." They reported that this reduction of self-preoccupation also reduced the need for medication, eliminated confusion, and made the recovery period shorter and more pleasant. Attempts by the staff to identify specific types of therapeutic music resulted in endorsement of soft, soothing, melodious, "after-dinner music with sweet orchestrations." Hymns, spirituals, and martial music were said to increase tension and were least acceptable for surgical use (Pickrell et al. 1950).

In the pediatrics ward, radio-phonograph music was used to provide pleasure for children and to simplify their custodial care. Using 45 rpm records and automatic changers, a wide variety of music could be arranged without changing records more than once each hour. In addition, electrical units such as X-ray equipment did not interfere with recorded music as they did with radio reception.

Children undergoing surgery were given music to help avoid unfortunate experiences which could leave irreparable psychological and physical scars. Nurses and aids used stories and songs to act out the operative procedure with dolls, followed by applying dressings, feedings, and use off a bedpan (Pickrell et al. 1950).

As with many scientific advances, the military began to examine the usefulness of medical applications of music for use in hospitals for wounded and disabled veterans. Although many investigations had been conducted previously, in 1947 a group consisting of retired Army Surgeon General Norman T. Kirk, Admiral Swanson, Chief of the Navy's Bureau of Medicine and Surgery, and General Hawley, Veterans Administration Chief of Medical Services, ruled that music could not be classified with quinine, penicillin, and infrared treatment as a therapy. They also disallowed use of the title "Music Therapist" and any further reports of accomplishments in music therapy until research validated such claims (Lewis et al. 1947).

Lewis and associates believed that no medically accepted techniques existed for using music with patients beyond mere entertainment during convalescence. However, they cited an unpublished report describing a two-year project in oral surgery using music with anesthesia. The result was that "with music, it has been possible to reduce the amount of standard anesthetic, with the result that patients recover rapidly and easily from the anesthetic and exhibit no evidence of cyanosis" (546).

In 1948, the use of music in dental procedures received renewed attention. The dangers of subnormal oxygen levels with nitrous oxide anesthesia had been observed and reported for over 50 years. The primary difficulty was anoxia and its serious effects such as temporary and permanent damage to the brain and to other organs although with more reversibility. After many chemical and remedial techniques were dismissed as too dangerous, expensive, or legally cumbersome, music was successfully employed as a diversionary tactic. Nitrous oxide oxygen anesthesia with music was devoid of oxygen deprivation, adequate for all types of dental procedures, and accepted without struggling or delirium. Patients emerged rapidly and completely from the anesthetic state with minimum chair occupation time, no need for assistance with leaving the dental chair, and with no undesirable effects in the poor risk patient (Cherry and Pallin 1948).

Despite the work and research completed during the first half of this century, published reports of music in physical medicine were widely scattered among journals and other periodicals. Physicians interested in such data had no complete and readily available source of information. Consequently, many investigations were begun in the belief that each was original.

One of these was a large-scale investigation begun in 1948 at the University of Chicago Clinics (Light et al. 1954). Their first experiment involved 200 patients receiving music during surgery under local, regional, and spinal analgesia. Patients were observed during surgery and their remarks before, during, and after surgery were compiled. Results indicated that selected music was beneficial to the patient prior to and during surgery. Other observations and conclusions were similar to those of Pickrell and colleagues (1950).

When the University of Chicago study began in February of 1948, a portable wire recorder was used; this was soon replaced by a tape recorder. Any phonograph or tape equipment, speakers, outlets, and earphones were made explosion-proof or were not used in the presence of explosive anesthetic agents. Later improvements involved three tape recorders installed in a special music room from which music could be supplied to each of six operating rooms, to the preoperative preparation rooms, and to the central supply room where surgical equipment was prepared.

These researchers found that music enabled them to reduce the previously heavy sedation necessary during surgery. This reduction supposedly saved the patient from toxic effects of larger dosages, and accelerated his or her postoperative recovery. Particularly in children, music was found helpful in producing a smooth, quiet induction of general anesthesia (Light et al. 1954).

In 1949, a group of Chicago surgeons used music in conjunction with the psychosomatic factor in physical illness. They performed a series of operations including 24 vagotomy operations for peptic ulcer, an illness with a largely psychogenic etiology. Routine medication had minimal effect on these normally tense and nervous people; they were therefore considered excellent candidates for the calming effect of music during surgery. Most requested semiclassical music and were reportedly enthusiastic about listening to the music. The researchers emphasized the importance of selecting music that would calm the patient without stimulating at any time, yet would maintain attention (Light et al. 1949).

Gillespie (1950) took a new approach to the relationship between anesthesia and music, drawing an analogy between a surgical team and a string quartet:

> By nature the anaesthetist is an "ensemble player." Very rarely, as is the case with a therapeutic block or a tracheo-bronchial toilet, is he the "soloist." It is much more usually his lot to be the second violin or the viola in a quartett. Perhaps the "cello" would be a better simile, since he provides the necessary "base" or "bass" (if a bad pun be permissible) for the performance. Yet although he rarely performs alone, his contribution is vital to the efficiency of the operation as a whole (115). An anaesthetist who has learnt to make his contribution a worthy part of an artistically perfect whole is entitled to a similar pride in himself (116).

With formation in 1950 of the National Association for Music Therapy, Inc. (NAMT), an organization became available for presentation and publication of music therapy applications. As a result, the number of published studies describing music therapy in general hospitals increased substantially during the next decade. These and subsequent reports included the use of music in radiology, emergency rooms, electroencephalography, waiting rooms, burn centers, and oncology units. NAMT sources also provide information regarding subsequent progress in musical applications in physical medicine.

References

Best, E. S. 1935. The psychology of pain control. *Journal of the American Dental Association* 22:256–267.

Boxberger, R. 1963. History of the National Association for Music Therapy, Inc. In *Music therapy 1962,* edited by E. H. Schneider. Lawrence, KS: National Association for Music Therapy.

Cherry, H., and I. Pallin. 1948. Music as a supplement in nitrous oxide oxygen anesthesia. *Anesthesiology* 9:391–399.

Columbia University to heal wounded by music. *Literary Digest* (1 March 1919):59–62.

Erdmann, A. F. 1934. Silent gramophone in local anesthesia and therapy. *Current Researches in Anesthesia and Analgesia, Supplement* 13:70–71.

Gatewood, E. L. 1921. The psychology of music in relation to anesthesia. *American Journal of Surgery, Anesthesia Supplement* 35:47–50.

Gillespie, N. A. 1950. Anesthesia and music. *Current Researches in Anesthesia and Analgesia* 29:114–116.

Gilliland, E. G. 1956. Music therapy rehabilitation. *Hospital Management* 81:46–48, 98–99.

"Healing" by music tried in hospitals. *New York Times* (20 March 1938):5.

Hyde, I. H. 1924. Effects of music upon electrocardiograms and blood pressure. *Journal of Experimental Psychology* 7:213–224.

Ilsen, I. M. 1926. How music is used in hospitals. *Musician* 31:15.

Kane, E. O. 1914. Phonograph in the operating room. *Journal of the American Medical Association* 62:1829.

Kuemmel, W. F. 1978. Music and medicine as interrelated in theory and practice. Cited in V. Moretti, Book Review, *Journal of Music Therapy* 15:157–159.

Lewis, R. D., H. Burris-Meyer, and R. I. Cardinell. 1947. Music as an aid to healing. *Journal of the Acoustical Society of America* 19:544–546.

Light, G. A., W. V. Haymond, H. M. Livingston, and J. Willard. 1949. Use of magnetic recorder "silent" music during operation. *Current Researches in Anesthesia and Analgesia* 28:330–338.

Light, G. A., D. M. Love, D. Benson, and E. T. Morch. 1954. Music in surgery. *Current Researches in Anesthesia and Analgesia* 33:258–264.

McGlinn, J. A. 1930. Music in the operating room. *American Journal of Obstetrics and Gynecology* 10:678–683.

Pickrell, K. L., J. T. Metzger, J. N. Wilde, R. R. Broadbent, and B. F. Edwards. 1950. The use and therapeutic value of music in the hospital and operating room. *Plastic and Reconstructive Surgery* 6:142–152.

200 test music cure. *New York Times* (29 June 1933):22.

Vescelius, E. 1918. Music and health. *Music Quarterly* 4:376–400.

Examination of Taylor's article reveals that the structure of the study differs considerably from that used in experimental and descriptive research. It does not contain method, results, or discussion sections. The form of historical research emerges from the data by using logical and critical thinking and varies from problem to problem. The structure of the narrative is not evident from the beginning of the project but takes shape as it is being written (Solomon and Heller 1982).

From reading Taylor's article, Janine can determine that the use of music to divert attention away from physical ailments has been used successfully for many years. This historical information provides a strong rationale for including music in Janine's music therapy program.

CURRENT STATUS OF RESEARCH IN THE PROFESSION

The advancement of research has been a primary purpose of the National Association for Music Therapy (NAMT) since it was founded in 1950 (NAMT 1950). In comparison to some professions established hundreds of years ago, however, this is a short history of research involvement. Therefore, a comparatively small quantity of research knowledge has been gathered by music therapists.

The first coordinated effort to share research findings came in 1951, when NAMT published philosophical, methodological, and research papers in its *Book of Proceedings.* This annual compendium primarily consisted of professional papers and presentations given at the organization's annual conferences.

In 1964, NAMT began publishing the *Journal of Music Therapy,* a periodical that disseminates original music therapy research. By 1973, music therapists had access to an additional forum for clinical and research papers in a journal entitled *Arts Psychotherapy: An International Journal,* now published under the title *Arts in Psychotherapy.* This journal includes papers from a variety of allied health professionals, such as psychologists, art therapists, and counselors, as well as music therapists. Still another journal, *Music Therapy,* was established by the American Association for Music Therapy (AAMT) in 1981 (this journal ceased publication in 1997). One year later, NAMT approved and commenced publication of *Music Therapy Perspectives,* a journal that addresses primarily clinical matters but which also includes data-based research. These four periodicals are by no means the only ones of professional interest to music therapists, who often read and write for journals in related fields such as counseling, special education, and psychology. However, the aforementioned journals do represent the primary collection of research information dedicated to the use of music in therapy.

SUMMARY

Descriptive, experimental, historical, philosophical, qualitative, and single systems research are all valuable forms of inquiry, and each type has its particular strengths and limitations. Descriptive research and qualitative research are used to determine current conditions (e.g., how a client feels about a particular type of music), whereas experimental and single systems research methods explore what will be (e.g., whether or not music has a significant effect on increasing verbal responses in a mentally retarded child).

Historical and philosophical research are less common than descriptive and experimental research, though no less important. Historical research is concerned with what was (the people, places, and events that have shaped the music therapy profession); philosophical research is involved with what might be (the definition, clarification, and speculation about the profession's future through logic and critical thinking).

One type of research is not inherently better than another. Rather, it is important for the researcher to select the method best suited to answer a particular question. In addition, one type of research can have an important effect on another. For example, the principles proposed by a philosophical researcher are often tested through experimental research methods. Or a series of experimental findings can assist a philosophical researcher in formulating new principles.

Finally, it is important to understand that research findings are always in flux. As a result of new and more sophisticated research methods, past studies may be refuted. And with each research finding, new questions emerge. Theories and methods will be continually tested and refined as a result of the cumulative efforts of researchers of the past, present, and future.

STUDY QUESTIONS

1. What are the three ways that research can influence music therapy practice?
2. Define descriptive research and provide one example of a research study that would use this technique.
3. Why is the related literature section of a research project important?
4. What function does the research abstract serve in research articles?
5. How are philosophical and historical research different?
6. How do the *Journal of Music Therapy* and *Music Therapy Perspectives* differ in their focus?
7. Which clinical populations have been studied most frequently by music therapists?
8. What was the purpose of NAMT's publication, *Book of Proceedings?*
9. What are at least two differences between qualitative research and experimental research?
10. Why is it important to use a baseline phase in single systems research before beginning treatment?

REFERENCES

Aigen, K. 1995. Interpretational research. In *Music therapy research: Quantitative and qualitative perspectives,* edited by B. Wheeler, 329–366. Phoenixville, PA: Barcelona Press.

Berg, B. L. 1998. *Qualitative research methods for the social sciences.* 3d ed. Boston: Allyn and Bacon.

Codding, P. A. 1988. A content analysis of the *Journal of Music Therapy. Journal of Music Therapy* 24:195–202.

Denzin, N. K., and Y. S. Lincoln, eds. 1994. *Handbook of qualitative research.* Thousand Oaks, CA: Sage.

Duerksen, G. 1968. The research process. In *Music in therapy,* edited by E. T. Gaston, 409–424. New York: Macmillan.

Feder, E., and B. Feder. 1981. *The expressive arts therapies.* Englewood Cliffs, NJ: Prentice Hall.

Gilbert, J. P. 1979. Published research in music therapy, 1973–1978: Content, focus, and implications for future research. *Journal of Music Therapy* 16:102–110.

Hanser, S. B. 1974. Group contingent music listening with emotionally disturbed boys. *Journal of Music Therapy* 11:220–225.

———. 1995. Applied behavior analysis. In *Music therapy research: Quantitative and qualitative perspectives,* edited by B. L. Wheeler. Phoenixville, PA: Barcelona Press.

Jellison, J. 1973. The frequency and general mode of inquiry of research in music therapy, 1952–1972. *Council for Research in Music Education Bulletin* 35:1–8.

Meyer, L. B. 1955. Learning, belief, and music therapy. *Fifth Book of Proceedings of the National Association for Music Therapy.* Lawrence, KS: National Association for Music Therapy.

National Association for Music Therapy (NAMT). 1950. *Constitution and bylaws of the National Association for Music Therapy.* Lawrence, KS: National Association for Music Therapy.

———. 1969. Constitution and bylaws of the National Association for Music Therapy, Article 2. *Journal of Music Therapy* 8:59–67.

Ottenbacher, K. J. 1986. *Evaluating clinical change: Strategies for occupational and physical therapists.* Baltimore: Williams and Wilkins.

Patton, M. Q. 1991. *How to use qualitative methods in evaluation.* Newbury Park: Sage.

Payton, O. D. 1988. *Research: The validation of clinical practice.* Philadelphia: F. A. Davis.

Phelps, R., L. Ferrara, and T. B. Goolsby. 1993. *A guide to research in music education.* 4th ed. Dubuque, IA: William C. Brown.

Phillips, K. H. 1989. Learning to read research. *Iowa Music Educator* 43:23–25.

Rainbow, E. L., and H. C. Froehlich. 1987. *Research in music education.* New York: Schirmer.

Solomon, A. I. 1980. Music for the feeble-minded in nineteenth century America. *Journal of Music Therapy* 11:119–122.

———. 1984. A historical study of the National Association for Music Therapy, 1960–1980. Unpublished Ph.D. diss., University of Kansas, Lawrence, KS.

Solomon, A. I., and G. N. Heller. 1982. Historical research in music therapy: An important avenue for studying the profession. *Journal of Music Therapy* 19:236–242.

Taylor, D. B. 1981. Music in general hospital treatment from 1900 to 1950. *Journal of Music Therapy* 18:62–73.

Wolfe, D. 1980. The effect of automated interrupted music on head posturing of cerebral palsied individuals. *Journal of Music Therapy* 17:184–206.

APPENDIX

A SESSION STRUCTURE FOR MUSIC PSYCHOTHERAPY

The following is an example of a music therapy session structure that integrates in a stepwise progression the two components of music psychotherapy: counseling and therapeutic music experience. The structure is flexible enough to allow for the use of various types of therapeutic music experiences, for example, instrumental improvisation, guided music listening, music and movement, as well as the application of different counseling techniques, such as reality therapy, person-centered therapy, and so forth. However, the structure of these stages allows a logical progression toward effective therapeutic change in music therapy. Stages may be repeated or interchanged as the therapeutic process and the needs of the clients require. This session format is oriented toward the "here and now" of the therapy group and concrete behavioral change within the therapy group structure; it is therefore particularly suited for music therapy in the psychiatric setting.

STAGE I: INTRODUCTION

This stage, which may last anywhere from 10 to 20 minutes, is necessary to orient the patients to the reality of the group, group rules, and the purpose of the group. It is divided into five substages.

1 *Orientation to group, time, and place:* The therapist introduces him- or herself, explains the general nature of the group, the length of the session, and rules of conduct, and also diffuses the patient's anxiety.

2 *Establishment of purpose of group:* The therapist explains the therapeutic purpose of the group and how the session structure and activities will give the patient the opportunity to accomplish therapeutic change.

3 *Assessment of current moods, issues of concern, and levels of behavior:* Patients are encouraged to talk about their current feelings, thoughts, important events, and issues of

Source: Michael H. Thaut. 1992. In *An Introduction to Music Therapy: Theory and Practice,* by William B. Davis, Kate E. Gfeller, and Michael H. Thaut, 278–281. Dubuque, IA: McGraw-Hill Companies.

concern. This discussion will facilitate the personal agenda setting in the next substage, and will give the therapist a feeling for the group's level of functioning and areas of therapeutic need.

4 *Establishment of individual and group goals:* The patient is asked to establish a personal agenda for the session under the guidance of the therapist. The patient should define in very simple words what is to be accomplished in the group in respect to his or her therapeutic progress. Group goals, for example, in regard to social interaction, can also be set.

5 *Preview of therapeutic outcome and benefit to the individual group member:* The therapist reviews personal goals with the patients and explains how the following stages in the session will help accomplish each goal. Thus, the patient has a clear point of reference throughout the session to help understand the therapeutic meaning of each activity and its expected benefit.

STAGE II: THERAPEUTIC MUSIC EXPERIENCE

The patient should be sufficiently prepared by stage I to enter the therapeutic music experience and to understand its intended therapeutic meaning. The therapeutic music experience should simulate and translate a therapeutically meaningful real-life experience into a musical activity. For example, music activities may re-create and model social interaction patterns, or may be used to teach the patient to communicate feelings and thoughts to others. Music may be used to facilitate recall of important experiences in life. Positive mood experiences through music may help access positive information about oneself, and thus may create a pleasurable emotional state in the patient and motivate her or him to seek behavioral change.

A therapeutic music experience may relieve the patient of anxiety, which may make him or her open to thinking about therapeutic change. Music therapy techniques to accomplish these goals include guided music listening, instrumental and vocal improvisation, group singing, music and movement, music and imagery techniques, music in conjunction with other arts media, and so on (Unkefer 1990).

STAGE III: STIMULUS REFLECTION

In this stage verbal interaction is used to clarify and interpret the therapeutic music experience. The three substages are:

1 *Stimulus verification:* The therapist and the patient discuss the qualities and properties of the musical stimulus or the musical experience. Questions pertaining to what was heard, what was done, what mood was conveyed, or how the aesthetic qualities of the experience were perceived will serve to clarify the group's perceptions and to ascertain the reality base of the patient's perceptions.

2 *Stimulus interpretation:* The patients are encouraged, with help from the therapist, to relate the musical experience to their own states of feeling and thinking. Questions pertaining to how the patients' feelings and thoughts were influenced by the music are important here.

3 *Stimulus evaluation:* The therapist guides the patient through the process of relating the therapeutic music experience to her or his personal agenda. The therapist and patient discuss how the therapeutic music experience can help accomplish the therapeutic goals of the patient.

STAGE IV: TRANSFER

In this stage the therapist guides the patient toward an understanding of the connection between the therapy experience and areas of therapeutic concern in the patient's life. This stage is divided into two closely related substages.

1 *Connection:* The therapist and patient discuss how the therapeutic music experience reflected problems and issues of therapeutic concern in the patient's life. The value of experiencing these problems and concerns in a different medium—music—should be clarified to the patient at this point.

2 *Application:* Based on the understanding accomplished in the connection stage, the therapist and patient are now ready to discuss specific applications of the therapeutic music experience to the patient's therapeutic progress. The therapist and patient clarify, define, and discuss applications of the knowledge and the behavioral experiences accomplished previously.

STAGE V: PLANNING

This stage is concerned with formulating concrete plans of therapeutic change and making commitments to carrying out those plans. At least parts of each plan should have short-term commitments that can be checked during the next session.

STAGE VI: REVIEW

The importance of the last stage is to give closure to the session and to review the purpose as well as the therapeutic outcomes of the session. The three substages are:

1 *Event summary:* The therapist and the patients review and summarize the events, experiences, and progress of the session.

2 *Therapeutic music summary:* The therapist and the patients clarify and review the role of the therapeutic music experience in therapeutic learning and change as it relates to each patient's personal agenda.

3 *Preview:* The therapist explains the time, the place, and the nature of the next meeting and reminds the patients of their commitments to working on their therapeutic plans.

REFERENCE

Unkefer, R., ed. 1990. *Music therapy in the treatment of adults with mental disorders.* New York: Schirmer.

SELECTED READINGS

Song Collections and Method Books and Articles

Bayless, K. M., and M. E. Ramsey. 1982. *Music: A way of life for the young child.* St. Louis, MO: C. V. Mosby.

Birkenshaw, L. 1982. *Music for fun, music for learning.* 3d ed. Toronto: Holt, Rinehart and Winston.

Bitcon, C. H. 1976. *Alike and different: The clinical and educational use of Orff-Schulwerk.* Santa Ana, CA: Rosha Press.

Bright, R. 1972. *Music in geriatric care.* New York: St. Martin's Press.

Bruscia, K. E. 1987. *Improvisational models of music therapy.* Springfield, IL: Charles C Thomas.

Cassity, M. D. 1977. Nontraditional guitar techniques for the educable and trainable mentally retarded residents in music therapy activities. *Journal of Music Therapy* 14:39–42.

Chavin, M. 1991. *The lost chord: Reaching persons with dementia through the power of music.* Mt. Airy, MD: Eldersong.

Chosky, L., and D. Brummitt. 1987. *120 singing games and dances for elementary schools.* Englewood Cliffs, NJ: Prentice Hall.

Clark, C., and D. Chadwick. 1979. *Clinically adapted instruments for the multiply handicapped: A sourcebook.* Westford, MA: Modulations.

Elliot, B. 1982. *Guide to the selection of musical instruments with respect to physical ability and disability.* St. Louis, MO: Magnamusic-Baton.

Ficken, T. 1976. The use of songwriting in a psychiatric setting. *Journal of Music Therapy* 13:163–172.

Graham, R. M., and A. S. Beers. 1980. *Teaching music to exceptional child: A handbook for mainstreaming.* Englewood Cliffs, NJ: Prentice Hall.

Graham, T. L. 1986. *Fingerplays and rhymes for always and sometimes.* 2d ed. Atlanta, GA: Humanics.

Haselbach, B. 1978. *Dance education: Basic principles for nursery and primary school.* London, England: Schott.

———. 1981. *Improvisation, dance, and movement.* St. Louis, MO: Magnamusic-Baton.

Henry, D., C. Knoll, and B. Reuer. 1986. *Music works: A handbook of job skills for music therapists.* Stephanville, TX: Music Works.

Hoshizaki, M. K. 1983. *Teaching mentally retarded children through music.* Springfield, IL: Charles C Thomas.

Karras, B. 1980. *Down Memory Lane.* Wheaton, MD: Circle Press.

———. 1989. *Moments to remember: Topics and ideas for reminiscence groups.* Mt. Airy, MD: Eldersong.

———. 1990. *Say it with music: Music games and trivia.* Mt. Airy, MD: Eldersong.

Knoll, C., and D. Henry. 1995. *Music Works: A handbook of job skills for music therapists.* Stephanville, TX: Music Works.

Krout, R. 1983. *Teaching basic guitar skills to special learners.* St. Louis, MO: Magnamusic-Baton.

———. 1995. *Beginning rock guitar for music leaders: Skills for therapy, education, recreation and leisure.* St. Louis, MO: Magnamusic-Baton.

Lathom, W. B., and C. T. Eagle, eds. 1984. *Music therapy for handicapped children,* vols. 1, 2, and 3. Lawrence, KS: Meseraull Printing.

Mettler, B. 1975. *Group dance improvisations.* Tucson, AZ: Mettler Studios.

Nelson, E. L. 1986. *The great rounds song book.* New York: Sterling.

Nordoff, P., and C. Robbins. 1971. *Music therapy in special education.* New York: John Day.

———. 1977. *Creative music therapy.* New York: John Day.

Palmer, H. 1981. *Hap Palmer favorites: Songs for learning through music and movement.* Sherman Oaks, CA: Alfred.

———. 1987. *Songs to enhance the movement vocabulary of young children.* Sherman Oaks, CA: Alfred.

Polisar, B. L. 1985. *Noises from under the rug: The Barry Polisar songbook.* 2d ed. Silver Spring, MD: Rainbow Morning Music Alts.

Rykov, M., and G. Hewitt. 1994. *Last songs: AIDS and the music therapist.* 2d ed. Toronto: Music Therapy Series of Metropolitan Toronto.

Schulberg, C. H. 1981. *The music therapy sourcebook: A collection of activities categorized and analyzed.* New York: Human Sciences Press.

Shaw, J. 1993. *The joy of music in maturity.* St. Louis, MO: Magnamusic-Baton.

Shaw, J., and C. Manthey. 1996. *Musical Bridges: Intergenerational music programs.* St. Louis, MO: Magnamusic-Baton.

Psychology and Anthropology of Music Resources

Berlyne, D. E. 1971. *Aesthetics and psychobiology.* New York: Appleton-Century-Crofts.

Dainow, E. 1977. Physical effects and motor response to music. *Journal of Research in Music Education* 25:211–221.

Hodges, D. A., ed. 1996. *Handbook of music psychology.* 2d ed. San Antonio: IMR Press.

Merriam, A. P. 1964. *The anthropology of music.* Evanston, IL: University of Chicago Press.

Meyer, L. B. 1956. *Emotion and meaning in music.* Chicago: University of Chicago Press.

Radocy, R. E., and J. D. Boyle. 1996. *Psychological foundations of musical behavior.* 3d ed. Springfield, IL: Charles C Thomas.

Springer, S. P., and G. Deutsch. 1985. *Left brain, right brain.* New York: Freeman.

Principles, Theories, and History of Music Development, Music Education, and Music Therapy

Alley, J. M. 1979. Music in the IEP: Therapy/education. *Journal of Music Therapy* 16:111–127.

Atterbury, B. W. 1990. *Mainstreaming exceptional learners in music.* Englewood Cliffs, NJ: Prentice Hall.

Borczon, R. M. 1998. *Music therapy: Group vignettes.* Gilsum, NH: Barcelona Press.

Boxberger, R. 1962. Historical bases for the use of music in therapy. In *Music Therapy 1961,* edited by E. H. Schneider. Lawrence, KS: National Association for Music Therapy.

Boxhill, E. H. 1985. *Music therapy for the developmentally disabled.* Rockville, MD: Aspen Systems.

———. 1998. *The miracle of music therapy.* Gilsum, NH: Barcelona Press.

Bright, R. 1997. *Music therapy and the dementias: Improving the quality of life.* St. Louis, MO: Magnamusic-Baton.

Brotons, M., S. M. Koger, and P. Pickett-Cooper. 1997. Music and the dementias: A review of literature. *Journal of Music Therapy* 34(4):204–245.

Bruscia, K. E. 1987. *Improvisational models of music therapy.* Springfield, IL: Charles C Thomas.

———. 1989. *Defining music therapy.* Spring City, PA: Spring House.

———. 1991. *Case studies in music therapy.* Gilsum, NH: Barcelona Press.

Cassity, M. D., and J. E. Cassity. 1995. *Multimodal psychiatric music therapy for adults, adolescents and children: A clinical manual.* St. Louis, MO: Magnamusic-Baton.

Clair, A. A. 1996. *Therapeutic uses of music with older adults.* Baltimore: Health Professions Press.

Clark, M. E. 1986. Music therapy-assisted childbirth: A practical guide. *Music Therapy Perspectives* 3:34–41.

Cohen, G., and O. L. Gericke. 1972. Music therapy assessment: Prime requisite for determining patient objectives. *Journal of Music Therapy* 9:161–189.

Darrow, A. A. 1985. Music for the deaf. *Music Educators Journal* 71:33–35.

Darrow, A. A., and G. N. Heller. 1985. Early advocates of music education for the hearing-impaired: William Wolcott Turner and David Ely Bartlett. *Journal of Research in Music Education* 33:269–279.

Davis, W. B. 1987. Music therapy in nineteenth-century America. *Journal of Music Therapy* 24:76–87.

———. 1993. Keeping the dream alive: Profiles of three early twentieth-century music therapists. *Journal of Music Therapy* 30(1):34–45.

DiGiammarino, M. 1990. Functional music skills of persons with mental retardation. *Journal of Music Therapy* 27(4):209–220.

Furman, C. E., ed. 1996. *Effectiveness of music therapy procedures: Documentation of research and clinical practice,* 2d ed. Silver Spring, MD: National Association for Music Therapy.

Gaston, E. T., ed. 1968. *Music in therapy.* New York: Macmillan.

Gfeller, K. E. 1984. Prominent theories in learning disabilities and implications for music therapy methodology. *Music Therapy Perspectives* 2:9–13.

———, ed. 1986. *Fiscal, regulatory, and legislative issues for the music therapist.* Washington, DC: National Association for Music Therapy, Inc.

———. 1987. Music therapy theory and practice as reflected in research literature. *Journal of Music Therapy* 24:176–194.

———. 1987. Songwriting as a tool for reading and language remediation. *Music Therapy* 6:28–38.

Gfeller, K. E., and A. A. Baumann. 1988. Assessment procedures for music therapy with hearing-impaired children: Language development. *Journal of Music Therapy* 25:192–205.

Gibbons, A. C. 1988. A review of literature for music development/education and music therapy with the elderly. *Music Therapy Perspectives* 5:33–40.

Gilbert, J. P. 1977. Music therapy perspectives on death and dying. *Journal of Music Therapy* 14:165–171.

Godley, C. A. 1987. The use of music therapy in pain clinics. *Music Therapy Perspectives* 4:24–28.

Goll, H. 1994. *Special education music therapy with persons who have severe/profound retardation: Theory and methodology.* New York: Peter Lang.

Hanser, S. 1985. *Music therapist's handbook.* St. Louis, MO: Warren H. Green.

Heller, G. N. 1987. Ideas, initiatives, and implementations: Music therapy in America. *Journal of Music Therapy* 24:35–46.

Isenberg-Grezeda, C. 1988. Music therapy assessment: A reflection of professional identity. *Journal of Music Therapy* 25:156–169.

Lucia, C. M. 1987. Toward developing a model of music therapy intervention in the rehabilitation of head and trauma patients. *Music Therapy Perspectives* 4:34–39.

Maranto, C., ed. 1991. *Application of music in medicine.* Silver Spring, MD: National Association for Music Therapy.

Maranto, C. D., and K. E. Bruscia, eds. 1987. *Perspectives on music therapy education and training.* Philadelphia: Temple University.

McDonald, D. T., and G. M. Simons. 1989. *Musical growth and development: Birth through six.* New York: Schirmer.

Michel, D. M. 1985. *Music therapy: An introduction, including music in special education.* 2d ed. Springfield, IL: Charles C Thomas.

Michel, D. M., and J. L. Jones. 1992. *Music for developing speech and language skills in children: A guide for parents and therapists.* St. Louis, MO: Magnamusic-Baton.

Munro, S. 1984. *Music therapy in palliative/hospice care.* St. Louis, MO: Magnamusic-Baton.

Peters, J. S. 1987. *Music therapy: An introduction.* Springfield, IL: Charles C Thomas.

Plach, T. 1997. *The creative use of music in group therapy.* 2d ed. Springfield, IL: Charles C Thomas.

Pratt, R. R., and R. Spintge, eds. 1996. *Music medicine, vol 2.* St. Louis, MO: Magnamusic-Baton.

Rainbow, E. L., and H. C. Froehlich. 1987. *Research in music education.* New York: Schirmer.

Rorke, M. A. 1996. Music and the wounded of World War II. *Journal of Music Therapy* 23(3):189–207.

Roskam, K. S. 1993. *Feeling the sound: The influence of music on behavior.* San Francisco: San Francisco Press.

Ruud, E. 1978. *Music therapy and its relationship to current treatment theories.* St. Louis, MO: Magnamusic-Baton.

Scartelli, J. P. 1989. *Music and self-management methods.* St. Louis, MO: Magnamusic-Baton.

Scovel, M. A., and B. Houghton, eds. 1990. *Reimbursement guide for music therapists: Phase one.* Washington, DC: National Association for Music Therapy.

Solomon, A. I. 1984. A historical study of the National Association for Music Therapy, 1960–1980. Unpublished Ph.D. diss., University of Kansas, Lawrence, KS.

———. 1993. A history of the *Journal of Music Therapy:* The first decade (1964–1973). *Journal of Music Therapy* 30(1):3–33.

Solomon, A. I., and G. N. Heller. 1982. Historical research in music therapy: An important avenue for studying the profession. *Journal of Music Therapy* 19:236–242.

Standley, J. M. 1986. Music research in medical/dental treatment: Meta-analysis and clinical applications. *Journal of Music Therapy* 20:69–87.

———. 1991. *Music techniques in therapy, counseling and special education.* St. Louis, MO: Magnamusic-Baton.

Standley, J. M., and C. A. Prickett, eds. 1994. *Research in music therapy: A tradition of excellence.* Silver Spring, MD: National Association for Music Therapy.

Steele, A. L., ed. 1985. *The music therapy levels system.* Cleveland, OH: Cleveland Music School Settlement.

Thaut, M. H. 1983. A music therapy treatment model for autistic children. *Music Therapy Perspectives* 1:7–13.

———. 1987. A new challenge for music therapy: The correctional setting. *Music Therapy Perspectives* 4:44–50.

———. 1988. Rhythmic intervention techniques in music therapy with gross motor dysfunction. *Arts in Psychotherapy* 15:127–137.

Unkefer, R., ed. 1990. *Music therapy in the treatment of adults with mental disorders.* New York: Schirmer.

Wheeler, B. 1983. A psychotherapeutic classification of music therapy practices: A continuum of procedures. *Music Therapy Perspectives* 1:8–10

———, ed. 1995. *Music therapy research: Quantitative and qualitative perspectives.* Gilsum, NH: Barcelona Press.

Wigram, T., R. West, and B. Saperston, eds. 1995. *The art and science of music therapy: A handbook.* Chur, Switzerland: Harwood Academic.

Wilson, B. L., ed. 1996. *Models of music therapy interventions in school settings: From institution to inclusion.* Silver Spring, MD: National Association for Music Therapy.

Related References and Resources

Bear, M., B. Connors, and M. Paradiso. 1996. *Neuroscience: Exploring the brain.* Baltimore: Williams and Wilkins.

Berg, G. L. 1998. *Qualitative research methods for the social sciences.* 3d ed. Boston: Allyn and Bacon.

Birren, J. E., and K. W. Schaie, eds. 1996. *Handbook of the psychology of aging.* 4th ed. San Diego: Academic Press.

Bleck, E. E., and D. A. Nagel, eds. 1982. *Physically handicapped children: A medical atlas for teachers.* 2d ed. New York: Grune and Stratton.

Corey, G. 1996. *Theory and practice of counseling and psychotherapy.* 5th ed. Pacific Grove, CA: Brooks/Cole.

Corey, M., and G. Corey. 1987. *Groups: Process and practice.* 3d ed. Monterey, CA: Brooks/Cole.

Corsini, R. J. 1989. *Current psychotherapies.* Itasca, IL: F. E. Peacock.

Cratty, B. J. 1979. *Perceptual motor development in infants and children.* Englewood Cliffs, NJ: Prentice Hall.

Crystal, D. 1980. Introduction to language pathology. Baltimore: University Park Press.

Cunningham, W. R., and J. W. Brookbank. 1988. *Gerontology: The psychology, biology, and sociology of aging.* New York: Harper and Row.

Delisa, J. A., ed. 1988. *Rehabilitation medicine: Principles and practice.* Philadelphia: Lippincott.

Diagnostic and statistical manual of mental disorders—IV. 1994. Washington, DC: American Psychiatric Association.

Donnellan, A., ed. 1985. *Classic readings in autism.* New York: Teachers College Press.

Dowling, J. E. 1992. *Neurons and networks: An introduction to neuroscience.* Cambridge, MA: Belknap Press of Harvard University Press.

Farber, S. D. 1982. *Neurorehabilitation: A multisensory approach.* Philadelphia: W. B. Saunders.

Feder, E., and B. Feder. 1981. *The expressive arts therapies.* Englewood Cliffs, NJ: Prentice Hall.

Feil, N. 1993. *The validation breakthrough: Simple techniques for communicating with people with "Alzheimer's type dementia."* Baltimore: Health Professions Press.

Gallahue, D. L. 1982. *Developmental movement experiences for children.* New York: Wiley.

———. 1982. *Understanding motor development in children.* New York: Wiley.

Groden, G., and M. G. Baron, eds. 1988. *Autism: Strategies for change.* New York: Gardner Press.

Kandel, J. H., J. H. Schwarz, and T. M. Jessell. 1995. *Essentials of neural science and behavior.* Stamford, CT: Appleton and Lange.

Kavale, K. A. 1988. *Learning disabilities: State of the art and practice.* Boston: College Hill Press.

Madsen, C. K. 1986. Research and Music Therapy: The necessity for transfer. *Journal of Music Therapy* 23(2):50–55.

Masdau, L., L. Sudarsky, and L. Wolfson, eds. 1997. *Gait disorders of aging.* Philadelphia: Lippincott Raven.

Meier, S. T. 1989. *The elements of counseling.* Pacific Grove, CA: Brooks/Cole.

Moursound, J. 1990. *The process of counseling and therapy.* Englewood Cliffs, NJ: Prentice Hall.

Ottenbacher, K. J. 1986. *Evaluating clinical change: Strategies for occupational and physical therapists.* Baltimore: Williams and Wilkins.

Papalia, D. E., C. J. Cameron, and R. D. Feldman. 1996. *Adult development and aging.* New York: McGraw-Hill.

Parente, R., and D. Herman. 1996. *Retraining cognition: Techniques and applications.* Gaithersburg, MD: Aspen.

Reisberg, D., ed. 1992. *Auditory imagery.* Hillsdale, NJ: Lawrence Erlbaum.

Shore, K. 1986. *The special education handbook.* New York: Teachers College Press.

Shott, S. 1990. *Statistics for health professionals.* Philadelphia: Saunders.

Spence, A. P. 1989. *Biology of human aging.* Englewood Cliffs, NJ: Prentice Hall.

Spivak, B. S., ed. 1995. *Evaluation and management of gait disorders.* New York: Marcel Dekker.

Strub, F. W., and F. W. Black. 1992. *Neurobehavioral disorders: A clinical approach.* Philadelphia: F. A. Davis.

Sullivan, P. E., P. D. Markos, and M. A. D. Minor. 1982. *An integrated approach to therapeutic exercise: Theory and clinical application.* Reston, VA: Reston.

U.S. Department of Education. 1988. *Summary of existing legislation affecting persons with disabilities.* Washington, DC: Office of Special Education and Rehabilitation Services.

Wade, D. T., R. Langton-Hewer, C. E. Skilbeck, and R. M. David. 1985. *Stroke: A critical approach to diagnosis, treatment, and management.* Chicago: Yearbook Medical Publications.

Walsh, K. 1994. *Neuropsychology: A clinical approach.* New York: Churchill Livingstone.

Warren, B., ed. 1993. *Using creative arts in therapy: A practical introduction.* New York: Rutledge.

Weiner, M. B., A. J. Brok, and A. M. Snadowsky. 1987. *Working with the aged.* 2d ed. Norwalk, CT: Appleton-Century-Crofts.

Yalom, I. 1983. *Inpatient group psychotherapy.* New York: Basic Books.

GLOSSARY

acquired hearing loss A hearing loss acquired after birth.
acuity Keenness of perception (often associated with vision or hearing).
adventitious Not present at birth.
aesthetics Sensitivity to art and beauty; also the study of people's responses to the fine arts.
Alzheimer's disease A type of dementia that causes a gradual, steady decline in cognitive function because of structural changes in the brain.
anaclitic depression A depressed state in an infant between the ages of 7 to 30 months that is caused by a separation from the primary caregiver. Symptoms include listlessness, lack of affect, anorexia, and depressed motor activity.
analgesic Something that reduces or eliminates pain (i.e., aspirin).
anoxia Deprivation of oxygen to the brain because of disease or trauma.
anxiety disorder A group of diagnoses characterized by unrealistic or excessive anxiety, panic attacks, or avoidance behavior.
aphasia Impaired ability to use or understand oral language.
apraxia Inability to carry out purposeful movements of the speech musculature in the absence of paralysis or other motor or sensory impairments. A milder form of apraxia is called dyspraxia.
aptitude Natural ability or capacity for learning.
arteriosclerosis A group of diseases characterized by thickening and hardening of arterial walls.
articulation The production of individual sounds in speech.
assessment A procedure completed prior to the start of treatment that provides an overall view of the client's history and present condition. This information is then used to develop treatment strategies and estimate duration of treatment.
association through contiguity The association of two separate events that are due to temporal proximity.
astigmatism Distorted vision because of an abnormal curvature of the cornea.
atlantoaxial instability A type of misalignment of the upper spinal column that is often found in people with Down's syndrome.

attending behavior The ability to carry out a task to completion.

audiologist A health care professional who deals with the science of hearing. An audiologist often tests hearing, fits hearing aids, and directs the rehabilitation of individuals with significant hearing losses.

auditory awareness The perception of sounds in the environment.

auditory nerve The nerve fibers that carry information from the inner ear (cochlea) to the brain, where the information is processed.

auditory training A rehabilitative process aimed at assisting persons with hearing impairments to maximize use of residual or usable hearing.

autonomic nervous system The part of the central nervous system that automatically regulates processes such as respiration, heart rate, and metabolism.

baseline (as used in behavior modification) The level at which a behavior occurs before any attempt to modify it.

behavior modification A systematic application of the theories of learning to weaken, strengthen, or maintain a target behavior.

central nervous system The brain and spinal cord.

central processing The categorization of an incoming stimulus using memory, reasoning, and evaluation.

cerebral aneurysm A bulge in the wall of an artery in the brain caused by a weakness in the tissue of the artery.

civilization First civilization appeared between 5,000 and 6,000 B.C. and is characterized by the evolution of written communication, the growth of cities, and achievement in medicine and science.

cochlea A small snail-shaped structure of the inner ear that contains sensory receptors important in the transmission of sound to the auditory nerve.

cochlear implant An assistive hearing device designed for individuals with profound sensorineural loss.

cognition The act or process of knowing, as in various thinking skills.

cognitive behavior modification A behavior modification technique that includes self-reinforcement and self-evaluation.

cognitive pain control The use of mental strategies for relieving discomfort.

communication The broad process through which people interact with each other.

conductive hearing loss Reduction in the ability to hear because of an anomaly of the outer or middle ear.

confidentiality Principles of confidentiality seek to protect the client's right to privacy within the boundary of the law.

congenital Existing at birth.

deaf This term refers to both the audiological condition characterized by little or no usable hearing and a label that is used to describe those people with hearing impairments who align themselves socially and politically with a community of Deaf as opposed to hearing people.

delusions Invalid beliefs that lack evidence in reality.

dementia An illness characterized by multiple cognitive deficits that include over a dozen similar conditions, including Alzheimer's disease.

descriptive research A type of research that describes "what is" under current conditions. Surveys are a common tool used to gather data for this mode of inquiry.

discrimination Ability to determine differences between two or more objects or events (i.e., determining the difference between the sounds of the words *had* and *bad*).

Down's syndrome A specific form of mental retardation resulting from a chromosomal abnormality.

duration recording A recording technique used to measure how long a particular behavior lasts. Duration may be measured in the total amount of time or in the percentage of time that a behavior occurs during a given period.

dysarthria Imperfect articulation of speech because of loss of muscle control as a result of damage to the central or peripheral nervous system.

dyslexia A disorder that results in failure in skills of reading. This term is frequently used when a neurological dysfunction is suspected as the cause of the reading problem.

embolus An obstruction of blood flow caused by a blood clot.

endocardium Lining of the heart.

endogenous Originating within the body.

etiology Cause or origin of a condition.

executive function The decision-making component essential to all adaptive behavior.

exogenous Originating from external causes, outside the body.

experimental research Investigates what "will be" if particular factors or conditions are in effect.

expression The ability to select an appropriate response to the incoming stimuli from a variety of choices.

expressionism As related to the philosophy of the arts, the belief that music's ability to evoke emotions and take on meaning results from the structural characteristics (embodied) of the music itself.

expressive language Production of language such as speaking and writing.

felt needs An approach to assessment that incorporates client interests, values, and attitudes into the treatment plan.

field of vision How much area the eye sees centrally or peripherally.

four cardinal humors A medical theory originating about 380 B.C. that influenced medicine for 2,000 years. A balance between the four humors (blood, phlegm, yellow bile, and black bile) resulted in good health, whereas an imbalance led to illness.

fragile X syndrome A genetic disorder that causes mental retardation.

frequency The number of sound waves per second generated by a sound-producing source (measured in hertz). The greater the number of waves per second, the higher the sound. As a point of reference, 440 Hz is the value assigned to the musical note A above middle C on the piano.

frequency recording An observational technique that is useful in recording occurrences of behavior under observation.

generalization The ability to take information learned in one setting and apply it to a different setting.

geriatrics A medical subspecialty concerned with the care of elderly patients and treatment of their medical problems.

gerontologist A person who specializes in one or more aspects of aging.

gerontology The scientific study of the phenomena of aging, involving the processes of aging and senescence, and including the related problems and achievements of older people.

goal A broad statement of the desired outcome of treatment.

gustation Relating to taste. The ability to perceive salty, sweet, sour, and bitter tastes.

hedonic Having to do with pleasure.

historical research Reflects "what was," assisting in the understanding of the past as it relates to the present.

homeostasis The ability of the body to maintain stability of chemical and physical states.

hospice In relation to terminal illness, the reduction and abatement of pain and other troubling symptoms. Hospice programs may include services of nurses, counselors, music therapists, clergy, and trained volunteers, depending on the particular needs of a given client.

Huntington's disease A relatively rare, inherited neurological disorder affecting motor control.

hyperkinesia Abnormally increased motor activity.

hypoactivity Less than normal amount of activity.

hypothermia A condition in which the body temperature is significantly below normal.

hypotonia A lack of muscle tone.

iconicity The imitation of a feeling, object, or event through the structural properties of an art form.

individualized education plan (IEP) This is a required individualized education plan for disabled children enrolled in public schools. This document is written by a team of special-education professionals in consultation with the child's parents or guardian and acts as the blueprint for determining the best possible educational program for each child.

intensity (as the word relates to acoustics) The degree of acoustical energy produced by a sound source. This term is related to the subjective term *loudness*.

interdisciplinary team A group of health professionals working together to coordinate a client's treatment plan.

intracranial hemorrhage Rupture of a blood vessel inside the cranium.

ischemia Deficiency of blood flow caused by an obstruction of a blood vessel.

iso principle A technique by which music is matched with the mood of a client, then gradually altered to affect the desired mood state.

language Verbal or nonverbal means for communicating thoughts or feelings generally involving a system of spoken, written, or gestured symbols known to a given community.

language arts Academic activities that utilize language, such as reading, speech, writing, and spelling.

limbic system A network of nerve centers in the brain involved with emotional and motivational states.

localization To fix an object, sound, or event in a particular place or locale.

mainstreaming Placing students with disabilities in a regular educational setting rather than in a special education placement.

masking The process of covering one auditory stimulus with the sounds of another (i.e., covering the undesirable sound of a dentist's drill with pleasant music).

mental retardation A term that refers to significantly subaverage general intellectual functioning existing concurrently with deficits in adaptive behavior, and manifested during the developmental period. Mental retardation may be caused before birth (prenatal), during birth (perinatal), or after birth (postnatal).

minimal brain dysfunction A mild neurological abnormality that causes learning problems in children with near-average intelligence.

mnemonic Meant to help the memory.

mobility Movement from present position to a desired location in space.

mood disorder A mental disorder characterized primarily by disturbance in mood such as depression or extreme elation.

moral treatment A progressive, late nineteenth-century therapeutic program for the mentally ill that included the use of art, reading, music, and physical education.

music therapy A behavioral science concerned with changing unhealthy behavior and replacing it with more adaptive behavior through the use of musical stimuli.

neurofibromatosis An inherited disorder of the nervous system and skin. Also called von Recklinghausen's disease.

neuroleptic drugs Medications used in the treatment of mental illness. Also known as antipsychotic drugs.

normalization The process of integrating objects, events, and interactions that resemble those of everyday life into a treatment environment.
object classification The identification of colors and shapes, for example.
objective Describes an immediate goal that may be viewed as a small step in the process of attaining a final goal.
olfactory Relating to the sense of smell.
orientation Utilization of sensory processes to establish one's position in relation to significant objects in the environment.
ossicles The three small bones (malleus, incus, and stapes) found in the middle ear that move in response to acoustical energy.
parallel play A stage of development in which very young children will play beside each other but not engage in social interaction.
paralysis Loss or impairment of motor function because of lesions of the neural or muscular mechanisms in the nervous system responsible for motor activity.
Parkinson's disease A neurological disorder that affects movement.
passive activities Music or other activities used in a rehabilitation setting with the regressed elderly that require very little verbal or physical response from the client.
patterned sensory enhancement (PSA) A music therapy technique that uses temporal, visual–spatial, and dynamic patterns in music to create structures for cuing movements.
perception The process of organizing or interpreting information taken in through the senses.
perceptual disorder A disturbance in the awareness of objects, relationships, or qualities of information taken in through the senses.
perinatal Refers to the time period shortly before, during, or after birth.
personality disorder A mental disorder in which a person exhibits extreme, inflexible personality traits that cause difficulty in work, school, and interpersonal relationships.
phenylketonuria (PKU) A genetic metabolic disorder that causes severe brain damage because of the body's inability to break down the chemical *phenylalanine.*
philosophical research Expresses a researcher's opinion about "what ought to be."
postlingual Occurring after the acquisition of the principle structures of adult speech and language.
postnatal Refers to the time period after birth.
potentiation Readiness.
prelingual Occurring in the period before acquisition of the principle structures of adult speech and language (approximately the first three years of life).
preliterate societies Cultures that possess no system of written communication and have no agricultural or political structure, or permanent housing.
prenatal Refers to the time period before birth.
prescriptive framework An approach to assessment in which the therapist designs a treatment plan based on the client's weaknesses and limitations, with little or no input from the client.
pressured speech A symptom often found among individuals suffering a manic episode in which the individual is extremely talkative and may feel an irresistible urge to keep on talking.
primary aging The systematic, genetically determined decline in the efficiency of organ systems in the body. The overall rate at which a person ages is determined by both primary and secondary aging.
psychogenic Distress caused by mental conflict or stress.
qualitative research A research style that is descriptive and focuses on people's percep-

tions and feelings. Qualitative research is conducted with individuals or small groups in the client's social environment over extended periods of time.

rational medicine The study of health and disease based on empirical evidence.

reality orientation A technique used with the elderly that emphasizes the repetition of information to reeducate clients who may be disoriented and confused. Accurate perception of person, place, date, time, and other environmental objects or events.

reception The perception of a visual, aural, or other sensory stimulus.

receptive language The ability to understand language in spoken or written form.

referential meaning The philosophical belief that the meaning in music arises from connections the listener makes between music and a nonmusical object or event.

refractive Referring to structures of the eye that focus light, such as the retina, cornea, and lens.

reliability Refers to the consistency with which a test measures a behavior or behaviors.

reminiscence A structured review of past life events and experiences. This is an important therapeutic tool used with elderly persons.

remotivation A therapeutic technique used with the elderly to stimulate thinking and verbal interaction and to improve social skills.

residual hearing Usable hearing (associated with people with hearing losses who can hear some sounds but not others).

resource room A specially equipped and staffed classroom to help disabled children with their particular difficulties.

retina A layer of light-sensitive cells at the back of the eyeball that receive a visual image and transmit the message to the optic nerve.

rhythmic auditory stimulus (RAS) A technique to facilitate rhythmic movement, especially gait.

schizophrenia A serious mental disorder in which an individual experiences profound alterations in thinking, sensory perception, affect, and behavior.

secondary aging Stress, trauma, and disease contribute to secondary aging. The overall rate at which a person ages is determined by both primary and secondary aging.

senescence The normal, inevitable decline in the efficiency of body systems. It is a normal aspect of aging and not considered dysfunctional.

sensorimotor Referring to an act such as walking or running that is dependent on the integration of sensory and motor mechanisms.

sensorineural hearing loss Loss in hearing usually because of defects in the sensory or neural mechanisms of the ear (cochlea and auditory nerve).

sensory modulation The processing of and responding to sensory stimuli in the central nervous system.

sensory training A rehabilitation technique used with the elderly to restore contact with the environment.

seriation The grouping of objects by size, number, or attribute.

short-term memory The ability to recall information shortly after it has been presented.

single systems research A type of research conducted with an individual or small group of clients in the client's social or therapeutic environment.

spatial relationships Concepts such as up/down and in/out are examples of spatial relationships.

speech-language pathologist A health care professional trained to assist individuals with disordered communication in the production of speech or use of augmentative communicative devices.

startle reflex Involuntary muscle response to loud, sudden sound.

syntax The grammar system of a language.
tactile Related to the sense of touch.
task analysis A method of breaking down a skill into smaller sequentially ordered steps.
temporal relationships The order of events in time, such as first, second, last.
tertiary aging Refers to changes that occur rapidly in the very old person.
therapeutic instrumental music playing (TIMP) A music therapy technique that exercises muscles and improves fine and gross motor skills.
thrombus A blood clot that obstructs arterial blood flow.
transient ischemic attack (TIA) A condition caused by temporary interruption of blood flow to the brain.
treatment plan A step-by-step plan designed to help a client reach a predetermined point of desired behavior.
validity How well a test measures what it is supposed to.
vestibulocochlear nerve A structure located in the inner ear that is involved in hearing and balance.

INDEX